CORE CURRICULUM COURSE

Perfection: Towards Spiritual Maturity

Copyright © 2020 Wendy Bowen

ALL RIGHTS RESERVED WORLDWIDE

Manifest International, LLC

ISBN: 978-1-951280-11-6

Scripture references in this book are from the New International Version of the Bible unless otherwise noted. Emphasis added by author for teaching purposes.

Scripture taken from the HOLY BIBLE, NEW INTERNATIONAL VERSION ® NIV ® Copyright © 1973, 1978, 1984, 2011 by Biblica, Inc. Used by permission of Biblica, Inc. All rights reserved worldwide. – Scripture quotations are taken from the Holy Bible, New Living Translation, copyright © 1996, 2004, 2007 by Tyndale House Foundation. Used by permission of Tyndale House Publishers, Inc. Carol Stream, Illinois 60188. All rights reserved. – Scripture taken from the New King James Version ®. Copyright © 1982 by Thomas Nelson, Inc. Used by permission. All rights reserved.

All Biblical definitions in this book are from Strong's Hebrew and Greek Lexicon, Gesenius' Hebrew-Chaldee Lexicon, and Thayer's Greek Lexicon

Some excerpts and adaptations from other books by Wendy Bowen, including: ACTS © 2015, Paul's Prayers © 2016, Biblical Healing © 2016, For Love © 2018

Cover Image Credit: rawpixel.com / Freepik

DEDICATION

To Jesus. The one and only perfect one.

Contents

Guide to this Course – Book Format		1
Course Introduction		2
Pre-Course Examination		4

UNIT ONE — OPEN EARS TO OBEY — 5
- Class 1.1 The Mystery Revealed — 6
- Class 1.2 Guidance from God — 13
- Class 1.3 Testing the Spirit — 21
- Class 1.4 Abiding & Obedience — 36
- Key Questions & Group Exercises — 42

UNIT TWO — THE WHOLE COUNSEL OF GOD — 45
- Class 2.1 Foundations & Whole Counsel of God — 46
- Class 2.2 Good News of the Kingdom — 50
- Class 2.3 Israel & One New Man — 65
- Class 2.4 God's Sovereignty Over ALL Nations — 77
- Key Questions & Group Exercises — 86

UNIT THREE — DIVINE NATURE — 89
- Class 3.1 Rend Your Heart — 90
- Class 3.2 I Desire Mercy — 98
- Class 3.3 Suitable for Service — 104
- Class 3.4 Motivational Gifts of the Father — 108
- Key Questions & Group Exercises — 114

UNIT FOUR — SKILLED IN RIGHTEOUSNESS — 116
- Class 4.1 It Is Finished — 117
- Class 4.2 Established in Righteousness — 124
- Class 4.3 Rest for Your Soul & Unbelief — 132
- Class 4.4 Established Together — 140
- Key Questions & Group Exercises — 143

UNIT FIVE — KINGDOM GOSPEL WITH SIGNS — 146
- Class 5.1 God's Passion for Souls — 147
- Class 5.2 Gospel of the Kingdom — 154
- Class 5.3 These Signs Will Follow — 164
- Class 5.4 If You Continue… — 171
- Key Questions & Group Exercises — 179

UNIT SIX — DISCERNMENT OF GOOD & EVIL — 181
- Class 6.1 Discerning the Schemes of the Enemy — 182
- Class 6.2 Yeasts of Jesus' Day & Today — 192
- Class 6.3 Deceitful Workers & Doctrines of Demons — 199
- Class 6.4 Enduring through the Great Apostasy — 215
- Key Questions & Group Exercises — 222

UNIT SEVEN — MINISTRY TO PREPARE THE BRIDE — 226
- Class 7.1 Making Disciples — 227
- Class 7.2 The Work of Ministry — 234
- Class 7.3 Bridal Love Made Ready — 246
- Key Questions & Group Exercises — 256

GUIDE TO THIS COURSE

This course is designed to provoke you to a deeper walk with Christ and function as a living demonstration of God's love and power through Jesus Christ.* You will learn how to walk in the obedience of faith and the whole counsel of God. You will become skilled in the word of righteousness and functioning from the power of the Holy Spirit. You will learn what is to come in the days ahead and your place of service in the Body of Christ.

SEVEN UNITS, FOUR CLASSES EACH, PLUS GROUP EXERCISES

Each Unit of the Perfection Course digs deeply into a specific element of spiritual maturity and Christ-likeness. Each Class contains various readings and spiritual exercises to help you KNOW the Word and DO what it says through practical application. Lord willing, we will soon have video teachings to supplement each class. Check for videos at www.manifestinternational.com/videos

Each Unit offers Key Questions and a Group Exercise for churches, home groups, or gatherings of believers who are taking the course together. The whole Curriculum can be completed in seven weeks or at your own pace.

We pray that God will pour out His Spirit of wisdom and revelation to you as you grow in your knowledge of Him and that you are richly edified in your walk with Jesus as you grow towards spiritual maturity and the fullness of God.

NOTES:

Book Format Notes: Please note that this course was initially assembled as an online course. It consists of writings, exercises, inspections, and other tools created for fostering spiritual growth. This book was created to make it easier for participants who desire the full course pre-assembled, rather than downloading each element individually.

Please be advised: This course is written for the mature and maturing believer in a style that assumes some level of knowledge and experience with the Word of God and the direction of the Holy Spirit. Therefore, we **strongly recommend completing the **Cornerstone Course** as a prerequisite to this course. The Cornerstone Course can be found at www.manifestinternational.com/cornerstone

PERFECTION COURSE – INTRODUCTION

INTRODUCTION

Hear the true story of an Olympic marksman. In Olympic competition, this marksman was ahead of his competition by such a wide margin that all he was required to do in the last round of shooting was to hit anywhere on the target – even the rung furthest from the bullseye would be sufficient to secure his gold medal. As the leader, he would shoot last after all his competitors registered their final scores. When it came to be his time to shoot, he took aim, fired, and hit a dead-on bullseye. But when he lowered his scope, it was revealed that he hit the target's bullseye *beside* the target he should have been aiming at. By not even hitting his target at all, he did not win gold, nor silver, nor bronze. An expert marksman who should have won - lost. In the same way, expert marksmen who proclaim Jesus with wrong aims, intents, selfish ambition, or as a means of personal gain will not be gold medal recipients no matter how wonderful their "results" may seem to be on earth.

Jesus is the only perfect one who has ever lived and will ever live. But Jesus said, "Be perfect as your heavenly Father is perfect." (See Matthew 5:48.) Perfection is the demonstration of the likeness of God. It is only attained through the total transformation of an individual from their old nature to the divine nature that God has granted to dwell inside of us as His children. Even the Apostle Paul openly confessed that he did not consider himself to have attained this, but Paul revealed something about the mindset of the mature believer.

> *Philippians 3:10-17:* **I want to know Christ**--yes, to know the **power of his resurrection and participation in his sufferings, becoming like him in his death, and so, somehow, attaining to the resurrection from the dead.** *Not that I have already obtained all this, or have already arrived at my goal, but I press on to take hold of that for which Christ Jesus took hold of me. Brothers and sisters, I do not consider myself yet to have taken hold of it. But one thing I do: Forgetting what is behind and straining toward what is ahead, I press on toward the goal to win the prize for which God has called me heavenward in Christ Jesus.* **All of us, then, who are mature should take such a view of things.** *And if on some point you think differently, that too God will make clear to you. Only let us live up to what we have already attained. Join together in* **following my example**, *brothers and sisters, and just as* **you have us as a model**, *keep your eyes on those who live as we do.*

Paul clearly laid out the mindset of those focused on eternal life with God and set his own life as the example of one walking towards this aim. The pattern of Paul's life reflected the pattern of the life of our crucified King, Jesus. This is a life focused on eternity and living life on earth as a citizen of heaven. The mindset of the mature is to know Christ and to be like Him as a pure and spotless Bride who has readied herself for His return.

Pressing on to Maturity

The author of the Book of Hebrews chastised readers about their complacency in pressing on towards maturity. They had grown so weary in their attempts to stand for Christ that they became stagnant and could not hear and perceive God's ways correctly.

> *Hebrews 5:11-14; 6:1-3: We have much to say about this, but it is hard to make it clear to you because you no longer try to understand. In fact, though by this time you ought to be*

teachers, you need someone to teach you the elementary truths of God's word all over again. You need milk, not solid food! Anyone who lives on milk, being still an infant, is not acquainted with the teaching about righteousness. **But solid food is for the mature, who by constant use have trained themselves to distinguish good from evil. Therefore let us move beyond the elementary teachings about Christ and be taken forward to maturity,** *not laying again the foundation of repentance from acts that lead to death, and of faith in God, instruction about cleansing rites, the laying on of hands, the resurrection of the dead, and eternal judgment. And God permitting, we will do so.*

Many of them could or should have been proficient enough in the ways of God to teach others and lead by example like Paul demonstrated. But they had stopped trying to understand what God is really looking for in Christ's followers.

How could this be? Because the road to maturity is laden with sharing in the sufferings of Jesus. The path to eternal life is a narrow and difficult way and few find it. (See Matthew 7:14.) Maturity is attained through successfully persevering in the faith through trials and tribulations of many kinds.

James 1:2-4 - Consider it pure joy, my brothers and sisters, whenever you face trials of many kinds, because you know that the testing of your faith produces perseverance. Let **perseverance finish its work so that you may be mature and complete, not lacking anything.**

The command of Jesus to His disciples is to love one another as He loves us. Total *agape* love is selfless surrender in willing charity without expecting to receive anything in return. To love as Jesus loves means first and foremost having agape love for God, whom we serve with all our heart, soul, mind, and strength, and having agape love towards others for whom God allows us to reach for His glory.

1 Timothy 1:5 - The goal of this command is **love***, which comes from a* **pure heart** *and a* **good conscience** *and a* **sincere faith***.*

Paul's concept of God's love was not an endorsement for lawlessness or sin at the expense of Christ's blood. There is a genuine love that emanates from real knowledge of God through Christ in contrast to a counterfeit love which is manufactured through a carnal heart that has not been purified, a seared conscience that has not been cleansed, and an insincere faith that has not been established in the righteousness of God. No matter how loving a person may appear to be, God knows their heart.

It is time to grow up and put away pretending and playing make-believe. It is time to engage with God and press on to know Him to the fullest extent available to us. It is time to put away tricks and showmanship, puffed up pride, false securities, and wrong motives. There is more of God that we have not and cannot know while we are aiming at the wrong target. Let us press on to maturity to know Him.

1 Corinthians 13:11 - When I was a child, I talked like a child, I thought like a child, I reasoned like a child. **When I became a man, I put the ways of childhood behind me.**

Perfection Course Elements

In the seven units of this course, we will dig into seven aspects of spiritual maturity. These elements of maturity are: 1) Open Ears to Obey; 2) Foundation of Christ & the Whole Counsel of God; 3) Functioning from Divine Nature; 4) Skilled in the Word of Righteousness; 5) Kingdom Gospel with Signs Following; 6) Discernment of Good and Evil; and 7) Fulfilling Ministry to Prepare the Bride. If we lack any of these elements, or if we are not quite fully like Jesus in any of these elements, then we have not yet attained spiritual maturity. This course was designed to be taken again and again as we grow. No matter how mature we become, there will always be more of God to press into.

May you be richly blessed as you grow in your knowledge of Him!

Pre-Course Examination & Questions
What is Spiritual Maturity?

Answer the following questions to the best of your ability. Examine your beliefs about spiritual maturity.

How are believers today led by the Holy Spirit?	What did Jesus accomplish through His death, resurrection, and ascension?	What does it mean to participate with divine nature?
What is the teaching of righteousness?	**What is the purpose of miracles?**	**How do we discern false teachings?**
What is the definition and purpose of ministry?	**What does spiritual maturity look like for a follower of Jesus?**	**What is one thing you are hoping to learn through this course?**

UNIT ONE:
OPEN EARS TO OBEY

KEY SCRIPTURE VERSE FOR UNIT ONE
We do, however, speak a message of wisdom among the mature, but not the wisdom of this age or of the rulers of this age, who are coming to nothing. No, we declare God's wisdom, a mystery that has been hidden and that God destined for our glory before time began. -1 Corinthians 2:6-7

CLASS 1: THE MYSTERY REVEALED
1 Reading, 1 Exercise, 1 Evaluation
The mystery of all ages has been revealed to us by the Spirit of the Lord. God has put His own Spirit inside of us so that we can live to reveal His glory.

CLASS 2: GUIDANCE FROM GOD
2 Readings, 1 Evaluation, 1 Exercise
God's purpose for mankind has not changed since creation. But now, God guides us by His Spirit into His purposes for our lives so that we can manifest His glory to all the earth.

CLASS 3: TESTING THE SPIRIT
2 Readings, 2 Exercises
As we turn ourselves over to guidance from the Holy Spirit, other voices of influence will seek to distort God's word or distract us from God's purposes. Therefore, we must learn to test the spirit.

CLASS 4: ABIDING & OBEDIENCE
1 Reading, 1 Evaluation, 1 Exercise
Jesus said if we love Him we will keep His commands. As we remain connected and faithful to Jesus, He guides us by His Spirit into all that He has for us.

KEY QUESTIONS

GROUP EXERCISES

PERFECTION COURSE – UNIT 1.1 READING

CHRIST IN YOU – THE MYSTERY REVEALED

God's original purpose for mankind has not changed. He created the world to be filled with people who would give Him glory by willingly and obediently tending and keeping the earth and everything in it according to His ways. This will happen – just not in the way it originally seemed.

In the Garden of Eden, the first woman gave way to the wiles of the evil one and disobeyed God's command not to eat of the tree of the knowledge of good and evil. Adam was with her and also disobeyed God's order. They did it because they were deceived into believing that disobeying God would make them wise and like God. Through this self-serving act of treason and anarchy against God, they whored themselves out into the service of the evil one. Through their attempt to usurp God's authority and become like God, iniquity was found in their hearts and innocence was lost. Their lack of knowledge and understanding of God's ways combined with their ignorance of the evil one's schemes left them vulnerable to his tactics of deception.

Since then, all of mankind – including you and me – have been usurpers, anarchists, and self-serving whores who attempt in numerous ways to be our own gods while unknowingly remaining in subjection to the evil one's many deceptions. All of mankind has fallen very short of the glory of God and God's original design and purpose for mankind.

> *Romans 3:10-18: As it is written: "There is **no one righteous, not even one**; there is **no one who understands**; there is **no one who seeks God. All have turned away**, they have together become worthless; there is **no one who does good, not even one**." "Their throats are open graves; their tongues practice deceit." "The poison of vipers is on their lips." "Their mouths are full of cursing and bitterness." "Their feet are swift to shed blood; ruin and misery mark their ways and the way of peace they do not know." "There is no fear of God before their eyes."*

Jesus is coming back for His Bride. He laid down His life to have her. Jesus came the first time to cleanse her from sin through His perfect life, sacrificial death, resurrection to eternal life, and ascension to the Father's right hand in heaven. He washes her with the water of the Word so that she can be holy and undefiled for her wedding day. The Bride that Jesus is coming for will have willingly cleansed herself from all whoredom, impurity, and iniquity in expectation of the return of her Bridegroom King. This Bride will be supernaturally strengthened to not bow to the wiles of the evil one but will stand in faith with boldness even at the expense of her own life in order to not rebel against the command of God.

> *Ephesians 5:29-32: After all, no one ever hated their own body, but they feed and care for their body, just as Christ does the church-- for we are members of his body. "For this reason a man will leave his father and mother and be united to his wife, and the two will become one flesh." **This is a profound mystery--but I am talking about Christ and the church**.*

The first Adam's wife was in a perfect paradise. Paradise was lost due to failure to correctly discern deception and, therefore, caving in to sin. At the end of the age, the Bride of Jesus will stand in a world of chaos, disorder, lawlessness, and deep darkness from the evil one's deceit and power over the world. She will gain paradise for eternity with Jesus by walking in the light of the truth and not bowing to any of the devices of the ancient serpent.

This is God's purpose for the church. People from every nation, tribe, and tongue are included in the salvation and inheritance obtained by Jesus through His death and resurrection to declare and reveal God's ultimate and eternal victory over the evil one. (See Revelation 5:9.)

> *Ephesians 3:4-11: In reading this, then, you will be able to understand my insight into **the mystery of Christ**, which was not made known to people in other generations as it has now been revealed by the Spirit to God's holy apostles and prophets. **This mystery is that through the gospel the Gentiles are heirs together with Israel**, members together of one body, and sharers together in the promise in Christ Jesus. I became a servant of this gospel by the gift of God's grace given me through the working of his power. Although I am less than the least of all the Lord's people, this grace was given me: to preach to the Gentiles the boundless riches of Christ, and **to make plain to everyone the administration of this mystery**, which for ages past was kept hidden in God, who created all things. **His intent was that now, through the church, the manifold wisdom of God should be made known to the rulers and authorities in the heavenly realms, according to his eternal purpose that he accomplished in Christ Jesus our Lord.***

What is the mystery that was so important to God that He kept it hidden for all ages until the fullness of time had come?

> *Colossians 1:26-27: the **mystery** that has been kept hidden for ages and generations, but is now disclosed to the Lord's people. To them God has chosen to make known among the Gentiles **the glorious riches of this mystery, which is Christ in you, the hope of glory**.*

Christ in you. The hope of the glory of God and eternal life with Him. Only Christ in us gives us this hope. This hope drives us to live by the power of Christ in us to resist the lusts and temptations of this world, our flesh, and the devil.

The only way that God could create a Bride for His Son, who would be able to withstand the days of evil in this world before He returns to make all things new, was to put His very own Spirit inside of us – His enemies. But, if God tried to put His Spirit inside of sinful flesh, we would instantly die. Therefore, before He could put His Spirit inside of us, He had to cleanse us of our sin so that we could become holy vessels able to hold His indwelling presence. This is why Jesus came the first time. The sinless life and sacrificial death of Jesus cleansed our sin through the shedding of His blood. His resurrection proves God's acceptance of His offering and that His life was truly and totally righteous. Death could not hold Him because eternal life is the divine promise to the righteous.

Through our faith in Jesus, we are cleansed from our sin and the Holy Spirit comes to dwell inside of us. (See Ephesians 1:13.) In fact, all of the blessings and benefits of the righteous become available to us freely by faith in what Jesus has done for us.

> *Colossians 2:2-3: My goal is that they may be encouraged in heart and united in love, so that they may have the **full riches of complete understanding**, in order that they may **know the mystery of God, namely, Christ, in whom are hidden all the treasures of wisdom and knowledge.***

God kept this hidden for ages because if the rulers of this world had known that this would be the ultimate result of Jesus' death on a cross, they would never have crucified Him.

> *1 Corinthians 2:6-16: We do, however, speak a message of wisdom among the mature, but not the wisdom of this age or of the rulers of this age, who are coming to nothing. **No, we declare God's wisdom, a mystery that has been hidden and that God destined for our glory before time began**. None of the rulers of this age understood it, for if they had, they would not have crucified the Lord of glory. However, as it is written: "What no eye has seen,*

what no ear has heard, and what no human mind has conceived"--the things God has prepared for those who love him-- **these are the things God has revealed to us by his Spirit.** *The Spirit searches all things, even the deep things of God. For who knows a person's thoughts except their own spirit within them? In the same way no one knows the thoughts of God except the Spirit of God.* **What we have received is not the spirit of the world, but the Spirit who is from God, so that we may understand what God has freely given us.** *This is what we speak, not in words taught us by human wisdom but in words taught by the Spirit, explaining spiritual realities with Spirit-taught words. The person without the Spirit does not accept the things that come from the Spirit of God but considers them foolishness, and cannot understand them because they are discerned only through the Spirit. The person with the Spirit makes judgments about all things, but such a person is not subject to merely human judgments, for, "Who has known the mind of the Lord so as to instruct him?"* **But we have the mind of Christ.**

Through His Spirit inside of us, God has given us the mind of Christ so that we can know Him, understand His ways and what He has done for us, and discern the deceptions of the enemy and ways of this world so that we are not ensnared into anarchy like the first woman was. The Holy Spirit in our hearts guides us into all truth—not just a little bit of the truth, but all the truth. This is why we are encouraged to keep on asking, seeking, and knocking so that we can continue to receive, find, and have more and more of God's goodness opened to us.

> *John 16:13: But when he, the Spirit of truth, comes,* **he will guide you into all the truth.** *He will not speak on his own; he will speak only what he hears, and he will tell you what is yet to come.*

> *Matthew 7:7-8:* **Ask** *and it will be given to you;* **seek** *and you will find;* **knock** *and the door will be opened to you. For everyone who asks receives; the one who seeks finds; and to the one who knocks, the door will be opened.*

When we do this, we discover that God has revealed the biggest mystery of all redemptive history to us so that we can steward the mystery to the rest of the world. The mystery is this: Jesus Christ was born as God in the flesh who came, died, was raised to everlasting life, ascended to heaven, and poured out His Spirit into our hearts so that we can be just like Him while we are still here on earth.

> *1 Timothy 3:16: Beyond all question, the* **mystery from which true godliness springs is** *great: He appeared in the flesh, was vindicated by the Spirit, was seen by angels, was preached among the nations, was believed on in the world, was taken up in glory.*

> *Romans 16:25-27: Now to him who is able to establish you in accordance with my gospel, the message I proclaim about Jesus Christ, in keeping with the* **revelation of the mystery** *hidden for long ages past, but now revealed and made known through the prophetic writings by the command of the eternal God, so that all the Gentiles might come* **to the obedience that comes from faith**—*to the only wise God be glory forever through Jesus Christ! Amen.*

The first Adam's wife was made out of his rib and he exclaimed, "Bone of my bone and flesh of my flesh." (See Genesis 2:23.) The second Adam's Bride is made not by flesh and blood but by the Spirit of the Lord indwelling jars of clay to bring Him glory through personal godliness exhibited by righteousness, holiness, purity, and obedience to God's commands from the heart. When He returns for her, He will recognize her by her likeness to Him. Knowing that she will reign with her King for eternity in the world to come, she lives on earth now for this eternal hope refusing to submit herself to the temporal temptations put before her in this world.

The Mystery Revealed: A New Creation in Christ

As we place our faith in Jesus, the nature of God and the very Spirit of Christ dwell inside of us and we are given power and ability to live as children of God and as a totally new creation in Christ.

> *John 1:12-13: Yet to all who did receive him [Jesus], to those who believed in his name, he **gave the right to become children of God**-- children born not of natural descent, nor of human decision or a husband's will, **but born of God**.*

> *John 14:23 - Jesus replied, "Anyone who loves me will obey my teaching. My Father will love them, and **we will come to them and make our home with them**.*

> *2 Corinthians 5:17 - Therefore, if anyone is in Christ, **the new creation has come: The old has gone, the new is here!***

> *2 Peter 1:3-4 - His divine power has given us everything we need for a godly life through our knowledge of him who called us by his own glory and goodness. Through these he has given us his very great and precious promises, so that through them **you may participate in the divine nature, having escaped the corruption in the world caused by evil desires**.*

Through faith in Christ, we have been given the right to participate with God's nature dwelling inside of us. But we must be born again by submitting ourselves to the regenerating power of the Spirit of the Lord to renew our minds into the will of God and away from our own Adamic inclinations toward sin, self-exaltation, anarchy, and usurping God's authority in our life.

> *John 3:5-8 - Jesus answered, "Very truly I tell you, **no one can enter the kingdom of God unless they are born of water and the Spirit**. Flesh gives birth to flesh, but the Spirit gives birth to spirit. You should not be surprised at my saying, 'You must be born again.' The wind blows wherever it pleases. You hear its sound, but you cannot tell where it comes from or where it is going. So it is with everyone born of the Spirit."*

> *1 John 3:9 - **No one who is born of God will continue to sin**, because God's seed remains in them; they cannot go on sinning, because they have been born of God.*

By the power of the Holy Spirit within us, we can live lives of purity and holiness to reveal God to the world. In fact, as we are led by the Spirit of the Lord, we prove ourselves to be the sons of God, calling out to our Father in Heaven to help us in our time of need through the trials and tribulations of this world.

> *Romans 8:13-17: For if you live according to the flesh, you will die; but **if by the Spirit you put to death the misdeeds of the body, you will live. For those who are led by the Spirit of God are the children of God.** The Spirit you received does not make you slaves, so that you live in fear again; rather, the Spirit you received brought about your adoption to sonship. And by him we cry, "Abba, Father." The Spirit himself testifies with our spirit that we are God's children. Now if we are children, then we are heirs--heirs of God and co-heirs with Christ, **if indeed we share in his sufferings in order that we may also share in his glory**.*

As believers, we have become stewards of the mysteries of God. To live them out and to share them with anyone who will listen. Jesus readily explained His parables to His closest followers while they remained a mystery to those without ears to hear. Moreover, if we obey Jesus, He calls us His friends; and as His friends, He shares with us everything the Father has shared with Him.

> *1 Corinthians 4:1: This, then, is how you ought to regard us: as servants of Christ and as those entrusted with the **mysteries God has revealed**.*

> *Matthew 13:11: He replied, "Because the **knowledge of the secrets of the kingdom of heaven has been given to you**, but not to them."*

> *John 15:14-15: You are my friends if you do what I command. I no longer call you servants, because a servant does not know his master's business. Instead,* **I have called you friends, for everything that I learned from my Father I have made known to you**.

The mystery revealed is that through Christ dwelling inside of us, we can be like Him. We can attain to spiritual maturity and the likeness of God as we await Christ's return.

> *Romans 8:29: For those God foreknew he also* **predestined to be conformed to the image of his Son**, *that he might be the firstborn among many brothers and sisters.*

> *Luke 6:40 - The student is not above the teacher, but* **everyone who is fully trained will be like their teacher.**

Therefore, we must press on to maturity by putting off our old self, reckoning ourselves dead to sin, and submitting ourselves to the leading of the Holy Spirit as He guides us into all righteousness and goodness. This was God's eternal purpose and the reason for Christ's sacrifice.

> *Titus 2:11-14: For the grace of God has appeared that offers salvation to all people. It teaches us to* **say "No" to ungodliness and worldly passions, and to live self-controlled, upright and godly lives in this present age**, *while we wait for the blessed hope--the appearing of the glory of our great God and Savior,* **Jesus Christ, who gave himself for us to redeem us from all wickedness and to purify for himself a people that are his very own**, *eager to do what is good.*

May God be glorified as we trust in His Son and reveal His love to the world. Let us strive to attain all that Christ attained for us.

Basic Training Exercise

DIVINE NATURE

2 Peter 1:3-4 NIV – His divine power has given us everything we need for a godly life through our knowledge of him who called us by his own glory and goodness. Through these he has given us his very great and precious promises, so that through them you may participate in the divine nature, having escaped the corruption the world caused by evil desires.

DESCRIPTION

God has given us what we need in order for us to be like Him. Godliness is the reason He created mankind – to reflect His image and His likeness. But since Adam, no one except Jesus has been able to do this fully.

When we believe Jesus, the Holy Spirit dwells in us. This is the same Spirit of the Lord that came upon Mary, causing her to conceive and give birth to the Son of God. The same Spirit that dwelt inside of Jesus to guide Him in a perfect and sinless life now dwells inside of us. We have divine nature inside us.

From the moment the Holy Spirit enters our hearts, a conflict begins between this divine nature and our own corrupt and fleshly desires. As we allow ourselves to be led by divine nature instead of our flesh, we become more and more like Jesus. The Spirit of the Lord within us will give us strength to resist our own urges and replace them with righteous thoughts and actions. The more the Holy Spirit transforms us in this way, the more of God's image we reflect.

Practicing participation in Divine Nature is about becoming increasingly conscious of the Spirit of God dwelling within us and choosing to obey His leadings as superior to our own inclinations.

PRAYER

Father, thank you for placing your Holy Spirit inside of me to help me become like Jesus. Help me submit to your guidance from within and strengthen me with your power for godliness. In Jesus' name, Amen.

Basic TRAINING
SPIRITUAL EXERCISES

PURPOSE:

To become increasingly godly and reflect God's image.

To be led by the Holy Spirit in righteous and pure thoughts.

To be empowered by the Holy Spirit for right words and actions.

SPIRITUAL FRUIT:

Holiness. Christlikeness. Godliness.

Increasing in the fruit of the Spirit listed in Galatians 5:22-23.

Growing evidence of our calling and election through the attributes listed in 2 Peter 1:5-7.

TALK WITH GOD

Jesus was perfect in all of His thoughts, words, and actions. How does this increase your respect and worship for Him? Tell Him about it.

How have you experienced the conflict between your own desires and what the Holy Spirit within you desires? In your life so far, who has been winning this conflict?

How does knowing that Jesus dwells inside you change your concept of approaching godliness? How does God want you to put this into practice in your life?

How is God inviting you to participate more deeply in His divine nature? What area of your thoughts, words, and actions does Jesus want you to reform right now?

Do you think it is possible for a person to be so renewed by the Holy Spirit that they do not sin? Why or why not? What is God's desire in this?

PRACTICE

1. Use the Talk with God points above to have a conversation with God about participating in Divine Nature. Listen to what He shares and put it into practice.

2. As you go through your day, find a way to regularly remind yourself that Jesus dwells inside of you. When you remember, take a moment to re-center your thoughts on Him. Allow Him to guide and strengthen you from within.

3. As you engage with others, remember that the Spirit of the Lord dwells inside of you. Turn yourself over to His guidance. How is Jesus engaging with this person? What is Jesus saying to them? It is not "what would Jesus do?" but "what is Jesus doing right now?" ... through you!

4. Journal to Jesus about the areas of your life or times of day when it seems to be more challenging to obey the Holy Spirit rather than your flesh. Seek the Lord for His insight and assistance with this.

ADDITIONAL SCRIPTURES:

Ephesians 4:23-24

2 Peter 2:20

1 John 3:9

1 John 5:18

Titus 3:5

Romans 7:14-20

Romans 8:1-15

Hebrews 1:3

Galatians 5:17-22

NOTES: _____

LIVING FOR GOD INSPECTION			
1 = Needs improvement	*2 = In Refining Process*	*3 = Doing Well for Now*	
Am I more focused on the things of God than the things of this world?			1 2 3
Am I spending enough time with God and communing with Him?			1 2 3
Am I enjoying the Word of God and prayer?			1 2 3
Am I regularly sharing faith with others?			1 2 3
Do I disobey God in anything?			1 2 3
Do I continue to do something which makes my conscience uneasy?			1 2 3
Do I pray about how I spend my time and with whom?			1 2 3
Do I pray about the money I spend?			1 2 3
Do I choose my own preferences, desires, or ideas over God's instructions or commands?			1 2 3
Do I have a healthy rhythm of life, service, and rest? Do I get enough sleep?			1 2 3
Do I spend my "free" time in holy activities or with worldliness, lusts, or sin?			1 2 3
Am I a hearer of the Word or a do-er of the Word? Am I self-deceived?			1 2 3
Am I doing the things I tell/teach others to do? Am I without hypocrisy?			1 2 3
Am I honest in all my acts and words? Do I exaggerate or lie?			1 2 3
Do I thank God that I am not like other people, like the Pharisee at the tax collector?			1 2 3
Is there anyone I fear, dislike, disown, criticize, disregard, or hold resentment towards?			1 2 3
Do I look at others with sexual/sensual lust or fantasy in my heart?			1 2 3
Do I dress to entice others with my physical appearance?			1 2 3
Am I in any way creating the impression that I am better than I really am?			1 2 3
Do I use my outward appearance as a façade, mask, or cover up for insecurity?			1 2 3
Do I pass on confidential information to other people? Can I be trusted?			1 2 3
Am I a slave to anything? (Habits, diet, dress, image, other people's approval, etc.)			1 2 3
Am I self-conscious, self-pitying, or self-justifying?			1 2 3
Do I deflect, blame-shift, self-deceive, or otherwise avoid God's dealings with me?			1 2 3
Am I living victoriously in all areas of life?			1 2 3
Am I jealous, impure, critical, irritable, touchy, or distrustful?			1 2 3
Do I grumble or complain? Am I angry or frustrated in any area of my life?			1 2 3
Have I been loving, joyful, at peace, patient, kind, faithful, gentle, and self-controlled?			1 2 3
Am I totally honest with myself about what God is doing in my life?			1 2 3
Am I totally honest with at least one person about what God is doing in my life?			1 2 3
Can I accept correction with an open heart and willingness to change for God's purpose?			1 2 3
Do I have difficulty submitting to authority which God has placed over me in life, work, or ministry? Do I ignore their counsel or go my own way in my heart?			1 2 3
The aim of our charge is love that issues from a pure heart, a good conscience, and a sincere faith. *1Timothy 1:5*			

# PERFECTION COURSE – UNIT 1.2.1 READING

Guidance from God*

As descendants of Adam, in our human minds, we can never figure out what Jesus would do. And even if we could, it would not be in our nature to do it. Without the Holy Spirit, even disciples who had walked with Jesus for three years did not know what to do. After the resurrection, they returned to their former occupations because they did not realize that their work for Messiah had only just begun. (See John 21:3.) During their time of waiting in Jerusalem in obedience to Jesus' command to them, they did what seemed right to them according to their own interpretation of Scripture. But when it came to the point of decision, they were stuck flipping a coin for divine guidance. (See Acts 1:26.) The point is that without the Holy Spirit, even those who walked most closely with God in the flesh were totally without the ability to know what they were supposed to do next and how they were supposed to execute God's will for their lives.

In this condition, Jesus did not want them to do a thing for Him or in His name. In this condition, the disciples were still focused on worldly things and interpreting things from a fleshly perspective. They still thought that it was time for the Messiah to come and conquer all of Israel's enemies in earthly and political battles for power and dominance. Their hearts were bent on war and judgment of God's enemies in the final and catastrophic *day of the Lord*, which they knew about from the Scriptures. (See Acts 1:6.) They were constantly arguing with one another over who was the greatest and who would have positions of power in Jesus' Kingdom. (See Matthew 18:1; Mark 9:34; Luke 9:46, 22:23-24.) They were also most likely expecting Jesus to come back imminently to lead them in His army, slaying all their enemies.

They were, indeed, entering into war. But this was a war for the hearts and souls of men. This war would only be won by doing what Jesus did by the guidance and power of God from within.

On the day of Pentecost, when the Holy Spirit was poured out from heaven, the 120 believers who received the Holy Spirit became animated by the Spirit of the Lord. Their war against evil began through the words of their mouths as they made known the completed work of the cross, declaring the enemy's defeat. (See Acts 2:7-11.)

Only after Christ's followers had received the Holy Spirit were their hearts transformed. Their hearts became circumcised and softened to be compassionate rather than conquering. All of their plans for the future were replaced with a higher calling to the Kingdom of God. From this day forward, Jesus would be leading them step-by-step as if He were there in person, but now He was *Christ-in-them* who would guide them into all truth and every good work He had prepared for them. The disciples became ambassadors of heaven who extended offers of peace to sinners, religious rebels, and enemies of God.

Manifesting Christ

We have the same assignment today that the first believers did – to manifest the love of Jesus as His representatives in the earth until He returns. Unfortunately, just like the first 120 believers, if left to ourselves without the Holy Spirit, we may as well be tossing a coin. Even "righteous" deeds are nothing but *filthy rags* before God when they are done without the leading of the Holy Spirit. (See Isaiah 64:6.) These works, no matter how good they may be, are eternally profitless. Unrestrained, our sinful nature is jealous, selfishly ambitious, greedy, and lusty. To live from this operating system results in every evil thing. Basically, when we do not obey the Holy Spirit, we are really no different from the people of the world.

The Holy Spirit is willing to guide us step by step, moment by moment into our Kingdom tasks. As believers, we have the opportunity to offer ourselves as Christ's willing and obedient subjects to allow Him to change us to live for Him and not for ourselves. (See Romans 12:1-2.)

This is a choice. It is not done for us just because we have put our faith in Jesus. Out of gratitude for the salvation God has given us in Christ, we must willingly offer ourselves to live by the guidance of the Spirit of the Lord. This is not rooted in obligation or dogmatic religious fear but in love and thankfulness, prompting us to the genuine pursuit of God. We do not become robots of God but retain our free will to live according to our own desires or live according to the guidance of the Holy Spirit that God has put within us. (See Romans 8:5-8,12-14.)

This said, the Christian life is not a democracy, it is a monarchy, and Christ is our King. Therefore, we do not ask Jesus to co-labor with us in our goals, dreams, and desires; rather, we co-labor with Christ to do the Kingdom works that He has designed for us. (See 1 Corinthians 3:9.) The Holy Spirit will not lead us into worldly wisdom or set our aims on the things of this world or the kingdoms of this world which are doomed to burn and perish. In fact, the things that the Holy Spirit is focused on will seem like foolishness to those who do not have the Holy Spirit. But Jesus' Kingdom is not of this world, and His wisdom is higher than any earthly wisdom. (See 1 Corinthians 2:12-16.) The Holy Spirit will not guide us into satisfying our own desires and lusts of our flesh but into the will of God which is for our holiness, purity, righteousness, and moral goodness. (See Galatians 5:16-25.)

When Christ died on the cross, we died with Him. Now, our calling is to live as if we are dead to our own ideas, plans, and concepts of good and godliness in order to live fully and exclusively for Jesus and His guidance for His Kingdom. We must live for God even if this involves pain, loss, suffering, or selfless acts.

> *Colossians 3:2-3: Set your minds on things above, not on earthly things.* **For you died, and your life is now hidden with Christ** *in God.*
>
> *1Peter 4:1-2 NLT: So then, since Christ suffered physical pain,* **you must arm yourselves with the same attitude he had***, and be ready to suffer, too. For if you have suffered physically for Christ, you have finished with sin.* **You won't spend the rest of your lives chasing your own desires, but you will be anxious to do the will of God.**

Without overstating it, living life according to the Holy Spirit is the occupation of the Christian life here on earth. God's purpose in sending Jesus was to cleanse us from our sin in order to restore us to right standing with Himself so that each of us draws near to Him and hears His voice.

Moreover, as we progress in the Christian life towards spiritual maturity, we do not become LESS dependent on the Holy Spirit; we become MORE dependent on Jesus and His guidance. We realize that we are not only dead in His death, but we are totally useless without Him. The more we do the things that Jesus did, which are completely out of the realm of human capacity, the more we NEED Him to guide, lead, and empower us for our Kingdom tasks. Even more so, if we undergo hardship, trials, and opposition, we NEED His comfort and strength in order to endure. Therefore, no matter what is happening in our lives, we NEED Jesus and God's guidance through the Holy Spirit.

Oftentimes, this means that, just like the first 120 disciples who eagerly and expectantly waited to hear from Jesus about what they were supposed to do next, we have to wait for the Holy Spirit to give us our divine marching orders. Waiting on God is challenging because our flesh naturally desires to fulfill itself, satisfy its lusts, and be exalted as powerful, busy, needed, useful, and successful. Additionally, our flesh is tempted to consider our natural abilities to procure results that seem like what God revealed His will to be to "make things happen" or "use our God-given gifts and skills." Sometimes, waiting for God seems irresponsible, complacent, or disobedient. Other times, we simply grow impatient, and the pressures of conformity and temptations towards "easier" or "faster" solutions, seem to bear down on us. When this happens, we are likely to resort to our own interpretations of God's Word or will and set out on a course of our own design rather than continuing to wait for God's guidance into His will, ways, and purposes. Rebellion against God often presents itself as the logical solution to our problems, the fulfillment of our truest desires, or even what God has promised. This is exactly what Eve thought before eating from the wrong tree.

This is serious stuff. God gave us His Spirit within us, but we retain our free will to obey the Spirit of the Lord or not. We have the ability to obey God or disobey Him. We have free will to acknowledge Jesus or to deny Him. We retain the right to submit to Christ or renounce Him. (See 2 Timothy 2:12.) This is why true waiting on God is the token mark of spiritual maturity and submission to God. Waiting acknowledges an authority higher than ourselves and submits willingly to that authority's timing and purpose. True waiting is not stagnancy because God will always be faithful to prompt us at the right time into the right action with the right motive for His purpose, which will always be rooted in eternity.

The only way that we will be able to *fight the good fight of faith* (see 1 Timothy 6:12; 2 Timothy 4:7) and endure through the trials of life is to listen to and obey the Holy Spirit DAILY and to constantly encourage one another in living our lives by the direction of the Holy Spirit. All we have to do is ASK God for wisdom and He will freely give it to us. (See James 1-:5-8.)

> *Hebrews 3:7-8, 12-15: So,* **as the Holy Spirit says: "Today, if you hear his voice, do not harden your hearts** *as you did in the rebellion, during the time of testing in the wilderness, (quoting Psalm 95:7-11) ... See to it, brothers and sisters, that none of you has a sinful, unbelieving heart that turns away from the living God.* **But encourage one another daily, as long as it is called "Today," so that none of you may be hardened by sin's deceitfulness.** *We have come to share in Christ, if indeed we hold our original conviction firmly to the very end. As has just been said:* **"Today, if you hear his voice, do not harden your hearts** *as you did in the rebellion."*

Keep it simple, listen to Jesus and do what He says. Stay available to the Lord and be flexible when He sends you in a different direction than what you were expecting. The true Christian life of spiritual maturity is a life that is yielded to God so that it can manifest the love of Jesus to all mankind.

> *John 10:27:* **My sheep listen to my voice; I know them, and they follow me.**

Examples from the Book of Acts

The Book of Acts gives us various examples of how God speaks to followers of Jesus. Sometimes, the Holy Spirit said *go* and other times *stay*. Sometimes, the Holy Spirit prevented believers from going where they desired to go and other times compelled them to go even in the face of great suffering.

Examples can be found in Acts 8:29-30, 10:19-21, 16:6-7, 18:21, 20:22-24, 22:18.

All of this is to say that Christ-followers no longer made decisions for themselves based on their own logic or way of thinking about things. They lived their lives by literally obeying the promptings of God through the indwelling Holy Spirit.

Prophecy, Dreams & Visions

Examples of prophecy, dreams, and visions are prevalent throughout the Book of Acts. In fact, once a believer received the Holy Spirit, it was normal for ordinary men and women to prophesy. Prophetic revelation is given to believers for ourselves and for one another to comfort us in our trials, encourage us into our Kingdom purpose, and build up our faith in Jesus Christ. (See 1 Corinthians 14:3, 12.) All believers are encouraged to eagerly desire to prophesy so that they may build up the Church. (See 1 Corinthians 14:1, 39.)

Examples can be found in Acts 15:32, 19:6, 21:8-9, 16:9-10, 18:9-11, 9:10-17, 10:9-20.

Visions God gave to believers photographically depicted something God was revealing, but He also spoke directly about its meaning. The people receiving the visions remained of sound mind and were able to converse with God to see what He was showing them and hear what He was giving them as an interpretation. God spoke through the vision, during the visions, and after the visions. Once the vision was received, the recipients set out to obey what God had instructed them or were led by the Lord into the situations, which would clearly demonstrate what the vision had portrayed. (See Acts 11:4-18.)

Prophecy can include rebukes and warnings for the purpose of helping one another stay on track in our walk of faith and holiness. For example, a prophetic warning was issued through Paul to the Ephesian elders regarding false teachers who would spring up out of the ranks of the Church. Paul and the elders also prophetically discerned that they would never see each other again. (See Acts 20:25-32.) God also uses prophecy to reveal His omniscience by disclosing the secrets of our hearts and by accurately foretelling the things which are to come. (See 1 Corinthians 14:24-25.) For example, prophetic discernment about the inner workings of Ananias and Sapphira's hearts was given to Peter in order to keep the Church unpolluted by those who were deceptive. (See Acts 5:3-9.)

Most of the time, prophecy, dreams, and visions are subject to interpretation. Sometimes, the Holy Spirit will give us the interpretation, but other times He will not, and we must receive by faith what the Lord has revealed to us in the way that He has given it to us. This said, revelation, which the Holy Spirit gives us, no matter which form it takes, will always be aligned with the *whole counsel of God*, His character, and the completed work of Christ, which helps us to *test the spirit* and discern that God is speaking. Sometimes, God's message is crystal clear but, most often, it seems as if we are seeing imperfectly like puzzling reflections in a dimly lit mirror. (See 1 Corinthians 13:12; Numbers 12:6-8.) This is by design and keeps us dependent on Christ and the Holy Spirit.

For example, prophetic insight was given to Paul and the believers in every city about the suffering that laid ahead for Paul as he journeyed on towards Jerusalem. The prophet Agabus even acted it out. (See Acts 20:22-23, 21:4, 10-15.) What these believers spiritually discerned was all true, but God's will in the matter was subject to interpretation. Everyone listening to the Holy Spirit knew that suffering awaited Paul if he went to Jerusalem, so they urged him not to go but Paul knew that it was God's will for him to go, in spite of the suffering that was in store. This is somewhat reminiscent of Jesus' encounter with Peter when Peter admonished Jesus that He would not have to suffer and die on a cross. (See Matthew 16:21-23; Mark 8:31-33.) In a similar way, the believers prophesying to Paul heard the Holy Spirit correctly, but their interpretation was carnal and selfish. On the other hand, Paul had already been imprisoned, whipped, beaten, stoned, and left for dead on account of the Gospel, and he was willing to go through it all again because the love of Christ compelled him to selflessness. He was ready to pay the ultimate price for Christ, and nothing would deter him from obeying God.

Prophetic revelation was also given to believers in order to speak warnings to His people regarding the things that were to come in the world. (See Acts 11:27-29.) Notice that Agabus' prophecy of famine was not given as a proclamation of judgment against the Roman world. Instead, it was interpreted as a grace of God for the preparation of His people because they perceived that the prophecy was given for the building up of the Church. To dig into this a little bit, no matter what Jesus taught, His resounding underlying message was always *repent for the Kingdom of Heaven is at hand*. When Jesus was asked about disasters and calamities happening in the world, this message remained the same. Essentially, Jesus instructed His followers not to consider those who experience catastrophe or misfortune to be worse sinners who were more deserving of God's apparent judgment. Rather, Jesus conveyed that disasters speak warnings that anyone who does not repent and place their faith in Him as Lord and Savior will suffer the ultimate calamity on the *day of judgment* which is to come. (See Luke 13:1-5.) Jesus never went on sin hunts to expose the reasons why bad things were happening in the world but steadfastly continued proclaiming to *repent for the Kingdom of Heaven is at hand* so that everyone could come to know Him and be saved. This is totally consistent with how God functioned throughout the Old Testament. God often gave conditional prophetic warnings of what would happen if people would not repent. This said, in most cases, God was clear that if people repented, He would relent of the impending calamity. (See Jeremiah 7:3, 18:8, 26:13, 36:3; Ezekiel 18:21; Joel 2:14; Jonah 3:10.) However, other times, God reached the limit of His mercy, and the sin of the people attained to full measure. By then, repentance would profit the people nothing because it was too late. Jesus prophesied about the coming *day of judgment* as an appointed time that has been set, which only God (not even Jesus and definitely none of us) knows, when God's vengeance will be poured out on the earth because the sin of all mankind has reached its full measure. (See Matthew 24:1-51; Mark 13:1-37; Luke 12:35-59, 21:5-38.) God's judgment and wrath was satisfied when He poured it out on Christ on the cross, and therefore, for everyone who has repented and placed their faith in Jesus, God relents of the judgment that we deserve. This is why the message of *repent for the Kingdom of Heaven is at hand* is of utmost importance and is the loving tone of all true prophecy. The day of God's wrath is yet to come and will bring destruction for everyone who has not placed their faith in Jesus.

Until then, the purpose of revelation for cities or nations is not to decree judgment or to bless ignorance or lawlessness. The purpose is to inspire faithfulness to the Lord and invite unbelievers into God's grace through faith in Jesus Christ. According to the apostle Paul, God marked out the boundary lines of all the nations and the appointed times when they would rise and fall since before the creation of the earth. His purpose was that everyone in all nations would seek Him and try to find Him or, in other words, that they would *repent for the Kingdom of Heaven is at hand*. (See Acts 17:26-27.) As God's foreordained plans are fulfilled on the earth, He reveals them to His people through prophetic revelation. (See Amos 3:7.) This encourages God's people and is a testimony to unbelievers of God's omniscience and that Christ is King. The Old Testament is filled with examples of this type of prophecy. For example, the Books of 1 and 2 Kings were written to encourage the people of Israel in their faithfulness to God, and are both packed full of historical accounts of God speaking through a person and then *it came to pass just as the man of God had said*. As a smattering of other examples, the prophet Isaiah prophesied the events of the reign of

Cyrus of Persia approximately 150 years before it came to pass, Jeremiah accurately predicted that the people of Israel would be in Babylonian exile for 70 years, 20 years before the 70 years began. Daniel accurately foretold the events in the lives of the kings of Babylon whom he served while he was in exile. (See Isaiah 44:28; Jeremiah 25:11-12; Daniel 2:29-45, 4:19-33, 5:13-31.) Interestingly, all of these prophets also prophesied things which are still yet to come. For us today, when believers prophesy about the things going on in the world and they come to pass, we are encouraged by knowing that God already knows the end from the beginning. Our faith is built up so that we are able to stand firm in Christ no matter what happens between now and when He returns. (See Isaiah 46:10; Revelation 1:8, 21:6, 22:13.) We will cover this in more depth in Unit Two of this course.

Angels

God also sent His angels to guide believers in the Book of Acts. Throughout the Old Testament, God sent angels to His people to bring words of encouragement, to assist with dramatic escapes, to fight battles with them and for God's people, and to reveal heaven's agenda. (See Genesis 18:2, 19:1-22, 32:1; Joshua 5:13-15; 2 Kings 6:17; Isaiah 6:5, etc.) Jesus Christ is the *Lord of Hosts* which means that He is the captain and commander of God's army of angels who carry out His commands. This is one of God's most commonly used names in the Scriptures, mentioned over 250 times. Angels can take the form of human beings who supernaturally appear and disappear, or they may be seen only through eyes which God has granted to see in the spiritual realm.

Angels were responsible for releasing Peter from prison on two occasions, once with John and once on his own. The second time it happened, it was so surreal that Peter thought it was a vision, but it wasn't. (See Acts 5:19-20, 12:7-11.) An angel of the Lord told Philip to take a certain road to his next divine appointment. (See Acts 8:26-27.) God sent an angel to Cornelius so that he would send for Peter and hear the Gospel of Jesus Christ. (See Acts 10:3-8, 10:21-22.) An angel appeared to Paul to encourage and reassure him in spite of the impending shipwreck. (See Acts 27:21-26.) An angel of the Lord struck Herod down dead when he did not give glory to God. This instilled the fear of God in many people, and they placed their faith in Jesus. (See Acts 12:23-24.) Angels ministered to believers constantly and were sent to care for God's people. (See Hebrews 1:14; Psalm 34:7, 91:4, 11-12.) Sometimes they were seen and sometimes not, but they were there carrying out God's commands.

The Same Yesterday, Today, and Forever

God speaks and guides us today the same way He guided the first followers of Christ in the Book of Acts.

PRAYER INSPECTION				
1 = Needs improvement	2 = In Refining Process		3 = Doing Well for Now	
Prayer Inspection – *praying at all times in all situations – nothing earthly, sensual, or demonic*				
Have I *asked* God what His will is in this situation?	1	2	3	
Have I *listened* to God for His perspective, wisdom, and insight into the situation?	1	2	3	
Am I praying this because God guided me about it or because it is what I want?	1	2	3	
Am I praying this because it is what I *think* God would want?	1	2	3	
Am I praying this to manipulate, control, or impose my will on a person or situation?	1	2	3	
Am I misusing or abusing Scripture in prayer?	1	2	3	
Am I misusing or abusing "*agreement*" between believers in prayer?	1	2	3	
Am I imitating a prayer technique or method to try to obtain or force results?	1	2	3	
Am I praying out of genuine love for God and others?	1	2	3	
Have I taken the planks out of my own eyes before praying for someone else to change?	1	2	3	
Am I praying according to the ways of God or of this world?	1	2	3	
Am I praying for my own promotion or for Jesus to be exalted?	1	2	3	
Am I praying a prayer of faith, or out of flesh or fear?	1	2	3	
Lord, teach us to pray… *Luke 11:1*				

Basic Training Exercise

OBEDIENCE TO THE MASTER

Romans 6:16-17 NIV - Don't you know that when you offer yourselves to someone as obedient slaves, you are slaves of the one you obey—whether you are slaves to sin, which leads to death, or to obedience, which leads to righteousness? But thanks be to God that, though you used to be slaves to sin, you have come to obey from your heart the pattern of teaching that has now claimed your allegiance.

DESCRIPTION

The Apostle Paul knew that He had been bought with a price. God purchased us for Himself with the precious blood of Jesus. This redemption sets us free from wrong "masters" so that we can obey God.

It is true that Jesus calls us His friends but He is also our King. The Kingdom is a monarchy, not a democracy. Our King has the right to give us orders, instructions, and daily tasks. Unfortunately, we often live according to our own agenda, desires, ambitions, the pattern of this world, or the expectations of others rather than turning ourselves over to obey God exclusively.

We are God's servants. A servant eagerly awaits their master's orders and executes them without argument or contradiction. The master sets the agenda each day for their own purposes and has the right to shift the focus of the servant anytime they need to.

To practice Obedience to the Master is about receiving daily "orders" from the Lord about the things that He has for us **today** so that we can obey Him even if it means we have to alter our own plans.

CONSIDERATIONS

Has there been a time when you knew that God was telling you to do something other than what you had planned? What was this like for you? What did you do? What difficulties do you encounter when thinking of yourself as a servant/slave? Why are you offended? Are you willing to allow God to change your plans today? This week? This year? For your life?

Category: Listening to God

ALL RIGHTS RESERVED © 2018 Wendy Bowen

www.manifestinternational.com

Basic TRAINING
SPIRITUAL EXERCISES

PURPOSE:

To listen to God's voice.

To discern the will of the Lord for us for today.

To present ourselves to God to do His will.

SPIRITUAL FRUIT:

Greater alignment with God's will.

Increased awareness of God in our daily life and routine.

Increased worship through offering of ourselves.

Improved clarity of God's desires for us.

PRAYER

Jesus, you are my King. Forgive me for the times I have treated You too casually by not listening to or obeying Your instructions. I come before You now as a servant to my Master to receive Your directions and to do Your will. Speak to me now so I can obey Your voice. In Jesus' name, Amen.

PRACTICE

1. Each morning, set a time and find a quiet and private place where you can spend time with God.
   - If you need to wake up earlier to make this time, do so.
   - Bring your Bible and a notebook to take note of anything significant the Lord may share with you.

2. Be still for a moment. Then, offer yourself to God.
   - Offer the day ahead to God, saying, "Jesus, I offer this day to you as a sacrifice. I desire to do Your will today."
   - Wait for anything He might say to you before you begin.

3. Begin to ask the Lord for His guidance for the day. Give Jesus enough time to respond to you. Take notes of your King's responses as needed. Use the following questions as a guide for your conversation.
   - King Jesus, what do you have for me today?
   - Is there anything You want me to do?
   - Is there anywhere You want me to go?
   - Is there anyone You want me to reach out to or serve?
   - Is there any issue in me that You want to address?
   - Is there anyone You want me to forgive or bless?
   - Is there anything You want me to acquire or give away?
   - Is there anything on my calendar today that is **not** Your will? How do You want me to handle that?
   - Is there any fruit of the Spirit that You desire for me to execute my tasks with today? (love, joy, peace, etc.)

4. Thank the Lord for His guidance. Ask Him to help you to do the things He has revealed to you **today**, without making excuses – especially the things you might not desire to do.

NOTES: _____

ADDITIONAL SCRIPTURES:

Psalm 123:2
John 10:27
1 Corinthians 6:20
1 Corinthians 7:23
Isaiah 30:21
Hebrews 3:7-15
Jeremiah 31:33
Romans 12:1
Philippians 2:6-8

20

PERFECTION COURSE – UNIT 1.3.1 READING

Testing the Spirit

In spite of the fact that the Holy Spirit was poured out so powerfully on the first believers in the early churches, even they were subject to error and turning to wrong spirits, counterfeits of Jesus, and so-called gospels. This was because even though they were indwelt by the Holy Spirit, they had not yet been fully transformed by the Holy Spirit and brought into the full reality of the Christian existence.

> *Galatians 1:6-8: I am astonished that you are so quickly deserting the one who called you to live in the grace of Christ and are **turning to a different gospel-- which is really no gospel at all**. Evidently some people are throwing you into confusion and are trying to pervert the gospel of Christ. But even **if we or an angel from heaven should preach a gospel other than the one we preached to you, let them be under God's curse**!*

> *2 Corinthians 11:3-4: But I am afraid that just as **Eve was deceived by the serpent's cunning, your minds may somehow be led astray from your sincere and pure devotion to Christ**. For if someone comes to you and **preaches a Jesus other than the Jesus we preached**, or if you receive **a different spirit from the Spirit** you received, or **a different gospel** from the one you accepted, you put up with it easily enough.*

> *1 John 4:1: Dear friends, **do not believe every spirit**, but **test the spirits to see whether they are from God**, because many false prophets have gone out into the world.*

As we set out to pursue God through obedience to the indwelling Holy Spirit, we will be vulnerable to the same counterfeits, deceptions, and wrong spirits that early believers were until, by reason of use, we have been trained by the Holy Spirit to discern good from evil. (See Hebrews 5:14.)

This means that we must test the spirit behind everything. If a spirit whispers something to us, or a prophet prophesies, or a teacher teaches, or a preacher preaches, or an angel comes to us, or we have a vision beyond description, or feel physical sensations all over our body, or we have spiritual experience beyond human comprehension but the message and direction of the spirit, prophet, teacher, preacher, angel, vision, sensation, or experience does not line up with the truth of God's Word or the teachings and commands of Jesus, it is a lie from the pit of Hell.

This calls for discernment. We cannot and MUST not accept everything as if it is from God. Even if it seems like God or is delivered in the name of God or the name of Jesus, if it does not line up with the truth of God, it is a lie from the evil one.

We must test the spirit. In the Book of Job, Job says that the "ear tests words like the tongue tests foods." (See Job 12:11.) Just like a trained tongue can taste the different ingredients mixed into a dish of food, the trained ear can distinguish when flesh, ignorance, prejudice, presumption, or evil has been mixed into the truth. Those who have ears to hear will HEAR what God is saying. Moreover, we have been given the Holy Spirit to discern not only by the ear but by the Spirit. Spiritual people test and discern ALL things by whether or not the Spirit within them bears witness to the truth. Therefore, each of us MUST learn to discern by the Spirit of the Lord.

This said, the following gives some Scriptural guideline to assist you in cultivating the ability to discern what is from the Holy Spirit and what is not so that you can know God's voice from the other "voices" trying to influence you.

Holiness

First and foremost, let's state the obvious. The Holy Spirit is HOLY and the Holy Spirit will lead us in holiness. To be holy means to be *set apart* or *consecrated* or *sanctified* to the Lord exclusively for His purposes. The first use of holy in the Scriptures is used to describe the seventh day which God sanctified to Himself as different from all the other days of the week. (See Genesis 2:3.) Holiness is not somberness or some feigned religiosity. It is more about being reserved for special use according to God's will and not man's purposes. For example, the priests and Levites were appointed by God to teach the people to distinguish the holy from the common. (See Leviticus 10:10; Ezekiel 44:23.) When we give ourselves to Jesus, we become sanctified by His blood so that we can become holy through the regeneration of the Holy Spirit's work within us. (See Hebrews 10:14; Titus 3:5.) We have been set apart from the world and its purposes for God and His purposes.

> *1 John 4:2-6:* **This is how you can recognize the Spirit of God: Every spirit that acknowledges that Jesus Christ has come in the flesh is from God, but every spirit that does not acknowledge Jesus is not from God.** *This is the spirit of the antichrist, which you have heard is coming and even now is already in the world. You, dear children, are from God and have overcome them, because the one who is in you is greater than the one who is in the world.* **They are from the world and therefore speak from the viewpoint of the world, and the world listens to them.** *We are from God, and* **whoever knows God listens to us; but whoever is not from God does not listen to us. This is how we recognize the Spirit of truth and the spirit of falsehood.**

<u>Exalts Jesus as God in flesh</u>: The Holy Spirit will acknowledge Jesus as God in the flesh, who came to the world and is now raised from the dead and seated at the right hand of God in heaven.

Any spirit that will not say the name of Jesus or cannot declare that Jesus is Lord, or says that Jesus was a good teacher but not God or the Son of God, or that Jesus didn't die, or that Jesus was not raised from the dead is NOT the Holy Spirit. (See also 1 Corinthians 12:3.)

<u>Not of this world</u>: The Holy Spirit will lead us in the ways of God and not the ways of this world. We have been chosen to be set apart from this world and declare the works of the world to be evil. (See John 7:7.)

Any spirit that aligns with the ways of this world or seeks to advance the ways of this world or its kingdoms is NOT the Holy Spirit. Jesus clearly forewarned that His followers would be hated by the world for following Him and proclaimed a curse on those who are well spoken of by the world because it is evidence of them being in the same spirit of the false prophets. (See John 15:18-20; Luke 6:26.)

Conviction of Sin, Righteousness, Judgment

Jesus said this about what the Holy Spirit does:

> *John 16:8-11 ESV - And when he [the Holy Spirit] comes, he will* **convict the world concerning sin and righteousness and judgment***: concerning sin, because they do not believe in me; concerning righteousness, because I go to the Father, and you will see me no longer; concerning judgment, because the ruler of this world is judged.*

<u>Convict the world</u>: The Holy Spirit shows the world to be wrong. Its works are evil and rebellious against God. The world proved this to be true when they unanimously rejected and crucified Jesus, who is God in the flesh walking in perfect obedience to the Holy Spirit. The whole world is guilty before God and the Holy Spirit will not endorse the world or its ways.

Any spirit which aligns with the methodologies of this world or does not dissuade you from the perspective and beliefs of this world is NOT the Holy Spirit. Any spirit which endorses lawlessness or neglects to bring correction for ungodly behaviors is NOT the Holy Spirit.

Sin: By definition, sin is missing the mark. Anywhere on the target that is not a bullseye is missing the mark of perfection. Jesus demonstrated a sinless life in total submission to God. The greatest mark to miss is the free gift of salvation offered by God when He gave His Son, Jesus, as a sacrifice for sin.

Any spirit prompting unbelief in who Jesus is or what He has done for us is NOT the Holy Spirit. Any spirit denying the human need for Jesus due to self-righteousness or self-sufficiency is NOT the Holy Spirit. Any person who says they have no sin is a liar and does not know God. (See 1John 1:8-10.)

Righteousness: Righteousness is Biblically synonymous with justice or what is right in any given situation. It can also mean right standing or right relationship. Jesus demonstrated God's perfect righteousness in His conduct and perfect relationship with God. The prophet Amos described Him as a plumb line which is the device used by builders to assess whether something is upright or not. (See Amos 7:7-8.) Even though He was hated in the world, He is now seated at the right hand of God.

Any spirit which allows for unjust or unrighteous behavior which is not upright is NOT the Holy Spirit. Any spirit that will not submit itself to the justice of God or will not accept and submit itself to God's dealings is NOT the Holy Spirit.

Judgment: The whole world is under the power of the evil one. (See 1 John 5:19.) But the ancient serpent was judged and triumphed over through Jesus' death and resurrection. (See Colossians 2:15.) Jesus is coming back to judge the world with fire and the wrath of God. (See 2 Peter 3:7.) The Holy Spirit will bring a deep sense of knowing that this world and everything in it is prepared for judgment by fire alongside a deep gratitude for the salvation Jesus gives us from the day of God's wrath.

Any spirit which distracts from, nullifies, minimizes, or leaves out the cross of Christ is NOT the Holy Spirit. Any spirit which claims that Jesus is not returning, that there will not be a day of judgment, that Jesus is delayed, or tries to predict the exact time of Jesus' return is NOT the Holy Spirit.

Exalt Jesus & Uphold His Teachings

Jesus also said this about what the Holy Spirit does:

> John 16:13-14 NIV - But when he, the Spirit of truth, comes, **he will guide you into all the truth**. He will not speak on his own; he will speak only what he hears, and he will **tell you what is yet to come. He will glorify me** because it is from me that he will receive what he will make known to you.
>
> John 14:26: But the Advocate, the Holy Spirit, whom the Father will send in my name, will teach you all things and will **remind you of everything I have said to you.**

Guide into all truth: The word for truth used here means the actual reality of something as it truly is. The Word of God is truth. The Holy Spirit will guide us into the full experience of faith and faithfulness to God and all of His ways. When our lives are submitted to the Holy Spirit, they will start to resemble the Bible and we will understand God's Word and ways due to our practical experience of it.

Any spirit which nullifies, distorts, or neglects God's Word is NOT the Holy Spirit. (See 2 Timothy 3:16.) Any spirit which promotes a pattern of life which is contrary to the Word of God is NOT the Holy Spirit.

Tell you what is to come: God knows the end from the beginning. On several occasions, Jesus told His disciples in advance what was going to happen so that they would be strengthened with fore-knowledge when it did actually happen. (See John 16:1.) The Holy Spirit will continue in this type of revelation and advance notification of what is to come in order to equip and prepare us for what God is doing so that we can stand through various trials and temptations.

Unfortunately, there are also many false spirits or fortune-telling, divination, or psychic readings that counterfeit the Holy Spirit to reveal the things that the false spirit has been charged with declaring. We will cover this more later. Just because someone is telling you what is to come is NOT evidence of the Holy Spirit. You must test the spirit.

Exalt Jesus: The Holy Spirit will never exalt Himself – only JESUS. The Holy Spirit will not exalt you – only JESUS. The Holy Spirit will speak of the one true God, the only Creator of Heaven and earth as the Father of JESUS because it is only through JESUS that we can access the Father and anyone who has learned from the Father turns to JESUS. (See John 6:45, 14:6.)

Any spirit exalting or declaring a non-specific, all-encompassing "god" is NOT the Holy Spirit. Any spirit exalting the spirit is NOT the Holy Spirit. Any spirit claiming to know God but that does not point to Jesus as the only way to God is NOT the Holy Spirit. Any spirit that exalts man, this world. or anything in it is NOT the Holy Spirit.

Remind of Jesus' teachings: Jesus has perfect theology because He is God. As such, Jesus is the living demonstration of perfect theology in all of His words and deeds. The Holy Spirit will bring to remembrance the teachings and life of Jesus as our guide and example of how to live for God.

Any spirit which contradicts, diminishes, or neglects the teachings of Jesus is NOT the Holy Spirit.

Four Kinds of Wisdom

The apostle James corrected the behavior of some early believers by calling upon them to recognize the source of the "wisdom" they were functioning in. Our wisdom is demonstrated through our actions and our motives. A basic definition of wisdom is right application and use of knowledge. As such, wisdom in action is the practical application of knowledge based on our understanding of the facts. Someone can have much knowledge about many things but if they do not apply this knowledge correctly, they are a fool. God's wisdom applies God's knowledge (and He knows everything) to do things the way that God does them (and He does all things well.)

> *James 3:13-18 NKJV - Who is wise and understanding among you?* **Let him show by good conduct that his works are done in the meekness of wisdom.** *But if you have bitter envy and self-seeking in your hearts, do not boast and lie against the truth [reality].* **This wisdom does not descend from above, but is earthly, sensual, demonic.** *For where envy and self-seeking [selfish ambition] exist, confusion and every evil thing are there.* **But the wisdom that is from above is first pure, then peaceable, gentle, willing to yield, full of mercy and good fruits, without partiality and without hypocrisy.** *Now the fruit of righteousness is sown in peace by those who make peace.*

Earthly: Earthly wisdom is according to the terrestrial, natural, and common order of things and sets its aim on the pleasures and good things of this earth. This kind of wisdom will seek stability and comfort by worldly standards and the pursuit of earthly things. This kind of wisdom might be referred to as "common sense" but remember, the Holy Spirit teaches us to distinguish between the common and the holy. Jesus' Kingdom is not of this world. The very things that are valued in this earth are of very little value in God's sight. (See Luke 12:15, 16:15.)

Sensual: Sensual wisdom is from our sensuality, lusts, passions, and animal nature. This kind of wisdom is rooted in our sinful nature and passions. These are the very things we are called to put to death and reckon ourselves dead to in order to not indulge our carnality. (See Romans 6:11-14; Galatians 5:17.)

Sensual wisdom can also be evidenced through unsanctified emotions and physical sensations, even if these emotions or sensations occur while we are doing something spiritual. For example, strong emotional outbursts during a time of prayer might be evidence of the Holy Spirit touching a heart or it might just be emotions that have not yet been renewed in the Lord. Emotions are the least stable element of our soul and following emotions as if they are evidence of the Lord speaking will result in much instability.

Similarly, physical manifestations or sensations which occur during times with the Lord are not always evidence that the Holy Spirit is speaking. We do not confirm the word of the Lord by the evidence of getting a goosebump or any other kind of outward sensory physical feeling or "presence." These things are of the senses and as such, it is sensual. I do not deny that these things happen. However, we discern the truth of God by the Holy Spirit and the truth, NOT by anything in the sensual realm. The Holy Spirit leads us by faith in the truth whether we "feel it" or not. If we follow manifestations in the sensory realm as if they are God's guidance or confirmation we will be led from goosebump to goosebump rather than from glory to glory and can very quickly fall into many errors.

Demonic: Satan's sin is rebellion against God through self-exaltation. Satan was designed by God to be the chief worshipper but at some point decided that he wanted worship for himself. Demonic wisdom takes the form of selfish ambition, self-exaltation, and attempting to usurp God's position of supreme authority and power. Any so-called "wisdom" which subjugates, enslaves, or looks down upon others, coveting what others have, is from the evil one.

In contrast, Jesus took on the form of a servant, the lowest place, and obeyed God even unto death on a cross at the hands of the very ones He was sent to save, forgiving them as they killed Him. He tells us to take up our cross, deny ourselves daily, and pour our lives out for God and others. Any spirit which is self-protective, unforgiving, holds a grudge, demands restitution, or seeks vengeance is NOT the Holy Spirit.

Wisdom from Above: Notice that the first quality of wisdom from above is pure. James specifically noted and highlighted this. God will never compromise truth in order to make peace. He will die first. This said, without going into each aspect in detail, the other attributes of wisdom from above will also encompass the nature and character of God, which is to love and give freely without expecting anything in return. Godly wisdom has no partiality or prejudice in any matter but sees all for what it really is. Godly wisdom is never hypocritical or pretending to be something it is not. Godly wisdom leads people to make peace in God's way. The way God made peace with us was by incarnating flesh and dying on a cross for us when we were His enemies. (See Luke 19:42; Romans 5:8-10.)

Setting Itself Up Against God

When false apostles were persuading the Corinthians believers away from the true teachings of Jesus and ways of God, the apostle Paul corrected them about their incorrect assessments of spiritual realities and wrong application of the truth.

> *2 Corinthians 10:4-5, 7: The weapons we fight with are not the weapons of the world. On the contrary, they have divine power to demolish **strongholds**. We demolish **arguments** [imaginations] and every **pretension that sets itself up against the knowledge of God**, and we **take captive every thought to make it obedient to Christ**... You are **judging by appearances**. If anyone is confident that they belong to Christ, they should consider again that we belong to Christ just as much as they do.*

Strongholds: In the Old Testament, a stronghold was a tower in the center of a city where people would run for safety when an enemy attacked. Spiritually speaking, a stronghold is anything we run to other than Jesus when we feel under an attack of the enemy. It is a false comfort. For example, the rich man's wealth is his stronghold because he thinks his security is in money. (See Proverbs 10:15, 18:11.) However, a wise man scales the city of the might and pulls down the stronghold they trust in. (See Proverbs 21:22.) The apostle Paul was a wise man. He made it his aim to identify and pull down every false trust anyone had put confidence in so that the name of Jesus could be their stronghold and salvation in all things. (See Proverbs 18:10; Psalm 62:7, 71:7, etc.) God will always lead us into living by FAITH, and the Holy Spirit will never exalt a false trust – only JESUS.

<u>Arguments, Reasonings, Computations, Imaginations</u>: Pride, carnal nature, logic, "figuring it out," and our own fabricated fantasies can cause us to resist God's dealings with us and fall into deception. In short, it is in our nature to not want God to be God because we want to be our own god. Yes, it is our glory to search out the matters of God. (See Proverbs 25:2.) But the true discovery of God and His ways does not puff us up with knowledge but causes us to humble ourselves more deeply before His excellence and wisdom. (See 1 Corinthians 8:1.)

Anything calculating or capitalizing on our natural abilities or the logic of this world is NOT the Holy Spirit. For example, it was a grave sin inspired by Satan when David took a census of Israel to assess his own military strength. (See 1 Chronicles 21:1.) By contrast, when God used Gideon to defeat the Midianites, he reduced Gideon's army from thirty thousand to three hundred so that Gideon would have no doubt that the victory had not been accomplished through his own strength.

Any desire fabricated by our lusts or false hopes is a fantasy. If pursued under the premise that God wants to give us the "desires of our heart," we have abused the word of God and will find ourselves disappointed. It is important to remember that our flesh desires what is contrary to God and that our flesh has no value to God apart from our willingness to submit ourselves to Him and obey Him.

<u>Pretensions or high things raised up against God</u>: Anything claiming or exalting itself as the solution to your problems that is not JESUS is NOT from the Holy Spirit. Anything done with the motive of self-protection, self-defense, self-advancement, or independence from God is NOT the Holy Spirit. Anything claiming to be a god that is not God is NOT the Holy Spirit.

In an even finer analysis, any false assumptions we have about Jesus, God or His Word are NOT the Holy Spirit. Any presumptions we have about God's will or the way He does things is NOT the Holy Spirit. Even our zeal for God without true knowledge of Him is NOT the Holy Spirit. Remember that with all of his religious zeal, the apostle Paul was zealously against Christians (and therefore against Jesus) until God finally got a hold of him and showed him the truth. All the religious leaders in Jesus' day completely missed the fact that Jesus was God in the flesh. This shows us that we cannot base our "spiritual" discernment on our own concepts of God. We must ASK God in every situation what He is doing and what He wants us to do.

<u>Judging by Appearances</u>: Man judges by appearances but God looks at the heart. (See 1 Samuel 16:7.) The Book of Proverbs warns about judging by appearances and being hasty to "take our neighbor to court" based on what we have seen. (See Proverbs 25:8.) It is very dangerous to presume that we know something based on what it appears to be. The truth of the matter may be very different from how it appears. Instead, we can ASK the Lord about anything and everything and He will tell us what we need to know about it or He might tell us to mind our own business.

It is also important to consider that by outward observation according to man's standards of success, Jesus was a failure. What is esteemed by men is an abomination to God and vice-versa. (See Luke 6:15.) The world assesses "success" primarily by money, power, status, followers, fame, and influence. God does not see it that way. When the crowds wanted to make Jesus king in an earthly manner, He pointed out that they only followed Him out of selfishness and challenged them with a hard teaching. Almost everyone abandoned Him. (See John 6:15-71.) We follow a King who was crucified by the powers of this world, not one who came to exalt Himself or strive to be chummy with the powers of this world.

Practical Experience: What Is and Is Not God

If you are reading this, it is assumed that you already have some basic understanding and experience with the Holy Spirit and how God communicates with us. Therefore, we will discuss here some of the ways God speaks and some things to look out for as you prepare yourself to listen to Him and obey.

Internal Impressions: God's guidance is INTERNAL. He put His Spirit INSIDE of us. Yes, I know that Gideon held out a fleece and the first disciples cast lots, but that was before the Holy Spirit was poured out at Pentecost. Now, God dwells WITHIN us and guides us from within.

Notice from the examples of the Holy Spirit's guidance in the Book of Acts that the direction was always simple and clear. It was not muddy or plagued by uncertainty, and it was usually given one step at a time. God's guidance is never forceful, condemning, pushy, or obsessive. The only exception to this is in the case of urgency, but even in urgency, the Lord is kind. Pressure, condemnation, fear of missing out, fear of missing God, fear of God's punishment or displeasure, obsessively recurring thoughts, and things like this are NOT from God. Imitation of others, copycatting, regurgitating what others say or teach, and any kind of hypocrisy that causes our words to be out of line with our actions is NOT from God. God has ordained good works for us, but His aim is on spiritual fruitfulness – which is the condition of our hearts. Good works done with wrong motives are not of God and will burn.

God guides us into the truth in love. He knows exactly where we are on our journey with Him and He is never in a rush. He prefers the slow-cooker method to genuine transformation over the microwave approach to busy-ness and activities that dodge the genuine work of His Spirit.

Scripture Reading: God can and does speak to us through His Word. He delights to reveal Himself to us and cause us to understand His will and His ways. His Word is absolutely perfect in every possible way and will never lie to you or lead you astray.

However, the evil one also knows the Scriptures. His first successful deception of man in the Garden of Eden was accomplished through distorting the command of God for selfish purposes. He is still doing the same thing with God's word today.

I realize that there are many teachings about the difference between a *logos* word and a *rhema* word. Essentially these teachings say that the logos word is the original context but the rhema word is the "right now" voice of God through the Scripture on any given subject. There may be some validity to the dissection of these two Greek words as it pertains to how God speaks. However, and unfortunately, these teachings have also been used by many people to wrench the Scriptures out of their Biblical and historical context to say something in the frame of "thus sayeth the Lord through His Word" that God never intended from those passages of Scripture and that God would never say. Usually, this involves applying the Scripture for personal gain or advancement. Hmmm... sounds an awful lot like Eden to me.

God can use His Scriptures to assure our hearts of something that He is doing. But it is important to consider that Jesus (who is the Word in flesh) never abused or misused Scripture to advance Himself. Moreover, Paul reasoned from the Scriptures to explain God's redemptive plan and said his hands were innocent of blood because he had declared the whole counsel of God. (See Acts 20:27.) A fully trained servant of the Lord will be skilled in dividing the Word of God accurately, not selfishly. (See 2 Timothy 2:15.)

Prophesy, Dreams, Visions: Prophetic words, dreams, and visions can be from God but are not always from God. We need spiritual discernment to weigh what is revealed before we act upon it as if it is guidance from God.

There are numerous examples of false prophets throughout the Bible who were all functioning in dreams and visions and saying "thus says the Lord" when God was not speaking to them or through them. It is no different today, even among well-meaning believers who desire to hear God and be used by Him to proclaim His Word. We ourselves must TEST everything to see if it lines up with the revealed will of God through the Scriptures and what God has already been speaking to us about individually.

It is also important to note that the false prophets in Scripture were always and only blessing people and proclaiming peace upon sinful rebels rather than urging them to repent before God. (See Lamentations 2:14.) The same is true today. Prophecies that bless sin, which are overly focused on nations, government, or politics, or which bless nations in sin are NOT from the Holy Spirit. Jesus only spoke of Caesar one time and it was to answer a question about paying taxes. (See Luke 20:22.) He knew that no ruler in the world had any authority other than what God had given them. (See John 19:11; Romans 13:1.) Jesus was constantly speaking and prophesying about His Kingdom, which is not of this world. (See John 18:36.)

False prophecies can be accompanied by events or even miracles which do occur. Miracle power is NOT confirmation that something is from God. If it is out of alignment with God's will, word, or ways, it is false. We will cover this in-depth in Unit Six of this course.

False dreams and visions can reveal Satan's plans and purposes in attempt to lure well-meaning believers out of the will of God and into shipwreck through a "supernatural encounter." Not everything supernatural is always from God. There are many false spirits and antichrists already released in the world and this will only increase until the return of Christ.

Please also note from the examples in the Book of Acts that believers receiving visions remained alert and in their right mind. They did not enter into a passive state of "emptying" but were mentally aware enough to converse with God while they were having the vision. Functioning in the Holy Spirit brings us into the fullness of God's design for mankind including mental faculties and does not make us drones or zombies stripped of free will or function. In contrast, passivity and emptying the mind according to other spirituality techniques is an open invitation for wrong spirits to enter in and counterfeit the workings of God.

<u>God in Circumstances</u>: Noticing coincidences is NOT guidance from God. Yes, God is sovereign over all things but we do not make life decisions based on external events or circumstances. The enemy is able to maneuver all manner of events in this world but that does not mean that they are acts of God or God's way of communicating. (See Job Chapter 1.)

There is a difference between divine guidance and divination. Divination by definition is observing signs or omens. When we interpret an event or occurrence as an omen or sign from God, we are functioning in divination, not divine direction. By contrast, the men of the tribe of Issachar *understood* the times and knew what Israel must do. (See 1 Chronicles 12:32.) They had divinely inspired intelligence to discern the will of God and the hand of God upon the events taking place. They knew that God knows the end from the beginning and assessed the circumstances in accordance with the revealed will and word of God. Similarly, Jesus rebuked the religious leaders in His day for their apparent inability to discern the times correctly, even though they read the weather very well. (See Luke 12:56.) Similar to the word used to describe what the men of Issachar did so well, the word Jesus used means to examine like a jeweler inspecting a jewel or metals for authenticity and imperfections. All of this is to say that we discern things that happen according to how they line up with the revealed will of God. We do not receive guidance and make decisions based on things that happen – no matter how coincidental they may seem.

<u>Angels</u>: God does send angels for many purposes to serve us who will inherit salvation. (See Hebrews 1:14.) Angels can be from God but are not always from God. We must be aware that Satan's messengers disguise themselves as angels of light and messengers of righteousness. (See 2 Corinthians 11:14.)

Without going into excessive teaching on angels, it is important to note that there is no example in Scripture of any human every commanding the angels. Even Jesus was ministered to by angels but did not call upon them or command them when He was in need. (See Matthew 4:11; 26:53.) God commands His angels concerning us. (See Psalm 91:11.) In all Biblical instances, the angels were commanded by God and appeared to mankind to tell them of God's plans and assist them in carrying out God's plans. If an angel comes to us with a message other than the truth of Christ, the angel and their message is cursed and condemned. (See Galatians 1:8.) Moreover, we do not worship angels – even ones sent by God. (See Revelation 19:10, 22:9.)

Do Not Be Deceived

The point of all these examples is to assist you in standing in the truth of God as you give yourself over to the guidance of the Holy Spirit. The Holy Spirit will never fail you or lead you astray. But the enemy is always deceiving and counterfeiting the work of God. Those who give way to his schemes have lost their connection with the Head of the Body, who is Christ.

> *Colossians 2:8, 18-19 NIV - See to it that no one takes you captive through **hollow and deceptive philosophy, which depends on human tradition and the elemental spiritual forces of this world rather than on Christ**. ... Do not let anyone who delights in **false humility** and the **worship of angels** disqualify you. Such a person also goes into great detail about what they have seen; they are **puffed up with idle notions by their unspiritual mind**. They have **lost connection with the head**, from whom the whole body, supported and held together by its ligaments and sinews, grows as God causes it to grow.*

If you have gone astray and lost your connection, repent. Submit yourself to God. Resist the techniques of the enemy which have snared you and receive afresh the mind of Christ.

THE PATTERN OF OBEDIENCE

The Bible is full of stories of those who obeyed God and those who did not. We could not possibly explore every Biblical example of what faithful obedience to God looks like. However, we will very briefly explore a few examples of obedience and disobedience to give a basic guideline of the ways we will be tempted to submit ourselves to God's guidance…or not.

Moses and the Israelites

Moses was a special child from birth, ordained by God from the womb to be the deliverer of His people. Moses was raised by Pharaoh's daughter in all the skills and knowledge of Egypt and, while in Egypt, came to know his calling as God's chosen deliverer. At that time, he **presumed** that his people would recognize that God had chosen him to be their leader and took action accordingly. This did not go well for Moses and he wound up fleeing to the wilderness of Midian for forty years. (See Exodus 1-3; Acts 7:20-29.)

After forty years, it was time for Moses to fulfill his calling. By the time God appeared to him in the burning bush, he was insecure and did not feel qualified to speak to or lead God's people. This was evidence of his readiness for such a serious task. God led Moses **step by step** to carry out His purposes to deliver Israel from Egyptian slavery and to bury Pharaoh and his army in the depths of the sea. When Moses **obeyed God's instructions by faith**, everything went exactly as God intended. Even the waters of the sea were parted by the hand of God to fulfill His promise to His people.

Once they arrived in the wilderness, the Israelites constantly tested God. Their **flesh craved** meat and they **did not wait for God's counsel**. (See Psalm 106:13.) They desired to return to Egypt and considered slavery in Egypt better than service to God. They tested God through **stubborn unbelief** that God would be able to fulfill His promises to them. (See Psalm 78.) When spies were sent in to explore the land that God had promised them, they were impressed with the land but **did not believe** that God could destroy their giant enemies. Due to their unbelief, God sentenced them to die in the wilderness until forty years were complete. At that time, they **presumed to take the land in their own strength** even though God was not with them. In a humiliating defeat, they were chased out by their enemies as if by a swarm of bees. (See Numbers 13-14; Deuteronomy 1:44.)

Joshua and the Israelites

When Joshua became the leader of God's people, he was instructed by Moses to **mediate on the Law of God day and night** and not let it depart from his mouth. (See Joshua 1:1-8.) Joshua had seen how God led Moses in victorious battles against giants on the eastern side of the Jordan River and Moses instructed him to approach his battles on the other side of the Jordan in the same fashion of **faith**.

During the battle of Jericho, Joshua **followed God's instructions precisely** and the walls of the city came tumbling down. However, at the next battle, Joshua **did not consult with God**, took counsel from others who **judged by appearances** and **presumed that it would be easy** to conquer such a small city. Instead, they were defeated. (See Joshua 7.) When Joshua **sought the Lord** about this, the Lord pointed out the problem and instructed Joshua on how to fix it, and they obeyed. God then sent them back into Ai and they conquered Ai.

In another instance, Joshua **did not consult the Lord** when Gibeonites came cloaked as friends from a distant land. Unfortunately, they were part of the peoples that God had instructed to destroy and not to offer any kind of treaty. Because Joshua **did not consult the Lord**, Israel entered into a treaty with them. (See Joshua 9.)

David and Saul

David was not a perfect man but he was a man after God's own heart. David was anointed by Samuel as a teenager but it was not yet his time to be king. He **did not presume** to become king **ahead of God's appointed time** and he **served faithfully** in the kingdom of Israel **under God's appointed leader** at the time, Saul. Unfortunately, Saul **became jealous** of David, the anointing upon his life, and the victories God gave him, so Saul tried to kill David. David had to flee for his life and live in caves as an outlaw. When David had the chance to kill Saul, he **refused to lay a hand against God's anointed leader**. Instead, he **waited patiently** for it to be his time to lead God's people.

Even though David was a skilled warrior, he **consulted the Lord before his battles**. (See 1 Samuel 23:1-29, 30:8-9; 2 Samuel 2:1-2, 5:17-25, 21:1, etc.) When David sinned and became aware of his sin, he **repented quickly**. (See Psalm 51.) When God decreed justice against David, David **accepted God's dealings** with him as righteous and true. (See 2 Samuel 12:10, 16:10.) When David sinned and it caused a plague to break out on the people of Israel, he **offered himself in their place**. (See 1 Chronicles 21:17; 2 Samuel 24:17.) It was constantly in David's heart to **build a house for God** to dwell in, and he spent the second half of his life making preparations for God's Temple to be the most splendid in all the earth.

In contrast, was Saul's kingship. Saul was also anointed by Samuel, who told Saul that after the Spirit of the Lord had changed his heart, he could do whatever he found fit to do. However, when it came to the important matters, Saul was told to **wait for his next instructions** from Samuel, who was God's representative at the time. (See 1 Samuel 9:15-8.) For a while, Saul experienced victory because the Spirit of the Lord was with him. Unfortunately, Saul eventually **grew impatient and found it difficult to wait** for Samuel to come and give him his next instructions. He started **looking at his circumstances and the strength of his enemies**. As things seemed to slip **out of his control and look formidable** for his people, Saul decided to **override God's orders with his own will**. He did what he thought he should do according to his **own way of seeing things** and, simply put, **protect his ego**. When the Lord did not respond to Saul the way Saul thought He should, Saul **consulted a medium** and engaged in the **spiritual practices of the nations** rather than earnestly and persistently seeking the Lord, the Most High God of Israel. It cost Saul his kingship. (See 1 Samuel 13:7-14, 15:23; 1 Chronicles 10:13-14.)

After God took the kingdom from Saul (though he remained in office as Israel's king) and put His anointing on David, Saul became **tormented by an evil spirit and murder filled his heart**. Saul came to his end by **falling on his own sword** because he didn't want to be tortured by his enemies or look weak to his people. Saul's trust in God's protection had completely given way to the **self-protection of his ego**.

The Hebrews 11 Hall of Faith

Hebrews 11 is known as the Bible's "Hall of Faith" because it lists many of the heroes of the Bible and how they obeyed God with all their heart, soul, and life. Abel, Enoch, Noah, Abraham, Moses, David, and others lived in close fellowship with God, were called a friend of God, who spoke with God face to face, and who were men after God's own heart. (See Genesis 5:21-24, 6:9, 17:1, 24:40; Exodus 33:11; Numbers 12:8; 1 Samuel 13:14; 2 Chronicles 20:7; James 2:23; Isaiah 41:8; Acts 13:22.)

Each of these men was **consumed with God's heart and His purposes**. They were **willing to look foolish by worldly standards** in order to **maintain close fellowship with the Lord** and **follow His instructions**. They did not use their faith or the power of God or the privilege of being God's people for their own gain, purpose, or advantage. They **discarded their own plans** in order to **keep their minds on the Kingdom of Heaven**. They **submitted themselves to God's will** even at the expense of their lives. Their hearts were focused on a city whose builder and maker was God, **not the kingdoms of this world**. For this reason, God was not ashamed to be called their God.

Hebrews 11 is also referred to as the great cloud of witnesses. They are not witnesses of us and our walk of faith and they are not cheering us on from heaven. Heaven's worship is entirely consumed with JESUS.

They are witnesses who can testify truthfully of the faithfulness of God and how eternal matters of God are far more important than anything of this world could ever be.

Jesus: the Author and Perfecter of our Faith

Hebrews 11 leads into Hebrews 12, which reveals that Jesus is the ultimate example of obedience to God and the ultimate champion of faith and faithfulness.

> *Hebrews 12:1-4: Therefore, since we are surrounded by such a great cloud of witnesses, let us throw off everything that hinders and the sin that so easily entangles. And let us run with perseverance the race marked out for us,* ***fixing our eyes on Jesus, the pioneer and perfecter of faith. For the joy set before him he endured the cross, scorning its shame****, and sat down at the right hand of the throne of God.* ***Consider him who endured such opposition from sinners****, so that you will not grow weary and lose heart. In your struggle against sin, you have not yet resisted to the point of shedding your blood.*

Jesus left the riches and glory of heaven to **take the lowly place** of being born in a barn. Jesus lived a **sinless life** from birth and **submitted Himself** to earthly parents even though He was God. Jesus was **skilled in the Scriptures** by age twelve but **waited for God** to release Him in **God's timing** to begin His earthly ministry, which was eighteen years later. During His ministry years, He was misunderstood, followed by people full of selfishness, and even His own disciples did not understand what He was saying most of the time. He was ridiculed, mocked, rejected, accused of blasphemy, and ultimately crucified as a criminal at the hands of those He had been sent to save.

> *Philippians 2:6-8: Who, being in very nature God,* ***did not consider equality with God something to be used to his own advantage****; rather, he* ***made himself nothing*** *by taking the very* ***nature of a servant****, being made in human likeness. And being found in appearance as a man, he* ***humbled himself by becoming obedient*** *to death--even death on a cross!*

Jesus was **not trying to make a name for Himself** or to build a ministry so that He could be famous. And yet, He is the most famous person who ever lived. He **humbled Himself** in absolute **submission and obedience to God**. Therefore, God is not ashamed to be called His God or His Father. God raised Him from the dead and gave Him the name above every name in heaven, on earth, and under the earth.

The Apostle Paul: the Pattern of Obedience

The Apostle Paul gave this example of Christ's mindset and then referenced the pattern of his own life as an example of one who is truly following Jesus in spite of the fact that he had started out as one of Christ's primary persecutors.[1] (Note: We will dig a bit more into discerning false apostles in Unit Six of this course.)

Paul had been a passionate Pharisee with the best training in the Scriptures that the world had to offer at that time. He had been on a mission to eradicate Christianity from the face of the earth and to kill any Christians who would not deny that Jesus is Lord. But after an encounter with the living Lord Jesus on the road to Damascus, Paul became a believer. Then, following his conversion, he went into the wilderness of Arabia for three years. During this time, the Lord revealed to Paul that all the Scriptures point to Him and have been fulfilled through His death and resurrection. Paul's extensive knowledge of the Scriptures was **converted from the perspective of a condemning Law-enforcer to the Lord's heart of love, grace, mercy, and faith.**

Paul's **approach to life was also completely renovated**. Following his conversion, Paul was rejected by his

---

[1] *The story of Paul's conversion and transformation can be found in Acts 9:3-9, 11:25-30, 13:1-3, 22:3-21, 26:1-23; Philippians 3:3-9; Galatians 1:13-2:1; 2 Corinthians 11*

old comrades as a traitor, heretic, brainwashed idiot, and runaway. At the same time, the people in the Church did not believe that Paul had really become a follower of Jesus so they were afraid of him and did not accept him either. Paul **did not care what they thought or what happened to his career** or any part of life as he had known it. This was his mindset:

> *Philippians 3:7-9: But whatever were gains to me I now consider loss for the sake of Christ. What is more, I consider everything a loss because of the surpassing worth of knowing Christ Jesus my Lord, for whose sake I have lost all things. I consider them garbage, that I may gain Christ and be found in him, not having a righteousness of my own that comes from the law, but that which is through faith in Christ--the righteousness that comes from God on the basis of faith.*

After the wilderness in Arabia, Paul spent over ten years in Cilicia, and historians are not certain exactly what he was doing while he was there. No doubt, Paul was **wholly devoted to the Lord**, but it did not seem that God was using Paul too powerfully at all, at least for a season. But, all the while, God was transforming Paul into the most influential advocate for Christianity that the world has ever known.

Eventually, believers from the church at Antioch came to fetch Paul and bring him back in order to **teach the church in the ways of the Lord**. Soon enough, the Holy Spirit set Paul apart for ministry and his missionary journeys began. Paul and his teams changed the world through the proclamation of the Gospel, first to the Jew and then to the Gentile, in every territory where the Lord sent him. Paul **endured through persecution, riots, beatings, imprisonments, and attacks by false teachers and joyously suffered for the name of Jesus**. He was eventually beheaded for our faith, is now with the Lord in glory, and will rule and reign with Jesus for 1,000 years. (See Revelation 20:4-5.) The Church as we know it today was largely established through Paul's simple devotion to Christ.

Not everyone is called to martyrdom, but every believer is called to **take up their cross, crucify their flesh, and follow Jesus**. Not everyone is called to give away everything that they own, but every believer is called **to love nothing more than Jesus and to cling to nothing of this world**. Not everyone is called to be the Apostle Paul, but every believer is called to **be like Jesus**.

This is the pattern of obedience.

Basic Training Exercise

FOUR KINDS OF WISDOM

James 3:15-17 NKJV - This wisdom does not descend from above, but is earthly, sensual, demonic. For where envy and self-seeking [exist], confusion and every evil thing are there. But the wisdom that is from above is first pure, then peaceable, gentle, willing to yield, full of mercy and good fruits, without partiality and without hypocrisy.

DESCRIPTION

Whether we are wise or not is revealed by our actions and the long-term outcomes our actions produce. A basic definition of wisdom is the right application of knowledge. A person with much knowledge who uses it incorrectly will prove to be a fool.

Jesus Christ IS the wisdom of God and the perfect demonstration of walking in God's ways. When He died on a cross, He looked like the world's biggest fool. But when God raised Him from the dead, those who crucified Jesus proved to be the foolish ones. In their selfish zeal of being wise in their own sight and in the ways of this world, they had killed God in the flesh. But God proved His wisdom, justice, and power through His Son's resurrection.

The Apostle James highlighted four different kinds of wisdom and only one of them is from above. He listed characteristics of these wisdoms to help us discern what we were placing our confidence in and basing our actions upon.

To put Four Kinds of Wisdom into practice is about asking the Lord to reveal the differences between the various influences which seek to guide our decisions so that we can align ourselves with His voice and His eternal purposes for our lives.

PRAYER

Father, thank you that you are the source of wisdom from above and you give it to us liberally when we ask for it. We ask now that you give us wisdom. Help us to discern the other wisdoms which are not of you and help us to resist them. In Jesus' name, Amen.

Category: Discernment

Basic TRAINING
SPIRITUAL EXERCISES

PURPOSE:
To discern the voices of the enemy which seek to lead us astray.

To turn from evil and walk according to the wisdom of God.

SPIRITUAL FRUIT:
Increased discernment of the attacks of the enemy.

Faithfulness to God and His voice and purposes.

Distinguishing holy from common.

Restored faith and hope.

Repentance from focus on self.

Purging of evil, pride, and discouragement.

CONSIDERATIONS

Consider these aspects of the four kinds of wisdom:

Wisdoms NOT from Above:
- **Earthly:** of this world or the natural order; "common sense"
- **Sensual:** satiating desires of the flesh; emotional; physical
- **Demonic:** self-exalting, ambitious, covetous, subjugating

Wisdom from Above:
- **First of All Pure:** uncompromising about the truth
- **Peaceable, willing to yield:** not insisting on its own way
- **Fruit of the Spirit:** reflective of the Lord's character
- **Impartial:** not tainted by personal preference
- **Without an act:** consistent in word and deed, not phony

PRACTICE

1. Ask the Lord to highlight to you a decision in your life for which you need wisdom. (Hint: this should be ALL decisions.)

2. As you consider this decision, listen to the thoughts going through your head for or against certain possible choices. Write your various thoughts on a piece of paper.
   - Do these thoughts line up with aspects of the wisdoms that are not from God or the wisdom that is from above?
   - If the thoughts do not line up with wisdom from above, ask the Lord to give you wisdom from above and listen to what He says.

3. With each thought you have written down, ask the Lord to show you what kind of wisdom that thought represents.
   - If the thoughts do not line up with wisdom from above, repent and thank God for showing you the ungodly source of the wisdom.

4. Ask the Lord to give you wisdom from above and listen to what He says.

5. Ask the Lord to help you to do whatever He says.

NOTES:

ADDITIONAL SCRIPTURES:
James 1:5
Proverbs 3:13-18
Ephesians 5:15-17
Proverbs 10:23
Colossians 3:16
Psalm 111:10
Proverbs 3:7
James 3:13
Colossians 2:8
Matthew 7:24
Matthew 11:19
Wisdom & Folly: Proverbs 9

Category: Discernment

Basic Training Exercise

AT HIS FEET

Luke 10:38-42 NIV – As Jesus and his disciples were on their way, he came to a village where a woman named Martha opened her home to him. She had a sister called Mary, who sat at the Lord's feet listening to what he said. But Martha was distracted by all the preparations that had to be made. She came to him and asked, "Lord, don't you care that my sister has left me to do the work by myself? Tell her to help me!" "Martha, Martha," the Lord answered, "you are worried and upset about many things, but few things are needed—or indeed only one. Mary has chosen what is better, and it will not be taken away from her."

DESCRIPTION

Jesus said that only one thing was needed in our life with Him. This thing is time At His Feet.

Two sisters, Mary and Martha, provide a vivid example of how we sometimes approach our life with Jesus. Both sisters loved Jesus. Martha busied herself with much serving and Jesus loved her. But Mary sat at His feet, positioned to hear, receive, and partake of everything that He may convey to her. He said that she chose the better portion; and the one that would remain with her forever.

As we walk with and worship Jesus, placing ourselves At His Feet is essentially doing the same things that Mary did. We let go of control, set aside our concerns, anxieties, and even other forms of service to God in order to allow Jesus to speak to us and minister to us however He sees fit. When we do this, we will be refreshed in His presence and receive from Him things that will remain with us forever.

PRAYER

Father, thank you allow me and encourage me to take time to rest in your presence and sit at the feet of Jesus. Help me to still my heart and mind as I prioritize your desires over my own forms of serving you. Speak to me Lord, I am listening. In Jesus' name, Amen.

Basic TRAINING
SPIRITUAL EXERCISES

PURPOSE:

To sit in the presence of Jesus and receive from Him.

To take a time out from other forms of serving to be with God.

To grow in our relationship with Jesus by offering our time to Him over other things.

SPIRITUAL FRUIT:

Closer relationship with Jesus through drawing near to Him.

Deeper rest in Christ.

Fuller experience of God's peace and love.

Re-alignment to Christ-centered priorities.

CONSIDERATIONS

How and when can you make time to sit at Jesus feet? What is required for you to choose this over other demands of life?

How long can you sit At His Feet? (Recommendation: Start with at least 20 minutes.) If needed, set a timer so you can relax and not be anxious about exceeding the time allotted.

Where will you sit At His Feet so distractions are minimized? Will you turn off or silence electronics or leave them behind?

Will you play gentle worship music or not? There is value in music or silence. Ask God what He desires for your time.

Prayerfully consider your bodily position for being at the feet of Jesus. (For this exercise, I recommend being comfortable.)

Bring your Bible and a notebook to write down what Jesus reveals to you.

PRACTICE

1. Once you are in the place and position for your time:
   - Invite the Holy Spirit to minister to however He desires.
   - Be still and quiet in His presence.
   - Open your heart to receive from the Lord. Listen to Him and receive all that He reveals, heals, speaks, imparts to you, or instructs you to do. Watch with the eyes of your heart for any visions He may want to show you.
   - Don't worry if you fall asleep. He gives you rest as a gift.

2. After your time At His Feet, take a moment to write down any impressions you had about what Jesus was saying or doing during your time together.
   - What is one thing you sense Jesus spoke to you?
   - How do you feel different after time with Him compared to before time At His Feet?
   - Thank God for what He has done during your time.

3. Resume your regular duties rested and refreshed by Jesus.

NOTES: _____

ADDITIONAL SCRIPTURES:

Matthew 11:28-30

Psalm 16:11

John 15:1-11

James 4:8

Psalm 27:4

Genesis 2:2

Hebrews 4:1-11

Romans 4:1-8

 PERFECTION COURSE – UNIT 1.4 READING

Abiding & Obedience

Jesus gave His followers a new command, "Love one another as I have loved you." (See John 13:34, 15:12-17.) By fulfilling God's perfect righteous standard for us and putting Himself inside of us, Jesus now calls us to be like Him and empowers us to do it. First, we have to receive the love of Jesus for ourselves so that we can love others as He loves us. This is entirely impossible without the indwelling Holy Spirit.

This is part of what I call God's "you first" policy. We cannot give out what we have not received for ourselves. If a "you first" policy seems selfish to you, then I urge you to consider how important it was to the Father that Jesus was assured of His love for Him. Before Jesus began His ministry and at certain other significant moments, God spoke from heaven in an audible voice in order for His Son and everyone else around to unquestionably know of His love and approval for His Son. (See Matthew 3:17, 17:5; Mark 11:1; Luke 3:22, 9:35.) In the same way, because of what Jesus did for us, we can be assured of God's love for us before we have done anything to deserve it. (See Ephesians 2:8-9.) In order for us to love others as Jesus loves us, we have to let Him love us first.

Simple Abiding

Jesus tells His followers to abide in His love. To *abide* means *to remain, not depart from, continue, endure in, to be held and kept,* and *to wait*.

> *John 15:1-10 ESV - "I am the true vine, and my Father is the vinedresser. Every branch in me that does not bear fruit he takes away, and every branch that does bear fruit he prunes, that it may bear more fruit. Already you are clean because of the word that I have spoken to you.* **Abide in me, and I in you.** *As the branch cannot bear fruit by itself, unless it abides in the vine, neither can you, unless you abide in me.* **I am the vine; you are the branches. Whoever abides in me and I in him, he it is that bears much fruit, for apart from me you can do nothing.** *If anyone does not abide in me he is thrown away like a branch and withers; and the branches are gathered, thrown into the fire, and burned.* **If you abide in me, and my words abide in you, ask whatever you wish, and it will be done for you. By this my Father is glorified, that you bear much fruit and so prove to be my disciples.** *As the Father has loved me, so have I loved you.* **Abide in my love. If you keep my commandments, you will abide in my love,** *just as I have kept my Father's commandments and abide in his love.*

The word for *abide* in this passage means *to remain, to not depart, to continue, to endure, to keep, to wait for,* and *to not become different*. When we place our faith in Jesus, learn His words and teachings, and hear His voice, we are to stay and not depart from what He said. We MUST continue, endure, and wait for Him to prove Himself faithful without turning our hearts away from what He said or giving up or giving in when trials and temptations come along.

While abiding can be difficult, it is not strenuous or strained. Staying connected to Jesus is as natural as a branch staying connected to a vine. The branch does not try to be a branch; it just is. The branch does not try to produce fruit; it just does. The branch does not ask itself, *Am I really a branch?*, *Am I a good enough branch?*, *Have I done enough branching today?*, *Does the vine approve of me?*, *Will I ever produce fruit?*, or *Are there better vines across town?* The branch does not come up with its own branching strategy or create a fruit fulfillment agenda. No. The branch is a branch because that's what it was made to be. A branch simply cannot live without the vine. The branch receives all of its sustenance and life from the vine, and all the branch has to do is allow the vine to fill it with sap and receive all that the vine has to give it. Then, the branch can't help but produce fruit – much fruit. Then, the vine and the gardener receive praise because the branch has fulfilled its purpose by simply abiding.

Abiding in truth and faith is the only work that God requires of us.

> *John 6:29 NLT - Jesus told them, "This is **the only work God wants from you: Believe** in the one he has sent."*

Jesus is the vine that we abide in as branches. When we believe that Jesus is whom He says He is and remain connected to Him, we can ask for anything, and He will give it to us. When we believe what He did for us, all things are possible. But we have to REMAIN in the simplicity of devotion to Him and not depart from Him and what He taught in favor of human wisdom or our own ideas. Genuine abiding organically produces genuine obedience – from the heart.

Simple Obedience

The Christian life is not a democracy. It is a monarchy—we have a King. Our King has commandments. If we truly believe that Jesus is Lord and King of all the earth and if we truly love Him for what He has done for us, we will keep His commandments even more seriously than we would submit ourselves to any king of this world. Jesus specifically says that His purpose in sending the Holy Spirit is to help us to keep His commandments. This is because doing so is contrary to our human nature.

> *John 14:15-18: "**If you love me, keep my commands**. And I will ask the Father, and **he will give you another advocate to help you** and be with you forever-- the Spirit of truth. The world cannot accept him, because it neither sees him nor knows him. But you know him, for **he lives with you and will be in you**. I will **not leave you as orphans**; I will come to you.*

God adopts us as His own and puts Himself inside of us so that we can hear His voice and obey Him. This means that we have no need for any other person to speak to God for us because we can speak to Him directly ourselves, as our Father. We no longer have to go to someone else to receive the word of the Lord to us because we can each hear God for ourselves. We no longer have to guess what God's will is for us. We can stop presuming and hypothetically imitating Jesus or other people whom we believe to be godly. We can simply listen to God for ourselves and be led by the Holy Spirit directly. (See 1 John 2:27; John 10:14,27; Hebrews 3:7-8, 4:7-11.)

Sometimes, our approach to obedience can become overly passive in the name of "God's sovereignty," thinking that God has predetermined His will, and it is both totally inescapable and unaffected by the choices of man. Other times, we can think that doing God's will lies entirely on our ability to obey Him perfectly or the rest of eternity could be altered by our decisions. Another methodology is to make plans according to what we believe to be the good things that God desires for us to be doing and then ask God to bless what we do.

However, none of these reflect the relationship of the Father and His child cooperating to bring about God's will on the earth. To put it plainly, God does have His will, and He gives us free will to cooperate with Him or not. God's will was Eden. Adam's free will messed it up. (See Genesis 3.) Jesus, on the other hand, surrendered His free will to do only what the Father wanted. On a daily and even a moment-by-moment basis, Jesus said and did only what He heard and saw His Father doing by living in obedience to the Holy Spirit. (See John 4:34, 5:19, 6:38, 12:49.)

Obedience is simple. All we have to do is listen to God and do what He says. In fact, this is our New Covenant form of worship. Under the old system, the life of an animal was offered to God as a sacrifice of worship. But Jesus as our perfect example of living the fulfillment of God's will, offered His own life through obedience to His Father, even unto death. Even though He could have used His *Son of God* status and power for His own benefit, He chose to submit Himself entirely to doing His Father's will by dying on the cross. We follow a crucified King.

> *Philippians 2:5-8 - In your relationships with one another,* **have the same mindset as Christ Jesus**: *Who, being in very nature God, did not consider equality with God something to be used to his own advantage; rather,* **he made himself nothing by taking the very nature of a servant**, *being made in human likeness. And being found in appearance as a man, he* **humbled himself by becoming obedient** *to death-- even death on a cross! (Also Romans 12:1.)*

Jesus does not ask us to do anything for Him that He has not already done Himself. We learn obedience by submitting to God's will and ways of doing things even at the expense of our desires, pride, plans, timing, reputation, and way of doing things. (See Hebrews 5:8, 12:3-11; James 1:4; Romans 5:3-5.) In everything that we encounter, the Holy Spirit reveals God's path for us, shows us God's standard of purity, and strengthens us to do things God's way so that, like Jesus, we live our lives in a way that says to God, "Not my will but Yours be done." (See Luke 22:42.) Anything we do from the motivation or reasoning of our flesh has absolutely no eternal value. (See John 6:63; Matthew 26:41.)

As we walk in obedience to the promptings of the Holy Spirit, we quickly discover that God's ways of doing things are much different from our natural inclinations, common sensibilities, short-term and long-term objectives, and earthly perspectives. God knows the end from the beginning and often uses supernatural or miraculous methods of executing His plans because His ways are a lot higher than ours and have a holy and eternal objective. (See Isaiah 55:8-11.) For this reason, He often leads us in ways that make absolutely no earthly sense whatsoever to demonstrate His love, mercy, and power and so that only HIS name is exalted.

God doesn't really need our help. He wants our cooperation as His children as He fulfills His eternal plans in all the earth. Sometimes, it seems that He tells us everything because we are His friends, and other times, it seems that we are on a need-to-know basis because if He told us everything our minds would explode. This said, when we trust that He loves us and is working for our good and the good of others, we are free to obey even when we don't know exactly what He is doing. In fact, we stop trusting in ourselves and our own ways and truly begin to know to the depths of our being that God is real and He is good to us. Through this, our mind, will, and emotions are changed to be like Jesus as we keep our attention on Him and press into deeper levels of knowing and doing God's will for our lives. (See Romans 12:2; James 3:15-17; Galatians 5:19-23; Philippians 2:13.) Although submission may sound like subjection, obedience to God is the only submission that leads to absolute liberty. When our abiding leads us into obedience to the truth, the truth will set us free.

Walking as Jesus Walked

The Biblical writer who best expressed this abiding and obedience relationship of us in Christ and Christ in us through the Holy Spirit was John. John emphasized Jesus' teaching about His relationship with God the Father and our relationship with Christ through the Holy Spirit. These are a mirror image of one another. When we are truly following Christ and living by the guidance of the Holy Spirit, we walk on the earth in the same way that Jesus walked on the earth by God's guidance. We even say the same things He said and do the same things He did. It is only through this abiding and obedient relationship that we are empowered to carry out God's purposes on the earth. In fact, this is the evidence that we truly know Him.

> *1 John 2:4-6 ESV - Whoever says "I know him" but does not keep his commandments is a liar, and the truth is not in him, but whoever keeps his word, in him truly the love of God is perfected. By this we may know that we are in him:* **whoever says he abides in him ought to walk in the same way in which he walked.**

COMMANDS OF JESUS - EVALUATION

"IF YOU LOVE ME, KEEP MY COMMANDS." JOHN 14:15

1 = Not obeying/Not enough   2 = Some/Partial Obedience   3 = Regular Obedient Application

Repent	1	2	3	Hearing Jesus/Listening carefully	1	2	3
Believe	1	2	3	Not judging	1	2	3
Following Jesus	1	2	3	Not condemning	1	2	3
Rejoicing at Persecution	1	2	3	Forgiving repeatedly	1	2	3
Reconciling with adversaries	1	2	3	Taking planks out of own eyes	1	2	3
Cut hand & Pluck eye (cut out sin)	1	2	3	Helping others with speck in eyes	1	2	3
No taking oaths	1	2	3	Not putting pearls before pigs	1	2	3
Not resisting evil person/people	1	2	3	Asking, Seeking, Knocking	1	2	3
Turning other cheek	1	2	3	Doing unto others as you want to you	1	2	3
Giving more than demanded	1	2	3	Entering through narrow gate	1	2	3
Going extra mile	1	2	3	Every effort through narrow door	1	2	3
Giving to everyone who asks	1	2	3	Watching out for false prophets	1	2	3
Loving enemies & persecutors	1	2	3	Receiving healing (Be clean, loosed)	1	2	3
Blessing those who hate you	1	2	3	Letting dead bury the dead	1	2	3
Be perfect/merciful as God is	1	2	3	Showing mercy, more than sacrifice	1	2	3
Doing good deeds in secret	1	2	3	Praying for laborers	1	2	3
Giving in secret	1	2	3	Proclaiming Kingdom	1	2	3
Few words in prayer (no babbling)	1	2	3	Healing sick, casting out demons, etc.	1	2	3
Praying the Lord's prayer	1	2	3	Freely receiving & giving	1	2	3
Fasting without show	1	2	3	Shaking dust off feet	1	2	3
Not storing treasures on earth	1	2	3	Not rejoicing in spiritual power	1	2	3
Storing treasures in heaven	1	2	3	Being wise as serpent, harmless as dove	1	2	3
Not worrying about your life	1	2	3	Not worrying about what to say	1	2	3
Heart not set on food or clothes	1	2	3	Speaking out what Jesus has revealed	1	2	3
Seeking Kingdom First	1	2	3	Not fearing man, fearing only God	1	2	3
Not worrying about finances/$$	1	2	3	Not supposing peace, but sword	1	2	3
Guarding against greed	1	2	3	Not stopping false teachers	1	2	3
Coming to Jesus for rest	1	2	3	Believing God	1	2	3
Learning of Jesus	1	2	3	Believing also in Jesus	1	2	3
Denying self, taking up cross	1	2	3	Keeping commands of God	1	2	3
Having no fear	1	2	3	Not separating marriages	1	2	3

Being aware of yeast: religion	1	2	3	Watching out that no one deceives you	1	2	3
Being aware of yeast: unbelief	1	2	3	Being ready for service	1	2	3
Being aware of yeast: worldliness	1	2	3	Not taking place of honor for self	1	2	3
Paying taxes to Caesar	1	2	3	Taking lowest place	1	2	3
Coming to God like a child	1	2	3	Not inviting friends to banquet	1	2	3
Going to those who sin against you	1	2	3	Inviting those who cannot repay	1	2	3
Selling possessions, giving to poor	1	2	3	Hating own life (compared to Jesus)	1	2	3
Being a servant of all	1	2	3	Hating family (by comparison)	1	2	3
Loving God	1	2	3	Using wealth to make heavenly friends	1	2	3
Loving neighbor as self	1	2	3	Hating money	1	2	3
Not chasing Kingdom, anointing	1	2	3	Rebuking those in sin	1	2	3
Being ready for Jesus' return	1	2	3	Not fearing end times wars and battles	1	2	3
Keeping watch for Jesus' return	1	2	3	Remembering Lot's wife	1	2	3
Showing mercy (Good Samaritan)	1	2	3	Praying to not fall into temptation	1	2	3
Generously giving to the poor	1	2	3	Being born again by the Spirit	1	2	3
Feeding the hungry, thirsty	1	2	3	Not turning God's house into marketplace	1	2	3
Taking in strangers	1	2	3	Worshipping in spirit and truth	1	2	3
Clothing the naked	1	2	3	No excuses (take up mat and walk)	1	2	3
Caring for the sick	1	2	3	Stop sinning, sin no more	1	2	3
Visiting prisoners	1	2	3	Not working for food that spoils	1	2	3
Taking Communion rightly	1	2	3	Not judging by appearances	1	2	3
Going to all nations (fulfill calling)	1	2	3	Judging with right judgment	1	2	3
Making disciples	1	2	3	Obeying teachings of Jesus	1	2	3
Baptizing others into faith	1	2	3	Obeying commands of Jesus	1	2	3
Teaching the teachings of Jesus	1	2	3	Washing feet of others	1	2	3
Feeding God's sheep, lambs	1	2	3	Doing the works as at first (first love)	1	2	3
Waiting on God	1	2	3	Not afraid of suffering	1	2	3
Witnessing for Jesus	1	2	3	Being faithful even unto death	1	2	3
Doing the works of Jesus	1	2	3	Holding on to what you have	1	2	3
Abiding in Jesus, remaining	1	2	3	Waking up! Re-Strengthening to finish	1	2	3
Loving one another as Jesus loves	1	2	3	Being earnest	1	2	3
Laying down life for others	1	2	3	Being hot or cold	1	2	3

Basic Training Exercise

COUNT THE COST

Luke 14:27-33 ESV. Whoever does not bear his own cross and come after me cannot be my disciple. For which of you, desiring to build a tower, does not first sit down and count the cost, whether he has enough to complete it? Otherwise, when he has laid a foundation and is not able to finish, all who see it begin to mock him, saying, 'This man began to build and was not able to finish.' Or what king, going out to encounter another king in war, will not sit down first and deliberate whether he is able with ten thousand to meet him who comes against him with twenty thousand? And if not, while the other is yet a great way off, he sends a delegation and asks for terms of peace. So therefore, any one of you who does not renounce all that he has cannot be my disciple.

Basic TRAINING
SPIRITUAL EXERCISES

PURPOSE:

To understand the terms and requirements of following Jesus.

To realistically assess our commitment to following Jesus.

To increase our willingness to give all for Jesus.

SPIRITUAL FRUIT:

Absolute surrender to God and following Jesus.

Increased humility.

Increased readiness to suffer and sacrifice for Jesus and His Kingdom.

DESCRIPTION

Jesus made the terms of following Him explicitly clear. When we agree to be a disciple of Jesus, we enter in knowing that it will cost us everything, like a king who knows that he does not have enough strength, soldiers, or resources to win the battle or the war.

We serve a God who gave up everything and died on a cross for us. The evidence of our understanding of what our God did for us is found in the cost we are willing to pay as we obediently follow Jesus.

Jesus imperatively said His disciples must take up our cross and renounce all that we have in order to follow Him. The cross is an instrument of death and as such, disciples must be willing to suffer humiliation, loss, and even pay the ultimate price if God so wills. Not that we pursue sacrifice of our own design but that we position our hearts in readiness to sacrifice whatever might be required of us on our path with God. There is no such thing as a 50% disciple, a good-times only disciple, or a have it my way disciple. We must be hot or cold, all in or not in at all.

Practicing Count the Cost is about examining our willingness to follow Jesus, even when it hurts and even if it costs us everything.

Category: Self-Denial

PRAYER

Father, thank you for paying the ultimate price for me. Help me to understand the worth of your sacrifice and increase my willingness to give my all for you. In Jesus' name, Amen.

CONSIDERATIONS

Consider the following aspects Jesus alluded to as the potential cost of following Him. Listed in no particular order:

- Hated by family, mother, father for name of Jesus.
- Homelessness: foxes have holes but not Son of Man.
- Losing/giving up all possessions to follow Jesus.
- Persecuted/ridiculed by family, friends, etc.
- Hated by world. Hated by all people.
- Death to self: arrogance, pride, selfishness, "my way," etc.
- Death to flesh: passions, sensual desires, preferences, etc.
- Ultimate price: death, loss of life for the name of Jesus.

TALK WITH GOD

In what ways have you followed God because He gives you what you want or has the power to bless you?

If Jesus never blessed you again, (material blessing, healing, guidance, etc.) would you still want to follow Him?

If you knew that God's purpose was for you to be martyred for Jesus, how would that change your walk of faith?

In what ways have you experienced persecution from family, friends, or others for following Jesus? What is your response?

In what ways have you been called upon to suffer or sacrifice for following Jesus? Did you do it? Joyfully?

In what ways has Jesus asked you to take up your cross and die to yourself or your flesh? How did it change you?

What do you think motivated Jesus to take up His cross? How did He do it? What example does that set for you?

After counting the cost, do you still want to be a disciple of Jesus? Why?

NOTES: _____

Category: Self-Denial

ADDITIONAL SCRIPTURES:

Matthew 5:10
Luke 9:58
Matthew 24:9
Luke 4:26
John 15:18-25
James 1:2-3, 12
Acts 14:22
Mark 8:36
Luke 9:23
Philippians 2:5-11
Matthew 6:24
1 John 2:15-17
Revelation 3:16

UNIT ONE – KEY QUESTIONS
Open Ears to Obey

Use this worksheet to test your grasp of the material and exercises of Unit One.

What is the mystery that God has revealed to us by His Spirit? (in your own words)	
Why did Jesus send the Holy Spirit?	**How does God speak to us today?**
In what ways can we test the spirit?	**What does obedience mean in the New Covenant?**
What is the goal of the spiritually mature person?	**What does it mean to abide in Christ?**
What is one thing you learned that you did not know before?	**What questions do you still have about this subject?**

UNIT ONE: GROUP EXERCISES

Group Training Exercise

NO AGENDA

PURPOSE:
Listen to God for His addenda and insight.

Share the insights of God with one another.

Encourage one another in our pursuit of God.

GROUP SIZE:
Any size group.

SCRIPTURES:
John 10:27
Jeremiah 33:3
Isaiah 30:21
John 16:13
Luke 11:28
Psalm 32:8-9

SCRIPTURE PORTION: 1 SAMUEL 3:4-10

Then the LORD called Samuel. Samuel answered, "Here I am." And he ran to Eli and said, "Here I am; you called me." But Eli said, "I did not call; go back and lie down." So he went and lay down.

Again the LORD called, "Samuel!" And Samuel got up and went to Eli and said, "Here I am; you called me." "My son," Eli said, "I did not call; go back and lie down." Now Samuel did not yet know the LORD: The word of the LORD had not yet been revealed to him.

A third time the LORD called, "Samuel!" And Samuel got up and went to Eli and said, "Here I am; you called me." Then Eli realized that the LORD was calling the boy. So Eli told Samuel, "Go and lie down, and if he calls you, say, 'Speak, LORD, for your servant is listening.'" So Samuel went and lay down in his place. The LORD came and stood there, calling as at the other times, "Samuel! Samuel!" Then Samuel said, "Speak, for your servant is listening."

DESCRIPTION

In the passage above, the Lord wanted to speak to Samuel and tried three times before Samuel knew to simply listen to God and what God wanted to say. Samuel was readily attentive to the order of man but not yet to the voice of God.

Sometimes, we are just like this with the Lord. Other times, we present ourselves repeatedly before Him with lists of requests of what we need, want, or long to see happen but fail to listen to Him about His desires. While there is nothing wrong with listening to people or prayers of petition, there is great value in taking the time to simply listen to God with No Agenda. When we take time to disconnect from the pulls of life and set aside our own demands, we can hear the heart and instruction of God.

As believers we are called to pray for one another, including listening to the Lord on one another's behalf. The word the Lord gave Samuel was actually for the house of Eli. When we come before God as a group with No Agenda, God can do wonderful and unexpected things among us.

GROUP PRACTICE

1. Pray and invite the Lord to speak to your hearts. Encourage each person to say quietly, "Speak, Jesus, for your servant is listening."

2. Take time in silence to sit and listen to what the Lord wants to reveal. (About 5-10 minutes is a good start.)
   - Resist the urge to bring your own ideas and requests to God.
   - Open your heart to hear anything God might want to speak to you about any subject pertaining to your life, other people's lives, or other matters.

3. When the allotted time is complete, write down what the Lord revealed to you.

   _____
   _____
   _____

4. Invite group members to share what the Lord has revealed to them during this time.
   - Were there any common themes of what God revealed to the members of your group?
   - Was the Lord highlighting any particular person, problem, or subject for prayer?
   - Was the Lord giving insight for the group or its members?

5. Pray for one another and exhort one another in your pursuit of God and His purposes.

6. Take a few moments as a group to discuss the difference between a typical prayer meeting with prayer requests and coming before the Lord with No Agenda.
   - How will you incorporate this into your group practice?

Category: Listening

Unit Two:
Whole Counsel of God

Key Scripture Verse for Unit Two
Therefore let us move beyond the elementary teachings about Christ and be taken forward to maturity, not laying again the foundation of repentance from acts that lead to death, and of faith in God, instruction about cleansing rites, the laying on of hands, the resurrection of the dead, and eternal judgment. And God permitting, we will do so. - Hebrews 6:1-3

Pre-Test of the Basics

Class 1: Foundations and Whole Counsel of God
1 Reading, 1 Exercise
Each individual believer must know and believe the basic foundations of the Christian faith for ourselves. But it doesn't stop at the basics. God has given us the Scriptures so that we can know Him and understand His ways according to the whole counsel of God.

Class 2: Good News of the Kingdom
1 Reading, 2 Exercises
The whole Bible tells the story of God's desire and design for His Kingdom. Jesus is King and the centerpiece of God's plan of redemption for mankind. Jesus is coming back to judge all evil and establish His Kingdom on earth forever.

Pre-Test of Israel Knowledge

Class 3: Israel & One New Man
1 Reading, 1 Prayer Guide
Jesus was born Jewish, a direct descendant of Abraham, Isaac, Jacob, and David. The Jewish people have, for the most part, rejected Jesus as their Messiah, but God's eternal plan for Israel has not changed.

Class 4: God's Sovereignty Over ALL Nations
1 Reading, 1 Exercise
There is no authority on the earth that has not been established by God. Jesus is returning to judge all nations and establish His Kingdom forever. Until then, He has made a way for people from all nations to be saved.

Key Questions

Group Exercises

Foundations Test

Do you know the elementary teachings of the Christian faith?

Answer the following questions. Examine what you know and believe about these elementary teachings.

What does it mean to repent from dead works?	What does it mean to have faith in God?	What is the doctrine of baptisms? *(Note: plural.)*
What is the laying on of hands?	**What is eternal judgment?**	**What will happen at the resurrection?**
How do we attain a clear conscience before God?	**What is permitted for followers of Jesus?**	**What is forbidden for followers of Jesus?**

PERFECTION COURSE – UNIT 2.1 READING

Foundations & Whole Counsel

When the author of the letter to the Hebrews spoke about going on to spiritual maturity, he first referenced the elementary teachings of the faith.

> *Hebrews 6:1-3 ESV - Therefore let us leave the elementary doctrine of Christ and **go on to maturity**, not laying again a foundation of **repentance from dead works** and of **faith toward God**, and of **instruction about washings**, the **laying on of hands**, the **resurrection of the dead**, and **eternal judgment**. And this we will do if God permits.*

Without these elements firmly in place in the hearts and lives of believers, they were not ready to press on to the meatier teachings of the Word and the Spirit. We should take heed of this before we press on with this course which is aimed entirely at spiritual maturity.

Each of the elements listed above were deliberately included and explained in the Cornerstone Course. You can review the answers in the Cornerstone Course as follows:

What does it mean to repent from dead works?	What does it mean to have faith in God?	What is the doctrine of baptisms? (Note: plural.)
Cornerstone Course: C1.3, C3.3, C1.4	Cornerstone Course: C1.3, C1.1, C6.1	Cornerstone Course: C3.1
What is the laying on of hands?	What is eternal judgment?	What will happen at the resurrection?
Cornerstone Course: C3.2	Cornerstone Course: C1.1	Cornerstone Course: C1.1
How do we attain a clear conscience before God?	What is permitted for followers of Jesus?	What is forbidden for followers of Jesus?
Cornerstone Course: C1.1, C1.2, C1.3	Cornerstone Course: C3.2	Cornerstone Course: C3.2

Please take the time to review these basics before pressing onwards. Building on the foundation of Christ is absolutely critical to your spiritual development.

The Whole Counsel of God

When the Apostle Paul was parting company with the elders of the Ephesian church, he declared himself to be innocent of their lifeblood because he had declared to them the whole counsel of God. (See Acts 20:20-27.) In the days of the early church, they did not have the New Testament yet. Scrolls of the Old Testament were studied extensively by Jewish scholars but only the wealthy could afford to have scrolls in their homes. Paul had been trained in the Scriptures by the best in the world in his day. After the Holy Spirit came into his life, his ability to fully understand the Scriptures was unlocked. He purposefully went to the Jewish synagogues of every city he traveled to in order to reason with them from the Scriptures that Jesus is the Messiah of Israel. When he was with Gentile believers, he taught from the Scriptures about God's eternal redemptive plan of salvation for all mankind and also used the Scriptures as a guide for pointing out what God deems to be right and wrong, good and evil, and clean and unclean. Paul honored the Word of God as the source of all good and proper doctrine, correction, and training for those who want to be God's servants. Peter also honored the Scriptures as the source of our strengthening for endurance in the times before the return of Christ.

2 Timothy 3:16-17: **All Scripture is God-breathed and is useful for teaching, rebuking, correcting and training in righteousness**, *so that the servant of God may be thoroughly equipped for every good work.*

2 Peter 1:19-21: We also have the **prophetic message as something completely reliable**, *and* **you will do well to pay attention to it**, *as to a light shining in a dark place, until the day dawns and the morning star rises in your hearts. Above all, you must understand that* **no prophecy of Scripture came about by the prophet's own interpretation of things**. *For* **prophecy never had its origin in the human will**, *but prophets, though human, spoke from God as they were carried along by the Holy Spirit.*

Abusing the word of God is something the evil one has been doing since the Garden of Eden. Usually, false teachers wrench Scripture out of context to promote techniques for establishing self-righteousness or to promote free blessings while endorsing lawless behavior. If we lose sight of the truth of God's Word, we will be vulnerable to their flatteries and false promises of being like God. However, the Word of God is only profitable if it is used properly. We must know what the Scripture says for ourselves so that we can discern truth from error and good teaching from false teaching.

1 Timothy 1:8-11: We know that **the law is good if one uses it properly**. *We also know that* **the law is made not for the righteous but for lawbreakers and rebels**, *the ungodly and sinful, the unholy and irreligious, for those who kill their fathers or mothers, for murderers, for the sexually immoral, for those practicing homosexuality, for slave traders and liars and perjurers--***and for whatever else is contrary to the sound doctrine that conforms to the gospel** *concerning the glory of the blessed God, which he entrusted to me.*

I like the comparison of a person who is charged with spotting counterfeit money, bills, and coins. It is said that the way these experts train is NOT by spending time examining the various counterfeits that are out in the marketplace but by spending the majority of their time with the genuine article. When their eyes have been given only to the real thing, they can spot a fake immediately because it does not conform to the pattern of genuine article. Similarly, the only way we will be able to discern false teaching is to know the truth and this means the whole counsel of God, from Genesis to Revelation.

God gave us His Word as a gift for our encouragement to help us stand through the trials of the life of faith. One of my favorite things about the Scriptures is that God, who does not lie, included accounts of the failures of His people at various points in time alongside the stories of their glory in Him. We can learn so much from the examples of faithfulness or faithlessness laid out in the stories of the Bible. (See Romans 15:4.) At times, reading the stories of Israel's failures might cause us to feel superior or as if we could not possibly make the same mistakes they did. It's easy to say from observation, especially because we can turn the page and know how the story turns out. But when God puts us in situations which demand our response of faith, it will be revealed that we are just as human as the Israelites were and they did not have the indwelling Holy Spirit. This is why their example is such a comfort and exhortation for us to NOT make the same mistakes they did and for us to keep pressing into the Holy Spirit to endure through trials and fight the fight of faith. (See 1 Corinthians 10:11.)

Therefore, let us press on to know and understand the whole counsel of the Word of God for ourselves. Let us seek first the Kingdom of God until we are firmly established the truth so that we can quickly discern false teachings when they batter our ears. Let us proclaim Jesus and the whole counsel of God to others so that their eternal blood is not on our hands.

Basic Training Exercise

FEAR OF THE LORD

Job 28:20-28 NLT – But do people know where to find wisdom? Where can they find understanding? It is hidden from the eyes of all humanity. Even the sharp-eyed birds in the sky cannot discover it. Destruction and Death say, "We've heard only rumors of where wisdom can be found." God alone understands the way to wisdom; he knows where it can be found, for he looks throughout the whole earth and sees everything under the heavens. He decided how hard the winds should blow and how much rain should fall. He made the laws for the rain and laid out a path for the lightning. Then he saw wisdom and evaluated it. He set it in place and examined it thoroughly. And this is what he says to all humanity: "The fear of the Lord is true wisdom; to forsake evil is real understanding."

DESCRIPTION

God is all powerful. It is His privilege as the Creator of the Universe and the Most High God. God is good. He is also perfectly just as the Judge of all the earth and King above every king.

At the end of the age, every person will stand before God and give an account for what they have done. The Fear of the Lord is to live today in a manner that reflects our recognition of God's eternal position of authority in our lives. If He is truly God and if He is truly our only judge, which He is, then our actions today should demonstrate our desire to be pleasing to the One who has this right. This rightly places emphasis on God over any other person or influence in our lives.

Putting the Fear of the Lord into practice is about aligning our lives with a healthy reverence for God in all that we think, say, and do because of who He is.

PRAYER

Father, I recognize that you are the only God and only judge of my eternity. Thank you for your mercy for times when I have not lived as if this is true. I ask you to examine my heart and help me to acknowledge you in everything I do. In Jesus' name, Amen.

Basic TRAINING
SPIRITUAL EXERCISES

PURPOSE:

To grow in understanding accurately what the Fear of the Lord is.

To develop in our own personal walk in the fear of the Lord.

SPIRITUAL FRUIT:

Fear of the Lord.

Right reverence for God, who He is, and how He likes things.

Repentance from sin.

Purification of motives and actions.

MEDITATION

Look up and slowly read through the Additional Scriptures listed on this page. Invite the Holy Spirit to give you insight about what it means to genuinely Fear the Lord.

TALK WITH GOD

How have you experienced the Fear of the Lord in your own life? How is God inviting you into deeper fear of the Lord?

Have you tended towards fearing God's punishment such as legalism or religion or in self-indulgence such as permissiveness or lawlessness? What is God saying to you about this?

What is the right balance between fearing God and experiencing His love and mercy? How is God advising you to maintain this balance?

How did Jesus demonstrate the Fear of the Lord? How is God asking you to apply this to your life right now?

PRACTICE

1. Invite the Holy Spirit to reveal some areas where your thoughts and actions are out of alignment with the Fear of the Lord. Write down what He says.

2. Ask God to reveal to you how/why these thoughts or behaviors lack reverence for God. For example:
   - Are they arrogant or self-sufficient? As if God didn't exist or was not there for you?
   - Are they contradictory to what you know of His will for you and/or written word?
   - Are they rooted in fearing or trusting something/someone other than God?
   - Are they unwise? Do they lead to bad consequences?

3. Ask God how He desires for your heart to change towards Him. Ask Him to grant you a deeper respect for who He is and how He wants you to do things.

4. Listen to what He says. Put it into practice.

NOTES: _____

ADDITIONAL SCRIPTURES:

Proverbs 3:1

Job 28:28

Proverbs 16:6

Psalm 25:14

Proverbs 1:7

Exodus 20:20

Proverbs 8:13

Revelation 20:11-15

Matthew 16:27

Psalm 19:9

Matthew 10:28

Isaiah 11:1-2

Ecclesiastes 12:13

Proverbs 14:27

Psalm 34:9

2 Corinthians 5:11

 PERFECTION COURSE – UNIT 2.2 READING

GOOD NEWS OF THE KINGDOM

All of humanity is in a war. It is an ancient war for worship. It is a war between God, who is the giver of life and worthy of all worship, and His adversary, an angel named Lucifer, who was created by God to be His chief worshipper but who rebelled because he wanted worship for himself and desired to usurp God's throne. Lucifer launched a rebellion against God which God speedily crushed. Lucifer was banished from heaven along with the angels who had joined in his rebellion, and he became known as Satan, which means *adversary* of God. Soon after this rebellion when God spoke creation into existence, Satan was thrown down to the earth in the form of a serpent. At this time, the earth was void and without form and the waste-waters of chaos covered the earth as the adversary's dwelling place. (This occurred between Genesis 1:1 and Genesis 1:2 and is reflected in more detail in Isaiah 14 and Ezekiel 28.)

In the Beginning (Genesis 1-4)

When God created all of creation, He made it as a gift for mankind, whom He would make in His image. God created mankind to bear His image, have eternal life, and to subjugate Satan as his punishment for rebellion against God. (See Genesis 1-2.) Everything about creation was designed to reproduce and multiply a fruitful bounty for mankind to enjoy without sweat and toil, and to rule over as kings. God's assignment for mankind was to tend to the earth and to be fruitful and multiply in order to fill the earth with descendants who would worship God in thanksgiving for the life He had given them and the world He created for them while enjoying sweet fellowship with God.

Unfortunately, all of creation and fellowship with God wasn't enough for Adam and Eve. The serpent deceived them into disobeying God by appealing to their seemingly harmless desires to be wise and to be like God, even though they had already been made in God's image. They gave way to the nature of a usurper and subjugated themselves to the one they were supposed to rule over. They had lived a life of innocence but they became rebels when they disobeyed God's command, sold out to God's adversary, and forfeited eternal life with God. The time of testing revealed that they worshipped themselves and wanted to be God rather than obey God.

God banished Adam and Eve from the Garden of Eden and from fellowship with Him. They were deposed as kings. God's adversary became the prince of this world. The adversary became the ruler of mankind and the creation was cursed. Adam and Eve were also cursed to eating their bread only through sweat and toil in the thorns and thistles of the cursed ground, and they would eventually die and return to the dust that God had created man out of.

It appeared that God's adversary had won the battle of the Kingdoms.

However, even in their punishment, God granted a ray of hope by promising that one of the woman's descendants, her seed, would crush the head of the serpent and re-establish God's Kingdom for mankind. This promised descendant is who we have come to know as the Messiah—the Anointed One of God. (See Genesis 3.)

Was this calling fulfilled by one of their immediate sons? No. Adam and Eve's rebellion against God's ways became evident in their children very quickly. Their elder son Cain, in the likeness of an usurper, killed their younger son Abel because Cain was jealous that God accepted Abel's blood sacrifice as an offering but did not accept his offering. For this, Cain was banished even further from Eden and driven from any hope of ruling the earth with God. (See Genesis 4.) As Adam and Eve had more children and the generations continued down the line, it became evident that every thought in the minds of Adam and Eve's descendants tended to evil all the time. (See Genesis 6:5.) They worshipped anything and everything except God and their selfish behavior resulted in wickedness and violence filling the earth. They continued to choose the ways of the adversary and displayed his likeness rather than God's.

A Remnant of One Man (Genesis 6-9)

Therefore, God started over again with a remnant of one, a man named Noah. In all the earth, God found only Noah to be blameless because Noah's heart was towards God and not himself. God instructed Noah to build an ark that would house a remnant of creation. It took Noah many years to build this boat and he looked very foolish because it had never rained on the earth. But Noah's building of the boat was a warning to the rest of mankind that judgment was coming upon their rebellion against God.

Once Noah and his family were safe, a great flood filled the earth, killing and destroying everyone and everything that was not inside Noah's Ark. Again, the waste-waters of chaos covered the earth as the dwelling place of God's adversaries.

After the flood had receded, God instructed Noah and his sons to fill the earth with descendants. God's ultimate purpose for mankind had not changed – He still sought a Kingdom of people who would fill the earth and worship Him rather than his adversary. God also entered into a covenant with Noah, promising that He would never again destroy the earth by flood.

Man's United Rebellion Against God (Genesis 11)

As generations continued to be born, mankind proved to have an innate determination to rebel against God. Instead of desiring to rule the earth as a Kingdom for and with God, they took rebellion to a whole new level and gathered together to build a kingdom for themselves. Nimrod led the way as the leader of the world in uniting all of mankind to work together to build a tower that would reach up to heaven. They built the Tower of Babel to make a name for themselves as a symbol of self-empowerment and rejection of God altogether. The world was united as usurpers. They may have hoped that the tower would be so high that they could escape the waters of another flood of judgment.

God saw this rebellion and scattered the peoples to the ends of the earth. He gave them different languages so that they would not be able to work cooperatively in this manner again, so as to impede any further rebellions of this sort.

At this point, God's destiny for mankind to be a Kingdom on the earth as His image bearers seemed all but lost and hopeless.

One Chosen Man (Genesis 12-50)

Therefore, God again selected one man as a remnant to carry forth His Kingdom purposes for mankind. God chose Abraham. Out of all the peoples in all the earth, Abraham was the only one who believed and obeyed God. God entered into a covenant with Abraham which was sealed with the blood of sacrifices. God promised to bless Abraham with a land of his own and make Him into a nation of people— a Kingdom that would bless all the nations of the earth. The Messiah, the One who would crush the head of the serpent and establish the Kingdom of God on the earth, was now promised to come through one of Abraham's descendants.

God also showed Abraham what His judgment looked like so that Abraham could teach His descendants to fear Him and walk blamelessly with Him. Abraham stood and watched as fire and brimstone was rained down from heaven on Sodom and Gomorrah, cities which had given themselves over wholly to wickedness, violence, and perversion.

Abraham believed God and this faith was credited to him as righteousness. This means that even though Abraham's behavior was not always completely kosher, God did not hold Abraham's errors against him, nor did He hold the sins of Abraham's ancestors against him. Abraham's faith was also evidenced by his actions. He left everything he had ever known in this world in order to follow God's call. He left his country, his father's household, and his father's traditions, and his ancestor's approach to religion and spiritual life. He set out looking to for the Kingdom of God on the earth. Even the Gentiles recognized Abraham as a prince among them. (See Genesis 23:6.)

Now that the Messiah was going to be born through Abraham, was it Abraham's immediate son who would bear God's image and trample the head of the adversary? No. Abraham and his wife Sarah waited a long time for an heir, even past the point of her menstruation and child-bearing years. Eventually, angels visited them and told them that they would have a son and they were to name him Isaac. Through a miraculous conception, Sarah became pregnant at age ninety, after being barren her whole life. Abraham was one hundred years old when their son Isaac arrived.

After a while, God tested Abraham's faith to see if he was a worthy steward of His Kingdom. When put to the test, would Abraham falter as Adam and Eve had? God told Abraham to go to Mount Moriah and offer Isaac, his only son, as a sacrifice. According to any reasonable concept of good and evil, this makes no sense whatsoever. But Abraham trusted God as the source of life who was even able to raise Isaac from the dead to fulfill His promises. In trust, he set out to obey God's command rather than rebel against Him. Before Abraham was able to slay Isaac on top of Mount Moriah, an angel stopped him and pointed out that God had provided a ram to be sacrificed instead. The angel also confirmed that Abraham, through his humble submission and faithfulness to God, had passed the test. Abraham had not taken matters into his own hands as Adam and Eve had. Now, most assuredly, the Messiah would come through Abraham's descendants to crush the head of the adversary and establish the Kingdom of God. Then, Abraham saw into the future and prophesied that on the same mountain, the Mountain of the Lord, God would see to the fulfillment of this promise.

God's covenant with Abraham was transferred exclusively to his son Isaac. Then, through another miraculous conception, Isaac and his wife Rebekah had twin sons, Esau and Jacob. Esau was the elder and apparent heir of the promises of God. However, God had fore-ordained that His promises would pass to Jacob. Long story short, through a series of events, Esau rejected his firstborn birthright and sold it to Jacob for a bowl of lentils and Isaac passed the blessing of God to Jacob. Therefore, God's covenant with Abraham transferred exclusively from Isaac to Jacob, whose name God later changed to Israel.

Jacob, aka Israel, had twelve sons who had sons and daughters and became the twelve tribes of Israel. Jacob's favorite son, Joseph, had two dreams from God showing that the rest of his family was going to bow down to him and serve him. Jacob, as God's covenant carrier in his generation who knew the prophecies and promises given to his fathers, took note of this. It is possible that Jacob considered that Joseph might be the promised Messiah who was going to establish the Kingdom of God on the earth. Joseph's brothers, however, rejected Joseph's dreams entirely and threw him in a pit to leave him for dead before selling him to some Gentiles passing by. The Gentiles brought Joseph to Egypt to serve as a slave. After many years and a series of divinely orchestrated events, Joseph was appointed second in command to Pharaoh, the most powerful man in the world at that time. Everything that God had revealed to Joseph came to pass. He had been granted great authority on the earth and eventually, all his brothers bowed down to him.

The God of Israel received great glory on a global basis during this time. Joseph had God-given wisdom and was a righteous image-bearer for God with no record of sin according to Scripture. When this was combined with Joseph's position of authority as second in command under Pharaoh, who was the most powerful man in the world at that time, Joseph was responsible for feeding the whole world during a time of global famine. However, God had a different kind of Kingdom in mind for His people. He had a plan to bring forth image-bearers who were second to no one but Him, the way it had originally been in the Garden of Eden with Adam and Eve. Furthermore, even though Joseph was considered a prince among his brothers in his generation, when the time came for Jacob to bless his sons and pass the covenant promises of God to the next generation, Jacob prophesied that the scepter of God's Kingdom would be carried through his son Judah.

One Chosen Nation: The First Passover (Exodus 1-15)

After Jacob's descendants had multiplied through the course of several generations, God chose the whole nation of Israel for His purposes. God sent Moses to deliver them from Egyptian slavery exactly as and when He promised He would. God worked miracles for Moses as His servant so that the Jewish people would see the power of the Kingdom of Heaven follow Moses as His chosen servant.

In judgment against Pharaoh, Egypt, and their false gods, God orchestrated nine ferocious plagues. Most of these plagues impacted Egyptians but did not touch the people of God. After these plagues, Moses told Pharaoh that God was going to send the Destroyer to kill all the firstborn sons in Egypt. At the same time, Moses told the Israelites to slaughter a lamb for each household and paint the lamb's blood on the doorpost of their homes. When God saw the blood on the doorposts, He would **pass over** the house and not allow the Destroyer to enter. The Israelites obeyed God and God was faithful to deliver them. They departed from Egypt and left behind Egyptian slavery by walking through the parted waters of the Red Sea on dry ground. When their enemies pursued them, the waters came crashing back down on them and buried them forever.

In one day, the nation of Israel was born and set apart to God as His special people. From this day forward, there was only ONE nation in the entire world which was in covenant with the one true God who created heaven and earth and everything in it. The rest of the world was hopeless and disconnected from God altogether because they were usurpers and rebels against God and His authority.

A Kingdom of Priests (Exodus 19-40)

Since God had spared the Israelites first born sons from destruction in Egypt, God now required His people to dedicate to Him every firstborn male as a priest of God. This would mean that almost every Jewish household would have a priest in it to keep the ways of God constantly before all of His people.

God's design for His special people was to be a Kingdom of priests who would worship Him, bear His image of righteousness, rule over God's adversaries, crush the evil one, and bless the whole world. (See Exodus 19:5-6.) God's purpose for Israel was to be a Kingdom for Him, like the Kingdom of Heaven on earth. At Sinai, God gave His people His Law and entered into covenant with Israel which was sealed with the blood of sacrifices. (See Exodus 19-24.) By obeying God's Law, they would maintain fellowship with God and He would dwell among them. Through observing the righteous standards of God's Law, they would bear His image, demonstrate God's likeness to the rest of the world, and be granted eternal life with God. (See Deuteronomy 4:5-8; Leviticus 18:5.)

The Law also established the Tabernacle of God as the predecessor to the Temple and God's sacrificial system by which Israel could atone for their sins through blood sacrifices. When individuals or the collective community of Israel rebelled against God in the likeness of Adam and Eve or committed violations of the Law, either knowingly or unintentionally, the Law requires the shedding of the blood of an unblemished sacrifice to atone for their sins. The Law commands that at God's designated place for sacrifice, the sins of the people must be confessed as they lay their hands upon a spotless sacrificial lamb, transferring their sins to the lamb. Then, the lamb is slaughtered, shedding its blood as atonement and dying the death penalty in the place of the person who had committed error. According to the Law, only blood can make atonement for the soul. (See Leviticus 17:11.) Without the shedding of blood, there is no atonement.

If Israel listened to God and obeyed the Law, they would be His royal Kingdom people and would rule the earth because God would raise them high above all other nations and all of His adversaries. On the other hand, if Israel went the way of Adam and Eve, whoring themselves out to the adversary through disobedience against God's commands, they would find themselves cursed, scattered, and cut off from God. (See Leviticus 26; Deuteronomy 28.)

One Mediator between God and Man (Exodus 20, Deuteronomy 5, 18)

When God appeared to the Israelites at Sinai, He manifested Himself in an all-consuming fire over the mountain, and the Israelites were afraid of God. They recognized that God was too holy for them to approach on their own and recognized that they would die if they entered God's presence or spoke to Him directly. God commended them for their recognition of His majesty and healthy fear of His power.

Out of reverence, the Israelites requested that Moses be the Mediator between them and God, and God granted their request. However, Moses promised that God would appoint a Prophet like Moses to be a superior Mediator between God and man – the Messiah.

Wilderness Rebellion (Exodus 32-33; Numbers 3, 13-14, 16, 21; Psalm 78, 105-106)

Unfortunately, the Israelites in the wilderness repeatedly rebelled against Moses and they constantly questioned his authority as God's only appointed leader and Mediator. Only a few months after they had walked through the Red Sea, they worshipped a Golden Calf and claimed that this was the god who had brought them out of Egypt.

After one year in the wilderness, it was time for Israel to inherit the Promised Land. Moses sent twelve spies into the Promised Land to bring back a report. Although all twelve agreed that it was a good land, only two of the spies believed that God was able to give it to them. The people of Israel rejected the report of the two spies and agreed with the unbelief of the ten spies. As a consequence for this rebellion, God was again ready to disinherit the people of Israel and start over with only Moses by multiplying Moses' descendants into a new generation which would inherit His promises and His Kingdom. However, Moses interceded for Israel and God relented. At that time, God decreed that Israel would have to stay in the wilderness for forty years until the entire generation from twenty years of age and older had died. None of them would be allowed to inherit the Promised Land. After God told them of this consequence, their nature as usurpers was made plain when they thought they could take the Promised Land without God's power and presumed to go into battle against Moses' warning not to. Their rebellion was crushed and they were chased out by their enemies as if by a swarm of bees.

Throughout the wilderness years, Israel grumbled against God and tested Him through unbelief and rebellion. On several occasions, they attempted to appoint leaders for themselves who would meet their demands to return to Egypt, even though they had been slaves there. As the consequence for such insolence, God was ready to destroy the Israelites and start all over again with a remnant of one man, Moses. But Moses prayed to God on Israel's behalf. Mercifully, God did not destroy them and start over but instead, let them live for the sake of His own holy name.

A New Generation & Time of Judges

When the time came for Israel to inherit the Promised Land, Moses transferred leadership of God's people to Joshua. Joshua led the people to conquering many nations within the territory that God had promised to His people.

After this, there were times when Israel did well in obeying the Law and remained faithful to God. At other times, however, they revealed the likeness of the adversary through disobedience to God. When they failed, adversaries were allowed to rule over them for a time. When they cried out to God for mercy, God delivered them. During this time, Israel's devotion to God and the Law waned. They were usurpers who wanted to do things their own way according to what was right in their own sight rather than what God had commanded them. Rather than being a demonstration of God's righteousness to the nations of the world, they conformed their behavior and their forms of worship to imitate the nations. They even worshiped their gods – who are the agents of God's adversary. Their moral condition became so degraded that they behaved as badly as Sodom and Gomorrah.

A Human King (1 Samuel 1-15)

Eventually, Israel asked God to give them a King so that they could be like all the other nations. In this, they were partially right and partially wrong. They knew they were supposed to be a Kingdom for God on the earth, but they were rejecting God as their rightful King. Nevertheless, God granted their request and appointed a man named Saul from the tribe of Benjamin as the first King of Israel. With their first human King, would Israel fulfill their destiny as a Kingdom of God on the earth? No. Saul did well at first in remaining true to God. Soon however, Saul sought to maintain his authority by disobeying God's commands. Therefore, the Kingdom was taken from him and given to David, a simple shepherd boy from Bethlehem of the tribe of Judah.

David was a man after God's own heart. God entered into covenant with David through which He promised to build His Kingdom through one of David's descendants. God would be a Father to David's descendant – the Messiah – and establish His Kingdom forever. (See 2 Samuel 7.) Unfortunately, soon after this, David made some royal missteps against the Law and God's ways. God would have been justified in putting David to death for his sins and revoking His covenant with David, but He never did. Even though there were short-term consequences within David's family and in Israel for David's errors, David was quick and sincere about admitting his faults, turning from his sins, genuinely entrusting himself to the Lord's mercy, and offering the blood sacrifices required by the Law for the atonement of his soul. In spite of his sins, this is what made David a man after God's own heart.

A Kingdom Divided (1&2 Kings, 1&2 Chronicles)

After David, Israel had a taste of what it would be like to be the Kingdom designed by God to bear His image and be a blessing to the whole world. David's son Solomon built the Temple in Jerusalem on the very same mountain where Abraham had offered Isaac and proclaimed God's provision for His Kingdom. Because Solomon recognized the high importance that God placed on the blood of sacrifices offered on His altar and the atoning power of blood for the sins of the people, he offered 22,000 oxen and 120,000 sheep and goats, shedding massive amounts of blood to dedicate the Temple of God. (See 1 Kings 8:63.) The glory of God filled the Temple, and the people of Israel were esteemed as the only people on earth in covenant with the Most High God, Creator of the Universe. People came from far and wide to worship the God of Israel and to hear the God-given wisdom of Solomon. This was the closest Israel had come so far to having a Kingdom which bore God's image and blessed the whole world.

However, Solomon was neglectful about obedience to God's instructions and gave way to rebellion in his own life, particularly through intermarriage with Gentile women who led him astray by their worldly ways and pagan gods. This insubordination resulted in the Kingdom of Israel being split in two after his lifetime. Ten out of the twelve tribes of Israel abandoned David's royal line to form the northern kingdom, while two tribes carried on with David's line to form the southern kingdom.

Both the northern and the southern kingdoms began to adopt the practices of the pagans in the land. In addition to this, the kings of the northern kingdom erected their own altars, created their own festivals to God, and appointed their own priests from the common people. These activities were in direct rebellion against God's explicit instructions that Jerusalem, the place where He had chosen to put His name forever, was the only place that sacrifices could be offered to Him. These things were also against the rules of the Law, which gives clear instructions about God's appointed feasts, priests, and Levites. The northern kingdom's rebellion against God and His ways went from bad to worse until the kingdom was scattered among the nations by the Assyrians in 722 B.C.E. in accordance with the consequences outlined in the Law. The kings of the southern kingdom had a little more success. Some were good, some bad; some were faithful, and some wretched. But eventually their collective disobedience led to their scattering and exile to Babylon, in accordance with the consequences outlined in the Law. Jerusalem was overthrown by Nebuchadnezzar, the King of Babylon, and the Temple of God was destroyed in the year 586 B.C.E.

In the centuries leading up to the destruction and exile of the northern and southern kingdoms, God faithfully sent Prophets to both kingdoms to warn God's people of what would happen to them if they did not repent, turn to Him as their one and only King, and keep His ways. Unfortunately, the people of Israel not only refused to heed the words and warnings of God's Prophets, but they persecuted and killed most of the Prophets for saying things that they didn't want to hear. They continued living their lives as they pleased, worshiping the gods of the nations rather than obeying the Law.

In due time, the words of the Prophets came to pass. Just like God's banishment of Adam and Eve from Eden into exile, God ejected His people from the Promised Land and scattered them to the four corners of the earth.

The Promise of a New Covenant

In spite of their banishment from the Land, God's Prophets revealed God's plans and promises for the future of Israel. God promised to forgive their transgressions, bring the exiles back to the Promised Land and more significantly, God promised to enter into a New Covenant with Israel which would prevent this cycle from recurring again. (See Jeremiah 31:31-37.) The New Covenant between God and Israel would not be like the covenant God had established with them at Sinai when He gave the Law through Moses. Due to the fact that they had proved again and again to be incapable of adhering to God's ways, obeying the Law, and heeding the warnings and directives of His Prophets, God would extend a great mercy to His chosen people through the New Covenant. God would write the Law on their hearts and give them a new heart and a new spirit. God would even place His own Spirit within them so that they would no longer be inclined toward Adam-and-Eve-style usurping and rebellion. Additionally, God would forgive all of their disobedience to the Law and no longer remember their sins against them. This would mean that there would no longer be any divinely instituted consequence for their error and rebellion, including the sins of their ancestors. This way, God's people would be able to obey Him from the heart and fulfill their God-given destiny as an image-bearing Kingdom of God and blessing to all the earth. (See Ezekiel 11:19-20, 36:26-27.)

The Promised Messiah, the Righteous King of Israel (the Prophets)

In the same way that God's existing covenants were established through God's chosen men Noah, Abraham, Moses, and David, God promised through His Prophets that this New Covenant would be given to Israel through His Servant, the Messiah.

According to the prophecies, the Spirit of the Lord would continually guide the Messiah to bring justice and vengeance against God's adversaries and establish the Kingdom of God. The Messiah would crush the head of the ancient serpent and Israel would be able to become a blessing to the whole earth. (See Isaiah 41:1-7; 61:1-3.)

Even in the midst of their exile, God continually reassured His people that He will never reject all of the descendants of Israel because of their rebellion. Instead, He would send the Messiah to establish justice on the earth as God's anointed King whom has been promised from the beginning and who lives in perfect righteousness and obedience to God, a standard that no one else has been able to live up to.

According to the Book of Daniel, which was written during the time of the Jewish people's exile in Babylon, several empires would rule the world before God's Messiah came to crush them all. God's people would even be oppressed and tormented by these evil empires until the time came for God to avenge them by sending the Messiah to establish the everlasting Kingdom of God. (See Daniel 2:44, 7:13-14, 21-27.)

The Messiah would fulfill God's righteous requirement of the Law of God without ever rebelling against God or trying to usurp God's authority for Himself. This would be the righteousness of the people of God. (See Jeremiah 23:5-6.) Even though the Messiah would be innocent of evil, He would be inflicted with the punishment of God that the people deserved. Like a spotless sacrificial lamb, the sins of the people would be laid upon the Messiah, and His soul would become an offering of atonement for their souls. The Messiah, the Righteous Branch, would suffer for the sins of the unrighteous. **(Read Isaiah 53.)**

Returned Exiles Prepare for their King (Ezra, Nehemiah, Haggai, Zechariah, Malachi)

At the appointed time after the Babylonian exile, God allowed many of the scattered Jews to return to the Promised Land. They were able to rebuild a Temple in Jerusalem and God allowed them to experience some level of spiritual re-awakening. However, this Temple was not as grand as Solomon's had been, and the glory of God never filled it. Plus, the Jewish people remained under the authority of a foreign King and were not re-established as an independent nation.

During this time, the Jewish people did not resemble a kingdom at all. Many of them were still scattered in the nations, and even in the Promised Land, they were subjected to Gentiles ruling over them. However, there was an eager expectation for the Messiah's arrival, partly because of the desire for liberation from foreign kings but mostly because of the words of God's Prophets.

No One Righteous (All of History)

During this time, out of fear that the increasingly lukewarm devotion of the Jewish people would lead them into another exile, the leaders of Israel created many rules and regulations in an attempt to establish and maintain holiness among God's people as they awaited Messiah. Various schools of interpretation sprung up with teachings of Scripture in accordance with their way of thinking. Some were extremely religious, forcing common people to maintain priestly standards of holiness. (Pharisees.) Others were very worldly, hoping to blend with the powers of the world in order to prosper as an earthly nation. (Sadducees.) Some wanted to instigate political revolt and throwing off the taxation of foreign powers through insurrection. (Zealots.) None of these groups were righteous in God's sight. They were all usurpers and rebels.

The rest of the nations of the world were still hopelessly disconnected from the one true God. Like their ancestors before them, they were usurpers and rebels who worshipped creation rather than the Creator and worshipped demons, the host of God's adversary, rather than God. There was no eternal hope for them. (See Romans 3:10-20.)

Yet again, it looked like God's plan for a Kingdom of descendants of Adam and Eve who would fill the earth and worship Him looked completely lost and hopeless.

Messiah's Birth (the Gospels)

At the exact time prophesied by Daniel, an angel visited a young Jewish woman from the tribe of Judah. The angel told Mary that even though she was a virgin, she would conceive a child by the power of the Spirit of the LORD, and she was to name Him Jesus. The name Jesus means God saves, because Mary's son would save the people from their sins. (See Matthew 1 and Luke 1, 3:23-38.) In accordance with the prophecies and promises of the Scriptures, God came to dwell with His people. Because Jesus was conceived by the power of the Spirit of the LORD, God was His Father. Jesus was also the seed of a woman descended from Eve—the One who would crush the head of the adversary. Jesus was formed in the womb in God's exact likeness to be God's perfect human image-bearer and King to reign on the eternal throne promised to David. (See Luke 1:32-35.)

Messiah's Kingdom Message

When the time came for Jesus to begin His earthly ministry, He had one simple and clear message: "Repent, for the Kingdom of God is at hand!" Jesus reached out exclusively to Jewish people teaching in synagogues and at the Temple in Jerusalem, encouraging them to turn from their sinful ways and live for God. Jesus spoke almost exclusively about the Kingdom of God. Jesus words, teachings, and actions demonstrated greater God-given wisdom than that of King Solomon. In every circumstance Jesus faced, He said only what God was saying and did only what God was doing because He had the Spirit of God inside of Him to guide Him. Jesus was God's perfect image-bearer. He demonstrated God's holiness, righteousness, power, and mercy. Jesus taught His followers that the Kingdom of God was the absolute top priority and the thing to be sought after above all else. (See Matthew 6:25-33.)

Jesus also demonstrated the power of the Kingdom of God by healing the sick, cleansing lepers, casting out demons, and raising the dead. In a similar way to how God had worked miracles for Moses so that the Jewish people would believe that he was God's appointed servant, God worked miracles through Jesus. In accordance with the prophecies pointing to the Messiah, the sick were healed, the blind saw, the deaf heard, the lame walked, the dead were raised, and good news was proclaimed to the poor. He sent His followers out to reach the Jewish people, proclaiming the message of the Kingdom of God and doing the miraculous works that He did in order to reveal that the Kingdom of God had come near. (See Matthew 10; Luke 10:8-12.)

Jesus was not on a self-promotional "Messiah Tour of Israel" but rather, preferred to keep His identify concealed so that only those who had a heart to perceive His message as coming from God would believe Him and follow Him. Those who recognized this discerned that Jesus spoke the words of eternal life which were from God and not the words of the knowledge of good and evil or rules and regulations like the religious leaders. This said, Jesus never rebelled against the Law nor did He encourage anyone else to do so. Jesus even said that the Law scribes and teachers who understand the things of the Kingdom of God have special advantages over those who do not have knowledge of the Law. (See Matthew 5:17-20, 13:52.) Moreover, Jesus raised the standard of obedience to God in God's Kingdom to be one that cut through to the motives of the heart, not just a measure of external actions. According to His teachings, looking at a woman lustfully is the same as committing the act of adultery and anger against someone is the same as committing the act of murder. The only way for His followers to be able to live up to such an impossible standard would be for them to be reborn by the Spirit of the Lord in keeping with the New Covenant. Without an internal renovation of the human heart and spirit in order to purify character and morality at their deepest levels, no person would ever be able to attain the standard of Jesus' teachings. For this, Jesus promised that the Holy Spirit, the Spirit of truth, would be sent from heaven to dwell inside His followers to enable them to live out His commands and teachings and participate in the Kingdom of God. (See John 14:15-17.)

All of this is to say that what God desired from the beginning of mankind for the establishment of His Kingdom on the earth is childlike trust and obedience to His commands from the depths of the heart. This kind of humble submission and faith in God is what God had found in Abraham and is exactly what Jesus taught His followers. (See Matthew 18:1-4.) Jesus' followers would only be able to fulfill this when the Holy Spirit was sent to dwell inside of them, in accordance with the New Covenant. This would change their hearts away from Adam and Eve's likeness back to the likeness of God.

Messiah's Kingdom

Jesus' followers, who were all Jewish, came from every kind of Jewish household and lifestyle. They regarded the depth of Jesus' understanding of the Scriptures, His miracles in healing the sick, commanding the weather, multiplying food to feed hungry people, and His mercy and compassion for people as confirmation that He was the Son of God. They openly recognized and acknowledged Jesus as the Messiah, the promised Anointed One of God, and the Prophet like Moses whom Israel must listen to. This revelation of Jesus' identity as King of the Kingdom of God was the foundation upon which God would be able to build His Kingdom on the earth.

> *Matthew 16:16-20 – Shimon Cephas answered,* **"You are the Messiah, the Son of the living God."** *Jesus replied, "Blessed are you, Shimon Bar Jonah, for this was not revealed to you by flesh and blood, but by my Father in heaven. And I tell you that you are Cephas, and* **on this rock I will build my congregation, and the gates of Hades will not overcome it. I will give you the keys of the Kingdom of Heaven; whatever you bind on earth will be bound in heaven, and whatever you loose on earth will be loosed in heaven."** *Then he ordered his disciples not to tell anyone that he was the Messiah.*

The religious leaders of Israel, however, did not follow Jesus or accept Him as the Messiah. By this time, the leaders of Israel, who were eagerly awaiting the arrival of the Messiah due to Daniel's prophecy, had also created many rules as a supplement to the Law which they claimed were the keys to obedience. Jesus did not submit Himself to their rules and pointedly rejected the ones which were a contradiction of the Law and the heart of God. (See Matthew 23.) Some of the religious leaders were so consumed with maintaining the traditions of the Jewish people and observing their religious rules that they had forgotten that being an image-bearing Kingdom for God is God's main purpose for Israel.

Additionally, some of the religious leaders had blended themselves into the marketplace of the world to such a degree that they had procured positions of political power and commercial authority. Leaders like this had turned God's house into a marketplace for personal gain and desired to "keep the peace" by maintaining the status quo with the world. They did not like the way Jesus drew great crowds that acknowledged Jesus as their King rather than the Roman Emperor because they feared that it would be seen as rebellion by all Jews against Rome and they would lose their positions of power. These religious leaders rejected Jesus as their King while submitting to Rome's authority.

Other Jewish leaders were looking for the Messiah to come and establish His Kingdom on the Day of the Lord with great terror by overthrowing their Gentile oppressors in a cataclysmic battle between God on Israel's behalf and the rest of the world. For them, Jesus' teachings of humility, sacrificial love, and mercy did not fit the profile of the Messiah they were looking for. These religious leaders rejected Jesus as their King because they lacked faith to see how God was fulfilling His promises right before their eyes. Though Jesus righteously longed for the day of judgment by fire, He knew that before judgment, God was doing something wonderful to make a way for the redemption of mankind.

> *Luke 12:49-50:* **I have come to bring fire on the earth, and how I wish it were already kindled! But I have a baptism to undergo**, *and what constraint I am under until it is completed!*

All of these religious leaders conspired together to stir up false accusations against Jesus as a deliberate attempt to prevent Israel from following Him and making Him their King. In a move to maintain their own authority, they sought to trap Jesus in His words and find contradictions against the Law in His life and teachings and sought ways to put Jesus to death and cut Him off from God's people.

Knowing in advance that all of this must take place, Jesus told His followers that He would be handed over to the religious leaders, and then to the Gentiles, and would beaten, scourged, and put to death. This was hard for His followers to understand because, like Abraham being asked to sacrifice his only son Isaac, this didn't make any sense. Peter even tried to rebuke Jesus for saying so but Jesus sharply said, "Get behind me Satan" because He recognized the voice of the usurper speaking through His friend. Peter was thinking from the world's perspective of war and victory through self-exaltation, whereas Jesus was on a mission to fulfill God's righteousness through obedience.

On the night before His death, Jesus shared a meal with His disciples. He prayed the blessing over the bread and broke it saying, "This is my body, broken for you." Then He prayed the blessing over the wine and said, "This is my blood of the New Covenant, which is poured out for the forgiveness of sins." That same night, Jesus prayed to ask God if there was any other way to offer atonement for His people but there was not. So, He submitted Himself to the will of God as revealed in the Scriptures, knowing that it must be fulfilled in order for God's Kingdom to be established.

At the appointed time, because Jesus knew the plan of God for Him to be cut off from the land of the living in fulfillment of the Scriptures, He allowed the religious leaders to arrest Him on charges of blasphemy for claiming to be God's only Son and prophesying that the Temple would be destroyed. Jesus could have used His own power to stop this, or He could have called out to God to put a stop to this unjust treatment, but instead, in accordance with the Scriptures, He did not open His mouth in self-defense. Like Abraham offering Isaac, Jesus had perfect faith in God as the source of life who had power even to raise Him from the dead in order to fulfill His promises. He trusted the prophetic promises about Himself which foretold that His death would be an offering of atonement which would establish the New Covenant between God and Israel and which would be sealed with His blood. When Pilate asked Jesus if it was true that He was a king, He did not deny it but affirmed His own destiny.

> *John 18:36-37 ESV: Jesus answered, "**My kingdom is not of this world**. If my kingdom were of this world, my servants would have been fighting, that I might not be delivered over to the Jews. But my kingdom is not from the world." Then Pilate said to him, "So you are a king?" Jesus answered, "**You say that I am a king. For this purpose I was born and for this purpose I have come into the world**--to bear witness to the truth. Everyone who is of the truth listens to my voice."*

The Crucified King & Eternal Passover Lamb

On the day of Passover, when the Passover lambs were being slaughtered in remembrance of the way that God delivered His people from Egyptian slavery, Jesus the Messiah, the eternal Passover Lamb, was slaughtered and shed His blood. On the same mountain where Abraham had offered Isaac as a sacrifice and said that God would provide for all of His promises, Jesus the Messiah offered Himself as the only Son and Lamb of God who makes provision for atonement for the sins of the world. Jesus was beaten, whipped, and scourged until He no longer resembled a human, and then He was hung upon a tree to die a horrifying, brutal, cursed death.

The sign above His head said, "King of the Jews" in Hebrew, Latin, and Greek the major languages of the world in that day. The whole world was out on notice that God was establishing His Kingdom through His chosen King of Israel, God's anointed Messiah. The cross was God's standard lifted up on the earth. All of mankind was exposed as usurpers. All of the descendants of Adam and Eve who, being more inclined to the ways of the adversary, didn't want God to rule over them and be their King. Even Jesus' own disciples abandoned Him in shocked unbelief at these turn of events.

During His crucifixion, He said to God, "Forgive them, for they know not what they do," and with His dying breath, He cried out, "It is finished!" knowing that the requirement for atonement of souls had been satisfied. Then, He committed His spirit into the hands of God and hung His head and died.

From a worldly perspective, God's plans for His Kingdom on the earth again looked hopeless.

But on the third day, in accordance with the Scriptures, God raised Jesus from the dead. Because He had lived in accordance with the Law perfectly, Jesus was an unblemished sacrifice and merited eternal life. Jesus served as the eternal Passover Lamb so that He *passes over* anyone who covers their soul with His blood to protect them from the Destroyer, namely death. Now, anyone from any nation, tribe, or tongue who believes in Him as the Suffering Servant and Messiah of Israel is redeemed from the curse of the Law which means that their sins no longer held against them by God. (See 1 Peter 1:18-19; 1 Corinthians 5:7.)

Crushing the Head of the Serpent

Jesus' resurrection proved that the offering of His soul for atonement for the sins and souls of mankind had been accepted by God. Through His resurrection, Jesus reversed the curse of Adam, crushed the head of Satan, and was granted the keys to the Kingdom of God.

The resurrected Jesus showed Himself alive to His followers for forty days. He gave them the keys to the Kingdom of God and commanded them to leave behind the life they had known and go, be fruitful, and multiply on the earth by making disciples of His Kingdom.

One New Man – One Mediator – the New Covenant

Through all of this, God was again starting with a remnant of one Man—His Son, Jesus, the promised Messiah of Israel. Moreover, God did this while remaining totally faithful to the Law and every promise He had made to the Patriarchs and Prophets of Israel. He fulfilled the Old Covenant and established the New Covenant through which the forgiveness of sins is available to anyone who believes that Jesus is the Son of God and that God raised Him from the dead. Faith in Jesus Christ as the King of the Kingdom of God is the only way to be included in God's people and the blessings of the righteous. He is the Mediator and Prophet, greater than Moses, appointed by God to represent mankind. (See John 14:6; Acts 4:12; 1 Timothy 2:5.)

After forty days of resurrection appearances, Jesus' disciples asked if He was going to establish His Kingdom by overthrowing all the kingdoms of the earth in the epic battle of the Day of the Lord. Jesus said it was not for them to know the times of God. He ascended to heaven from the Mount of Olives in Jerusalem, it was promised that He would return to the same place in order to fulfill the remaining Scriptures about the Messiah. At that time, bring judgment on all God's adversaries and anyone who does not accept Him as their King. Until then, Jesus' disciples are called upon to fulfill God's purpose for mankind by making disciples of God's Kingdom in readiness for the world to come.

Must Be Born Again by Faith (Acts & Beyond)

When Jesus ascended to and arrived in heaven, He sat down at the right hand of God. Ten days later, the Holy Spirit was poured out from heaven to all who believed in Jesus, who were gathered together at the Southern Steps of the Temple in Jerusalem. Similar to how a consuming fire dwelt over Sinai when the Law was written on tablets of stone and given to Israel, flames of fire hovered over the heads of Jesus' followers as the Law was written on the tablets of their hearts. (See Acts 2, Joel 2:28-29.)

The New Covenant between God and Israel, which had been sealed with the blood of the Messiah, which He shed for the forgiveness of sins, was now fully established and functional. Followers of Jesus now hold the keys to the Kingdom of God, bearing His image from the heart through the Holy Spirit, with delegated authority and power from heaven for the purpose of establishing God's Kingdom on the earth.

In the days and years that followed, the good news of Jesus the Messiah was initially spread only to Jews. After about ten to fifteen years, Jesus' Jewish followers came to understand that the New Covenant was also intended to be extended to Gentiles as long as they believed in Jesus, the Messiah of Israel. From then on and including now, anyone in any nation, Jew or Gentile alike, who confesses the name of Jesus and believes in their heart that God raised Him from the dead will have their sins blotted out and can live for God and His Kingdom. Like God's covenant with Abraham, righteousness is credited to us who believe by faith, not like the covenant with Moses which required perfect obedience to God's Law. This is really good news! (See John 1:12-13, 3:3-6; Romans 1:16-17.)

This said, our faith is revealed by what we do. We must be born again which includes an entire renovation of our human nature by the Holy Spirit who enables us to deny and crucify our sinful nature of the rebellious usurper who wants to be our own god rather than let Jesus be our King. (See Galatians 5:19-24.) We must allow the Holy Spirit within us to strengthen us in righteousness so that we do not give way to temptation like Adam and Eve did. Our faith will be tested and our actions will reveal what we truly believe. God's mercies are sure through our faith in Jesus but we will only be people after God's own heart if our repentance from error is swift and real from the heart.

Judgment Day to Come (Matthew 24, Mark 13, Luke 21, Revelation)

As Jesus promised, He will return to avenge all evil and judge the world. This time, it will not be by water as it was in the days of Noah, but by fire as it was for Sodom and Gomorrah. It will be a time similar to the outpouring of plagues in Egypt when God protected those who were His while He poured out judgments on those who defied Him. There will be wars, earthquakes, tsunamis and strange tides, and every type of plague, disease, and disaster in this world as the cursed creation groans for its rebirth by fire.

The times before the return of Jesus will be consumed with false prophets and false teachers using the tactics of the ancient serpent to prey upon the elect of God. Through teachings and techniques claiming to establish God's likeness through deeper spirituality, divine power, prophetic omniscience and things like this, the adversary will deceive many into counterfeit worship. The antichrist will set up his kingdom in absolute blasphemous rebellion against God, while imitating God's power with all manner of signs and wonders, and declaring himself to be God. There will be a great apostasy in the Church as many will fall away from worshipping God to worship the beast and take his mark.

Similar to the days of Noah, people will be going about their normal lives up until the moment judgment begins. Moreover, even Jesus does not know the exact day and hour of His return but says that it will come like a thief in the night when no one is expecting it. Similar to those who were inside Noah's Ark, we will be spared from the wrath of God through our faith in Jesus. Therefore, we are told to keep watch, be ready, and faithfully fulfill our duties as His servants until He returns. Even if the other servants in God's house begin to beat us and treat us shamefully while they themselves begin to eat, drink, and be merry because the Master is delayed. We must be vigilant in keeping the commands of our King.

In the end, just like in the beginning, all of mankind will sell themselves out to worship the ancient serpent – the beast – except for those who have their names written in the Lamb's Book of Life and endure in their faith. (See Revelation 13.) When the time for God's wrath comes upon the world, God will judge the living and the dead according to whether or not their names have been written in the Lamb's Book of Life. The dead will be raised and judged – some to everlasting life in God's Kingdom and some to everlasting contempt and punishment in the fires of hell. All usurpers and rebels will be destroyed. God will take vengeance on the beast, the ancient serpent who deceived mankind away from worshipping the one true God. (See Revelation 19:19-21; Daniel 12:1-2.) Then, God will establish His Kingdom and we will live with Him forever in the new heavens and the new earth after the old heavens have been rolled away like a scroll and the new earth has been created without any waters of chaos. (See Revelation 21:1-8.)

God's plan for mankind will be fulfilled. God's ultimate defeat of His adversary will be complete. God will have a people who will fill the earth and worship Him in Spirit and in truth from their hearts. And He will reign and dwell with us forever. Amen.

Basic Training Exercise

CHRIST REVEALED (TYPES & SHADOWS)

Luke 24:27 NIV – And beginning with Moses and all the Prophets, he explained to them what was said in all the Scriptures concerning himself.

DESCRIPTION

Jesus plainly said that all Scripture testifies about Him. From the beginning of mankind, God had Jesus in mind. This includes His perfect life, sacrificial death, resurrection, ascension, and eternal Kingdom.

Finding Jesus in all of Scripture can be easy in some passages and more challenging in others, forcing us to press into God for revelation. He can be found in people, things, holy objects, in ways that New Testament writers called "types" or "shadows." He is also discovered in the vivid words, metaphors, and predictions of the Prophets.

Practicing Christ Revealed is about discovering Jesus in all of Scripture. It helps us to marvel at how God has been disclosing parts of the mystery of His eternal plan of redemption since before the world began.

EXAMPLE

Genesis 4:1-16 – The Story of Cain and Abel

What are some ways that this passage reveals or points to Christ?

1. Adam and Eve may have thought that one of their sons would be the One to crush the head of the serpent. Jesus is that Son.
2. Evil Cain killing righteous Abel is like the wicked world crucifying righteous Jesus because He was acceptable to God.
3. Abel's blood cried out to God to be avenged. Christ's blood cries out to God for forgiveness of sins and then ultimately for eternal vengeance.
4. Cain was forced into exile away from God's presence with a mark on him. Those who do not believe Jesus will accept the mark of the beast and spend eternity away from the presence of God.

Category: Word of God

Basic TRAINING
SPIRITUAL EXERCISES

PURPOSE:

To accurately understand God's meaning and imagery used in Biblical texts.

To read the Bible objectively and impartially seeking out what God is speaking.

To identify key themes in the Bible and know how they point to Jesus the Messiah and fit into the greater picture of redemption.

SPIRITUAL FRUIT:

Deeper knowledge of God through His Word.

Increased revelation of Jesus and God's purposes for mankind.

Improved understanding of how God revealed Jesus throughout His Word.

Greater faith through hearing the Word of God.

PRAYER

Father, thank you sent Jesus to fill me with the Holy Spirit who teaches me and leads me in all truth. Holy Spirit, fill me now with wisdom and revelation. Explain the Scripture to me in a way that reveals Christ and helps me turn to Him in my heart. In Jesus' name, Amen.

PRACTICE

1. As you read your Bible, ask the Holy Spirit to highlight something within the text you are reading.

2. Answer the following question about the contents of your text. Try to find Scriptures to support your answers.
   - How does this passage anticipate the life, death, and/or resurrection of Jesus?
   - Can you hear Jesus speaking in this passage of His suffering and victory? (i.e. the Psalms) If so, how?
   - How is this a metaphor for God's redemptive work? (i.e. the Feasts of God, Tabernacle, etc.)
   - How has Jesus already fulfilled prophecies in the text?
   - Will the text's prophecies be fulfilled when Jesus returns?
   - How is this a "type" of Christ? (King, Prophet, Priest, etc.)
   - How is this a metaphor for something Jesus is? (i.e. light, life, way, truth, offering for sin, God's tabernacle, etc.)
   - How do the failures, faithlessness, and imperfections in the characters expose humanity's need for a Savior, eternal blood sacrifice, and righteous King? (i.e. through the Law, sin, curse, human weakness, imperfect leadership, etc.)
   - How is Jesus the perfect example of the application of God's wisdom this passage speaks about?

3. Summarize briefly how this has given you deeper insight in to the redemptive work of Jesus.

NOTES: _____

ADDITIONAL SCRIPTURES:

John 5:39-40

Colossians 2:17

Hebrews 10:1

Luke 24:25

Acts 3:24

John 1:45

Galatians 4:21-31

Category: Word of God

Basic Training Exercise

CONTEXT, CONTEXT, CONTEXT

Romans 15:4 NIV – For everything that was written in the past was written to teach us, so that through the endurance taught in the Scriptures and the encouragement they provide we might have hope.

DESCRIPTION

When we read the Scriptures to delve deeper into our knowledge of God, it is important to understand the context surrounding any passage we may be reading. There is always an original voice, audience, purpose, and history surrounding what God intended when He first spoke those words. By asking questions such as: who, what, where, when, how, and why, we gain insight into God's heart, plan, and purposes. Plus, we grow in our confidence that we are not misquoting or misunderstanding Him.

Practicing Context, Context, Context is about pulling our interpretive lens back to see the bigger picture of what God is saying in any given passage.

EXAMPLE (ABBREVIATED)

Scripture: Jeremiah 29:11: For I know the plans I have for you," declares the LORD, "plans to prosper you and not to harm you, plans to give you hope and a future.

1. **First Impression** – A promise of blessing for my life.
2. **Who** – The Prophet Jeremiah, mid-life, in a written letter. Called by God at a young age, rejected by leaders due to his prophecies of impending doom.
3. **To Whom** – The surviving exiles of Judah who have been deported to Babylon as captives.
4. **What** – Announcement of seventy years of exile. Exiles encouraged to live decently. False prophets denounced. Preceded and followed by false prophecies promising imminent blessing.
5. **Audience Interpretation** – Exile in Babylon was going to be long but God would eventually restore them and bring them back to the land of Judah.
6. **Look Again** – God's plan of discipline and redemption for Israel.

Category: Word of God

Basic TRAINING
SPIRITUAL EXERCISES

PURPOSE:
To accurately and objectively understand what God is saying in His Word.

To gain insight into God's redemptive plan through identifying the original setting of the text.

SPIRITUAL FRUIT:
Deeper knowledge of God through His Word.

Increased revelation of God's ways and dealings.

Improved understanding of what God is speaking through His Word.

PRAYER
Father, thank your Word is truth. I ask you now to grant me wisdom and understanding of what you are truly saying in your Word the way you originally intended it. Help me to grow in my knowledge of you by learning of your ways through your Word. In Jesus' name, Amen.

PRACTICE

1. As you read your Bible, ask the Holy Spirit to highlight a particular verse to you. (We'll call this the "Verse.")
   - Summarize your First Impression of the verse.

2. Use the following questions as a guideline to research some information about the context of your Verse.
   - Who is speaking? The person who wrote the Book, a person in dialog, God, or someone speaking for God?
   - To whom is the speaker speaking? Why?
   - What are the highlights in the lives/backgrounds of the speaker and the audience up to this point?
   - Where does it take place? Is it referring to another place?
   - When was it first spoken? Is it referring to its own present time, the past, the future, or the end of time?
   - Is it part of a greater story, proclamation, or dialog? When does the full story/speech begin and end?
   - What is being said in the Verse? Summarize it in your own words, including how it fits into the full story/speech.
   - Are there any symbols or figures of speech being used? How did the original speaker or audience interpret or understand these symbols from their culture background?

3. Look Again at the Verse by considering the following:
   - How does the context clarify what God is really saying?
   - Does the context alter or confirm your interpretation of what God is speaking through your Verse? If so, how?
   - Summarize what the Verse is about in its proper context.

NOTES: _____

ADDITIONAL SCRIPTURES:
2 Timothy 3:16
Acts 20:27
1 Corinthians 2:13
Isaiah 55:11
Matthew 24:35
Jeremiah 23:29
Joshua 1:8
Psalm 119:105

Israel Foundations Test

Do you know the significance of Israel?

Answer the following questions. Examine what you know and believe about Israel and the Jewish people.

Why did Jesus have to be Jewish?	Has God rejected the Jewish people?	Is God still in covenant with the Jewish people?
Are Jewish people already saved?	**How do Jewish people get saved?**	**Who is the Israel of God?**
What does One New Man mean?	**Are Jews the rightful onwers of the land of Israel?**	**Will all Jews return to Israel?**

PERFECTION COURSE – UNIT 2.3 READING

Israel & One New Man

God established an everlasting covenant with Noah that He would never judge the earth again by water.

God established an everlasting covenant with Abraham that Abraham would be the father of many nations and that his descendants would possess the land of Canaan as an everlasting possession. God also promised to be Abraham's God, to bless all the nations of the earth though him, and to curse anyone who cursed Abraham.

God established a covenant with the nation of Israel at Sinai that they would be His special possession and holy nation. If Israel obeyed the terms of this covenant, they would be richly blessed above all other nations on the earth, but if they disobeyed the terms of this covenant, they would be plagued, judged, oppressed by enemies, scattered among the nations, and made to be a horror in all the earth.

God established an everlasting covenant with David that one of David's descendants would be the Messiah of Israel who would establish a Kingdom with everlasting dominion.

The people of Israel consistently failed to be able to meet the requirements of the Old Covenant and so through His prophets, God promised to establish a new and everlasting covenant with Israel. This New Covenant would be through the Messiah, David's descendant, who would BE the covenant between God and Israel and extend its benefits even to the Gentiles. (See Jeremiah 31:31-34; Isaiah 42:6.)

Jesus fulfilled these prophecies and established the New Covenant. He is the Messiah born in the line of David. He is the covenant between God and Israel and the New Covenant's mediator. His blood was shed for the forgiveness of sins and as the seal of the New Covenant.

> *Hebrews 8:10-13:* [Quoting Jeremiah 31:31-34] **This is the covenant I will establish with the people of Israel** *after that time, declares the Lord. I will put my laws in their minds and write them on their hearts. I will be their God, and they will be my people. No longer will they teach their neighbor, or say to one another, 'Know the Lord,' because they will all know me, from the least of them to the greatest. For I will forgive their wickedness and will remember their sins no more."* **By calling this covenant "new," he has made the first one obsolete**; *and what is obsolete and outdated will soon disappear.*

Take note: Who is the New Covenant with? Israel. Who is the New Covenant for? Everyone who believes that Jesus is Lord. It is not a covenant with Gentiles as if God has neglected or rejected the Jewish people.

This said, when the Jews in Jesus' day claimed that they had access to the Kingdom of God and eternal life because they were descendants of Abraham, Jesus rebuked them and informed them that biological relation to Abraham is not enough to qualify anyone for eternal life and the world to come. (See John 8:31-59.) What is required is not to be descended from Abraham but to **be like** Abraham by doing the things that Abraham did: **believing God**. (See Romans 4:13; Galatians 3:29.)

> *Romans 9:6, 8: It is not as though God's word had failed. For* **not all who are descended from Israel are Israel.** *... In other words,* **it is not the children by physical descent who are God's children**, *but it is the* **children of the promise who are regarded as Abraham's offspring.**

During his life, Abraham declared from the mount where the Temple eventually stood that God Himself would provide the atoning sacrifice for the forgiveness of sins. (See Genesis 22.) God fulfilled what Abraham saw and declared by sending Jesus.

The New Covenant – One New Man

God's covenant with Abraham was sealed and symbolized through circumcision. According to the Old Covenant Law of Moses, anyone who was not circumcised was not allowed to participate in the Passover Feast commemorating God's deliverance of His people. Under the Old Covenant, only the nation of Israel had a relationship with God, and everyone else (collectively referred to as Gentiles, foreigners, and strangers) was completely excluded from the covenant and its blessings unless they were circumcised into God's covenant with Israel. At Sinai, God said that if Israel obeyed Him, they would be His special people and royal (kingdom) priesthood. But now because Jesus obeyed God in perfect righteousness, we who believe Him have become a new generation of humanity. God has chosen us out of every nation and background and ethnicity to participate in this new people in Christ. (See 1 Peter 2:9; Revelation 5:9-10.) In the New Covenant, we are spiritually circumcised through baptism. When we enter the waters, we symbolize putting to death our Adamic nature and it is rolled away as we emerge out of the waters as a new creation in Christ. We are born again as sons and daughters of God. There is neither Jew nor Gentile, only believers who have put their faith in Jesus. Our circumcision is of the heart. (See Romans 2:28-29; Philippians 3:3.)

> *Colossians 2:11-12: In him [Christ]* **you were also circumcised with a circumcision not performed by human hands.** *Your whole self ruled by the flesh was put off when you were circumcised by Christ, having been buried with him in baptism, in which you were also raised with him through your faith in the working of God, who raised him from the dead.*

When we put our faith in Jesus and the Holy Spirit comes to dwell inside of us, we become a new creation. We are a new species on the earth, a new generation, a new nation of people which was born by the power of God.

> *Ephesians 2:15-19: by setting aside in his flesh the law with its commands and regulations.* **His purpose was to create in himself <u>one new humanity</u>** *out of the two, thus making peace, and* **in one body to reconcile both of them to God through the cross,** *by which he put to death their hostility. He came and preached peace to you who were far away [Gentiles] and peace to those who were near [Jews].* **For through him we both [Jews & Gentiles] have access to the Father by one Spirit.** *Consequently, you are no longer foreigners and strangers, but* **fellow citizens with God's people and also members of his household,**

There are sixty-eight uses of "Israel" in the New Testament and they consistently refer to Israel as the natural descendants of Abraham, Isaac, and Jacob and followers of Moses. It is impossible to realistically interpret these verses to allegorically or metaphorically refer to the Church. However, two uses of the word Israel in the New Testament refer to Israel in a context other than natural descendants of the patriarchs.

> *Galatians 6:15-16: Neither circumcision nor uncircumcision means anything;* **what counts is the new creation.** *Peace and mercy to* **all who follow this rule--to the Israel of God.**

> *Romans 11:25-26: I do not want you to be ignorant of this mystery, brothers and sisters, so that you may not be conceited:* **Israel has experienced a hardening in part until the full number of the Gentiles has come in, and in this way all Israel will be saved.** *As it is written: 'The deliverer will come from Zion; he will turn godlessness away from Jacob.*

Both of these verses explicitly point to the inclusion of Jews and Gentiles as part of God's promises to Israel which were fulfilled in Christ. God has chosen a people from every nation, tribe, and tongue (including the natural descendants of the patriarchs) to be included in His promises to Israel. As such, those who believe Christ, whether Jew or Gentile, are the "Israel of God."

God Has NOT Rejected the Jewish People

Just because Jesus fulfilled the New Covenant does not mean that God has rejected the Jewish people who are still under the Old Covenant. Believers in early church in Rome became confused about this matter when Emperor Claudius expelled the Jews from Rome around 49 A.D. The believers in the church at Rome began to regard this expulsion as evidence that God had rejected the Jews and was punishing them for rejecting Jesus as their Messiah. However, the Apostle Paul strongly rebuked them for this error.

> *Romans 11:1, 11 ESV: I ask, then,* **has God rejected his people? By no means!** *For I myself am an Israelite, a descendant of Abraham, a member of the tribe of Benjamin. ... So I ask,* **did they stumble in order that they might fall? By no means!** *Rather, through their trespass salvation has come to the Gentiles, so as to make Israel jealous. (Also Romans 9:3-5, 10:1.)*

Jesus is Jewish. Jesus is the King of Israel. Every book in the Bible was written by Jews, for Jews, about Jews, and to Jews. All of Christ's apostles and first followers were Jewish and witnessed almost exclusively to Jews for the first ten years of Christianity. In fact, the inclusion of the Gentiles in the New Covenant was so controversial at first that the hot theological debate of the early Church was whether or not non-Jews had to be circumcised in their flesh in order to be included considered part of God's people at all. (See Acts 15:1-29.)

Jews were chosen by God first, loved by God first, and will be judged first when Christ returns. (See Romans 1:16, 2:9-11.) For this reason, it was the Apostle Paul's practice in all of his travels to witness first to the Jewish people in any given city before sharing the good news with Gentiles. For the most part, the Jews rejected this message and the people spreading it. Even so, Jews are still loved by God because of the covenant promises He made to Abraham, Isaac, and Jacob. This said, Jews who do not believe that Jesus is Lord are enemies of gospel message. They are fighting against the righteousness of God, which is by faith, while trying to establish their own righteousness by works of the Law.

> *Romans 11:28-29: As far as the* **gospel is concerned, they are enemies for your sake**; *but as far as* **election is concerned, they are loved on account of the patriarchs**, *for God's gifts and his call are irrevocable.*

> *Romans 10:3: Since they did not know the righteousness of God and* **sought to establish their own, they did not submit to God's righteousness**.

When the Jewish people rejected and continue to reject Jesus as their Messiah, they disqualify themselves from admittance into the New Covenant through their unbelief. If they repent of unbelief and place their faith in Jesus, God will readily accept them. **(Read Romans 11:17-24.)** In fact, the hearts of the Jewish people were hardened to the Gospel message so that the Gentiles, who were already enemies of God because of sin, could come to know Jesus and be saved. It is still God's will that the Jewish people come to know Him and believe that Jesus is the fulfillment of His promises for their Messiah. Their inclusion in the New Covenant through faith in Christ is absolutely and undoubtedly the will of God. (See Romans 11:12.) In fact, throughout history, God consistently maintained a faithful remnant of His people by His grace. (See Romans 11:5.)

Therefore, let us not be conceited but grateful regarding the Jewish heritage of our faith and let us be merciful to God's chosen people by giving them top priority as we witness for Christ. God's promise to Israel has not failed but it must be received by FAITH.

God Has NOT Replaced the Jewish People

Certain people throughout the centuries to believe that the Church has replaced Israel. This is a lie. Jesus fulfilled God's Old Covenant with Israel and as such is the rightful heir of all of God's blessings and promises to Israel which He extends in the New Covenant to everyone who believes in Him. However, just because Christ fulfilled the Old Covenant does not mean that God has revoked it.

When the writer of Hebrews wrote to Jewish believers in the early church, he stated that through the institution of the New Covenant, the Old Covenant was made obsolete and would soon disappear. (See Hebrews 8:13.) The words used describe something that has been made old, become worn out through time or use, or is about to be done away with – not something that has already been done away with. For example, when the automobile was invented, it proved itself to be a superior form of transportation but this did not mean that people could no longer travel by horse and buggy. Some might think that a horse and buggy is too slow, dangerous, or that water and hay are difficult sources of fuel. But if this is all you have ever known and what your people have always used then, an automobile looks like a strange contraption and probably a death wish. Even though automobiles may have been made available, people were still free to use a horse and buggy if they wanted to.

You get the point. God has not nullified the Old Covenant with Israel and it is still intact for those who have not aligned themselves with the New Covenant through faith in Jesus. However, the Old Covenant is not an everlasting covenant and will soon fade away, having been worn out from use. In the meantime, there are still people in the world today under the Old Covenant even while there are believers and adherents to the New Covenant.

Moreover, Jesus being Jewish actually served to CONFIRM God's promises to the patriarchs of Israel.

> Romans 15:8: *For I tell you that Christ has become a servant of the Jews on behalf of God's truth,* ***so that the promises made to the patriarchs might be confirmed***

Who are the patriarchs? Abraham, Isaac, and Jacob whose name was changed to Israel. While the Old Covenant with Moses was NOT an everlasting covenant, God's covenant with the patriarchs preceded His covenant with Moses and IS everlasting. So, what is it that God promised the patriarchs? In an EVERLASTING covenant, God promised Abraham a land, a nation, a name, to be his God and bless him, and that his offspring would inherit the world. (See Genesis 12:2-3, 15:18, 17:4-8.) Jesus did not negate or replace these promises but rather confirmed them. These promises still stand firmly in place and will be ultimately and literally fulfilled.

God has not become anti-Semitic. His Son is still Jewish. It is a dangerous misunderstanding of God's character for us to think that He has in any way broken His word to His covenant promises to His people or replaced them with another group of people. If He has been fickle in keeping His promises to them, then we should be very concerned that He might back out of His New Covenant assurances to us.

The truth is that God sustains His people by His mercy as a witness to all nations that He is still their God and to give them ample time to repent and come to know that Jesus is their Messiah. They are beloved to Him on account of the patriarchs. Love is patient.

God Has NOT Revoked or Broken His Covenant with the Jewish People

Just because Jesus fulfilled the New Covenant does not mean that God revoked the Old Covenant or is not still enforcing its terms upon natural descendants of Jacob who are under the Law of Moses.

In fact, the Old Covenant Law is still being sovereignly enforced and the words of God's prophets regarding Israel continue to be fulfilled. The Law clearly outlines the blessings and the curses which will come upon the Jewish people based on their obedience or disobedience to God's requirements. These can be found in Leviticus 26 and Deuteronomy 28. The Leviticus version includes God's schedule of increasingly severe punishments for persistent disobedience. **(Read Leviticus 26.)**

In summary, if Israel persisted in rebellion and disobedience to God they would experience every kind of plague and disease, crop failure, famine, drought, terror, defeat by enemies, the sword of the Lord, and having their cities overthrown and demolished. Ultimately, they would be cast out of the land that God had given them and scattered among the nations to perish.

Moreover, in the last days of Moses, before the people of Israel entered the Promised Land, the Lord instructed Moses to write down a song as a witness against His people. **(Read Deuteronomy 30, 31 & 32.)** God knew that His people would experience the fullness of the blessings and the curses laid out in His Law even before they had entered the Promised Land. He knew that they would be scattered and exiled among the nations of the earth for their rebellion against Him. But God in His great mercy, also made a way for their return to the land and to His blessings.

God does not break His promises. God does not violate His covenants. God explicitly promised that in spite of great calamities and afflictions that would come upon His people, He would never fully reject them or completely destroy them because this would be a violation of His covenant with them.

Moreover, in the promise of the New Covenant, God affirms His promise that He will again joyfully plant His people in the land promised to their ancestors. (See Jeremiah 32:40-41.) Additionally, God promised that at that time, He would be ready to circumcise their hearts so that they could willingly obey Him and experience eternal life with Him. This has always been His will and plan.

> *Deuteronomy 30:1-7: When **all these blessings and curses I have set before you come on you** and you take them to heart wherever the LORD your **God disperses you among the nations**, and when you and your children return to the LORD your God and obey him with all your heart and with all your soul according to everything I command you today, then the LORD your God will restore your fortunes and have compassion on you and **gather you again from all the nations where he scattered you. Even if you have been banished to the most distant land under the heavens, from there the LORD your God will gather you and bring you back.** He will bring you to the land that belonged to your ancestors, and you will take possession of it. He will make you more prosperous and numerous than your ancestors. **The LORD your God will circumcise your hearts and the hearts of your descendants, so that you may love him with all your heart and with all your soul, and live.** The LORD your God will put all these curses on your enemies who hate and persecute you.*

Historical Fulfillment

After Israel entered the Promised Land, their obedience waxed and waned. When Israel disobeyed God, God sent prophets to continually warn them and exhort them to return to the Lord and His ways. If they ignored the prophets, they experienced the beginnings of the punishments listed above. When they repented, God restored them to His favor because of His rich mercy towards them. However, their obedience was usually short-lived and they resumed their rebellion. So, God persistently and consistently urged His people to repent so they would not experience the curses of the Law. However, their repeated, persistent, and unabashed rebellion against God ultimately forced God's hand in delivering the consequences He forewarned them about would result from their disobedience.

When God's people divided into northern and southern kingdoms, the northern kingdom rebelled egregiously against God, and therefore, within a few hundred years they experienced defeat by the Assyrians and were scattered into exile in the nations in 722 B.C. God divorced Himself from the northern kingdom but prophesied that they would ultimately (in the last days) return to Him in recognition that God's covenant remained with David's descendant as the promised Messiah. (See Jeremiah 3:8; Hosea 3:5.) The southern kingdom was inconsistent in their obedience depending on who was king. The good kings would attempt reform to bring the people back into submission to God and His Law, but after they were gone, the people returned to neglecting the commands of God in favor of the ways of the world. Therefore, in 586 B.C., the Kingdom of Judah was trampled and overthrown by the Babylonians and they were exiled to Babylon and scattered among the nations. In keeping with His promise to David, God never divorced the Kingdom of Judah even though their sins exceeded that of the northern kingdom. (See Jeremiah 3:8-14.) Before the southern kingdom was exiled, God told them in advance exactly how long their exile would be. Once the land had enjoyed its Sabbaths, God's people would seek Him in the midst of their exile and He would hear them and bring them back to their land. (See Jeremiah 29:10-14.)

Many of God's prophets prophesied that God's plan for His people, collectively referred to as Israel, included restoration to the land, rebuilding the city of Jerusalem and the Temple, and living in the blessings of God to be a great kingdom on the earth as His shining light to the nations. Exiles longed to return to the land and see these prophetic promises fulfilled. However, while in exile, Daniel had a series of visions which foretold much hardship on the way to restoration. **(Read Daniel 7, 8 & 11.)**

Daniel's visions and their interpretations explicitly outline a sequence of increasingly fierce world empires leading up to one kingdom which would take over the whole world. From this kingdom would emerge a leader who, with total world dominance, would oppress God's people until the Messiah came to overthrow his empire and establish God's eternal kingdom. Because of these visions, Daniel realized that God's people had not responded correctly to God's discipline through repentance and returning to obedience to God. God's restoration of His people and establishment of His Kingdom would not come as easily or swiftly as the exiles hoped because they had not returned to the Lord with their whole heart.

> *Daniel 9:13-14: Just as it is written in the Law of Moses, all this disaster has come on us, yet we have not sought the favor of the LORD our God* **by turning from our sins and giving attention to your truth**. *The LORD did not hesitate to bring the disaster on us, for the LORD our God is righteous in everything he does;* **yet we have not obeyed him**.

According to the word of God through Jeremiah, after seventy years of exile was completed, God would keep His promise and allow the exiles to return to the land and rebuilt the Temple. But God informed Daniel that this would happen in a time of great trouble. Then, the Messiah would come and would be cut off from His people and a wicked world ruler would desecrate and demolish the Temple and the city of Jerusalem. War would increase, Jerusalem would be trampled by Gentile empires, and desolations would continue until the end. But in the last days, the Messiah would come riding on the clouds to demolish all other kingdoms and hand His Kingdom over to His people in total fulfillment of His promises to Israel through the prophets.

> *Daniel 7:13-14: In my vision at night I looked, and there before me was one like a son of man,* **coming with the clouds of heaven**. *He approached the Ancient of Days and was led into his presence. He was given authority, glory and sovereign power; all nations and peoples of every language worshiped him. His dominion is an everlasting dominion that will not pass away, and* **his kingdom is one that will never be destroyed**.

The world empires proceeded in succession according to the visions God had given to Daniel. First, Babylon was overthrown by Persia. Then, according to God's promise, after seventy years of exile were completed, a decree was made that the Jewish people could return to the land of Judah and rebuild the Temple of God. About forty thousand exiles returned to the land at this time but many Jewish people remained in the lands of exile and to varying degrees, blended themselves in with the cultures of the nations of their exiles. Nevertheless, in the midst of great opposition, the Temple of God was rebuilt by the exiles under Zerubbabel with the encouragement of Prophets Haggai and Zechariah. During the rule of the Persian Empire, antisemitism spiked in the highest levels of the government and a decree was issued for the annihilation of all Jewish people in the entire empire. But God had positioned Esther as queen of Persia to advocate for her people before the king and a new decree was issued for their defense. (See the Book of Esther.) After this, more exiles returned with Ezra, the scribe, who sought to re-train God's people in the Scriptures and ordered a massive separation of intermarriage with pagan wives in order to purify God's people. Later, Nehemiah returned to Jerusalem and rebuilt the wall of the city, as its governor, while Ezra remained its religious leader. Several years after this, the Prophet Malachi pointed out that the people's worship was already hypocritical and weak and reminded them of Messiah coming to judge.

Next, according to Daniel's vision, Persia was conquered by Greece under Alexander the Great. He sought to "Hellenize" the world to a uniform Greek culture and language in order to create a one world order. But Alexander died young and his empire was divided among four generals. During this time, the Jewish people in the land of Judah found themselves bargaining for peace between the rulers in the south (Egypt/Ptolemy) and the rulers in the north (Assyria/Seleucid) and subjugating themselves under one or the other depending on the agreement reached. While the Pharisees were advocating strict adherence to priestly standards of purity for all residents of Judah and Jerusalem, the Sadducees, who controlled the High Priesthood and Sanhedrin, advocated compromise with the Hellenists to open Jerusalem up as a commercial center along the trade routes. This division among God's people led to unrest and rebellion which was ultimately crushed by Antiochus IV, of Assyria. This is when the story of Hanukkah happened. Antiochus cut off the daily sacrifice, desecrated the Temple by sacrificing pigs, and stood on the Temple Mount declaring himself to be God. Judah Maccabee led a revolt against him, took back the Temple, and rededicated it to God. From this, the Maccabees began the Hasmonean dynasty and the Jews essentially ruled themselves for about 100 years.

But soon the Romans arose as a world power. They were so strong and fierce that the Jewish people willingly subjugated themselves rather than try to fight these ferocious warriors. The Roman style of government allowed for many freedoms within the kingdoms conquered by Rome, as long as they still paid taxes and did not revolt against Rome's authority.

Then, Jesus was born, proclaimed God's Kingdom, and was rejected and cut off from God's people who crucified Him on a cross. But God raised Him from the dead and He ascended into heaven on the clouds, promising to return riding on the clouds to fulfill the remaining prophecies of the Messiah and establish His Kingdom forever.

However, Jesus had made it clear during His ministry that for their rejection of Him, Jerusalem, the Jewish people, and the Temple would experience another destruction and scattering into exile in the nations. Jerusalem would continue to be trampled by Gentiles until the time of the Gentiles was complete and the Jewish people would not see Him coming on the clouds until they called out blessing His name. (See Luke 21:24-27; Matthew 23:37-39.) Therefore, in 70 A.D., the Romans overthrew Jerusalem and destroyed the Temple. In the years that followed, the Jewish people were again forced into exile in the nations and the promised land became desolate. This time, there was no prophetic indication of how long this exile would last or how long the land would remain desolate to keep its Sabbaths.

Over the next eighteen hundred years, Jerusalem would be owned and trampled on by empire after empire of Gentiles while the Jewish people remained in exile in the nations. While in exile, the Jewish people repeatedly experienced cycles of blessings and curses. They would flee from one place due to persecution or expulsion to start again in a new place with nothing. Then, they would re-devote themselves to God, work hard, experience God's blessings, and be exalted to top places in government, commerce, banking, philosophy, and other arenas. As new generations became more entitled to the blessings without reverence for the source of them, they blended with the pagans of the nations and their practices through intermarriage and unfaithfulness to God's Law. Soon, the punishments of the curse of the Law would begin to come upon them including escalating persecution and ultimately the sword and expulsion from wherever they lived. They would flee to a new place and the cycle would repeat itself.

The most historic example of this was the holocaust of World War II when Jews were expelled from their homes and ravaged mercilessly by Gentile nations. In fulfillment of God's word, it has become the most visceral object of horror that the world has ever known. (See Deuteronomy 28:37.) Please note, the curse is no excuse for persecution, antisemitism, or hateful behavior towards the Jewish people. It simply explains God's sovereignty over this grotesque mistreatment and destruction of His people.

But after these events, God did what only God could do and made a way for the Jewish people to return to the very land that He had promised to their ancestors. What a miracle! In 1948, the nation of Israel was born in a day. Jewish people who had survived the horrors of war flocked to their homeland.

Continued Fulfillment

The return of the Jewish people to the land God promised to them through their ancestors is called making Aliyah (ah-lee-ah.) There are almost seventy specific promises in Scripture pertaining to the return of God's people to the land promised to their ancestors. God knows where each and every single Jewish person is in the world and not one of them will be left behind. (See Ezekiel 39:27-28.) God does all of this for His own namesake in the sight of the nations and to assert His absolute sovereignty over all things in the sight of His adversaries. (See Deuteronomy 32:26-27, 36-43.)

The return of God's people to the Land of Israel after two thousand years of exile is an even greater miracle than parting the waters of the Red Sea to grant them escape from Egypt. It is such an awesome wonder that almost no one in Church history considered that God would LITERALLY fulfill these passages of Scripture and this is what led to some very incorrect theological positions about God's heart and plans for the Jewish people. However, God will fulfill His plan of gathering all of the Jews out of the nations by sending His agents to gather them.

> *Jeremiah 16:14-16 - "However, the days are coming," declares the LORD, "when it will no longer be said, 'As surely as the LORD lives, who brought the Israelites up out of Egypt,' but **it will be said, 'As surely as the LORD lives, who brought the Israelites up out of the land of the north and out of all the countries where he had banished them.'** For I will restore them to the land I gave their ancestors. But now I will **send for many fishermen**," declares the LORD, "and they will catch them. After that I will **send for many hunters, and they will hunt them down** on every mountain and hill and from the crevices of the rocks."*

God will send fishers and hunters to gather the Jewish people from all the nations under heaven. Fishers use a net which gently drags the fish to the shore, preserving the life of the fish until they arrive safely in the harbor. Hunters however, hunt with intent to kill. When the time for the hunters comes upon the world, there will be another horrifying persecution of the Jewish people on a global scale. At that time, Jews will be evicted from every nation in which they live in a time of great wrath. Not all of them will enter the land of Israel but God will preserve a remnant and restore them to the land.

> *Ezekiel 20:33-38, 44: "As surely as I live," declares the Sovereign LORD, "I will reign over you with a mighty hand and an outstretched arm and with outpoured wrath. **I will bring you from the nations and gather you from the countries where you have been scattered--with a mighty hand and an outstretched arm and with outpoured wrath. I will bring you into the wilderness of the nations and there, face to face, I will execute judgment upon you.** As I judged your ancestors in the wilderness of the land of Egypt, so I will judge you," declares the Sovereign LORD. "**I will take note of you as you pass under my rod, and I will bring you into the bond of the covenant. I will purge you of those who revolt and rebel against me. Although I will bring them out of the land where they are living, yet they will not enter the land of Israel.** Then you will know that I am the LORD."... You will know that I am the LORD, when **I deal with you for my name's sake** and not according to your evil ways and your corrupt practices, you people of Israel, declares the Sovereign LORD.'"*

Even after the people have been restored to the land of Israel, there will be a time of great trouble, wars and desolations until the end when Jesus returns on the clouds to establish His Kingdom. This time has become known as the time of Jacob's Trouble and I believe it is the same type of thing Daniel saw in his visions of the times preceding the arrival of the Messiah. **(Read Jeremiah 30.)**

The Days to Come

The Jewish people will experience the full discipline of God and this will continue to suffer at the hands of Gentile oppressors in their land. But ultimately, God will vindicate His people and destroy all the nations under heaven which have stood against them – ALL the nations of the earth. This day will not come until the strength of God's people has been broken so that God can be completely glorified by the miracles and wonders He will work to save and deliver His people.

> *Deuteronomy 32:36-43:* **The LORD will vindicate his people** *and relent concerning his servants* **when he sees their strength is gone** *and no one is left, slave or free. He will say: "Now where are their gods, the rock they took refuge in, the gods who ate the fat of their sacrifices and drank the wine of their drink offerings? Let them rise up to help you! Let them give you shelter! See now that I myself am he! There is no god besides me. I put to death and I bring to life, I have wounded and I will heal, and no one can deliver out of my hand. I lift my hand to heaven and solemnly swear: As surely as I live forever, when I sharpen my flashing sword and my hand grasps it in judgment,* **I will take vengeance on my adversaries and repay those who hate me.** *I will make my arrows drunk with blood, while my sword devours flesh: the blood of the slain and the captives,* **the heads of the enemy leaders.** *Rejoice, you nations, with his people, for he will avenge the blood of his servants; he will* **take vengeance on his enemies and make atonement for his land and people.**

> *Daniel 12:6-9:* *One of them said to the man clothed in linen, who was above the waters of the river, "How long will it be before these astonishing things are fulfilled?" The man clothed in linen, who was above the waters of the river, lifted his right hand and his left hand toward heaven, and I heard him swear by him who lives forever, saying, "It will be for a time, times and half a time.* **When the power of the holy people has been finally broken, all these things will be completed.”** *I heard, but I did not understand. So I asked, "My lord, what will the outcome of all this be?" He replied, "Go your way, Daniel, because the words are rolled up and* **sealed until the time of the end.**

In that day, God will circumcise the hearts of the Jewish people to come fully into the New Covenant through faith in Jesus as their Messiah. (See Ezekiel 39:22.) God will gather all the nations of the world and their armies to surround Jerusalem and fight against God, His city, and His people. But God will vindicate His people and turn Jerusalem into a cup of His wrath upon His adversaries. (See Joel 3:1-2; Zechariah 12:2-9.) ALL nations will fight against Jerusalem and God's people. Then, Jesus will come riding on the clouds and set His feet on the Mount of Olives. (See Zechariah 14:2-4.)

Jesus came the first time in a literal body to a literal place. He literally lived, He literally fulfilled the prophecies of the prophets. He literally died and was cut off. He was literally raised from death and literally ascended to heaven. He literally established a New Covenant with Israel, which is entered into by faith. This covenant literally extends the mercy and grace of God to Gentiles who put their faith in Him. He will literally return just as the prophets have foretold and judge all the nations of the earth. In that day, there will be one nation remaining – a holy nation and royal priesthood, purified by the blood of Jesus through faith in Him. God will literally establish a new earth and we will literally dwell with God forever. Hallelujah!

INGRAFTED IN MESSIAH
Post Card Handout

Jew and Gentile Ingrafted by Faith into Messiah
A visual demonstration of Romans 11

1.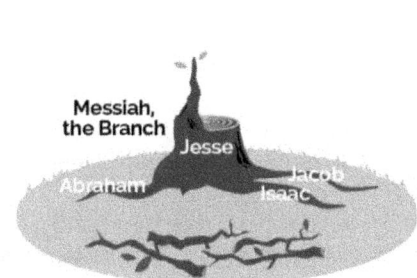

A. Natural branches broken off because of unbelief. (Rom 11:20)
B. A shoot comes up from the stump of Jesse, a Branch bearing fruit from his roots. (Isaiah 11:1)

2.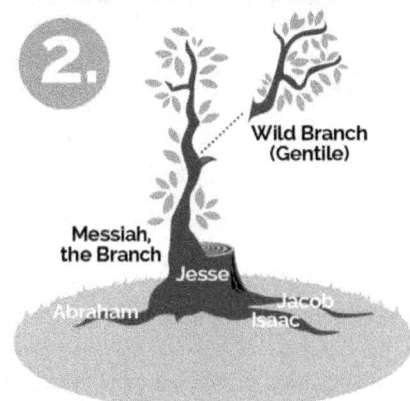

C. Gentiles (wild branches) grafted in by faith in Messiah. (Rom 11:17, 20)
D. Jewish hearts partially hardened until the fullness of Gentiles comes in. (Rom 11:25)

3.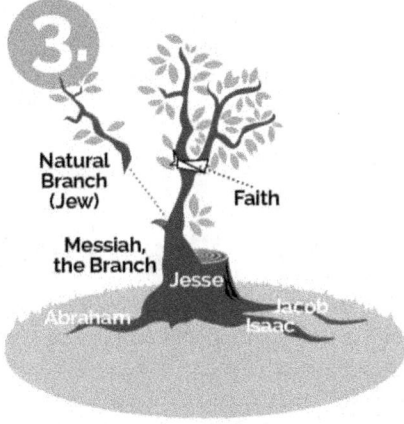

E. Jews (natural branches) grafted back in by faith in Messiah. (Rom 11:24)
F. Jew and Gentile are justified by faith. (Rom 3:22-30; Gal 5:6)

4.

G. All who call upon the name of the Lord will be saved. (Rom 10:11-13; Joel 2:32)
H. Great riches in the inclusion of both Jew and Gentile in Messiah. (Rom 11:12; Col 3:11)

Further Study: Romans 9-11, Ephesians 2, Isaiah 11 and 49, Jeremiah 23 and 33, Galatians 3, Romans 4, Zechariah 3 & 6

ALL RIGHTS RESERVED © 2016 Wendy Bowen - www.firsttothejew.com

PRAYER GUIDE FOR ISRAEL & THE JEWISH PEOPLE

ISRAEL & JERUSALEM

- Give no rest to the Lord until He establishes the peace of Jerusalem. (Isa 62:6-7; Psalm 121, Psalm 122)
- Israel to be a light to the nations, revealing God's holiness and power to the nations. (Isa 49:6; Zech 12:1-9)
- The Lord to take delight in His people and for them to delight in Him. (Zeph 3:14-17; Isa 62:1-5; Psalm 149)
- The people of Israel to know that God's plans for them are for good, to give them a hope and future. (Jer 29:11)

SALVATION OF THE JEWISH PEOPLE

- The Jewish people to seek the truth in God with all their heart and find Yeshua. (Deut 4:29-31; Jer 29:12-13, 33:3)
- The fullness of Gentiles to come in so that Jewish hearts may soften and all Israel may be saved. (Rom 11:25-26)
- Outpouring of Holy Spirit leading Jewish people to genuine repentance. (Zech 12:10; Daniel 9:4-19; Ezek 36:31)
- The Lord to circumcise the hearts of the Jewish people into the New Covenant. (Deut 30:6; Rom 2:29; Jer 31:31-34)
- The Lord to remove the veil and give the Jewish people a new heart and a new spirit. (2Cor 3:16; Ezek 36:26)
- Jewish people grafted into Messiah through faith, redeemed from the curse of the Law. (Rom 11:24, Gal 3:13)

THE WITNESS OF THE CHURCH TO THE JEWISH PEOPLE

- Be thankful and inclusive towards the Jewish people rather than conceited. (Rom 11:18-20; Gal 3:28; Eph 2:14-15)
- Have right revelation and correct doctrine about Israel and the Church. (Rom 11:1; Rom 11:28; Gen 12:1-3)
- Prioritize witnessing to the Jewish people in a Jewish context of Scripture and Messiah. (Rom 11:1-6; 1Cor 1:22-24)
- Support Messianic ministries and outreaches to the Jewish people. (Rom 1:16; Rom 10:14-17; Rom 15:27)
- Jewish believers to be unified, filled with love, and protected as a living witness of Yeshua. (John 17:11,23)
- Provoke the Jewish people to jealousy through righteousness, boldness, signs & wonders. (Rom 11:11; Acts 4:29-30)
- Give no unnecessary offense to the Jewish people in lifestyle or witnessing. (1Cor 10:32-33; Acts 15:21)

ALIYAH – THE RETURN OF THE JEWISH PEOPLE TO ISRAEL

- The Jewish people to respond to the call to return to the Land of their ancestors in these last days. (Isa 11:10-16)
- The Lord to be proved holy in the sight of the nations by gathering the Jewish people out of every nation to which they have been scattered, not leaving any behind. (Jer 23:7-8; Ezek 39:27-28; Ezek 20:41; Ezek 36:36; Ezek 28:25)
- The Jewish people to return voluntarily before the Lord sends His fishers and hunters to gather them. (Jer 16:16)
- The Jewish people in the land to prosper so that they come to know Yeshua as Messiah. (Duet 30:1-9; Ezek 36:30)

END-TIMES EVENTS DISCERNMENT & FULFILLMENT

- Discern the times, urgency for salvation, and God's ultimate purpose of redemption. (Luke 12:54-59; Jer 30:1-24)
- Israel to receive the Lord's supernatural protection as a witness to the nations. (Zech 12:2-9; Psalm 91)
- The Lord to judge nations setting themselves against Jerusalem. (Joel 3:1-4; Micah 4:11-13; Deut 32:36; Zech 14:1-4)
- The Lord to establish His Kingdom and set His glory upon Israel. (Dan 7:13-27; Ezek 39:21-22; Joel 3:17)

A Ministry of:

www.firsttothejew.com

ALL RIGHTS RESERVED © 2020 Wendy Bowen

PERFECTION COURSE – UNIT 2.4 READING

God's Sovereignty Over All Nations

God's purpose in ALL things is that HIS NAME is exalted on the earth – as it should rightfully be.

What do the heroes of the Hebrews 11 Hall of Faith have in common? They were all looking for a city and a Kingdom built by God which was not of this world. Their attention was not on the nations of this world or the political powers of this world because they knew that the nations of this world are a drop in the bucket to God. (See Isaiah 40:15, 17.) Their focus was exclusively on God and His Kingdom as they longed to see it manifest on the earth. We would be wise to follow their example instead of subscribing to a watered-down, political "gospel" that has no basis in the reality of the life of Jesus and what is coming in the days ahead before He establishes His Kingdom on earth.

We must narrow our focus on the Kingdom of God and widen our perspective of how God actually rules in the nations of the world. In fact, if we do not understand and accept God's absolute sovereignty over the nations of the earth and their authorities, we will be distracted from our true worship of God by turning our hope to world rulers. Ultimately, this will cause us to be ensnared into worshipping the beast in the end times – the adversary of God, who is the antichrist. We will cover the end-times piece of this more in Unit Six of this course but for this segment, we are going to focus on how God has demonstrated His authority over all international events from the beginning of time. He is God. There is none other.

God remains absolutely sovereign over all the nations of the earth and appoints ALL authorities on the earth. From the authority of a husband or father in a household to the authority of a president or emperor. No matter how they think they have attained it, it is God who appointed them to their position. This is true whether they know Him, believe Him, or even acknowledge His existence. (See Daniel 2:20-22, 4:17; Isaiah 45:1-6; Proverbs 21:1.) God appoints authorities whom we consider to be good/righteous and authorities whom we consider to be bad/evil. God uses them as His servants to carry out His justice on the earth, good or bad, however He sees fit and whether they know that God is using them or not. God speaks to them through dreams and other forms of communication. Examples include: Pharaoh in Abraham's day and Joseph's day, Pharaoh Necho in Josiah's day even though Josiah did not believe that God would speak to a foreign king, Nebuchadnezzar's dreams, visions, and divination which was ultimately controlled by God, Ahasuerus' sleepless night, Pilate's wife's dream, etc. God sometimes sends His own prophets to speak to or anoint foreign kings who do not know Him. Examples include: Jonah to Nineveh and Elisha anointing the king of Assyria. God also uses His prophets to declare what will happen in the nations as evidence that He is the One who is actually in charge. Whatever we may think of the authorities over nations, all of them are appointed by God. Through them, God sovereignly asserts His authority over all the earth. **(Read Romans 13:1-7.)**

God's view of world justice in the nations is completely different than the human perspective. His patience with nations spans hundreds if not thousands of years. He endures long and sends witnesses to give warnings, He responds to their repentance with mercy, He waits until justice is required and then, He sends it swiftly. (See Jeremiah 18:7-10.) As an example, consider that God sent the Prophet Jonah to warn Nineveh (a Gentile city) of impending disaster if they did not repent. The king of Nineveh ordered a fast to humble themselves before the God of Heaven. God saw this and relented of the disaster that He planned, much to Jonah's dismay. However, within one hundred years, the people of Nineveh had returned to their sins again warranted judgment. At that time, God warned them through the Prophet

Nahum but they did not repent. So, God destroyed the city of Nineveh to a degree that its ruins were not identified for thousands of years. (See the books of Jonah and Nahum.)

The truth is that the whole world, every nation, and all of mankind already stands condemned. (See John 3:18-21.) It is only because of God's great mercy that He allows us to continue to live and set up nations and governments here on earth. But even in this, God rules over all. God appointed the times of the rise and fall of nations and empires before nations were even started. (See Acts 17:26-31.)

God's desire is to be sought and found by people in all nations. (Matthew 7:7; John 6:44-45.) God has made a way for everyone from any nation, tribe, or tongue to be saved. God knows that all of world history will culminate in the Day of the Lord when He gathers together all the nations for judgment. It is not God's desire that anyone should perish on that day. But when that day comes, anyone who has not put their trust in Jesus Christ will be condemned for eternity.

Examples of God's Judgment: Noah, Babel, Sodom & Gomorrah (Genesis 6-19)

The Book of Genesis gives us three vivid examples of God's judgment on the wickedness of mankind. Each of these prophetically foreshadow the great day of God's judgment that is still yet to come.

In the days of Noah, ten generations of man had passed since Adam. By this time, the hard labor of sweat and toil in the cursed land of thorns and thistles had driven mankind to wickedness in their hearts and violence against one another. They had conjugated with spiritual beings to create a species of giants on the earth. Mankind was absolutely NOT reflecting the likeness of God and so, God regretted that He had made mankind. So, He called upon Noah to build an Ark to spare a remnant of mankind and creation from the judgment of flood He was about to send. Noah built the Ark and God sent the flood. All of mankind and everything with the breath of life in it was destroyed from the face of the earth. Only eight people were in the Ark plus one male and one female of each creature. God promised He will never judge the earth again by water. Noah's sons had children and eventually, their descendants grew into nations. All people spoke the same language.

Soon, Nimrod arose as a mighty hunter who built cities. He gathered all nations together in unity to build a tower up to the heavens to make a name for themselves. They may also have been attempting to avoid any future flood by building a tower high enough to escape – this would be their stronghold and their fortress. God saw this and changed all languages so that they could no longer communicate easily or join together for more tower building. At that time, God scattered humanity all over the earth. Everyone had to start again with nothing in a new territory that they had not known before.

In every culture in the world today, varying versions of these two stories are recorded and have been accepted as historical and factual events which took place in the dawnings of humanity.

In the days of Abraham, the cities of Sodom and Gomorrah had grown so wicked with abominations that the outcry of their victims rose up to God's ears in heaven. He could no longer tolerate the evil in these cities. So, He sent angelic messengers to confirm just how evil they were and the men of Sodom wanted to rape and sodomize God's messengers. Therefore, God rained fire and sulfur down from heaven to demolish the cities from the face of the earth. This time, only four people were rescued, minus one who looked back.

God allows wickedness, perversion, violence, and evil to exist in the world. God knows it is happening and has kept record of it all. Every lie ever told, every selfish sin ever committed, every misstep, every hateful thought, every act of meanness and cruelty, every perverted and unclean trespass, and all other manner of iniquity that anyone ever does is all known by God. As Creator of the world and mankind, it is God's sovereign right at any time to execute vengeance through any kind of judgment He sees fit, in order to vindicate the innocent, punish the guilty, and reestablish order on the earth.

If it were not for Jesus, we all rightfully deserve these judgments. This said, these judgments are only a preview of what is yet to come.

God's Right and Reason for Judging

God created heaven and earth and mankind. Anyone who says otherwise is a liar and a blasphemer. In most societies, anyone who denied the authority of their earthly king would be called a traitor and would be instantly put to death. How much greater is God than any earthly king? God in His great love gave us free will to acknowledge Him or not and to serve Him or not. In His great mercy, He does not pour out wrath swiftly but turns us over to our own depravity and the consequences of our ungodly decisions. All of creation testifies to the glory of God but mankind continues in rebellion against God and denial that He even exists. **(Read Romans 1:18-32.)** Is it not right for God to judge this however He sees fit?

But God does not always judge by water or fire or scattering. In fact, God precisely said the reason why He was expelling the seven nations dwelling in the land. Sin. Even though none of these nations were in covenant with God, their conduct was beyond reprobate in perversity and godlessness, particularly their sexual sin and sinful spiritual practices with their pagan gods. **(Read Leviticus 18.)** When it reached a limit which warranted God's judgment upon them, judgment came in the form of war, being overthrown by another people, and expulsion from their land. (See Leviticus 18:24-28; Deuteronomy 18:9-12.)

Truthfully, God could have destroyed the earth by fire many thousands of years ago because the wickedness, violence, and rebellion against Him which quickly resumed after the floodwaters receded in Noah's day. God could have done it in the days of Babel, but He didn't. Instead, He did something else. God called Abraham.

A People for the Sake of His Name

When God entered into covenant with Abraham and told him what his descendants would experience in the future, He revealed something about His sovereign hand over the nations of the world. At that time, the Amorites were the predominant people group living in the land that God had promised to give to Abraham's descendants. (See Genesis 15:13-16.)

Abraham believed God and lived in a land not his own for the majority of his life, being a witness for the one true God and telling people that his descendants would inherit the land of the Amorites. While in Egypt, Abraham's great-grandson, Joseph, became the second-most powerful man in the world and the God of Israel became known among the nations. A couple of generations later, they were forced into slavery and were mistreated for the next four hundred years.

God knew about the mistreatment and did not prevent it. What do you think of a God like that? It is the same God who multiplied His people over the course of four generations in the midst of this mistreatment in order to fulfill what He had spoken to Abraham. (See Deuteronomy 10:22.)

Moreover, God did not see fit to punish the wickedness of the Amorites while Abraham was still alive. Their sin had not yet come to the full measure of deserving to be expelled from their land. However, after four hundred years, God's time of mercy would be expired and their behavior would warrant God's judgment. This time, instead of sending fire and sulfur on the nation, God sent another nation to overthrow them, destroy them, and kick them out of their land.

Consider God's mercy for the Amorites even while His own people were mistreated. What do you think of a God like that? It is the same God who delivered His people by great displays of His power and through the midst of plagues and disasters in the land where they were slaves.

When the time came for God to deliver His people from Egyptian slavery, He called upon Moses to deliver the warnings to Pharaoh of what would happen if Pharaoh did not let God's people go. But God was also sovereign over Pharaoh's heart and hardened it so that Pharaoh would not let them go. This was

God's plan all along so that His name would be exalted on the earth. (See Exodus 9:16.)

God made a name for Himself by rescuing the smallest nation on the earth from slavery in the most powerful nation in the world. The whole world heard about the plagues of blood, frogs, lice, flies, pestilence, boils, hail, locusts, darkness, and death of firstborn sons that God released upon Egypt and how Pharaoh and his army had drowned in the midst of the sea after God's people walked through it without hindrance. It became known all over the world that the God of Heaven had chosen a people for Himself. Even forty years later, the nations feared the God of Israel because of these events. (See Joshua 2:10.) In fact, the story is still known all over the world today.

In Egypt, the Israelites did not deserve to be delivered. Even though they remembered God's promise to Abraham, they neglected their worship of God and turned to the idols of the land of Egypt during their time of slavery. But for the sake of His name in the sight of the nations, God delivered them. In the wilderness they often rebelled against God and He could have rightfully destroyed them. But for the sake of His name in the sight of the nations, God spared them. Their behavior did not warrant them inheriting the Promised Land. But God's promise was already known among the nations and therefore, for the sake of His name, God gave it to them and worked wonders on their behalf. **(Read Ezekiel 20:1-44.)**

God's interactions with Israel are always for the sake of His own name. If His people are blessed, it is so that all the nations of the world can know His goodness. If His people are bad, God must execute justice upon them to maintain His holy name in the sight of the nations. Even today, and even if they mess everything up beyond recognition of the likeness of God, God will not destroy them completely – for the sake of His name in the sight of the nations. (See Psalm 67; Ezekiel 36:22-23.)

Throughout the book of Judges, Kings, Chronicles, and the Prophets God's sovereign execution of justice for or against His people is clearly laid out. When the people were faithful to God, the fear of God fell on their enemies so that they would not attack. Those who did attack were sorely embarrassed. When God's people were unfaithful to Him, God orchestrated, appointed, and ordained enemies to rise up against them to attack them and oppress them.

When King Solomon's heart turned to other gods because of his pagan wives, God promised ten of Israel's tribes to Solomon's servant, Jeroboam. After Solomon's death, the kingdoms of God's people were divided in what looked like civil war, rebellion, and anarchy but was actually ordained by God.

Eventually, God appointed the Assyrians to conquer the northern kingdom of Israel and vomit them out of their land and into exile. The southern kingdom of Judah saw this act of judgement and knew by God's prophets that it was the will of God. However, this did not lead them to repent out of reverent fear of God and instead, they continued in their sin. So, God appointed the Babylonians to conquer them and vomit them out of their land and into exile. It was God who appointed the Gentile rulers and nations to conquer His own people. (See 2 Kings 17:6-8; Habakkuk 1:6; Jeremiah 21:2-7.)

God's prophet Habakkuk had a difficult time understanding how God could use the unrighteous, brutal, and godless Gentile nation like Babylon to judge God's own chosen people. But God, in His great mercy and for His own namesake, did not annihilate His people even though they behaved worse than the pagan nations in their vile practices and false spirituality against His commands. (See Ezekiel 5:6-7.) Instead, when His people demonstrated that they wanted to be like the nations, He turned them over to their own evil desire and sent them into exile in the nations.

They deserved to be punished like Sodom and Gomorrah but God left a remnant of survivors for the sake of His name in the sight of all the nations. (See Isaiah 1:9.) He is known as their God and He is a God who cannot and does not lie. All His words to His people will be fulfilled – for the sake of His name in the sight of all the nations.

God also assured His people through His prophets (particularly Jeremiah, Isaiah, and Habakkuk) that He would ultimately avenge His people by punishing those whom He had used to punish them. The Babylonians destroyed Assyria because Assyria thought they had power to overthrow and destroy God's people as if they were stronger than God. (See Isaiah 10:5-19.) Babylon was overthrown by the Persians (or Medes) because the Babylonians thought in their hearts that they had ascended to the power of God. (See Jeremiah 50-51; Isaiah 14:1-27.) Moreover, other neighboring nations who looked on and mocked while Judah and Israel were humiliated by their oppressors would also suffer consequences from God. Edom, Moab, Ammon, and the Philistines no longer exist. (See Ezekiel 25 and the Book of Obadiah.)

Since God called a people for His name's sake, He will show Himself mighty on their behalf, even if it takes hundreds or thousands of years before His justice comes. The first example of this is when the Amalekites attacked the newly born nation of Israel when they first came out of Egypt. God promised that He would judge and destroy the Amalekites because of this. But it was not until almost four hundred years later, when Saul was king of Israel that God ordered that the Amalekites be destroyed. (See Exodus 17:14; Deuteronomy 25:17; 1 Samuel 15.) Unfortunately, Saul did not completely destroy the Amalekites, and a descendant of their king Agag became the enemy of the Jews in the days of Esther. (See Esther 3:1.) But that's another story.

God's Judgment on and through Nations

As we have already seen, God uses nations to judge other nations to execute justice according to His righteousness and mercy. From the world's viewpoint, it may appear that one nation has a stronger army or better strategy than the one they conquer. But God can work through many or few and no one can supersede His sovereignty by their own might.

To recap, God used Egypt to suppress His people while they multiplied and then judged Egypt with mighty plagues of judgment. God overthrew seven nations in the land He had promised to Abraham through supernaturally empowered warfare on behalf of His people in judgment of their sins against Him. God split His own kingdom due to their compromise and false worship. God used the Assyrian Empire to judge and scatter ten tribes of His people. God used the Babylonian Empire to judge the Assyrians for doing so with such hubris. God also used Babylon to judge and scatter Judah and Jerusalem.

At that time, God also used the Babylonians to conquer and judge many nations and bring them into subjection under one world empire. Even though Nebuchadnezzar thought he had conquered the world by his own power, it was God who turned the whole world over to Nebuchadnezzar's authority and even referred to Nebuchadnezzar as His servant. (See Jeremiah 27:3-8; Daniel 2:37-38, 5:18-19.) Babylon became the cup of God's wrath upon the nations of the world in that day and God poured out His vengeance upon the nations through the dominant rule of Nebuchadnezzar. **(Read Jeremiah 25, 50-51.)** In fact, for doing such a good job in conquering so many nations, God gave Nebuchadnezzar the land of Egypt as a bonus. (See Ezekiel 29:18-20.)

Babylon became the center of global trade and the wealthiest empire in the entire world. Jewish exiles in the land of Babylon must have been awed by Babylon's opulence and indulgence, being either repulsed or tempted by it in their hearts. When Nebuchadnezzar became proud and exalted himself as a god, God humbled him. When Nebuchadnezzar acknowledged God's rule, he issued a proclamation throughout the world that the God of Israel reigns on high. (See Daniel 2-4.) In spite of His people's exile from their land, God's name was honored in the sight of the nations. Nebuchadnezzar's grandson, Belshazzar, had seen his grandfather experience God's humbling but did not choose to humble himself. Therefore, while Belshazzar was holding a feast, God put an end to Babylon. (See Daniel 5.) In one day – in one hour – the Babylonian Empire fell. It became like Sodom and Gomorrah. (See Jeremiah 50:40.)

God used the Persian Empire to judge Babylon and to set His people free from exile so that His Temple could be rebuilt in Jerusalem. God warned His people to get out of Babylon and leave behind their luxuries and lawless lifestyle to return to Him and His ways and His land. Later in the Persian Empire, the fear of God fell on God's people when their annihilation was decreed. But God again made a name for Himself through His people by their vindication on the day of Purim. After that, His people became more serious about separating themselves from the world and purifying themselves for God.

After Persia, Alexander the Great heard the vision of Nebuchadnezzar for one world order and took it on as his own personal mission. As quick as a leopard with wings, Alexander conquered the world and began to "Hellenize" every society with Greek culture and language. But Alexander died young and his empire was divided among four of his generals.

During this time, Greek replaced Aramaic as the primary international language of the day. Jewish exiles who remained in the nations learned Greek rather than Hebrew or Aramaic and for the most part, lost their ability to read or understand the Scriptures for themselves. A committee was assembled to translate the Scriptures into Greek. The translation is known as the Septuagint. The common, literate, Jewish person would now be able to read the Scriptures that typically only priests, scribes, and scholars could access.

Eventually, God raised up Rome to be the ruling force in the world. God used Rome to bring judgment on His people for their faithlessness and rejection of Jesus as their Messiah. The Temple was destroyed, the land was made desolate and the people were exiled. Those among the Jewish people who thought they could rebel against Rome were utterly crushed. The last remaining hold-outs on the mountain of Masada committed group suicide rather than be subject to Roman punishment. It is said that the Christian believers who heeded the words of Jesus to escape from the city when they saw the signs of the end had escaped the city and their lives were spared – even though the world did not end at that time.

These events were prophesied in advance by God's prophets, particularly Daniel, who saw the empires rise and fall according to God's plan. This gives us both the assurance that God is truly sovereign over the events in the nations and also gives us a basis of understanding God's ways of dealing with the nations whether they know Him or not. The point is that it is God who determines who rises and who falls and for what purpose according to His much larger, longer, and more all-encompassing view of the people involved and the measure of justice that is required at any given time.

Babylon – the Harlot of the End Times

The ancient city of Babel was built by Nimrod, who assembled all the peoples of the world together to build the tower of Babel. This tower has always been a symbol of mankind's assertion of independence from God, rebellion against Him, and spiritual attempts to access heaven's power through their own means in order to subvert and deny God's authority. In the ancient Akkadian language, the site of the tower of Babel was called the Gate of God. In essence, their desire was to access God and the heavenly realm in order to make a name for themselves on the earth. In a moment's time, it was shut down.

The world empire of Babylon and its king, Nebuchadnezzar, was raised up by God as an agent of His wrath. God used Babylon to conquer many nations and join them together as one people under one man who thought he was a god. In addition to its ferocious and conquering strength, Babylon was known for its luxury, opulence, and indulgent lifestyle. Their gods were revered as more powerful than the other nation's gods. Nebuchadnezzar even set up a statue of himself and demanded to be worshipped as a god. Babylon's world-dominating empire was thought of as so strong and mighty that it could never fall. But it fell in one day – in one hour.

These realities of Babylon's history prefigure a reality that is yet to come – a spiritual Babylon. Historical Babylon has become the Biblical symbol of mankind's self-indulgent, defiant rebellion against God. The prophet Daniel was told that his visions of Babylon's fall were for the time of the end. **(Read Daniel 8 & 11.)** As such, there is still a global one world order which has been prophesied by God and one world ruler who will deceive the nations and rule all peoples. The one world order yet to come is a new type of Babylon. It will be raised up by God to intoxicate the nations with luxury and indulgence and gather the world together as one. (See Revelation 17:4-6.) The aim of this ruler is to be worshipped by the whole world. He will use flattery and deception to corrupt, oppress, and destroy God's people, if it is possible. As such, and as God's New Covenant people, we have been warned to not fall prey to the numbing effects of Babylon's complacency, comfort, and luxury. We must also be ready to suffer persecution, captivity, or death for refusing to worship the antichrist and remaining loyal to Jesus. (See Revelation 13:7-10.)

But in a day – in an hour – this one world Babylon will come to an abrupt end. **(Read Revelation 18.)** All the nations and peoples of the world who have been gathered together will be shocked and appalled at Babylon's downfall.

The End: The Days of Noah, Egypt, and Sodom & Gomorrah

Jesus said that the day of judgment to come will be like the days of Noah. People will be doing normal things and carrying on with life up until the very moment that Jesus returns.

The Book of Revelation vividly describes the times of the end of the world. Like the series of plagues poured out on the land of Egypt before Israel was delivered as a nation, a succession of increasing disasters will cover the earth. In those days of great tribulation as the seals of the scroll are broken and the trumpets are blown, God will make a distinction between those who are His and those who are not, just as He did for His people when plagues were poured out on Egypt. In the end, God will deliver those who have remained faithful to Jesus and Jesus will return in triumph over the world to save us.

When the time for God's wrath has come, God will pour out desolations on the earth like never before. God will unleash a global assault like the destruction of Sodom and Gomorrah. On that day, nothing will escape the fiery destruction of the wrath of God.

God's Will Until That Day

When Jesus came the first time, He proclaimed the message, "repent for the Kingdom of Heaven is at hand!" He spoke almost exclusively about the Kingdom of God, how it would and would not come, and who would and would not be included in it. He warned that only those who both heard His message and put it into practice would be blessed. His priorities were not set on the things of this world but in establishing the Kingdom of God in people's hearts so that we could be saved from the wrath of God. He was warning them that the Kingdom of God will ultimately overthrow ALL kingdoms of this world.

Jesus never once scheduled an appointment to meet with Caesar or any of the world's rulers to discuss governing the world. He sought only to please God and did not entangle Himself in civilian affairs. (See 2 Timothy 2:4.) At that time, Caesar was living an absolutely licentious lifestyle on a remote island but Jesus never spoke of it. Jesus never spoke of Caesar at all except for one time when He was asked about taxes. At that time, He told people to submit to the governing authorities by paying their taxes. He knew that Caesar's authority over the world was given to him by God. When Jesus stood before Herod, He was on trial and did not say a word to defend Himself. When Jesus stood before Pilate and Pilate asserted His right to put Jesus to death, Jesus made it clear that Pilate had no authority except that which God had given to him. Jesus allowed the rulers of this world to reject, mock, ridicule, abuse, torture, and ultimately kill Him. His Kingdom is NOT of this world.

Jesus' first followers also gave us an example to follow. They recognized that all the nations were raging against God's anointed one and against them. As they eagerly awaited Christ's return in glory, they realized that the fulfillment of the prophetic scriptures pertaining to the oppression of God's people by world powers was imminently upon them. They were thrown in prison and persecuted for following Jesus. Their prayer had nothing to do with politics, governments, or world leaders. The focus of their prayers was entirely on boldness to proclaim the day of wrath to come and the salvation made available by God through faith in Jesus Christ. (See Acts 4:24-31.)

In the midst of global tumult and great misunderstanding about Christianity in its earliest days, Christians were ruthlessly persecuted. Nevertheless, the apostles adamantly admonished believers to submit to the governing authorities, even at the expense of their lives. (See Romans 13; 1 Peter 2; Revelation 2:10, 12:11.) When false teachers encouraged believers to pray against the rulers and governments of this world, Paul addressed their ignorance of the Scriptures and the mercy of God. In the same way that the prophet Jeremiah had told exiles in Babylon to pray for the peace of Babylon, Paul instructed that we are to pray FOR the rulers of this world so that we may live peaceable lives in this world. (See Jeremiah 29:4-7; 1 Timothy 2:1-6.) This does NOT mean that our hope shifts away from God to the rulers of this nation or that our prayer lives are to become consumed with praying for the nations. Instead, we must recognize that we are strangers and exiles here in this world who pray for our oppressors and persecutors until Jesus comes.

It is not God's will that any should perish. It is God's will for everyone to know that He has appointed His Son, Jesus, to judge the living and the dead on the day of God's wrath. Everything that God does in the nations of the world is for the singular purpose that all people might seek after Him. If they seek Him, He will be found by them. And He will receive all the glory. Rightfully so.

Basic Training Exercise

PRESSING ON TO SUCCESS

Philippians 3:12-14 NIV – Not that I have already obtained all this, or have already arrived at my goal, but I press on to take hold of that for which Christ Jesus took hold of me. Brothers and sisters, I do not consider myself yet to have taken hold of it. But one thing I do: Forgetting what is behind and straining toward what is ahead, I press on toward the goal to win the prize for which God has called me heavenward in Christ Jesus.

DESCRIPTION

Jesus is God's image of perfect success. Yet, His life did not match the world's view of triumph. Instead, Jesus willingly laid down His life to fulfill God's purpose. When He tells His followers to take up our cross and follow Him, He means denying ourselves as He did, including letting go of our own opinions, desires, cultural norms, preferences, and concepts of success.

For example, when measured by certain standards, the Apostle Paul had much to boast about. However, Paul knew that the world's standards of measurement are worthless in the sight of God. Paul had one objective in life and it was to know Jesus and be like Him, no matter the cost to his life, ego, or agenda.

Pressing on to Success is about entering into a deeper commitment to following Jesus, surrendering ourselves to God, and moving towards His purposes for our lives, no matter the cost.

STUDY/MEDITATION

Read Philippians 3:4-14 slowly and prayerfully. Read it two or three times, asking the Holy Spirit to speak.

How did the Apostle Paul's image of success change when He came to know Jesus?

What was Paul's aim in life with the Lord? What was his burning desire?

What did Paul have to lose, give up, or walk away from in order to follow Christ?

Why was Paul willing to give up these things?

Category: Self-Denial

Basic TRAINING
SPIRITUAL EXERCISES

PURPOSE:

To detach from, let go of, cut off, release, and repent of anything hindering my walk with Jesus and attaining His likeness.

To silence the past and look onwards to the future in the new mercies of God.

To take steps necessary for the advancement of God's Kingdom purpose for my life.

SPIRITUAL FRUIT:

Increased freedom to obey God today.

Advancement in God's purpose for your life.

Alignment with God's perspective and purpose.

Restored focus on Christ.

PRAYER

Father, thank you for sending Jesus to be the perfect example of pressing on in your purposes. Help me by your Spirit to forget the past and take new steps of faith towards all you have for me. In Jesus' name, Amen.

TALK WITH GOD

In your life right now, in what ways/areas is Jesus asking you to "forget what is behind" and press on to follow Him?

How are your standards of success or failure affecting your obedience to God? How is your boldness for God affected by your self-image, fears, or insecurities?

Are your desires, opinions, preferences, behaviors, or cultural norms hindering your advancement in God's purposes? If so, which ones? What does God say about these things?

Are there material objects or relationships that God is asking you to let go of? How is He asking you to go about doing this?

PRACTICE

1. Write down your past or present definition of success and its attributes. What does success look like to you? How do you measure success?

2. Write down what you believe God's idea of success is.

3. Compare your definition and God's view of success.
   - How does your view differ from God's?

4. Write a new definition of success for your life.
   - Ask Jesus to refresh your focus on His desires for your life.
   - Ask Him if there is anything from your past that you need to let go of or give/throw away. (It could be a past trophy, a sentimental object, or an old mindset, etc.)

5. Ask God what steps of faith He is calling you to take as you pursue Christ and His likeness. Do what He says.

ADDITIONAL SCRIPTURES:

Colossians 2:13-15

Matthew 16:23-26

Luke 14:26

Romans 8:38-39

1 Corinthians 9:24

John 12:25

Luke 9:51

NOTES: _____
_____
_____

Category: Self-Denial

UNIT TWO – KEY QUESTIONS
Foundations & Whole Counsel of God

Use this worksheet to test your grasp of the material and exercises of Unit Two.

Why is it important to have an understanding of the whole counsel of God? (in your own words)	
Why is mankind doomed to God's wrath?	**What is the good news of salvation?**
Why did Jesus have to be Jewish?	**How will God keep His promises to Israel?**
How does God rule the nations?	**How will the day of wrath be like God's prior judgments? How will it be different?**
What is one thing you learned that you did not know before?	**What questions do you still have about this subject?**

UNIT TWO: GROUP EXERCISES

Use the Prayer Guide for Israel to pray for Israel as a Group. AND/OR Do the following exercise:

Group Training Exercise

SUCCESS IN GOD'S KINGDOM

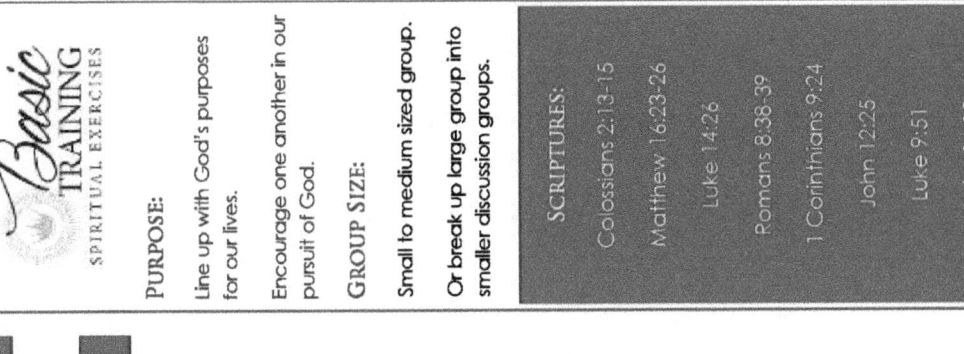

PURPOSE:
Line up with God's purposes for our lives.

Encourage one another in our pursuit of God.

GROUP SIZE:
Small to medium sized group.

Or break up large group into smaller discussion groups.

SCRIPTURES:
Colossians 2:13-15
Matthew 16:23-26
Luke 14:26
Romans 8:38-39
1 Corinthians 9:24
John 12:25
Luke 9:51
Luke 16:15
Hebrews 12:1-3

DESCRIPTION

Jesus is God's perfect example of success. However, in many ways and by worldly standards, Jesus was a failure. Similarly, the Apostle Paul was at the top of his game and one of the leaders in the world before he came to know Jesus as his Messiah. Then, he left all of his worldly acclaim behind to follow and die for the one who had died for him. The same is true for the other apostles, even though they had left behind less revered fishing and tax collecting businesses.

This reveals something important to us about what success in God's Kingdom is and is not. All of us must keep our eyes on Jesus and God's idea of success so that we do not become ensnared by the ways of this world.

As believers, we are called to encourage one another to obey God and provoke one another to good works in God's kingdom. We not only have to count the cost of following Jesus for ourselves but also to exhort one another to count the cost and pay it willingly because of the worthiness of Jesus and His eternal Kingdom.

SCRIPTURE PORTION: PHILIPPIANS 3:8-14

Philippians 3:8-14 NIV - What is more, I consider everything a loss because of the surpassing worth of knowing Christ Jesus my Lord, for whose sake I have lost all things. I consider them garbage, that I may gain Christ and be found in him, not having a righteousness of my own that comes from the law, but that which is through faith in Christ—the righteousness that comes from God on the basis of faith. I want to know Christ—yes, to know the power of his resurrection and participation in his sufferings, becoming like him in his death, and so, somehow, attaining to the resurrection from the dead. Not that I have already obtained all this, or have already arrived at my goal, but I press on to take hold of that for which Christ Jesus took hold of me. Brothers and sisters, I do not consider myself yet to have taken hold of it. But one thing I do: Forgetting what is behind and straining toward what is ahead, I press on toward the goal to win the prize for which God has called me heavenward in Christ Jesus.

GROUP PRACTICE

1. Pray and invite the Lord to speak to your hearts. Allow a moment of stillness before the first reading.

2. Have one person read the Scripture Portion out loud and slowly while others listen.

3. What are your past/present ideas of success? Describe it.
   _____
   _____
   _____

4. What is God's view of success? Describe it.
   _____
   _____
   _____

5. In your life right now, what is Jesus asking you to "forget" from the past in order to "press on" to God's purpose?
   _____
   _____
   _____

6. Have each member of the group share with the group:
   - What they discovered about how their concept of success differs from God's.
   - One growth area they would like the group to pray for them.

7. Pray for one another and exhort one another in your pursuit of God and His purposes.

Category: Self-Denial

ALL RIGHTS RESERVED © 2019 Wendy Bowen

UNIT THREE:
DIVINE NATURE

KEY SCRIPTURE VERSE FOR UNIT THREE
If you love those who love you, what reward will you get? Are not even the tax collectors doing that? And if you greet only your own people, what are you doing more than others? Do not even pagans do that? Be perfect, therefore, as your heavenly Father is perfect. - Matthew 5:46-48

CLASS 1: RENDER YOUR HEART
1 Reading, 1 Scripture Worksheet, 1 Evaluation
God is looking for believers who offer themselves to Him completely. We must be willing to let God transform us from our old way of doing things to a new creation in Christ.

CLASS 2: I DESIRE MERCY
1 Reading, 2 Exercises, 1 Evaluation
As God's representatives on earth, He wants His heart of mercy to shine through to the lost and hurting world. Our ability to show mercy can be an indication of our understanding of how God has shown mercy to us.

CLASS 3: SUITABLE FOR SERVICE
1 Reading, 1 Evaluation, 1 Exercise
Much work "for God" is done without God's guidance, power, or character. Being suitable for service includes doing the right things for God at the right time, in the right way, and for the right reasons.

CLASS 4: MOTIVATIONAL GIFTS
1 Reading, 1 Evaluation, 2 Exercises
God works His nature inside of us through spiritual gifts. We flow in these gifts for the benefit of others as a reflection of the heart of God.

KEY QUESTIONS

GROUP EXERCISES

PERFECTION COURSE – UNIT 3.1 READING

Render Your Heart

When Paul chastised the Corinthian church for being immature, he referred to their behavior as "carnal." The word in Greek is *sarkikos*, rooted in the word *sarx*, which means animal nature. They had put their faith in Jesus but were still behaving like beasts by giving way to the lusts of their flesh rather than the desires of the Spirit. In the same letter, Paul referenced a "natural" man. This word is *psychikos*, rooted in the word *psych* from which we get the word psychology. This is the same word used by James for sensual wisdom. The natural man is ruled by his natural senses and considers spiritual things to be foolish because he is consumed with mental or moral ascent of his own rationale. But Paul also speaks of a "spiritual" person, or *pneumatikos*, rooted in the word *pneuma*, meaning spirit. This person is governed by the Spirit of the Lord and not by their own carnality, sensual lusts, or unsanctified thoughts. (See 1 Corinthians 2-3.)

Paul knew a little something about being transformed from a natural person to a spiritual person. Paul did not receive the Gospel message the first time he heard about Jesus. Quite the contrary, it infuriated him. He was a natural person, completely consumed with his own perspective on things and self-righteous attainment of much so-called knowledge of God. Paul knew the Scriptures and prophecies about the Messiah of Israel as well as or better than anyone in the world. But because Paul lacked the Holy Spirit, all of his interpretations of the Scriptures did not lead him to recognize God when God was standing right in front of him in the flesh of Jesus! But then one day, on his way to Damascus with a mission to imprison more Christians, Paul had an encounter with Jesus. His life was changed forever.

> *Acts 26:14-15: We all fell to the ground, and I heard a voice saying to me in Aramaic,'Saul, Saul, why do you persecute me?* **It is hard for you to kick against the goads.**' *Then I asked, 'Who are you, Lord?' 'I am Jesus, whom you are persecuting,' the Lord replied.*

A *goad* is an iron tool used to prod cattle along in the way that their masters want them to go and *kicking against the goads* was a proverbial expression for *resisting the obvious to the point of self-destruction*. All of Scripture pointed to Jesus like a master's *goad* directing Paul's path. But Paul had no ability to be anything but goaded until Jesus revealed Himself. Then, in a moment's time, everything Paul thought he believed about Jesus was changed. After this dramatic encounter, Paul went through a transformation. He laid aside his own way of thinking to become a man entirely ruled by the Spirit of the Lord.

Cut to the Heart

On the day of Pentecost, Peter quoted the Book of Joel. Joel had cried out to the people of Israel, summoning them to humble themselves before the Lord with fasting and prayer, to weep over their sin with genuine contrition, and to return to the Lord with their whole heart. God appealed to His people to drop the outward show and come back to Him in sincere faith and heartfelt devotion. The day of the Lord's judgment upon all nations is at hand and only those who render their hearts to God will be spared.

> *Joel 2:1-3, 12-13: 1 "Blow the trumpet in Zion; sound the alarm on my holy hill. Let all who live in the land* **tremble, for the day of the LORD is coming.** *It is close at hand-- a day of darkness and gloom, a day of clouds and blackness. Like dawn spreading across the mountains a large and mighty army comes, such as never was in ancient times nor ever will be in ages to come. Before them fire devours, behind them a flame blazes. Before them the land is like the garden of Eden, behind them, a desert waste--* **nothing escapes them"**... *"Even now," declares the*

*LORD, "**return to me with all your heart**, with **fasting and weeping and mourning. Rend your heart and not your garments. Return to the LORD your God**, for he is gracious and compassionate, slow to anger and abounding in love, and he relents from sending calamity."*

On the day of Pentecost, people had again become religious in their outward demonstration of devotion without really meaning it in their hearts. They were functioning as natural people, devoid of the Spirit of the Lord, ruled by their own natural thoughts and desires. But now, Peter declared the word and it went out like a double-edged sword, piercing through the soul and exposing the motives of the heart while the Holy Spirit brought conviction of sin, righteousness, and judgment. Many people in Jerusalem were cut to the heart and begged to know what they needed to do to get right with God.

*Acts 2:36-40: "Therefore let all Israel be assured of this: God has made this Jesus, whom you crucified, both Lord and Messiah." When the people heard this, **they were cut to the heart** and said to Peter and the other apostles, "Brothers, **what shall we do?**" Peter replied, **"Repent and be baptized, every one of you, in the name of Jesus Christ for the forgiveness of your sins. And you will receive the gift of the Holy Spirit**. The promise is for you and your children and for all who are far off--for all whom the Lord our God will call." **With many other words he warned them; and he pleaded with them, "Save yourselves from this corrupt generation."***

I have heard that receiving the message of the Gospel could be compared to receiving a beautifully wrapped gift, only to open it and discover inside a bottle of mouthwash. What Jesus has done for us is the most wonderful and poignant expression of love the world has ever known. But in order to receive this love, we must first admit that we need His salvation. The call to following Jesus and remaining in Him requires us to stop denying our issues, blame-shifting to deflect God's dealings with us, and hiding behind excuses for ungodliness as self-made pardons for behavior unworthy of God.

Understandably, when Stephen made a speech similar to Peter's to another crowd on a different day, they were also cut to the heart but gnashed their teeth at Stephen and then stoned him to death. (See Acts 7:51-54.) They were not yet ready to deal with the planks in their own eyes.

Peter's Pentecost message remains the cry of God's heart to all people today. God's desire has always been for a people who will worship Him from the heart in pure and simple devotion and submission to His ways. (See Deuteronomy 10:16.) But all of mankind has turned away from God and all people are living lives of sin and error, folly and complacency, and religion and hypocrisy. Everyone is pretending to be good outwardly while plotting selfish schemes inwardly, and judging one another relentlessly while indulging their own selfish lusts to the max. The day of judgment is coming upon the world for this. Everyone who has not rendered their heart to Jesus is lost, without hope, and is destined for eternal destruction in a place where the fire never goes out and where there is torment, weeping, and gnashing of teeth.

After the days of Joel, when the time came for judgment on the city of Jerusalem, Ezekiel had a vision of a man dressed in white linen. (See Ezekiel 9.) This man in linen was commissioned by God to identify those who had genuinely rendered their hearts to God. They would be the ones who wept, sighed, and grieved over the sin and horrendous lack of regard for God in the city. On these people, the man in linen was ordered to place the mark of God, which would seal them and spare them from destruction.

Have you been cut to the heart?

The Need for Re-birth

All of us need to be transformed from being natural people to becoming spiritual people. God knows if we have been outwardly religious for selfish reasons (i.e. to look good, be regarded as holy, to get something from God, etc.) God knows if our lips are praising Him while we hold murder in our hearts. God knows that our hearts are inherently wicked and that without the Holy Spirit, we are helpless and hopelessly enslaved to our own sinful nature. This is why we must be born again by the Spirit of the Lord who writes the word of God upon our hearts and transforms us from the inside out.

When John was writing his gospel account of the life and ministry of Jesus, he relayed this emphatically. For example, in John 2, Jesus went to the Temple in Jerusalem where He turned over tables and made whips to drive out the merchants and their livestock merchandise. The nature of man is totally selfish, even at the expense of God and the sanctity of God's house. Immediately following this, Nicodemus came to Jesus, believing that He must be sent by God. Jesus explained to Nicodemus that no one can enter the Kingdom of God unless they are born again by the Spirit. However, Nicodemus was focused on earthly things, whereas Jesus was focused only on heavenly, eternal things. Jesus allegorically explained to Nicodemus that for this, the world was about to kill Him as an enemy. Only those who were reborn by the Spirit of the Lord would perceive the ways of God in the midst of the world's hostility.

Similarly, in the Book of Luke, chapter 18 contains stories in succession which reveal a deeper intent. Jesus told the story of the Pharisee, with his self-proclaimed piety and righteousness, who looked down on the Tax Collector who humbled himself before God in genuine contrition. This is followed by an exhortation to childlikeness. Then, in living demonstration of this parable, the Rich Young Ruler approached Jesus thinking that he had attained some level of righteousness through his own outward observances and application of the laws and statutes of God. But Jesus knew this man's heart and challenged him to shift his focus to heavenly things by giving all of his earthly things away. This man went away sad. God sees no value in outward religion if the heart is still set on its own desires and self-exaltation. Only those who will humble themselves like children in the hands of God will receive the fullness of what He has done for us.

The most poignant example of this is in Matthew 16 when Peter professed that Jesus is the Messiah and the Son of God. Jesus praised Peter for this revelation in thanksgiving that God had revealed this to Peter directly. Now that His disciples had the clear picture of who Jesus really is, Jesus began to speak to them about how He must suffer and die and be crucified. The same Peter who acclaimed Jesus as the Son of God now took the Son of God to the side to rebuke Him for His erroneous thinking. But it was Peter who had the wrong idea. Jesus rebuked Peter sharply, saying, "Get behind me, Satan! You have on your mind the ways of man and not of God." Even though Peter believed who Jesus was, he had not yet been cut to the heart. As such, his profession of faith went no further than his mind and his lips. His heart was still ruled by selfishness, the ways of this world, and the evil one.

All of us are in jeopardy of Peter's mistake if we will not allow ourselves to be cut to the heart and transformed by the Holy Spirit. Jesus made it clear that not everyone who calls Him Lord will enter the Kingdom of Heaven. Those who say they believe and even who work mighty things in Jesus' name but have not been deeply changed and transformed into spiritual people will be rebuked as ones who have instead worked for Satan and his agenda.

> *Matthew 7:21-23:* **Not everyone who says to me, 'Lord, Lord,' will enter the kingdom of heaven**, *but only the one who does the will of my Father who is in heaven. Many will say to me on that day, 'Lord, Lord, did we not prophesy in your name and in your name drive out demons and in your name perform many miracles?'* **Then I will tell them plainly, 'I never knew you. Away from me, you evildoers!'**

The unregenerate Peter proclaimed his own steadfast love but lacked the self-awareness to know the evil that was still within him. He went on to deny Jesus three times. Then, Peter was cut to the heart. He wept bitterly and was grieved to the depths of his soul. The depths of the depravity of his own humanity has been revealed to him and he would never be the same. When Jesus went to restore Peter to Kingdom service by the sea of Galilee, Peter had a new understanding of himself and could not honestly profess that truly selfless *agape* love was within him. Nevertheless, it was this very same Peter who went on to be filled with the Holy Spirit and proclaimed the message of repentance and the need for being cut to the heart. Peter had a new understanding of the wickedness of the human heart and the need for salvation from the corruption of his generation. It was this regenerated Peter who went on to be crucified upside down because he did not consider himself worthy to be martyred in the same way that Jesus had died.

Have you been reborn?

Offer Yourself

In Peter's last message from prison before he died for Christ (which is the letter we know of as 2 Peter) he exhorted believers as strongly as possible not to be shortsighted in their faith the way that he had been so that they would not stumble. When we put our faith in Jesus, the Holy Spirit comes to dwell inside of us. The divine nature of God dwells within us to guide us. In order to be a spiritual person, Peter said we have to participate and be a partaker of God's nature within us. Essentially, this means to partner with God for His purposes rather than resist Him for our purposes.

> 2 Peter 1:3-4: *His divine power has given us everything we need for a godly life through our knowledge of him who called us by his own glory and goodness. Through these he has given us his very great and precious promises, so that through them **you may participate in the divine nature, having escaped the corruption in the world caused by evil desires***.

True transformation of the heart can only be done by God Himself. This said, God will never subvert our free will. He does not turn us into robots or domineer over us to force us to do what He wants. That is not love. God asks us to willingly participate with Him and to turn ourselves over to Him in childlike confidence and willing surrender. Obedience is a choice. We are slaves to whomever and whatever we choose to obey. Outside pressures may influence our choices, but no one else controls our hearts or motives.

When Peter denied Jesus, he neglected his eternal best interest for the sake of his temporal protection. His motive was understandable. But his denial of Christ exposed his heart. We may never be put in the same position as Peter was. But we each face decisions every day which give us the opportunity to submit to God or to the pressures of this world and other people. If we profess with our mouth that Jesus is Lord but choose with our choices to follow another, we have not yet rendered our hearts completely.

When Paul persecuted Christians by imprisoning and killing them, he thought he was being exceedingly zealous for the right cause and for the sake of the name of God. But the blindness of his heart was exposed when he saw the Lord. We may never be as zealous as Paul was and our persecution of true believers may not be as obvious. But we each face decisions every day where we take a stand in our heart for what we believe to be right and what we believe to be wrong. If we serve God with all our might but fail to know the heart of God, we will constantly be kicking against the goads because our hearts have not yet been pricked.

Through the death and resurrection of Jesus, we have been set free from slavery to sin and have become a new creation. But we must also choose to live as this new creation by not indulging the old natural nature that still resides in the members of our flesh and tempts us to behave like beasts. We must daily deny the demands of our own fleshly lusts and passions in order to submit ourselves totally to the purity of the likeness of Christ. We must choose to serve God rather than ourselves and our own agendas – even the agendas we think are for God's Kingdom. We must daily lay our lives down as a sacrifice to Jesus, relinquishing all our ideas of what God is doing, why He is doing it, how He is doing it, through whom He will choose to do it, and in what timing He will do it. We must allow ourselves to be entirely governed by the Holy Spirit so that we can become truly spiritual people.

Have you rendered your heart?

www.manifestinternational.com

Put Off Old & Put On Christ
Scripture List & Worksheet

Directions:
1. Read through and meditate on the following Scriptures. Notice how we are called to renounce our old ways and put on Christ to live by His divine nature to lead us in godliness.
2. Allow the Holy Spirit to highlight to you how the Lord is calling you into deeper repentance and obedience in some of these areas.
3. Ask God to help you put into practice what the Holy Spirit reveals to you.

Ephesians 4:17-32: So I tell you this, and insist on it in the Lord, that you must no longer live as the Gentiles do, in the **futility of their thinking**. They are **darkened in their understanding** and separated from the life of God because of the **ignorance** that is in them due to the **hardening of their hearts**. Having **lost all sensitivity**, they have given themselves over to **sensuality** so as to indulge in **every kind of impurity**, and they are **full of greed**. That, however, is not the way of life you learned when you heard about Christ and were taught in him in accordance with the truth that is in Jesus. You were taught, with regard to your former way of life, to **put off your old self**, which is being **corrupted by its deceitful desires**; to **be made new in the attitude of your minds**; and to **put on the new self, created to be like God in true righteousness and holiness**. Therefore each of you must **put off falsehood and speak truthfully** to your neighbor, for we are all members of one body. "In your anger do not sin": **Do not let the sun go down while you are still angry**, and **do not give the devil a foothold**. Anyone who has been stealing must **steal no longer**, but must work, doing something useful with their own hands, that they may have something to **share with those in need**. **Do not let any unwholesome talk come out of your mouths**, but only what is **helpful for building others up** according to their needs, that it may benefit those who listen. And **do not grieve the Holy Spirit of God**, with whom you were sealed for the day of redemption. **Get rid of all bitterness, rage and anger, brawling and slander, along with every form of malice. Be kind and compassionate to one another, forgiving each other, just as in Christ God forgave you.**

Romans 6:11-14: In the same way, **count yourselves dead to sin but alive to God in Christ Jesus**. Therefore **do not let sin reign in your mortal body so that you obey its evil desires. Do not offer any part of yourself to sin as an instrument of wickedness**, but rather **offer yourselves to God** as those who have been brought from death to life; and **offer every part of yourself to him as an instrument of righteousness**. For sin shall no longer be your master, because you are not under the law, but under grace.

Romans 13:12-14: The night is nearly over; the day is almost here. So **let us put aside the deeds of darkness and put on the armor of light**. Let us **behave decently**, as in the daytime, **not in carousing and drunkenness, not in sexual immorality and debauchery, not in dissension and jealousy**. Rather, **clothe yourselves with the Lord Jesus Christ, and do not think about how to gratify the desires of the flesh**.

Colossians 3:1-14: Since, then, you have been raised with Christ, **set your hearts on things above**, where Christ is, seated at the right hand of God. **Set your minds on things above, not on earthly things**. For you died, and your life is now hidden with Christ in God. When Christ, who is your life, appears, then you also will appear with him in glory. **Put to death, therefore, whatever belongs to your earthly nature: sexual immorality, impurity, lust, evil desires and greed, which is idolatry**. Because of these, the wrath of God is coming. You used to walk in these ways, in the life you once lived. But now you must also **rid yourselves** of all such things as these: anger, rage, malice, slander, and filthy language from your lips. **Do not lie to each other**, since you have **taken off your old self with its practices and have put on the new self, which is being renewed in knowledge in the image of its Creator**. Here there is no Gentile or Jew, circumcised or uncircumcised, barbarian, Scythian, slave or free, but Christ is all, and is in all. Therefore, as God's chosen people, holy and dearly loved, **clothe yourselves with compassion, kindness, humility, gentleness and patience**. Bear with each other and forgive one another if any of you has a grievance against someone. Forgive as the Lord forgave you. And over all these virtues **put on love, which binds them all together in perfect unity**.

Ephesians 5:1-20: Follow God's example, therefore, as dearly loved children and **walk in the way of love**, just as Christ loved us and gave himself up for us as a fragrant offering and sacrifice to God. But among you there must **not be even a hint of sexual immorality**, or of **any kind of impurity, or of greed**, because these are improper for God's holy people. Nor should there be **obscenity, foolish talk or coarse joking**, which are out of place, but rather thanksgiving. For of this you can be sure: **No immoral, impure or greedy person--such a person is an idolater--has any inheritance in the kingdom of Christ and of God**. Let no one deceive you with empty words, for because of such things God's wrath comes on those who are disobedient. Therefore do not be partners with them. For you were once darkness, but now you are light in the Lord. **Live as children of light (for the fruit of the light consists in all goodness, righteousness and truth) and find out what pleases the Lord**. Have **nothing to do with the fruitless deeds of darkness**, but rather expose them. It is shameful even to mention what the disobedient do in secret. But everything exposed by the light becomes visible--and everything that is illuminated becomes a light. This is why it is said: "Wake up, sleeper, rise from the dead, and Christ will shine on you." Be very careful, then, how you live--**not as unwise but as wise**, making the most of every opportunity, because the days are evil. Therefore **do not be foolish, but understand what the Lord's will is. Do not get drunk on wine, which leads to debauchery. Instead, be filled with the Spirit**, speaking to one another with psalms, hymns, and songs from the Spirit. **Sing and make music from your heart to the Lord**, always giving thanks to God the Father for everything, in the name of our Lord Jesus Christ.

Hebrews 3:12-13: See to it, brothers and sisters, that **none of you has a sinful, unbelieving heart that turns away from the living God**. But **encourage one another daily**, as long as it is called "Today," so that none of you may be hardened by sin's deceitfulness.

Hebrews 12:1-4: Therefore, since we are surrounded by such a great cloud of witnesses, let us **throw off everything that hinders and the sin that so easily entangles**. And let us **run with perseverance the race marked out for us**, fixing our eyes on Jesus, the pioneer and perfecter of faith. For the joy set before him he endured the cross, scorning its shame, and sat down at the right hand of the throne of God. Consider him who endured such opposition from sinners, so that you will not grow weary and lose heart. In your struggle against sin, you have not yet resisted to the point of shedding your blood.

James 1:19-22: My dear brothers and sisters, take note of this: Everyone should be quick to listen, slow to speak and slow to become angry, because human anger does not produce the righteousness that God desires. Therefore, **get rid of all moral filth and the evil that is so prevalent and humbly accept the word planted in you, which can save you**. Do not merely listen to the word, and so deceive yourselves. **Do what it says.**

2 Peter 1:5-8: For this very reason, **make every effort to add to your faith goodness**; and to goodness, **knowledge**; and to knowledge, **self-control**; and to self-control, **perseverance**; and to perseverance,

godliness; and to godliness, **mutual affection**; and to mutual affection, **love.** For if you possess these qualities in increasing measure, they will keep you from being ineffective and unproductive in your knowledge of our Lord Jesus Christ.

Practical Application:

3 Things I Need to "Put Off"	3 Things I Need to "Put On"
1.	1.
2.	2.
3.	3.
How God is Showing Me to Do This:	How God is Showing Me to Do This:

MOTIVE INSPECTION		
1 = Needs improvement	2 = In Refining Process	3 = Doing Well for Now

Motive Inspection – *for all decisions large and small – no provision for the flesh*

Have I prayed about this?	1	2	3
Am I doing this because God spoke to me or guided me to do it?	1	2	3
Am I doing this out of religious obligation or to earn God's approval, favor, or love?	1	2	3
Am I doing this because it is "the right thing to do?" (Rather than from genuine love.)	1	2	3
Am I doing this because it is what other people do or want me to do?	1	2	3
Am I doing this to imitate or appease other people? Am I doing this to be accepted?	1	2	3
Am I doing this to serve God or my own desires?	1	2	3
Am I doing this to glorify God?	1	2	3
Am I doing this to be promoted, look heroic, or advance my own agenda or reputation?	1	2	3
Am I doing this to reach more people for Jesus?	1	2	3
Am I doing this to serve God or conform to this world's pattern? Am I double-minded?	1	2	3
Am I obeying God's instructions completely or am I compromising?	1	2	3
Am I doing this out of faith or fear?	1	2	3

All a person's ways seem pure to them, but motives are weighed by the LORD.
Proverbs 16:2

 PERFECTION COURSE – UNIT 3.2 READING

I Desire Mercy

In the days of Hosea, God commanded Hosea to marry a prostitute. Hosea provided a good home for her and they had children. But as a married woman, she returned to her prostitution and even sold herself over to a pimp. In complete disregard for the provision of her husband, she announced that her prostitution had produced for her all the wonderful things she had attained. Imagine Hosea's humiliation and the scorn he must have endured from others looking down on this. The penalty for adultery was death and Hosea could have rightfully cast the first stone to kill his wife. But instead, God told Hosea to buy his wife back out of prostitution, and he did. At that time, Hosea ordered her that she would not be prostituting herself anymore and that even he would not be having marital relations with her for some time. She could no longer use sex to attain what she desired. Even if it meant Hosea giving up his marital right as a husband, it was more important that she learn and experience what real love and mercy is.

One of the token marks of spiritual maturity is mercy. This is evidenced by our ability to treat our enemies the same way we treat our friends, no matter what they have done to us.

> *Matthew 5:43-48:* You have heard that it was said, 'Love your neighbor and hate your enemy.' But I tell you, **love your enemies and pray for those who persecute you, that you may be children of your Father in heaven.** He causes his sun to rise on the evil and the good, and sends rain on the righteous and the unrighteous. If you love those who love you, what reward will you get? Are not even the tax collectors doing that? And if you greet only your own people, what are you doing more than others? Do not even pagans do that? **Be perfect, therefore, as your heavenly Father is perfect.**

> *Luke 6:27-36:* But to you who are listening I say: **Love your enemies, do good to those who hate you, bless those who curse you, pray for those who mistreat you.** If someone slaps you on one cheek, turn to them the other also. If someone takes your coat, do not withhold your shirt from them. Give to everyone who asks you, and if anyone takes what belongs to you, do not demand it back. **Do to others as you would have them do to you.** If you love those who love you, what credit is that to you? Even sinners love those who love them. And if you do good to those who are good to you, what credit is that to you? Even sinners do that. And if you lend to those from whom you expect repayment, what credit is that to you? Even sinners lend to sinners, expecting to be repaid in full. But **love your enemies, do good to them, and lend to them without expecting to get anything back.** Then your reward will be great, and **you will be children of the Most High, because he is kind to the ungrateful and wicked. Be merciful, just as your Father is merciful.**

After Adam and Eve sinned in the Garden of Eden, God could have killed them. What they did was wrong. God could have punished them by cutting off their entire food supply on earth. He could have allowed them to plant food only to vindictively wash it away with droves of rain. He could have done many things to make life exceedingly miserable for them. But in His great mercy, He did not do any of these things. Although there were pre-disclosed consequences for Adam's disobedience, including separation from God, God did not starve or kill Adam for his rebellion. It was not until ten generations later, when all of Adam's descendants had repeatedly persisted in evil works and wickedness, that God finally put rebellion to an end with the flood. Only after about one thousand years did God's mercy run out.

God is slow to anger and full of mercy.

In spite of the fact that all of mankind is constantly in utter rebellion against Him, He still causes the sun to come up and the light to shine each day so that we can live. He has the ability to withhold rain or cause terrifying hail to fall on those who disregard Him. The day will come for that. But God overlooks these offenses and turns His divine cheek to more abuse by ungrateful people without withholding what they need for their sustenance even though He could.

Mercy is God's nature. As the incarnation of God and all that God's nature entails, Jesus was moved with compassion for people who were hurting and wandering like sheep without a shepherd. They had all been subjected to sin and sickness and death but instead of leaving them in their condition as God's righteous judgment upon them, Jesus' heart went out to them with mercy.

> *Matthew 14:14:* When Jesus landed and saw a large crowd, **He had compassion on them and healed their sick.**
>
> *Matthew 20:34:* **Jesus had compassion on them** and touched their eyes. Immediately they received their sight and followed Him.
>
> *Mark 6:34:* When Jesus landed and saw a large crowd, **He had compassion on them**, because they were like sheep without a shepherd. So He began teaching them many things.
>
> *Mark 8:2:* "**I have compassion for these people**; they have already been with Me three days and have nothing to eat." (Then Jesus miraculously fed the 4,000.)
>
> *Luke 7:12-13:* As He approached the town gate, a dead person was being carried out-- the only son of his mother, and she was a widow. And a large crowd from the town was with her. **When the Lord saw her, His heart went out to her** and He said, "Don't cry."

Mercy does not say that wrong is right. God is absolutely righteous and just. When Jesus died on the cross for our sins, He was not saying that sin is not sin. Jesus took the righteous punishment for sin so that we could receive mercy from God. Now, He calls upon us to be like Him and take up our cross and turn the other cheek to offenses so that others can receive His mercy.

Mercy is what God has always wanted to see in His people who are supposed to be the earthly representatives of His likeness. It was Hosea who spoke on behalf of the Lord, "I desire mercy, not sacrifice, and knowledge of God rather than burnt offerings." Anyone can bring a lamb and offer it on the altar to try to be good for God or to get God to do good things for them. But to make yourself into the lamb being offered on the altar by allowing yourself to be humiliated so that others can know love is something altogether divine – only the nature of God can do.

Self-righteous people have difficulty with mercy. The Pharisees disdained Jesus for calling a Tax Collector and for eating with sinners. (See Matthew 9:13.) In one way, they were right. God did call His people to be holy. But Jesus rebuked them by quoting Hosea. God desires mercy. Similarly, Pharisees challenged Jesus for allowing His disciples to pluck grain on the Sabbath when this type of "work" should have been forbidden. (See Matthew 12:7.) By the letter of the Law, they were right. But again, Jesus rebuked them. God desires mercy.

James, the leader of the Jerusalem church and the author of the Book of James, taught believers about living lives of genuine mercy. The royal law is God's Old Covenant Law which was given through Moses. It has commands which must be obeyed in order to be righteous. But Jesus came to fulfill this Law for us so that we can be righteous by faith in Him. Thus, by His mercy, we have been set free from the demands of the royal law and have been called to a higher one – the "perfect" or mature law that gives liberty. This is the law by which we will be judged – whether or not we have exhibited the divine nature of God within us by showing mercy the way He does.

> *James 2:8-13:* If you really keep the royal law found in Scripture, "Love your neighbor as

yourself," you are doing right. But if you show favoritism, you sin and are convicted by the law as lawbreakers. For whoever keeps the whole law and yet stumbles at just one point is guilty of breaking all of it. For he who said, "You shall not commit adultery," also said, "You shall not murder." If you do not commit adultery but do commit murder, you have become a lawbreaker. **Speak and act as those who are going to be judged by the law that gives freedom, because judgment without mercy will be shown to anyone who has not been merciful. Mercy triumphs over judgment.**

James 1:25: But whoever looks intently into **the perfect law that gives freedom**, *and continues in it--not forgetting what they have heard, but doing it--they will be blessed in what they do.*

Jesus laid down His life for us so that we could be free. As His followers, He gave us only one command. This is His command:

John 15:12-17: **My command is this: Love each other as I have loved you.** *Greater love has no one than this: to lay down one's life for one's friends. You are My friends if you do what I command. I no longer call you servants, because a servant does not know his master's business. Instead, I have called you friends, for everything that I learned from My Father I have made known to you. You did not choose Me, but I chose you and appointed you so that you might go and bear fruit--fruit that will last--and so that whatever you ask in My name the Father will give you.* **This is my command: Love each other.** *(Also John 13:34-35.)*

Without the nature of Jesus dwelling within us, it is absolutely impossible for anyone to fulfill His New Covenant command. Without participating in divine nature, we will be unable to love the way Jesus did. Spiritual fruitfulness and the evidence of our participation with divine nature has nothing to do with how many people we serve, how well we preach, teach, or lead worship, how rich or poor we are, how much revelation we have, or how much we sacrifice for God and His Kingdom. Any of us could do any of these things with a host of wrong motives. We may actually be aiming for recognition, revenge, success, expecting some form of repayment, or trying to earn a reward from God rather than being motivated by genuine love for God and for others. True spiritual fruit is produced through God's nature in our motives.

Galatians 5:22-23: But the **fruit of the Spirit is love, joy, peace, forbearance, kindness, goodness, faithfulness, gentleness and self-control.** *Against such things there is no law.*

Therefore, when others sin against us, hurt us, offend us, cause us harm, or owe us something, we must recognize that their debt to us is small by comparison to the mercy that we have received from God. When we truly understand this, forgiving others comes easily. If we do not understand the mercy that we have received from God, it can be difficult to forgive others and therefore, we put ourselves in jeopardy of losing what Jesus died to give us. (see Matthew 18:23-35)

Matthew 6:14-15: "For **if you forgive** *other people when they sin against you,* **your heavenly Father will also forgive you.** *But* **if you do not forgive** *others their sins,* **your Father will not forgive your sins.**"

Mark 11:24-25: "Therefore I tell you, whatever you ask for in prayer, believe that you have received it, and it will be yours. And when you stand praying, if you hold anything against anyone, **forgive them, so that your Father in heaven may forgive you your sins.**"

Luke 11:4a: **Forgive us our sins, for we also forgive** *everyone who sins against us.*

What God desires is mercy. He wants to see His likeness reflected in us. Although miracle power, preaching, testifying, or even serving are all valid and good things, if we desire to demonstrate God's likeness to others, we must learn to show mercy.

Basic Training Exercise

LOVING YOUR ENEMIES

Matthew 5:43-45 NIV – "You have heard that it was said, 'Love your neighbor and hate your enemy.' But I tell you, love your enemies and pray for those who persecute you, that you may be children of your Father in heaven. He causes his sun to rise on the evil and the good, and sends rain on the righteous and the unrighteous.

DESCRIPTION

While we were enemies of God and totally hostile to Him in our thoughts and actions, Christ died for us and forgave us completely. Now, as His followers, He calls upon us to love our enemies the way that He loved us when we were His enemies. Although we may not be nailed to a cross literally, it might require taking up our cross to suffer in order to release our enemies to freedom. This is the mercy that God desires for each of His children to have in our hearts.

Practicing participation in Loving Your Enemies is about working towards deep and genuine forgiveness and blessing in our hearts, even for those who have hurt us badly.

MEDITATION

Use these to reflect on God's mercy to you:

God does not make me earn His love. It is a free gift.

While I was ungodly and an enemy of God, He loved me enough to die for me.

God loves me without expecting anything in return.

God does not hold a grudge against me and He remembers my sins no more.

Jesus died to set me free from the things that kept me in bondage and hostile to Him.

Nothing and no one can separate me from God's love for me or thwart God's plan for my life.

When people do things to hurt or offend me, I reckon that part of me dead in Christ so I am free to love them without reservation.

Category: Divine Nature

Basic TRAINING
SPIRITUAL EXERCISES

PURPOSE:

To reveal God's nature in us by loving our enemies.

To love, bless, and pray for those who have treated us shamefully.

To forgive as Christ has forgiven us.

SPIRITUAL FRUIT:

Godliness. Mercy. Forgiveness.

Freedom from bitterness, resentment, accusations against others.

Growing in genuine love for others without partiality.

PRAYER

Father, thank you that you sent your Son Jesus to die for me when I was your enemy. Help me now to be like you by blessing, praying for, and loving my enemies. In Jesus' name, Amen.

PRACTICE

1. Write a list of the people who have hurt you or who you would consider to be your "enemies."
   - Those who cursed or slandered you, denigrated, abused, or humiliated you, misunderstood or wounded you through their words or actions, etc.

2. Consider the ways that your enemy's treatment of you triggered unloving, unforgiving, or ungodly reactions in you.
   - Does it spike in you offense, anger, pride, self-defensiveness; jealousy, competition, selfish ambition; revenge, withdrawal, or wanting their downfall, etc.

3. By faith, take up your cross and reckon that part of you dead in Christ. (See Galatians 2:20; Romans 6:11.)
   - You are dead to yourself by faith. Dead people aren't offended or angry; competitive or vengeful, etc.

4. One enemy at a time, ask the Holy Spirit to work in your heart towards genuine and total forgiveness and blessing. Use the following as a guide:
   - Father God, in Jesus' name, I pray for _____.
   - Father, thank you that you love _____ and sent Jesus to die for _____ to forgive all their sins, as you did mine.
   - Father, in Jesus' name, I forgive _____ and release them totally from the harm they have done to me.
   - Father, in Jesus' name, I ask you to bless and prosper _____'s life, family, health, and the work of their hands.
   - Father, in Jesus' name, show me how to love _____ in word and in deed the way that you love me.

ADDITIONAL SCRIPTURES:

Romans 5:6-10

Colossians 1:21-23

Leviticus 19:18

Matthew 18:23-35

1 John 4:21

Matthew 5:21-22

Romans 12:19-20

Luke 23:34

Matthew 9:13

NOTES: _____

Category: Divine Nature

Basic Training Exercise

BE PERFECT – BE MERCIFUL

Matthew 5:43-48 NIV - You have heard that it was said, 'Love your neighbor and hate your enemy.' But I tell you, love your enemies and pray for those who persecute you, that you may be children of your Father in heaven. He causes his sun to rise on the evil and the good, and sends rain on the righteous and the unrighteous. If you love those who love you, what reward will you get? Are not even the tax collectors doing that? And if you greet only your own people, what are you doing more than others? Do not even pagans do that? Be perfect, therefore, as your heavenly Father is perfect.

Luke 6:33-36 NIV - And if you do good to those who are good to you, what credit is that to you? Even sinners do that. And if you lend to those from whom you expect repayment, what credit is that to you? Even sinners lend to sinners, expecting to be repaid in full. But love your enemies, do good to them, and lend to them without expecting to get anything back. Then your reward will be great, and you will be children of the Most High, because he is kind to the ungrateful and wicked. Be merciful, just as your Father is merciful.

DESCRIPTION

We all want to receive a perfect score when we stand before God. Jesus says that to be perfect (the same word for mature) is to love our enemies and those who hate us, even when they are ungrateful and wicked. If Jesus waited for us to deserve His kindness, He would still be waiting to come. Instead, He came to save us when we had gone astray. He paid the price for us, knowing we can never possibly repay Him. He died for us when we were dead in sin. He continues to love us through our fears, failures, missteps, and rebellion.

Now, He asks us to be like Him. The Holy Spirit will help us to do what none of us can do unless Christ is in us. This is the way towards perfection.

Practicing Be Perfect – Be Merciful is about showing others the mercy and kindness that Jesus has shown to us when so that they can know His love.

Category: Christlike Care

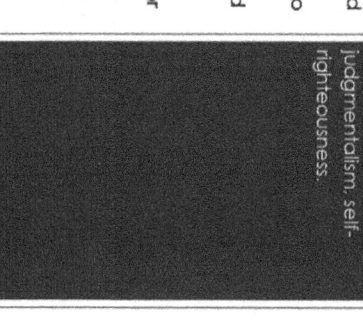

PURPOSE:
To love people the way God loves.

To be empowered by the Holy Spirit for revealing the mercy of Christ.

SPIRITUAL FRUIT:
Love. Mercy.

Increasing in patience, selflessness, humility, and compassion.

Reduction of criticism, judgmentalism, self-righteousness.

PRAYER

Father, thank you that you sent Jesus to give His life for me when I did not deserve it and could not repay you. Teach me how to love those who I consider unworthy. Show me how to be perfect like you. In Jesus' name, Amen.

CONSIDERATION

Why is it so tempting to want mercy for ourselves and judgment for others? How is God changing your heart on this?

Have you tended toward being lenient (passive/lawless) or severe (legalistic/religious)? Which one is God emphasizing in your life right now? What is God's perspective on this?

PRACTICE

1. Remember a time when you were not fully following Jesus.
   - How were you trying/hoping to solve your own problems?
   - What was the result of your attempts/solutions?
   - Why were you in need of a Savior?

2. Consider someone in your life who you consider to be sinful, wicked, rude, ungrateful, or otherwise unworthy of blessing.
   - Why do you think what they are doing is unacceptable to God? How is it different than what you did?
   - Why do they need a Savior?

3. Ask the Lord to reveal to you how He wants you to bless them without condemning them or condoning their sin. Do what He says.

4. Take note of any resistance that comes up in your heart.
   - Ask the Lord to help you identify the root of this resistance.
   - Ask the Holy Spirit to help you to obey God and bless them in spite of your natural resistance.
   - Take note of what happens in your heart when you obey God by blessing them.

5. Keep the person in prayer with your new heart of mercy.

NOTES: _____

_____

ADDITIONAL SCRIPTURES:
Colossians 1:21
Romans 5:8
John 15:12
1 Corinthians 13
John 8:11
John 3:17
John 5:14
Ephesians 5:2
1 John 3:16-18
1 John 4:20-21

Category: Christlike Care

FORGIVENESS INSPECTION

1 = Needs improvement	2 = In Refining Process	3 = Doing Well for Now			
Am I thankful that Christ died for my sins?			1	2	3
Do I recognize my own need to be forgiven for things I do wrong?			1	2	3
Am I able to acknowledge that even though my intentions are good, my actions are not always right?			1	2	3
Do I move forward trusting that God's mercies to me are new every morning?			1	2	3
Have I forgiven those who hurt me in the past?			1	2	3
When someone wrongs me, do I allow God to avenge me?			1	2	3
When someone wrongs me, do I "punish" or pay them back through acts of revenge, spitefulness, withdrawal of affection, or the silent treatment?			1	2	3
When someone hurts me, do I expose them to others through gossip or slander even in the form of "prayer request"?			1	2	3
When someone wrongs me do I communicate with them directly and follow the protocols laid out by Jesus according to Matthew 18:15-17?			1	2	3
When someone wrongs or hurts me, do I forgive them?			1	2	3
Is forgiving others easy for me?			1	2	3
Do I forgive freely, without expecting repayment or restitution?			1	2	3
Do I need to "understand" in order to forgive, or do I forgive because God forgave me?			1	2	3
Am I willing to forgive even if it costs me something?			1	2	3
Do I withdraw myself without communicating to the offender that they have hurt me?			1	2	3
Do I pretend to forgive others just to avoid conflict?			1	2	3
Do I hold a grudge?			1	2	3
Do I rejoice in my "enemy's" tragedy?			1	2	3
When I forgive someone, do I consider myself spiritually superior or look down on them for "not knowing what they are doing?"			1	2	3
When I forgive someone who has wronged me, do release them entirely and continue to love them? (Without putting them on probation period.)			1	2	3
When I forgive someone who has wronged me, do I let it go without bringing it up again to remind them of their fault?			1	2	3
Do I sincerely pray for and love my enemies and those who treat me shamefully?			1	2	3

Then Peter came to Jesus and asked, "Lord, how many times shall I forgive my brother or sister who sins against me? Up to seven times?" Jesus answered, "I tell you, not seven times, but seventy-seven times.
Matthew 18:21-22

PERFECTION COURSE – UNIT 3.3 READING

Suitable for Service

Even though Jesus is Lord, He did not come to lord over people. He came to serve them and give His life as a ransom for their souls. He did not come to serve His own appetites but He always made sure that everyone around Him had plenty to eat. He did not come to demand worship but to demonstrate what true worship is by offering Himself entirely to God. He humbled Himself and took on the nature of a servant, subjecting Himself entirely to His Father's will at all times.

We are made for good works which God prepared in advance for us and God wants us to be zealous for good works and serving Him by serving others. (See Ephesians 2:8-10; Titus 2:14.) This said, we can never allow ourselves to be so consumed with serving God by doing things for Him that we forget to allow His nature to penetrate ever more deeply into our own lives. Jesus loved Martha but said that Mary chose the one thing that was needed. (See Luke 10:38-42.) Even though the apostle Paul had served and trained so many other people, he recognized the need for spiritual discipline in his life and maintaining his own connection with the heart of God so that he would not be disqualified from the eternal prize. He compared ministry service to running a race. It is a marathon, not a sprint. We need to maintain our own grasp of God and perseverance in the truth because our souls and the souls of others are at stake.

> 1 Corinthians 9:24-27: Do you not know that in a race all the runners run, but only one gets the prize? **Run in such a way as to get the prize.** Everyone who competes in the games goes into **strict training**. They do it to get a crown that will not last, but we do it to get a crown that will last forever. Therefore **I do not run like someone running aimlessly**; I do not fight like a boxer beating the air. **No, I strike a blow to my body and make it my slave so that after I have preached to others, I myself will not be disqualified for the prize.**

> 1 Timothy 4:16: **Watch your life and doctrine closely.** Persevere in them, because if you do, you will save both yourself and your hearers.

Jesus came to fulfill the eternal will of God – not to enslave Himself to the temporal needs of men, or even His own needs. Even though God came to earth in the flesh, people still died. There continued to be the poor, the sick, and the orphan, and corruption continued in people's hearts and the governments of the world. Knowing that He was going to be crucified, Jesus could have taken up the cause of abolishing the death penalty but instead, He proclaimed one message: Repent – the Kingdom of God is at hand.

Many people do many wonderful things in the name of the Lord. But not everyone "working for the Lord" is actually working with the Lord and doing His will. Some people are very "anointed" with power for miracles, prophetic gifts, or revelation for teaching. But many of these will stand before Jesus and discover that they have been working iniquity. (See Matthew 7:21-23.) Many people are running to and fro after every whim and demand of the people. Others are chasing after opportunities to build their ministry or make a name for themselves. Some people are simply eager to demonstrate their own gifts and revelation or to feel needed. But their service to others is actually self-service in disguise.

Jesus taught that we will know the real workers by the fruit they reveal in their lives. There is a difference between works and fruit. There is a difference between anointing and fruit. There is a difference between service and fruit. The question is always whether the works, anointing, and service are for God, from God, and from a sincere heart of devotion to God. Anyone running about "serving God" without actually knowing Him, being transformed by Him, and submitting themselves to His guidance is beating the air.

Along these lines, Paul noted that a runner running a race must run the race according to the rules and he gave some indication as to what those rules are for people in ministry service. In his letters to Timothy and Titus, Paul urged them not to rush into appointing people to leadership before their character had been revealed, tested, and proven. Here are some of the attributes Paul listed of those qualified for leadership service.

> *1 Timothy 3:1-13: Here is a trustworthy saying: Whoever aspires to be an overseer desires a noble task. Now the overseer is to be above reproach, faithful to his wife, temperate, self-controlled, respectable, hospitable, able to teach, not given to drunkenness, not violent but gentle, not quarrelsome, not a lover of money. He must manage his own family well and see that his children obey him, and he must do so in a manner worthy of full respect. (If anyone does not know how to manage his own family, how can he take care of God's church?) He must not be a recent convert, or he may become conceited and fall under the same judgment as the devil. He must also have a good reputation with outsiders, so that he will not fall into disgrace and into the devil's trap. In the same way, deacons are to be worthy of respect, sincere, not indulging in much wine, and not pursuing dishonest gain. They must keep hold of the deep truths of the faith with a clear conscience. They must first be tested; and then if there is nothing against them, let them serve as deacons. In the same way, the women are to be worthy of respect, not malicious talkers but temperate and trustworthy in everything. A deacon must be faithful to his wife and must manage his children and his household well. Those who have served well gain an excellent standing and great assurance in their faith in Christ Jesus.*
>
> See also, 1 Timothy 5; 2 Timothy 2; Titus 1.

Servants of God are just that – servants. Their character, nature, and motive of all work will ultimately be tested by God and revealed for how genuine it has truly been according to God's will and purposes.

> *1 Corinthians 3:11-15: For no one can lay any foundation other than the one already laid, which is Jesus Christ.* **If anyone builds on this foundation using gold, silver, costly stones, wood, hay or straw, their work will be shown for what it is**, *because the Day will bring it to light. It will be revealed with fire, and the* **fire will test the quality of each person's work**. *If what has been built survives, the builder will receive a reward. If it is burned up, the builder will suffer loss but yet will be saved--even though only as one escaping through the flames.*

The basis of all genuine ministry is Jesus Christ. Any so-called ministry built on anything else is not ordained by God. Moreover, only service to God which is fully led and empowered by the Holy Spirit will prove itself to be gold, silver, and precious stones which stand the test of fire and receive a reward. Service to God which is done out of other motives or by human strength will prove itself to be wood, hay, or straw and will have no eternal value – no matter how "good," "godly," or "in fulfillment of God's word" we may think it to be. Consider that Abraham was allowed to produce an Ishmael by his own flesh but that resulted in heartache for him. By contrast, that Jesus did not rush as the Savior-on-call when Lazarus was dying but waited several days before making His way to where Lazarus was. (See John 11.)

Jesus was at all times submitted to the will of His Father, saying only what He heard the Father saying, teaching only what the Father taught, and doing only what He saw the Father doing with the right character and motive. In everything He did, He represented and exhibited the nature of His Father. Let us grow in our submission to God and allow Him to transform our hearts and lives to be like Jesus so that we produce good fruit, walk in the good works that God has ordained for us, and ultimately receive the reward for our service.

SUITABLE FOR SERVICE - EVALUATION

"If anyone aspires to the office of overseer [leadership], he desires a noble task." 1Timothy 3:1

1 = Needs Refining				2 = In Refining Process				3 = Purified by Fire			

Criterion	1	2	3	Criterion	1	2	3
Blameless. Above reproach, impossible to charge with offense.	1	2	3	Not lover of money, not covetous, not greedy or eager for gain	1	2	3
Husband of one wife	1	2	3	Not teaching for gain	1	2	3
Sober-minded, abstaining from alcohol entirely or moderate use	1	2	3	Not recent convert, novice, newly planted, new, young, recently born	1	2	3
Self-controlled, curbing desires and impulses	1	2	3	Not double-tongued, saying different things to different people (to deceive)	1	2	3
In right mind, sane, moderate	1	2	3	No depravity, riots, excess, prodigality	1	2	3
Respectable, good behavior, modest, well arranged, orderly	1	2	3	Not insubordinate, unruly, disobedient, rebellious, unable to control	1	2	3
Hospitable, generous to guests	1	2	3	Not arrogant, self-willed, self-pleasing	1	2	3
Able to teach, skillful in teaching				Not quick tempered, prone to anger	1	2	3
Gentle, patient, moderate, fair, equitable, mild, appropriate	1	2	3	Not deceivers (religion/error), seducer, misleading others	1	2	3
Manages own household well	1	2	3	Not empty/idle talk, of senseless things	1	2	3
Children are submissive, under control, in subjection, subordinate	1	2	3	Not lazy, idle, shunning work one ought to perform, ineffective	1	2	3
Good reputation with outsiders, witness, testimony, record	1	2	3	Not quarrelsome with words, physical force, or litigation/lawsuits	1	2	3
Dignified, honest, good character	1	2	3	Not a liar, one who breaks faith	1	2	3
Lover of good, promoter of virtue	1	2	3	Not glutton, belly, living for stomach	1	2	3
Holy, devout, undefiled by evil	1	2	3	Not promoting myths, fables, clichés	1	2	3
Patient when wronged, forbearing	1	2	3	Hates a bribe	1	2	3
Full of the Holy Spirit and wisdom	1	2	3	Disciplined, robust, restraining lusts	1	2	3
Able to instruct in right doctrine, comfort, exhort to one's side	1	2	3	Able to rebuke (tell one's fault) to those who contradict	1	2	3
Rendering justice to others in manner of dealing with them	1	2	3	Trustworthy	1	2	3

Deacon: *Greek: diakonos, meaning "servant"*

Responsibilities: To tend to the physical needs among the believers. To free up the apostles and elders for their work in the ministry, and for study of the Word and prayer.

Elder: *Greek: presbuteros, meaning "aged, mature"*

Responsibilities: To pastor or shepherd God's church, meaning to feed, lead, guide, and nurture. To administrate, rule, and represent the Church. To teach and preach. To pray for the sick.

---

*Based on 1Timothy 3, 5; 2Timothy 2; Titus 1; 1Peter 5; Acts 6, 20; James 5; Exodus 18:21

Basic Training Exercise

PRAY, OBEY, WALK AWAY

Mark 1:38 NIV - Jesus replied, "Let us go somewhere else--to the nearby villages--so I can preach there also. That is why I have come."

DESCRIPTION

Serving God is a wonderful thing. It is such a joy to serve God by serving others who are in need of His various types of service, love, compassion, and help.

If we never sense the unction from the Lord to serve others, we may not be listening to the Holy Spirit. On the other hand, if we serve others beyond what God has asked of us, we will burn out.

Each of us need to keep our spiritual "gas tank" full by keeping our eyes and Jesus and spending time with Him to be refilled with His Spirit.

As such, putting Pray, Obey, Walk Away into practice is about seeking the Lord for His direction about what He wants us to do for anyone in any situation so that we can do His will: nothing more, nothing less.

CONSIDERATIONS

Has there been a time when you "blessed" someone with your mouth but did nothing to actually help them?

Have you ever served someone to the extent that you became entangled in their issues or demands until it became a hindrance to your own walk with God?

Have you ever been "burned out" from ministry? In hindsight, how did it happen?

In what ways did Jesus Pray, Obey, and Walk Away? Who did He take His directions from? Did He give people what they demanded or what they needed?

PRAYER

Father, thank you that you sent Jesus to demonstrate love and obedience. Teach me how to listen to what you want me to do for others and to willingly do it without adding to or subtracting from your guidance. In Jesus' name, Amen.

Category: Christlike Care

Basic TRAINING
SPIRITUAL EXERCISES

PURPOSE:

To love others well.

To do the good works God has prepared for us without going beyond what God ordained.

To love others without creating co-dependence or becoming their savior.

SPIRITUAL FRUIT:

Love for others.

Wisdom and discernment of what the will of the Lord is for us in various situations.

Readiness to serve God and others.

Godly boundaries for ourselves and with others.

PRACTICE

1. Ask the Lord to highlight someone to you who He wants you to serve in some way.

2. PRAY: Ask the Lord what He wants you to do for the person.
   - Resist the urge to come up with your own ideas of what they need or what you could do for them.
   - Accept if God limits your involvement to praying for them without engaging directly with them.
   - Be willing to do what God says even if He asks you to do something you do not like to do.
   - Listen to the Lord for His instructions.

3. OBEY: Do whatever the Lord told you to do for this person.
   - Do not add anything or take anything away from what God told you to do.
   - Do what God told you to do secretly if possible. If it is not possible to do it secretly, be sure to give God all the glory for giving you the idea of what they needed.
   - Resist the urge to linger on the subject once you have obeyed God.

4. WALK AWAY: Excuse yourself or move on so that their gratitude goes only to God.
   - Resist the urge to consider yourself to be "involved" in their situation.
   - Do not do anything further in the situation unless and until God tells you to do so.
   - Move on and go back to Step One. If the Lord highlights the same person to you again, do what He says. If the Lord does not highlight the same person again, do not further involve yourself.

5. Praise the Lord for helping you to care for people without going beyond His instructions. Thank Him that the works and rest He guides you in keep you filled and ready for service.

NOTES: _____

ADDITIONAL SCRIPTURES:

James 2:16

Matthew 7:12

1 John 3:17

Matthew 15:35-36

Deuteronomy 15:7

1 John 4:20

Mary/Martha
Luke 10:38-42

Category: Christlike Care

PERFECTION COURSE – UNIT 3.4 READING

Motivational Gifts of the Father

When we offer our lives in service to God, He will lead us into serving others. His desire for us to bear His image as a reflection of His divine nature so that He is glorified. He is a good Father who equips us and gifts us with everything we need to do what He has asked of us. God's spiritual gifts are not about us being gifted. They are about Him and us representing Him to others as we serve them.

The Book of Romans, Chapter 12, is all about motives. Believers are urged to offer themselves completely to the will of God in service to Him which is done from a sincere heart with the right motives.

> *Romans 12:9-21: Love must be sincere. Hate what is evil; cling to what is good. Be devoted to one another in love. Honor one another above yourselves. Never be lacking in zeal, but keep your spiritual fervor, serving the Lord. Be joyful in hope, patient in affliction, faithful in prayer. Share with the Lord's people who are in need. Practice hospitality. Bless those who persecute you; bless and do not curse. Rejoice with those who rejoice; mourn with those who mourn. Live in harmony with one another. Do not be proud, but be willing to associate with people of low position. Do not be conceited. Do not repay anyone evil for evil. Be careful to do what is right in the eyes of everyone. If it is possible, as far as it depends on you, live at peace with everyone. Do not take revenge, my dear friends, but leave room for God's wrath, for it is written: "It is mine to avenge; I will repay," says the Lord. On the contrary: "If your enemy is hungry, feed him; if he is thirsty, give him something to drink. In doing this, you will heap burning coals on his head." Do not be overcome by evil, but overcome evil with good.*

Paul lists these attributes of genuine love **after** his explanation of spiritual gifts but they serve as the evidence that we are actually functioning from God's divine nature as we flow in these gifts. In fact, the spiritual gifts listed in this chapter are called "motivational" because they pertain to the character of the one using the gifts. Each person has been given various gifts according to the grace of God to serve other members of the Body.

> *Romans 12:4-8: For just as each of us has one body with many members, and these members do **not all have the same function**, so in Christ we, though many, form one body, and each member belongs to all the others. **We have different gifts, according to the grace given** to each of us. If your gift is **prophesying**, then prophesy in accordance with your faith; if it is **serving**, then serve; if it is **teaching**, then teach; if it is to **encourage**, then give encouragement; if it is **giving**, then give generously; if it is to **lead**, do it diligently; if it is to show **mercy**, do it cheerfully.*

Not everyone has the same role and function just like the hand and the foot of a natural body do not have the same function. This said, the hand and the foot are motivated to keep the whole body and all of its parts in top functionality – in fact, their very sustenance depends on it.

Motivated by Love

These motivational gifts have been distributed by God, our Father. As He works His own nature in us, these gifts flow from the Father's heart of love and compassion for people. The Father's heart is nurturing, truthful, selfless, and willing to do all that is required to train up a child in the way they should go and nurture His nature in them. As such, let us consider what these gifts look like from a parent's heart motivated by love and nurturing development to maturity.

Prophesying: A good parent teaches us right from wrong, warns us when we are getting off track or doing something wrong, encourages us when we are doing well or need a boost of courage, and talks with us about the outcomes of our choices and the things to come in the future.

Serving: A good parent cooks our meals, dresses us, changes our dirty diapers, notices what we need as we grow through different phases of life and enter into various projects and challenges, and helps us do things that we cannot do for ourselves or need assistance with.

Teaching: A good parent teaches us our A,B,C's and right from wrong, equips us with knowledge and skills we will need to succeed, guides us into the truth, and helps us understand the important things of life for surviving and thriving in this world.

Encouraging/Exhortation: A good parent speaks the truth in love to us, admonishes us to stay on the right path, do the right things at the right time with the right people and, with a positive outlook about our potential, helps us to set goals and cheers us on to attaining them.

Giving: A good parent willingly provides the best that they can for us, notices what we need and delights to supply it for us, and will willingly spend their last dime to make sure that we have what we need without begrudging us for costing them something.

Leading: A good parent leads by example and steers the whole family in the right direction, establishes solid boundaries and a predictable rhythm of life so that we feel safe and secure, gives discipline when we step out of bounds, and delegates responsibilities among the family and expects everyone to fulfill those responsibilities. Their objective is for the household to run well and for each person to be on the path to becoming a responsible adult who is capable of ruling our own house someday.

Mercy: A good parent comforts us when we are hurting, feels our pain as if it is their own, forgives us when we make mistakes or behave badly, continues to accept and love us even if we continue to do wrong, and will do anything to help us get ourselves back on the right path. A good parent never gives up.

As God allows and enables us to flow in any of these motivational gifts, we will love the children of God as if they are our own children, pouring ourselves out to them in kindness, hope, and desire for their good. Note: This does not mean that we assume parental authority in their lives, but is more aimed at tapping into the tireless, unending stream of love flowing from the Father's heart in these various ways.

Jesus' Example

Every believer has been gifted by God for service through these motivational gifts. Personally, I believe they are part of how God designed us in the womb. Even unbelievers will demonstrate aptitude in certain areas of care for others or an ease of willingness or ability to serve in certain ways. But until we are flowing in these gifts from the unending resources of God's love, it is unsanctified and fleshly.

Typically, we will have predominant gifts which seem to be our default mode and comes more easily to us. But Jesus demonstrated that spiritual maturity includes being able to function with any of these motives depending on what the situation demands based on the person we are serving. Let's look at how Jesus functioned in these gifts.

Prophesy: At the well, Jesus perceived the truth about the woman's marital situation and spoke it plainly. He perceived that Nathanael was an honest man of integrity. Jesus discerned that Satan was speaking through Peter and rebuked him sharply. He talked to His followers about what was to come, warned them about the hazards of following Him, and informed them of the rewards of it.

Serving: Jesus had compassion on the crowd who had not eaten and stayed longer to make sure they were fed. He stayed behind to dismiss the crowd while His disciples went on to the next place. Jesus took the lowest place and was not ashamed to do dirty work – He washed the feet of His disciples.

Teaching: Jesus was always teaching. He taught in the synagogues, in the fields, on the mountains, and at the Temple. He had compassion for the people because they were like sheep without a shepherd and so, He taught them many things. He wanted them to learn the ways of God and eternal life.

Encouraging/Exhortation: The Sermon on the Mount is a gigantic exhortation to right living in the Kingdom of God. Jesus also consistently promoted and prodded His disciples towards right responses and behavior, including warning them about how to behave in situations they had not yet faced.

Giving: Jesus gave up the splendor of heaven to come to earth and be born in a manger. Jesus gave generously to the poor as part of His ministry but more significantly, He gave His life – all of Himself, holding nothing back – for the sake of our salvation.

Leading: Jesus led by example of perfect Godly character in His application of truth and mercy. He carved out a new path and called His followers to set a new course for their lives which aligned with God's purposes. He trained His disciples in the ways of God and then delegated responsibility to them, giving them clear commands and instructions for how He wanted them to carry out His commission.

Mercy: Even though Jesus knew that God had given Him the right to judge, He instead chose to show mercy. He forgave sin, healed the sick, was a friend to sinners, and took the brutal punishment He did not deserve while extending forgiveness to the ones killing Him.

As we become more like Jesus by submitting ourselves to the Holy Spirit, we will be able to function from any one of these motives at the right time and in the right way so that we constantly reflect God's image to the people we are with.

But again, God's spiritual gifts are about Him and representing Him, not about us being gifted. If we think we are gifted in some area and set out to serve others with "our" gift, we are likely to do the exact opposite of what God wants in any given situation. For example, someone wanting to exhibit "their" gift of prophecy and truth-telling might rebuke someone who really needs a touch of mercy. Or vice versa, someone who only knows how to flow in the gift of mercy might show mercy to someone who really needs a prophetic rebuke. You get the picture. The only way to be like Jesus is to do things the way that He did – which is to be totally submitted to God at all times, being led by the Holy Spirit in all situations and serving people the way God guides in the moment.

Therefore, as we flow in motivational gifts, let us all aim to bear God's image and be motivated rightly in our exercise of the gifts God has given us for His purposes and for His glory.

Genuine Love Inspection

1 = Needs improvement				2 = In Refining Process				3 = Doing Well for Now			

Genuine Love = *Based on Romans 12:9-21.*

Statement	1	2	3	Statement	1	2	3
I am sincere.	1	2	3	I rejoice with those who rejoice.	1	2	3
I hate what is evil.	1	2	3	I mourn with those who mourn.	1	2	3
I cling to what is good.	1	2	3	I live in harmony with others.	1	2	3
I am devoted to others in love.	1	2	3	I am not proud.	1	2	3
I honor others over myself.	1	2	3	I associate with the lowly.	1	2	3
I am not lacking in zeal or fervor.	1	2	3	I am not conceited.	1	2	3
I am joyful in hope.	1	2	3	I do not repay evil for evil.	1	2	3
I am patient in affliction.	1	2	3	I do what is right.	1	2	3
I am faithful in prayer.	1	2	3	I live at peace with everyone.	1	2	3
I share with the needy.	1	2	3	I do not take revenge.	1	2	3
I practice hospitality.	1	2	3	I bless my enemies.	1	2	3
I bless my persecutors.	1	2	3	I am not overcome by evil.	1	2	3
				I overcome evil with good.	1	2	3

Dear friends, let us love one another, for love comes from God.
Everyone who loves has been born of God and knows God.
1 John 4:7

Basic Training Exercise

MOTIVATION: PROPHECY

Romans 12:6 NIV - We have different gifts, according to the grace given to each of us. If your gift is prophesying, then prophesy in accordance with your faith.

MOTIVATIONAL GIFTS

The Spiritual Gifts in the book of Romans pertain to our way of doing things or our mode of conduct in our interactions with others. Each one is an expression of God's love. Jesus demonstrated that it is possible for us to function in any of these gifts as the situation calls for when we serve others. *Note: These gifts are different than those in Ephesians 4 and 1 Corinthians 12.*

DESCRIPTION

This gift of Prophecy could be summarized as, "I love you enough to tell you the truth." This gift is one of God's ways of speaking through us with His discernment and loving guidance for right and wrong, including warnings or exhortations towards the future. Jesus demonstrated this gift in the way He perceived things accurately and spoke truthfully into the lives and situations of others. He knew what people did and what they thought even if they were not speaking. He knew what people needed to do to align themselves with God and He told them. His main message was, "Repent, for the Kingdom of God is at hand."

This gift is from the heart of God and carries no desire to tear people down. Even in challenging situations or when confronting sin, this gift is motivated by helping others to see the truth in order to be restored and to advance in their life with God. We do this in proportion to how strong our faith is in the message from God.

Evidence of mature development of this gift is the ability to accurately and supernaturally discern what is happening in the lives of others and to deliver a straightforward message from the Lord which sheds light on the situation for the recipient. It will come without a hint of condemnation and be full of love.

PURPOSE:

To speak the truth of God into the lives of others.

To discern situations accurately so that we can help others align with God's will.

To represent God as His spokesperson and convey His insights or instructions to people.

SPIRITUAL FRUIT:

Speaking the truth in love.

Correct discernment of good and evil.

Compassion coupled with words of restoration and redemption.

Considerate warnings and rebukes to those who need correction.

PRAYER

Father, thank you that Jesus had perfect discernment and delivery of truth in every situation He faced. Help me to grow in this motivational gift of prophecy so that I can see correctly and help guide others in your truth. In Jesus' name, Amen.

PRACTICE

1. Ask the Holy Spirit to highlight a challenging situation in the life of someone you know.
   - Write down your view of the situation, the facts which led up to it, and where you see things going if it continues.
   - Take note of your thoughts and feelings about the situation. Are you angry, sad, frustrated, scared, etc.?

2. Now, ask the Holy Spirit to give you very clear (black & white) discernment of good & evil in this situation. Consider:
   - Who is this person? Where are they coming from? Why?
   - Is this a result of sin/obedience; unbelief/faithfulness; arrogance/ignorance/wrong beliefs; unfortunate events?
   - What does God's Word say regarding His will about this?

3. Take a moment to remember that Jesus died for this person to be forgiven and free by grace through faith. Then:
   - Ask God to give you His heart for them and His insights into the situation. (Notice how this may be different than your own thoughts and feelings about it.)
   - Ask God to tell you what is needed for alignment with His will. This could include things like repentance, faith, patience, endurance, or specific actions/instructions, etc.
   - Ask Him about the outcome He foresees, desires for them, or promises in His Word. (Use Scripture wisely.)

4. Share the insights from God with the person directly. Do this according to the faith you have that you have heard God.
   - If your faith in the message is not strong, cushion your delivery with, "I sense that the Lord *might be* saying..."
   - If you have strong faith for prophesying, deliver it gently but clearly with boldness but without condemnation.

NOTES: _____

ADDITIONAL SCRIPTURES:

Woman at Well, John 4:4-26

Nathanael, John 1:47-51

Luke 5:22

Matthew 23

Hebrews 5:14

John 8:44-45

Luke 11:17-19

2 Timothy 4:1-4

Luke 3:3-20

Amos 7:14-16

Ezekiel 2:1-10

112

Basic Training Exercise

MOTIVATION: SERVING

Romans 12:6-7 NIV - We have different gifts, according to the grace given to each of us ... If it is serving, then serve.

MOTIVATIONAL GIFTS

The Spiritual Gifts in the book of Romans pertain to our way of doing things or our mode of conduct in our interactions with others. Each one is an expression of God's love. Jesus demonstrated that it is possible for us to function in any of these gifts as the situation calls for when we serve others. Note: These gifts are different than those in Ephesians 4 and 1 Corinthians 12.

DESCRIPTION

This gift of Serving could be summarized as, "I love you enough to help you and take care of your needs." God loves through us by helping us to notice the needs of others and help them through serving them.

Jesus made it abundantly clear that He came to serve not to be served. Our humble king washed the filthy feet of His disciples. He noticed the hunger of the people who had come to hear Him speak and made sure their bellies were full before going home. He told a parable about sheep and goats that those who serve the least are the ones who reflect His heart.

The word used to describe this gift of serving is the same word for Deacon which literally means waiter. Functioning in this gift (whether serving food or not) is like being a waiter in a restaurant. A waiter notices and serves basic needs, remembers special requests, is willing to go the extra mile to make the experience pleasant, and has stamina for completing the task. However, like Jesus, our true service is for God. He was never enslaved to the demands of men.

Evidence of mature development of this gift is the ability to notice the needs of others and meet them according to God's will and purposes. It will come without a hint of self-aggrandizing or subjugation and will be full of willingness, compassion, and love.

PURPOSE:

To notice the needs of others and help them according to God's will.

To humbly serve others rather than looking to be served.

SPIRITUAL FRUIT:

Speaking the truth in love.

Correct discernment of good and evil.

Compassion coupled with words of restoration and redemption.

Considerate warnings and rebukes to those who need correction.

PRAYER

Father, thank you that Jesus came not to be served but to serve. Help me to grow in this motivational gift of serving so that I can notice and attend to the needs of your people with your grace. In Jesus' name, Amen.

CONSIDERATIONS

Do you typically like to serve or be served? Why?

Is it challenging for you to notice the needs of others? Or to serve the needs of others? How so?

PRACTICE

1. Ask the Holy Spirit to highlight one person in your life to practice serving. If you are married, choose your spouse.

2. Each day for one week, take note of their needs such as:
   - Are they struggling to accomplish something?
   - Do they have any projects that are delayed due to inability to make time or need of assistance?
   - What chores do they have that need to be done?
   - What errands do they need to do? ...Etc. etc.

3. After one week of noticing, present your findings to Jesus.
   - Ask God to highlight the one thing that you can do to serve this person which would mean the most to them.
   - If you are capable of doing this thing, ask God to show you how He wants you to do it for them.
   - If you are not capable of doing this thing, ask God to help you make arrangements for it to be done or ask God to highlight something else from your list.
   - Ask God to give you a willing heart which desires to serve.

4. Do what God has shown you to do to serve this person.
   - Serve them with a willing heart, not a grudging one.
   - If possible, do it quietly without announcing it to them.
   - Do it without expecting anything in return, just to serve.
   - When they thank you, give God all the glory for it!

ADDITIONAL SCRIPTURES:

Washing Feet:
John 13:1-17

Feeding Hungry:
Matthew 15:32

Deacons:
Acts 6:1-6

Matthew 20:28

Mark 10:45

Philippians 2:7

Luke 10:38-42

NOTES: _____

www.manifestinternational.com

UNIT THREE – KEY QUESTIONS
Divine Nature

Use this worksheet to test your grasp of the material and exercises of Unit Three.

How do believers participate with God's divine nature? (in your own words)	

WHY and HOW do we render our hearts to God?	Whose responsibility is it to crucify our flesh?

How is spiritual fruit produced?	Why is mercy an important reflection of God's nature?

What is the difference between fruit and works?	What is the motivation of spiritual gifts?

What is one thing you learned that you did not know before?	What questions do you still have about this subject?

UNIT THREE: GROUP EXERCISES

Option One:
Share with one another what you discovered through the Motive Inspection & Forgiveness Inspection. Pray for one another to become more like Christ and a reflection of God's divine nature.

AND/OR

Option Two:
Put the Motivational Gift Exercises for Prophecy and Serving into practice in a group setting.

Unit Four:
Skilled in Righteousness

Key Scripture Verse for Unit Four
Anyone who lives on milk, being still an infant, is not acquainted with the teaching about righteousness. But solid food is for the mature, who by constant use have trained themselves to distinguish good from evil. - Hebrews 5:13-14

Class 1: It Is Finished
1 Reading, 1 Worksheet
By grace through faith in Jesus, we receive His perfect record of righteousness. We can stand before God free of guilt, shame, and accusation, ready to receive all of His blessings!

Class 2: Established in Righteousness
1 Reading, 1 Evaluation, 1 Exercise
Those who have the faith of Abraham are established in righteousness through their faith in Christ.

Class 3: Rest for Your Soul & Unbelief
1 Reading, 2 Exercises
We receive salvation and all of its benefits by grace through faith. Either Jesus finished it or we have to. Our only job now it to receive God's grace freely by faith and resist all forms of unbelief.

Class 4: Established Together
1 Reading, 1 Evaluation, 1 Exercise
We are called to help one another stay strong in the Lord and firm in His purposes for our lives. The Church will only fulfill God's purpose when we stand in Christ together.

Key Questions

Group Exercises

PERFECTION COURSE – UNIT 4.1 READING

It is Finished

Through the offering of His body, Jesus made a way for everyone who believes in Him to be righteous before God. Before taking His final breath, Jesus cried out, "IT IS FINISHED!" At that very same moment, the veil in the Temple was torn from top to bottom - meaning that access to God, His presence, and His blessings have been made available to us. Jesus' sacrifice and the shedding of His blood have reconciled us to God so that in God's sight, we have been justified, made holy, and are without blemish. We can have an absolutely clear conscience from sin.

> *Colossians 1:19-22: For God was pleased to have all his fullness dwell in him, and through him to reconcile to himself all things, whether things on earth or things in heaven,* **by making peace through his blood, shed on the cross**. *Once you were alienated from God and were enemies in your minds because of your evil behavior.* **But now he has reconciled you by Christ's physical body through death to present you holy in his sight, without blemish and free from accusation.**

> *Hebrews 10:19-22: Therefore, brothers and sisters, since we have confidence to* **enter the Most Holy Place by the blood of Jesus, by a new and living way opened for us through the curtain, that is, his body**, *and since we have a great priest over the house of God, let us* **draw near to God with a sincere heart and with the full assurance that faith brings**, *having our* **hearts sprinkled to cleanse us from a guilty conscience** *and having our bodies washed with pure water.*

The writer of Hebrews said that the spiritually immature are unskilled in the word of righteousness. I believe it is, therefore, safe to assume that the mature ARE skilled in it. Are you? Here is a refresher for you of what Jesus did for us to establish us in righteousness by faith.

Acts of Sin Forgiven

Under God's Old Covenant regulations, only one man, the High Priest, was allowed to enter into His presence behind the veil in the Temple, and this was only once per year on the Day of Atonement after specific blood sacrifices of bulls, sheep, and goats had been offered. (See Leviticus 16; Deuteronomy 12.) Anyone else who attempted to enter into God's presence at any other time instantly dropped dead. Needless to say, even the one man who was allowed to go behind the veil at the appointed time did so with fear that he might not make it out alive.

The standard of God for entering into His presence is purity and holiness. No one has been able to attain this level of purity and holiness because when we sin, err, or make mistakes, intentionally or unintentionally, our sins create a blemish on our record and a debt which must be paid. None of us are perfect.

Therefore, the only way to attain this is through the shedding of blood of an unblemished sacrifice of atonement. (See Leviticus 17:11.) Moreover, the sacrifice must be equal in worth to the cost of the error according to God's value system in order to reconcile accounts and pay the debt in full.

Jesus lived His life without sin. Therefore, He had no need to offer a blood sacrifice to atone for His sins and maintained connection with God at all times. Additionally, His own blood and body qualified as an unblemished sacrifice of atonement for the sins of all mankind. Knowing this, even though He was the Son of God, totally innocent, and could have stopped His trial, beating, and crucifixion at any moment, Jesus willingly laid His life down in order to fulfill God's eternal plan of redemption.

> *Isaiah 53:4-7, 10: Surely he took up our pain and bore our suffering, yet we considered him punished by God, stricken by him, and afflicted.* **But he was pierced for our transgressions, he was crushed for our iniquities; the punishment that brought us peace was on him, and by his wounds we are healed. We all, like sheep, have gone astray, each of us has turned to our own way; and the LORD has laid on him the iniquity of us all.** *He was oppressed and afflicted, yet he did not open his mouth; he was led like a lamb to the slaughter, and as a sheep before its shearers is silent, so he did not open his mouth. ... Yet it was the LORD's will to crush him and cause him to suffer, and* **though the LORD makes his life an offering for sin**, *he will see his offspring and prolong his days, and the will of the LORD will prosper in his hand.*

This willing and obedient sacrifice of His beloved Son has infinite value in God's sight, more than millions upon millions of offerings of lambs, goats, bulls, birds, grain, oil, new wine, and all the silver and gold in the world. This means that through the shed blood of Jesus, our sins have been paid for in full. We are completely forgiven, without blemish, continually clean, and purified from all sin. We have perpetual right standing with God as if we had never sinned and have been made holy and perfect in God's sight. Our right standing with Him no longer has anything to do with our own performance or measuring up to His standard because it is now completely secure through our faith in Jesus' blood that was shed for us.

> *Ephesians 1:7: In him* **we have redemption through his blood, the forgiveness of sins**, *in accordance with the riches of God's grace.*

> *1 John 1:7: But if we walk in the light, as he is in the light, we have fellowship with one another, and* **the blood of Jesus, his Son, purifies us from all sin**.

Redeemed from the Curse, Sinful Nature, & Personal Attributes

Through His death, Jesus allowed all punishment for sin and every accusation against all of mankind to be unleashed upon Himself. The curse of the Law from the Old Covenant outlines God's schedule of retribution for all forms of disobedience and these penalties include all forms of sickness and demonic oppression, death, and exile from God's presence. (For the curse of the Law, read through Deuteronomy 28 and Leviticus 26.)

What this means is that at the cross, the record of charges against us for everything that we have done or not done or will ever do to deserve God's punishment was brought before God. God's wrath and vengeance were poured out upon Jesus. At the same time, while Jesus was on the cross, we were being crucified with Him. When He died, we died with Him. Every descendant of Adam was included in Christ's crucifixion.

> *Galatians 2:20-:* **I have been crucified with Christ** *and I no longer live, but Christ lives in me. The life I now live in the body, I live by faith in the Son of God, who loved me and gave himself for me.*

> *2 Corinthians 5:14: For Christ's love compels us, because we are convinced that* **one died for all, and therefore all died**. *(See also John 12:32.)*

Jesus died and was fully confirmed as dead before they took Him down from the cross and buried Him. Needless to say, the death penalty is the ultimate punishment. But consider carefully that the death penalty also brings to an end the possibility of the offender being able to commit further offenses. Not to mention that in any righteous court, there is no double jeopardy. This means that we cannot be tried again and condemned for crimes that have already been justly punished. Accordingly, because the death penalty has already been satisfied in full, we have no further possibility of warranting God's punishment. This also means that the curse of the Law is rendered void against us.

> *Galatians 3:13:* Christ **redeemed us from the curse of the law** by becoming a curse for us, for it is written: "Cursed is everyone who is hung on a pole."
>
> *Colossians 2:14-15:* Having **canceled the charge of our legal indebtedness, which stood against us and condemned** us; he has taken it away, nailing it to the cross. And having disarmed the powers and authorities, he made a public spectacle of them, triumphing over them by the cross.

When Jesus died and was buried, we died and were buried. Through this, God removed every hindrance of our humanity and nullified every genetic and generational limitation. Nothing about our race, gender, family history, nationality, or personality has any impact on God's love for us because the nature that we inherited from our first ancestor Adam is as good as dead in God's sight. Even our circumstances and our personal advantages or disadvantages have no influence on God's plan for us or blessings towards us. Think of it this way. Dead people don't have anything going for them and they are far too dead to be disadvantaged by anything. In Christ's death, we are dead.

> *Romans 6:3-7:* Or don't you know that **all of us who were baptized into Christ Jesus were baptized into his death? We were therefore buried with him through baptism into death** in order that, just as Christ was raised from the dead through the glory of the Father, we too may live a new life. For if we have been **united with him in a death like his**, we will certainly also be united with him in a resurrection like his. For we know that **our old self was crucified with him so that the body ruled by sin might be done away with**, that we should no longer be slaves to sin—because anyone who has died has been set free from sin.
>
> *Colossians 3:3:* For **you died**, and your life is now hidden with Christ in God.
>
> *Galatians 6:14:* **May I never boast except in the cross of our Lord Jesus Christ**, through which **the world has been crucified to me, and I to the world**.

Being dead and buried with Christ is exactly what we have going for us! There is no longer anything from our human nature that can hinder us from receiving God's love and blessings. Hallelujah!

Transferred to the Kingdom of Light

In Jesus' death and burial, it truly seemed that death and the grave had triumphed as the Son of God descended into the place prepared for the devil and his angels. But on the third day, God resurrected His beloved Son, Jesus Christ, out of the grave in an imperishable body. Jesus was begotten again (or born again) by God and was delivered out of the domain of the evil one. The power of sin, the curse, death, the devil, and the powers of darkness were overcome and neutralized by the resurrection power of God. The gates of Hell did not prevail against the Son of God in His death, and everyone who believes Him was with Him. (See Matthew 16:18.)

When Jesus was raised from the dead, we were raised with Him. God created a New Covenant people for Himself. This means that the devil and all of his workers have no right to harm us because powers of darkness have no authority over our lives as children of the light. We never have to fear death (or anything else) again because we have been given everlasting life.

> *Colossians 1:13-14:* For he has **rescued us from the dominion of darkness and brought us into the kingdom of the Son he loves**, in whom we have redemption, the forgiveness of sins.
>
> *John 5:24:* Very truly I tell you, whoever hears my word and believes him who sent me has eternal life and will not be judged but **has crossed over from death to life**.
>
> *Hebrews 2:14-15:* Since the children have flesh and blood, He too shared in their humanity so that **by His death He might break the power of him who holds the power of death—that is, the devil**—and free those who all their lives were held in slavery by their fear of death.

As if that is not enough, when Christ ascended to heaven after forty days of resurrection appearances, we also ascended with Him. Consequently, we are seated in Christ at the right hand of God.

> *Ephesians 2:4-6: But because of his great love for us, God, who is rich in mercy,* **made us alive with Christ** *even when we were dead in transgressions—it is by grace you have been saved. And* **God raised us up with Christ and seated us with him in the heavenly realms in Christ Jesus.**

Yes, even while we are here in the imperfections of our flesh and the brokenness of this dark world, we are truly and totally accepted by God as righteous and unblemished. We live in the throne room of heaven. Hallelujah!

A New Creation in Christ

Through His life, death, burial, resurrection, and ascension, the Old Covenant has been fulfilled, and the New Covenant has been established. God created a whole new people group, a new type of humanity for Himself to be His New Covenant people.

> *2 Corinthians 5:17: Therefore, if anyone is in Christ,* **the new creation has come: The old has gone, the new is here!**

After Jesus ascended to heaven, He poured out the Holy Spirit into the hearts of all who believe in Him. The Holy Spirit gives us the power and ability to live as children of God and as a totally new creation in Christ. We who believe the Gospel are a heavenly people in earthly tents of flesh and a resurrected people in un-resurrected bodies. We have been reborn as children of God so that we can live the way that Jesus lived when He was on the earth in the flesh. We can literally do the things that He did in the way that He did them by the power of God as the Holy Spirit guides and empowers us.

Through His righteousness, Jesus made righteousness available to anyone who believes Him. Through our faith in Jesus, that Jesus is the Son of God and that God raised Him from the dead, we are established in righteousness.

ESTABLISHED IN RIGHTEOUSNESS

In righteousness you will

	OLD SELF		CRUCIFIED WI...
Old Man	**Examples**		**Selection of Scriptures**
Nature of Sin Descended from Adam	Anything that you were born with or into. Race, gender, genes, height, age... Generational curses, family patterns of behavior... Heritage, nationality, region, tribe... Sensual mind, depravity, futile thinking, vanity, hardness of heart, selfishness, narcissism...		Galatians 2:20 - I have been crucified with Christ and I no longer live, but Christ lives in me. The life I now live in the body, I live by faith in the Son of God, who loved me and gave himself for me. Romans 6:6 - For we know that our old self was crucified with him so that the body ruled by sin might be done away with, that we should no longer be slaves to sin
Acts of Sin Trespasses Iniquities	Anything done by you, including your inner motives. Lying, cheating, moral failures, errors, accidents, behavioral patterns, bad habits, addictions... Sexual immorality, adultery, fornication, impurity, lust... Acts of wickedness, evil, murder, deception... Evil desires, pride, competition, selfish ambition, slander, covetousness, obscene talk, hatred, anger, the way you have treated others ...		Colossians 1:21-22 - Once you were alienated from God and were enemies in your minds because of your evil behavior. But now he has reconciled you by Christ's physical body through death to present you holy in his sight, without blemish and free from accusation. Ephesians 1:7 - In him we have redemption through his blood, the forgiveness of sins, in accordance with the riches of God's grace
Curse of the Law Afflictions Oppressions	Any limitation on your ability to receive blessing. Lack, defeat, missed opportunities, inability to advance, lack of joy, hopelessness, heaviness, self-loathing... Sickness, disease, physical limitations, weakness, mental torment, miscarriages, stillbirths, barrenness... Subjugation to others, broken relationships, oppression...		Galatians 3:13 - Christ redeemed us from the curse of the law by becoming a curse for us, for it is written: "Cursed is everyone who is hung on a pole." Ephesians 1:3 - Praise be to the God and Father of our Lord Jesus Christ, who has blessed us in the heavenly realms with every spiritual blessing in Christ.
Kingdom of Darkness False Spirituality Religion	Any involvement you have had with works of the devil. All forms of non-Christian spirituality, including occult involvement, divination, consulting the dead, idol worship, astrology, horoscopes, freemasonry, karma, fortunes told to you or about you, curses spoken to you or about you, spells cast, witchcraft, unwise vows... Any form of erroneous Christian religious activity, trying to attain righteousness through good works, piety, asceticism, ordinances or traditions of man, legalism, false humility, self-righteousness... Principles of nature, ways of this world, philosophy...		Colossians 1:13 - For he has rescued us from the dominion of darkness and brought us into the kingdom of the Son he loves. Colossians 2:23 - Such regulations indeed have an appearance of wisdom, with their self-imposed worship, their false humility and their harsh treatment of the body, but they lack any value in restraining sensual indulgence. Colossians 2:8 - See to it that no one takes you captive through hollow and deceptive philosophy, which depends on human tradition and the elemental spiritual forces of this world rather than on Christ.
Personal Attributes Advantages Disadvantages	Anything you regard as an advantage or disadvantage. Skills, birthrights, status, location, wealth/poverty, marriage/singleness/divorce, what you or your people are known for... Successes/failures, experiences, education level, physical abilities/limitations, looks/appearance... The way you were raised, the way others have treated you, the lifestyle you are accustomed to...		1 Corinthians 1:27-29 - But God chose the foolish things... God chose the weak things... God chose the lowly things of this world and the despised things-and the things that are not-to nullify the things that are, so that no one may boast before him. Galatians 6:14 - May I never boast except in the cross of our Lord Jesus Christ, through which the world has been crucified to me, and I to the world.

The old has gone, the new is here! – 2 Corinthians 5:17

*Worksheet on page 120.

...be established... far from oppression... fear... tyranny... terror... – Isaiah 54:14

TH CHRIST	ESTABLISHED IN RIGHTEOUSNESS
Reckon Your Old Self Dead	**New Creation Life by Grace through Faith**
Surrender all your desires to God as if you are dead. Crucify your need to be right, to fit in with the crowd, to be recognized, or to be accepted. Surrender your ways of doing thing and "the way that we have always done it." Stop regarding anything about yourself or your life as a limitation on God's ability to use you.	*By faith, I believe that:* I was crucified and died with Jesus. My old nature is dead. The desires of my flesh, body, and its members are dead. I have been raised to new life with Jesus. I am a new creation in Christ.
Receive forgiveness as a free gift because of the blood of Jesus. Believe that the record of your errors, faults, failures, and the required divine punishment for them have been canceled at the cross. Regard guilt, shame, fear, and remembrance of sin as an attack of the enemy. You are forgiven. Stop defending yourself. Let God defend you.	*By the blood of Jesus:* My sins are forgiven, as if I had never sinned. Guilt, shame, and fear of punishment for my sins, past, present, and future have no place in me. In Christ's righteousness I am holy, spotless, and blameless in God's sight. There is no justifiable accusation against me.
Recognize areas of oppression, affliction, or subjugation in your life. Believe that God paid for those areas to be blessed through the blood of Jesus. By grace through faith, receive the blessing of your full inheritance in Christ.	*In the name of Jesus:* The curse of the Law is broken off of my life. All oppression, torment, and scorn must cease. Curses from my family lineage are null and void without right to oppress me or to restrict God's blessings in my life.
Renounce forever any and all involvement with all forms of false spirituality and works of darkness. Believe that the blood of Jesus atones for your sin and protects you from works of darkness and all of its effects and ramifications. Renounce religious legalism. Stop doing anything from a motive of earning favor with God. Believe that Jesus fulfilled the requirements of God for you. Stop believing that the ways of this world, natural principles, or philosophy dictate the path of your life. Regard guilt, shame, condemnation, and fear as an attack of the enemy.	*In the power and authority of the name of Jesus:* I command Satan to leave me now. I declare that any and all attachment to false spirituality is null and void in my life, including fortunes told about me, divination, false prophecies; spells cast, curses spoken against me; and unwise vows that I have made. I believe that my right standing with God is based on what Jesus did for me, not on my personal piety. I receive God's righteousness as a free gift. I place my faith is in God's wisdom and power, not man's wisdom or any other spiritual forces.
Stop placing confidence in anything that you have regarded as a personal advantage. Deny yourself and your own strength. Trust God. Stop believing that anything you have regarded as a disadvantage in your life has any power to prevent God from blessing you or using you. Trust God. Start believing God makes the way for you according to His plans for you because of the work of Jesus.	*By grace through faith, I believe that:* I am crucified to this world, common sense, and the knowledge of good and evil. I am crucified to pride in my accomplishments. I am not the product of my past but the product of the perfect obedience of Christ. My record of success or failure has no impact on God's ability to bless me and use me for His Kingdom.

NEW CREATION LIFE

www.manifestinternational.com

RIGHTEOUSNESS WORKSHEET
Accompanies Established in Righteousness Chart

Isaiah 54:9, 14-15: "To me this is like the days of Noah, when I swore that the waters of Noah would never again cover the earth. So now I have sworn not to be angry with you, never to rebuke you again. ... ***In righteousness you will be established****: Tyranny will be far from you; you will have nothing to fear. Terror will be far removed; it will not come near you. If anyone does attack you, it will not be my doing; whoever attacks you will surrender to you.*

1. In your life right now, what is your biggest area of struggle? Consider the following:
    a. Are there unchangeable aspects of who you are that you feel are holding you back?
    b. Are there areas in your life or your past where you still feel guilt, shame, or remorse?
    c. Are there areas where you feel stunted or cannot seem to break through to blessing?
    d. Are there patterns or cycles of disease, oppression, loss/accident/calamity, or demonic oppression?
    e. Are there ways you feel your own abilities or profile qualify or disqualify you for serving God?

2. **From Column One: Old Man**, which category does this struggle fit into? This category is your **Target Area** for today. (You can repeat this exercise for all Target Areas one at a time as the Lord leads.)

3. **Use Column Two: Examples**, to identify ways in which you feel oppressed or blocked from God's blessing

4. **Use Column Three: Selection of Scriptures**, to find Scriptures in your Target Area which speak to Christ's forgiveness, redemption, or nullification of this issue.
    a. Slowly read and speak these Scriptures out loud three times.
    b. What do these Scriptures say about what Jesus did for you?
    c. If these Scriptures are true (which they are) how does this impact your life?
    d. How do you know now that God is not holding you back in this area?

5. **Use Column Four: Reckon Your Old Self Dead**, to repent of wrong beliefs in your Target Area.
    a. Follow the instructions in the column in the way that the Lord guides you. For example, through prayer, journaling, confession, worship, acts of faith, etc.

6. Now that your old self is dead in Christ, how does this give you a fresh start and a clean slate?
    a. How does this change how you view yourself and God's ability to bless you and use you for His Kingdom?
    b. How does this change who you can be or who you want to be for God?
    c. How is God asking you to walk in freedom from sin, the curse, flesh, and darkness?
    d. How will you continue to walk in faith rather than slipping back into old patterns?

7. **Use Column Five: New Creation Life by Grace through Faith**, to declare the truth of God into your life and command the enemy's schemes of oppression off/out of your life.
    a. Speak the declarations in your Target Area out loud. Repeat them until you believe them in your heart.

8. Praise God for what He has done for you. Jesus is King!

9. **BONUS**: Skilled in Righteousness.
    a. Use this Righteousness Chart and Worksheet as a guide for ministering the truth of Christ's freedom and deliverance to others.

PERFECTION COURSE – UNIT 4.2 READING

Established in Righteousness

In the days when religious leaders were abusing and misleading the people of God, Jeremiah prophesied about the Messiah to come. God promised to raise up a King who would execute God's righteousness and would therefore BE the righteousness of the people and for the people.

> *Jeremiah 23:5-6 ESV: Behold, the days are coming, declares the LORD, when I will raise up for David a righteous Branch, and he shall reign as king and deal wisely, and shall execute justice and righteousness in the land. In his days Judah will be saved, and Israel will dwell securely. And this is the name by which he will be called:* **'The LORD is our righteousness.'**

When Isaiah prophesied about the work of God for His people, He referenced the days of Noah. In Noah's day, the vile wickedness of mankind was washed away in the flood and humanity received a fresh start. God swore He would never again judge the earth by flood. This is symbolic of what happens in our lives when we put our trust in Jesus. Our sinfulness and our pasts are washed away by the blood of Jesus and we receive a fresh start with God. God swears He has established us in righteousness and is no longer angry.

> *Isaiah 54:4, 9, 14-15: Do not be afraid; you will not be put to shame. Do not fear disgrace; you will not be humiliated.* **You will forget the shame of your youth and remember no more the reproach** *of your widowhood. ...* **To me this is like the days of Noah, when I swore that the waters of Noah would never again cover the earth.** *So now* **I have sworn not to be angry with you, never to rebuke you again. ... In righteousness you will be established:** *Tyranny will be far from you; you will have nothing to fear. Terror will be far removed; it will not come near you.* **If anyone does attack you, it will not be my doing;** *whoever attacks you will surrender to you.*

This righteousness is only available through faith in Jesus Christ who shed His blood to wash our sins away. When we believe that Jesus is Lord and that God raised Him from the dead, we are established in the righteousness of Christ with a perfect record before God.

The Faith of Abraham

Trust in God's victory over death is the type of faith that God has required since the beginning of His redemptive work of salvation through Abraham. Abraham's faith was credited to him as righteousness. Even though he was an imperfect man with the rebellious nature of Adam just like me and you, Abraham had right standing with God because of his faith. But God tested Abraham's faith by requesting that Abraham offer up his one and only son, Isaac, the very son through whom all the promises that God had made to Abraham were going to be fulfilled. Abraham willingly offered Isaac on the altar of sacrifice because he believed that God was able to raise the dead and that God would be faithful to fulfill every promise that He had made, regardless of how bizarre it seemed from a worldly point of view.

> *Hebrews 11:17-19:* **By faith Abraham**, *when God tested him,* **offered Isaac as a sacrifice**. *He who had embraced the promises was about to* **sacrifice his one and only son**, *even though God had said to him, "It is through Isaac that your offspring will be reckoned."* **Abraham reasoned that God could even raise the dead, and so in a manner of speaking he did receive Isaac back from death.** *(Referring to Genesis 22:1-18.)*

When we believe that God has raised Jesus from the dead, we exhibit the faith of Abraham. This is why Abraham is called the father of the faithful and we are his spiritual offspring.

This said, the author and perfecter of our faith is Jesus. Leading us all by His example, Jesus was a man in a flesh like ours who entrusted Himself into the hands of His heavenly Father. With faith even greater than Abraham's, Jesus believed that God would raise Him from the dead and would fulfill every promise of His eternal inheritance. Jesus believed that God would not abandon Him in death and that His reward would be an eternal inheritance.

> *Hebrews 12:1-2: Therefore, since we are surrounded by such a great cloud of witnesses, let us throw off everything that hinders and the sin that so easily entangles. And let us run with perseverance the race marked out for us,* **fixing our eyes on Jesus,** <u>**the pioneer**</u> **[the one who sets the example and leads the way] and perfecter of faith.** *For the joy set before him he endured the cross, scorning its shame, and sat down at the right hand of the throne of God.*

Abraham's faith was credited to Him as righteousness when He first believed God. But his faith was put to the test when confronted with death. It was the test of his faith in God's power over death which proved the genuineness of his faith and assured the fulfillment of all of God's promises to Him. Jesus had perfect faith from birth. But it was the confrontation with the cross that proved that He truly believed God. For us, our faith is credited as righteousness when we first believe Jesus. But this faith will be put to the test through trials and persecutions of all kinds. Will our faith stand the test?

No Knowledge of Good and Evil

In the historical account of Israel, when Moses sent spies into the Promised Land, ten out of the twelve spies did not believe that God was able to conquer their enemies and give them the land. The community of Israel believed the ten spies, even though they had seen God deliver them from Egypt and walk them through the Red Sea. Therefore, God informed them that the entire generation that did not believe would be unable to inherit the Promised Land. (See Numbers 13-14.)

When the census was taken to determine who would and would not receive the promised inheritance, only those under twenty years old who had no knowledge of good and evil were qualified. When the Israelites presumed to try to obtain the promise in their own strength without honoring God's word or requirement of faith, they were humiliated and chased out by their enemies as if chased by a swarm of bees. (See Deuteronomy 1:19-46.)

For us, because of Jesus' life, death, and resurrection, God's requirements for receiving His blessings have been fulfilled. Consequently, we are no longer judged to be blessed or cursed according to the standard of the Old Covenant but according to the terms of the New Covenant, which is by faith. (See Hebrews 7:12; Romans 8:1-2.) There is no condemnation for us or for our sins and it is no longer sin which causes us to fall out of God's good graces – lack of faith in Christ's righteousness is.

As such, anyone desiring to be justified and receive blessing from God through any form of legalism (which is the knowledge of good and evil) is required to keep the whole Law perfectly, something which no one in history except Jesus has ever been able to do.

> *Galatians 5:3-4: Again I declare to every man who lets himself be circumcised that he is obligated to obey the whole law.* **You who are trying to be justified by the law** *have been alienated from Christ; you* **have fallen away from grace.**

> *James 2:10: For whoever keeps the whole law and yet* **stumbles at just one point is guilty of breaking all of it.**

All of this is to say that sin is no longer the issue of our righteousness - faith is! By faith, we have the righteousness of Jesus as a free gift and, therefore, we have access to God and all of His blessings that otherwise would never be available to us.

> *Romans 3:22-24:* This **righteousness is given through faith in Jesus Christ to all who believe**. There is no difference between Jew and Gentile, for all have sinned and fall short of the glory of God, and **all are justified freely by his grace** through the redemption that came by Christ Jesus.
>
> *Romans 5:1-2:* Therefore, since we have been **justified through faith**, we have peace with God through our Lord Jesus Christ, through whom we have **gained access by faith into this grace** in which we now stand. And we boast in the hope of the glory of God.

For us to think we can attain God's promises in our own striving and strength instead of simple faith in Jesus means that we have shifted our attention to the knowledge of good and evil rather than faith in Jesus' sacrifice. If this is the case, then the evil one has deceived us into religion, legalism, and performance-based spirituality, which is essentially the same thing the serpent did when he persuaded Adam and Eve to eat from the forbidden tree when they already had everything they needed from God. What God desires for us is to be like little children who have no knowledge of good and evil as it pertains to our right standing with Him so that we can freely receive all that Jesus died for to share with us.

> *Matthew 18:3:* And he said: "Truly I tell you, unless you change and **become like little children**, you will never enter the kingdom of heaven."
>
> *Mark 10:15:* Truly I tell you, anyone who will not receive the kingdom of God **like a little child** will never enter it.

According to Your Faith

At one point during Jesus' ministry, two blind men followed Him crying out to Him for mercy. He stopped and asked if they believed He was able to heal them. When they affirmed their belief, Jesus said, "According to your faith, let it be done to you." (See Matthew 9:27-29.) Their sight was completely restored. On another occasion, a Centurion came to Jesus on behalf of his dying servant and Jesus said, "Let it be done just as you have believed." His servant was totally healed. (See Matthew 8:13)

We receive from God what we truly believe Jesus has done for us. If we believe God is our Provider, then we experience His supernatural provision according to our faith. If we believe God is our Deliverer, then we experience God's unexplainable hand of deliverance in our lives according to our faith. If we believe God is our Healer, then we receive miraculous healing from Him according to our faith. If we partially believe God, or believe God for some things and not others, then we partially receive from God just as we have believed.

When Jesus chastised His disciples for being of little faith, the word He used does not actually mean small or tiny in the same way that we interpret little. It means not trusting enough or not having enough confidence. It was not that Jesus' disciples did not trust Him at all—of course they did! They had dropped everything in their lives to follow the man they believed to be the Messiah. They had seen Him work countless miracles right in front of them, and they had even worked miracles in His name. It was only in certain scenarios that they did not trust Him or believe in His love enough to attain results.

It is safe to admit to having little faith. There is no condemnation for those who are in Christ Jesus, and that includes no condemnation for little faith. Condemning little faith is completely unhelpful and can do serious damage to the faith that does exist - like crushing a seedling before it has time to sprout.

Moreover, God does not require great or gigantic faith. He is looking for pure faith. Jesus said that faith as small as a mustard seed can move a mountain. But, this mustard seed is not a hybrid mix with other garden plants. Our faith cannot be in Jesus plus anything else—just Jesus. Pure faith is simple trust in God and trust in God's nature. God is love. His love demolishes all of our fears of condemnation and punishment. His love removed every obstacle that stands in the way of us receiving every blessing from Him. His love pours out endless streams of mercy and compassion. His love heals us in our hearts, our souls, and our bodies.

Because of what Jesus did for us, sin, the curse of the Law, and the devil are no longer the problem. Fear and unbelief are the problems. Fear and unbelief lead us to do things that spring from the knowledge of good and evil, but these things have no weight before the throne of God. God is not moved by begging, groveling, false attempts at humility and self-deprecation, or grandiose gestures of piety and faithfulness. He is not moved by our promises to be good, to serve Him, or to give to His Kingdom as if He needed anything from us or as if the work of Jesus is incomplete in any way. If we really meant these things, we would already be doing them. If we think God will be moved with compassion for our situation if we pray the right prayer, have the right person pray, or have a lot of people praying the same thing, then we have completely missed the point of what Jesus did for us. God is not the one who needs to move. God moved two thousand years ago when He gave His Son as an all-sufficient sacrifice for everything we will ever need for every trial we will ever face between now and when we go to heaven. God did a perfect work. Jesus said, "It is finished." The Holy Spirit's job is to teach us and remind us of this as our present truth. We need to simply trust God, move ourselves out of His way, and receive all that is His will for us.

We do not have to chase after the Kingdom or the power of God or every new wind of teaching that passes through the Church. In fact, doing so only reveals our immaturity and will most likely lead to fatigue, burn out, false hope, religious acts, and possibly deception because unfortunately, many ministries are built today on selling the knowledge of good and evil. We only think that we find it helpful to have more knowledge because we have grown so accustomed to a diet of the knowledge of good and evil. We convince ourselves that knowledge is power, but this is the lie that the devil has been selling from the beginning. But God put the same power that raised Christ from the dead inside us to equip and empower us to receive everything Jesus died to give us. All we need to do is believe it!

Actually, what takes the greatest faith of all is to repent and put our trust wholeheartedly and unreservedly in Jesus and His sacrifice for us as the greatest demonstration of God's love for us. The word for repentance the New Testament Greek means *change your mind* and the Old Testament Hebrew word for repentance means *to turn around*, implying a total change of direction in our actions. To say that we believe God but continue to trust in anything or anyone but God is not real repentance. We can say that we believe all sorts of things, but what we really believe is evidenced by the actions we take. Praying a prayer of repentance is not necessarily real repentance. God knows if we are honoring Him with our lips but far from Him in our hearts.

In addition to this, we cannot treat our walk of faith as if it is a walk with a psychologist rather than a Savior, Deliverer, and Healer. Jesus did not come to die on a cross, be raised from the dead, ascend to heaven, and pour out the Holy Spirit so that we could do endless self-inspections to uncover our past hurts and offenses and how they have shaped our lives. At His death, Jesus did not say, "It is a work in progress," but instead said, "It is finished!" No matter what events may have caused us harm or damaged our hearts and minds, if the offenses took place in the past, are occurring in the present, or happen in the future, the repentance we enter into as we walk with Jesus is one of bringing everything in our lives into alignment with the fact that He did a perfect work. If we have sinned, we must receive His forgiveness and move on with our lives by obeying His voice. If others have sinned against us, we must forgive them and move on with our lives by obeying His voice. When we do this, our lives will no longer be shaped by our past or our wounds but by the finished work of Jesus and by fulfilling His purpose for us in His Kingdom.

We must also be careful about abusing God's love, grace, and mercy for us to comfort ourselves in our lack of repentance. We do this when we say things like, "I have been wounded and God knows that it is hard for me," or, "God knows my weakness and He loves me anyway." Yes, God does love us all the time. But if His lovingkindness is truly at work in our lives, then it will lead us into deeper repentance and trust in Jesus for our salvation, deliverance, healing, and sustenance. The Christian life is not about being broken in our sin but being broken from our sin. In fact, for us to profess faith in Jesus without aligning our lives with what He did for us is hypocrisy, vanity, and self-deception. Faith in a God who enables false dependencies of our flesh is a perversion of the Gospel of Jesus Christ, who died on a cross for us to blot out our past, give us heaven on earth, and set us free from reliance on anything but Him. Instead of distorting God's love and mercy to settle for less than Jesus died to give us, we must press into real faith until the Kingdom of God manifests in our lives.

God is such a loving heavenly Father that He is willing and able to work with us wherever we are on this spectrum of faith and regardless of whatever mistakes we may have made in our lives or our journeys of faith. However, if we think we are faith superstars who know it all, or that God delights to pander to our fleshly weaknesses, then God will most likely let us stay stuck in the same place for as long as we think so.

Receiving by Faith

Approximately half of Jesus' healing miracles in the Scriptures are linked to the faith of someone involved. This same concept can be applied to just about any blessing we desire to receive from God which we know to be His will for us.

Matthew 8:13: Then Jesus said to the centurion, "Go! **Let it be done just as you believed** *it would." And his servant was healed at that moment.*

*Matthew 9:29: Then He touched their eyes and said, "***According to your faith*** let it be done to you."*

Matthew 15:28: Then Jesus said to her, "Woman, **you have great faith!** *Your request is granted." And her daughter was healed at that moment.*

Mark 2:5: When **Jesus saw their faith***, He said to the paralyzed man, "Son, your sins are forgiven."*

Luke 8:48: Then He said to her, "Daughter, **your faith has healed you.** *Go in peace."*

Luke 17:19: Then He said to him, "Rise and go; **your faith has made you well***."*

Luke 18:42: Jesus said to him, "Receive your sight; **your faith has healed you***."*

Notice that Jesus did not judge or condemn anyone in any way for their sin before healing them. He did not require confession of sin, proof of repentance, or any other preconditions for meriting a miracle. Though He occasionally tested the genuineness of the prospective recipient's faith and the engagement of their will, He was always able and willing to heal the sick that came to Him in faith.

*Matthew 9:28: When He had gone indoors, the blind men came to Him, and He asked them, "***Do you believe that I am able to do this?***" "Yes, Lord," they replied.*

*John 5:6: When Jesus saw him lying there and learned that he had been in this condition for a long time, He asked him, "***Do you want to get well?***"*

*Luke 5:12-13 NLT: In one of the villages, Jesus met a man with an advanced case of leprosy. When the man saw Jesus, he bowed with his face to the ground, begging to be healed. "Lord," he said, "***if You are willing, You can heal me*** and make me clean." Jesus reached out and touched him. "***I am willing," He said. "Be healed!***" And instantly the leprosy disappeared.*

*Mark 9:21-24 NLT: "How long has this been happening?" Jesus asked the boy's father. He replied, "Since he was a little boy. The spirit often throws him into the fire or into water, trying to kill him. Have mercy on us and help us, if you can." "***What do you mean, 'If I can'?***" Jesus asked. "***Anything is possible if a person believes***." The father instantly cried out, "I do believe, but help me overcome my unbelief!"*

In contrast, those who thought they could earn blessings from God based on their own righteousness received nothing from Jesus. For example, when the religious people in Jesus' day became upset and offended because of the people Jesus chose to heal, bless, and spend time with, He rebuked them for being blinded by their own pride and religion. Moreover, those who demanded a sign from Jesus (even in their hearts) as proof of His godly identity received nothing from Jesus but a rebuke.

*Matthew 9:12-13 NLT: When Jesus heard this, He said, "**Healthy people don't need a doctor--sick people do**." Then He added, "Now go and learn the meaning of this Scripture: '**I want you to show mercy**, not offer sacrifices.' For **I have come to call not those who think they are righteous, but those who know they are sinners**."*

*Matthew 16:4: **A wicked and adulterous generation looks for a sign**, but none will be given it except the sign of Jonah." Jesus then left them and went away.*

In spite of all of their religious piety and good works, Jesus worked no miracles for them.

This is why it is a good practice to engage our will in faith by putting our faith into action. We can ask God to give us a step of faith to help us engage with Him. For example, Jesus told a man with a withered hand to stretch it out, something that had been impossible for him before. His hand was not healed before he stretched it out, but while he stretched it out. (See Matthew 12:13.) When Jesus, Peter, and Paul told lame men who had never walked to stand up and walk as if they had never not walked, the men were healed when they put their faith into action and obeyed. (See Mark 2:11; Acts 3:6, 14:9.) When Jesus told the ten lepers to go show themselves to the priests, they did not receive their healing in the presence of Jesus but *as they went*. (See Luke 17:14.) When Jesus told the nobleman that his son would live and not die, he *took Jesus at His word* and demonstrated faith by returning home. (See John 4:50.) Their faith was revealed by their actions. This said, I do not recommend haphazardly creating rules like this for ourselves because God is not obligated in any way by our self-induced mandates.

God will guide you by His Spirit into all that He has for you. Listen to Him and do what He says. The point is for us to step out of hope and into faith. Abraham, the father of the faith, did not waver from believing the promise of God or in God's ability to fulfill His word, even though his circumstances appeared completely contradictory to everything God had said. He continued to live his life as if God's promises were true until they came to pass just as God had promised. (See Romans 4:20.) When the time came, Abraham had to go into Sarah and do his part in order for Isaac to be miraculously conceived. In the same way, we must each put our own faith into practice if we are to receive everything that Jesus died to give us.

FAITH INSPECTION				
1 = Needs improvement	*2 = In Refining Process*	*3 = Doing Well for Now*		
Is Jesus Christ real to me?		1	2	3
Do I believe God? Do I take God at His Word?		1	2	3
Do I believe that Jesus is Lord?		1	2	3
Do I believe that God raised Jesus from the dead?		1	2	3
Do I have lingering doubts against the sufficiency of Christ's sacrifice for me?		1	2	3
Do I hold feelings of guilt, shame, condemnation?		1	2	3
Am I resting in Christ's sufficiency for all aspects of my life? (As opposed to striving.)		1	2	3
Am I double-minded?		1	2	3
Am I placing my faith or confidence in any of my own natural abilities, qualities, or strengths, or on any particular set of circumstances rather than on Christ?		1	2	3
Do I have even the slightest reliance on anything or anyone other than God?		1	2	3
Am I trusting God more than common sense and the ways of this world?		1	2	3
Am I relying on God to work by His Spirit in what He has placed before me to do?		1	2	3
Is Jesus Lord of my life? Do I serve/obey Him as I would serve/obey an earthly King?		1	2	3
Do I use my faith to advance the will of God rather than my own desires?		1	2	3
Does my approach to the Christian life make me stand out from the ways of this world?		1	2	3
Do I regularly see God move on my behalf? (As opposed to natural efforts & outcomes.)		1	2	3
Do I believe God to heal my sickness and infirmities in my mind and body?		1	2	3
Do I believe God to provide for my food and clothing?		1	2	3
Am I content in Christ in all situations, whether abounding or abased?		1	2	3
Do I experience persecution for living a godly life in Christ Jesus? (2 Timothy 3:12)		1	2	3

For in the gospel the righteousness of God is revealed--a righteousness that is by faith from first to last, just as it is written: "The righteous will live by faith."
Romans 1:17

Basic Training Exercise

FROM FAITH TO FAITH

Romans 1:16-17 ESV – "For I am not ashamed of the gospel, for it is the power of God for salvation [deliverance, healing, sustenance/provision, life] to everyone who believes, to the Jew first and also to the Greek. For in it the righteousness of God is revealed from faith for faith, as it is written, 'The righteous shall live by faith.'"

DESCRIPTION

Through our faith in Jesus, and what He did for us through His death and resurrection, we have been made righteous before God. Therefore, have free access into all the benefits of being in right standing with God. We receive all these benefits by faith. By definition, in the Romans verse above, the word used for salvation includes salvation, deliverance, healing, and sustenance/provision. Therefore, the Gospel of Jesus Christ is the power of God on our behalf for every problem we will ever face.

It is God's desire for us to trust Him and live by faith in every area of our lives. We bring God glory when we allow Him to move on our behalf in ways that only He can. This said, similar to training muscle groups of our bodies, we may have exercised our faith in one area but remain weak in another. Plus, even when we feel that we are standing strong in faith, there are always new levels of trust that the Lord desires to take us to so that He can receive greater glory in our lives.

Therefore, to practice From Faith to Faith is about building our faith in God and what He did and desires to do for us by turning over new areas of our lives to a deeper commitment of trusting Him.

PRAYER

Father, I believe that I am righteous before you because of the work of Jesus. Increase my faith in more areas of my life so that I can bring you greater glory. Show me how to exercise my faith by trusting you more in all things. In Jesus' name, Amen.

Category: Miracles

Basic TRAINING
SPIRITUAL EXERCISES

PURPOSE:

To grow in faith and application of trusting God in our lives.

To identify and prune our lives of areas of faithlessness.

To increase in obedience and understanding of God's will and ways.

SPIRITUAL FRUIT: Faith and faithfulness.

Deeper experience of God's ways and work on our behalf.

Repentance from self-reliance over trust in God.

Purified motives and approach to life.

PRACTICE

1. Ask God to reveal to you an area where He desires for your faith to grow. (We'll call it your Focus Area.)
   - For example, living by faith in His salvation, deliverance, healing, sustenance/provision, sanctification, miracles, or any other situation in your life right now.

2. For ten (10) days, consciously, deliberately, and totally submit your Focus Area to God. (Ten represents total.)
   - Pray, "Father, I turn _____ over to you. I place my trust in you and your ways above my own thoughts, abilities, and resources. Guide me in the way you want me to go. In Jesus' name, Amen."

3. Ask the Lord to give you one or two Scriptures to believe in and build your faith upon for your Focus Area. (Note: Using only one or two will help you center your faith.)
   - Read these Scriptures out loud every morning when you wake up and every night before you go to bed. Read them throughout the day whenever you are able.
   - Spend at least ten (10) minutes per day in prayer about your Focus Area. In your times of prayer, alternate between quoting your Scriptures and praying in tongues. Also, try singing your Scriptures and singing in tongues.

4. Over the course of the ten days, allow the Lord to build your faith in Him for your Focus Area.
   - Renounce presumption that you understand God's ways.
   - Listen to any guidance He gives you. Do what He says.
   - Resist the wisdom of this world. Resist the lies of the devil.

5. After the ten days is completed, take note of the following:
   - What did God do in your situation?
   - How do you see things differently than you did before?
   - In what ways were you tempted to believe lies from the enemy or trust in your own strength?
   - How does knowing that you are righteous in Christ help you to trust God with situations in your life?

NOTES: _____

ADDITIONAL SCRIPTURES:

Hebrews 11:1, 6
James 2:17-18
Colossians 2:8
1 Corinthians 1:24, 2:5
Proverbs 3:5-6
Genesis 15:6
Habakkuk 2:4
John 6:29
Jude 1:20

Category: Miracles

PERFECTION COURSE – UNIT 4.3 READING

Rest for your Soul & Unbelief

God loves us so much that He removed every obstacle that stood in the way of our ability to receive His blessings. Plus, He continually gives us a clean slate as if we had never sinned. Therefore, instead of chasing experiences of passion or hiding ourselves in doubt and shame, we can fearlessly rest with peace in our hearts and receive God's blessings and guidance.

Rest for Our Souls

Soon after God had delivered Israel out of Egypt, the Israelites grumbled out of hunger and expressed their desire to return to Egypt where they had eaten as much as they wanted. They seemed to have forgotten that the food they ate in Egypt was not free. They had been slaves, working under harsh task masters to build cities for an evil ruler. And so, the first command God gave to the Israelites after they had departed from Egypt was given as a permanent reminder that He had redeemed them from a life of slavery. Before the Ten Commandments were given at Sinai, God instruction was to keep the Sabbath on the seventh day. For six days they could gather what God provided for them. But on the seventh day, they were required to rest from all work and observe the Sabbath. (See Exodus 16.)

The Hebrew word for *sabbath* means to *cease from exertion, to rest from labor*, and is used in other places to indicate *doing away with* something or *failure to produce*. Accordingly, to observe the Sabbath requires devoting the day to complete rest and doing no ordinary work. Later, when God gave the Law to His people, the Sabbath became the fourth commandment. Anyone who desecrated the Sabbath or failed to observe the Sabbath must be cut off from the people of God or be put to death.

This is significant because since the fall of Adam, all of mankind has been under the curse of sweat and toil with thorns and thistles. Everyone must work hard for their food and provision or die of starvation. Workaholism would seem to be the only correct approach to survival but instead, God gave His people rest. Observing the Sabbath became a new sign that symbolizes inclusion in the redeemed people of God. (See Exodus 16:29, 31:13,17; Deuteronomy 5:15.)

In addition to every seventh day being a day of rest for the people of Israel, there are a number of other days throughout the year on which the Law prohibits ordinary work, particularly connected to the Feasts of God. (See Leviticus 23.) Instead of working overtime at specific times during the year that are important for securing a good harvest, the Law requires God's people to observe multiple days of mandatory rest as an act of worship. No ordinary work is permitted at all, as they trust in God's faithfulness to abundantly supply all they need and take time to rejoice in all He has done. The most extreme example of this mandatory rest is on the Day of Atonement when all Israelites are required to do no ordinary work and humble themselves before God through fasting. Anyone who does any work or does not deny themselves on the Day of Atonement will be cut off from the people and destroyed by God.

> *Leviticus 23:28-32 NKJV: And **you shall do no work on that same day**, for it is the Day of Atonement, to make atonement for you before the LORD your God. For **any person who is not afflicted in soul on that same day shall be cut off** from his people. And **any person who does any work on that same day, that person I will destroy** from among his people. You shall **do no manner of work**; it shall be a statute forever throughout your generations in all your dwellings. "It shall be to you a sabbath of solemn rest, and **you shall afflict your souls**; on the ninth day of the month at evening,*

from evening to evening, you shall celebrate your sabbath.

Needless to say, God takes rest very seriously. This is because rest is an outward display of covenant relationship with Him. Rest proves trust in Him. Rest demonstrates gratitude for His redemption. Rest is an act of faith. Rest is an act of worship.

Without the shed blood of Jesus for atonement, we would still be subject to the Law of God, earning blessings or meriting curses through our own works and would be slaves to sin. You could say that we would be subject to a spiritual form of sweat and toil with thorns and thistles for our souls. But through Jesus' death and resurrection, we have been set free from the labor of the Law so that we can be at rest in His provision of righteousness and mercy. Jesus became our perfect sacrifice of atonement so that we can rest in our redemption as God's children. (See Romans 3:25.) Jesus said it this way:

> *Matthew 11:28-29: "Come to me, all you who are weary and burdened, and **I will give you rest**. Take My yoke upon you and learn from Me, for I am gentle and humble in heart, and **you will find rest for your souls**."*

In other words, and as is reflected in Hebrew translations of the New Testament, Jesus is saying, "Come to me and I will give you Sabbath, a Sabbath for your soul." Jesus redeemed us from slavery to sin and from the curse of spiritual sweat and toil because our blessings no longer depend on our own obedience but His! This means that we can rest, cease from, and put away all of the things we are doing or not doing from a motive of earning God's blessings because we recognize that they will fail to produce anything of eternal value. Now, the only thing that has any value before God is our faith in Jesus.

When Jesus cried out on the cross, "It is finished," He either meant that it is finished or He meant that it is not quite done yet. Either the blood of Jesus works or it doesn't. Either He paid the price in full for our sins or He didn't. Either He took all of our punishment upon Himself or we can still be penalized. Either He conquered the devil or the devil still reigns over us. But if Jesus has done all of these things, which He has, then the only thing for us to do now is to be at rest in our hearts, immovably certain of God's faithfulness, power, ability, and willingness to bless us because of what Jesus has done for us.

Entering into rest on the Day of Atonement called for people to afflict their souls. While fasting from food was required to afflict the body, afflicting the soul also involves the mind, will, and emotions. Accordingly, in order for us to honor and observe the eternal Sabbath that Jesus has given to us through His atonement, we must crucify our mind, will, and emotions to align ourselves with His perfect work. This means that we must cease from religious regulations, human commands, the ways and wisdom of this world, doing "good things," and anything else we might be trusting in somehow thinking we will earn or deserve God's favor or produce anything of value through them. We must also guard our freedom carefully from all forms of legalism, self-justification, and any teachings that imply that the blood of Jesus is not completely sufficient for our salvation, deliverance, healing, and sustenance.

> *Colossians 2:20-23: **Since you died with Christ to the elemental spiritual forces of this world, why, as though you still belonged to the world, do you submit to its rules**: "Do not handle! Do not taste! Do not touch!"? These rules, which have to do with things that are all destined to perish with use, are based on merely human commands and teachings. Such regulations indeed have an appearance of wisdom, with their self-imposed worship, their false humility and their harsh treatment of the body, but they lack any value in restraining sensual indulgence.*

> *Colossians 2:16-17: **Therefore do not let anyone judge you by what you eat or drink, or with regard to a religious festival, a New Moon celebration or a Sabbath day**. These are a shadow of the things that were to come; the reality, however, is found in Christ.*

> *Galatians 4:8-9: Formerly, **when you did not know God, you were slaves to those who by nature are not gods**. But now that you know God--or rather are known by God--**how is it that you are***

turning back to those weak and miserable forces? Do you wish to be enslaved by them all over again?

Galatians 3:1-3: You foolish Galatians! Who has bewitched you? Before your very eyes Jesus Christ was clearly portrayed as crucified. I would like to learn just one thing from you: **Did you receive the Spirit by the works of the law, or by believing what you heard?** *Are you so foolish? After beginning by means of the Spirit,* **are you now trying to finish by means of the flesh?**

Romans 4:4-5: Now to the one who works, wages are not credited as a gift but as an obligation. However, **to the one who does not work but trusts God who justifies the ungodly, their faith is credited as righteousness.**

Galatians 5:1: **It is for freedom that Christ has set us free.** *Stand firm, then, and* **do not let yourselves be burdened again** *by a yoke of slavery.*

Rest is an indication of our understanding that God's mercy and blessings are truly undeserved and cannot be earned through any kind of work. Our rest in Him serves as a sign between Him and us that we trust in His redemption and that we are humble enough to admit that we have nothing of value to add to His atoning work. If we are stressed because we are trying to deserve God's blessings through our own efforts, then our souls are not at rest. We must instead strive to enter into the rest that Jesus has provided.

Hebrews 4:9-11 ESV: So then, there remains **a Sabbath rest for the people of God**, *for whoever has entered God's rest has also rested from his works as God did from His. Let us therefore* **strive to enter that rest**, *so that no one may fall by the same sort of disobedience.*

Peace with God

The Hebrew word for peace is shalom and, in addition to peace from war, shalom includes completeness, soundness, wholeness, safety, good health, prosperity, tranquility, contentment, friendship, and ease. Shalom is a state of being where everything is working exactly as it should, and there is perfect harmony between all the many facets of life. Shalom with God is when we have right standing with Him because every hindrance to our relationship has been removed.

Since the fall of Adam, there has been an ongoing war between God and man. When there was no way for anyone to have peace with God, God made a way by sending His Son. As an example of God's approach to war and peace, when He sent the nation of Israel to war against enemy nations, He instructed them to first proclaim peace. (See Deuteronomy 20:10) Israel would extend an offer of peace to their enemies and, if this offer was accepted, the enemies would become servants of Israel. If the offer of peace was not accepted, the enemies would be destroyed. Shalom could only be attained through submission to the God of Israel.

In line with this, when God sent Jesus into the world which had become His enemy, Jesus came to proclaim peace. Jesus extended an offer of shalom with God to the Jews, who could not attain righteousness through their own efforts, and He extended the offer of shalom to Gentiles who previously had no hope of peace with the One True God.

Ephesians 2:17: **He came and preached peace** *to you who were far away and peace to those who were near.*

*John 14:27: "***Peace I leave with you; my peace I give you.** *I do not give to you as the world gives. Do not let your hearts be troubled and do not be afraid."*

As is true in any war, terms of peace require a settling of accounts so that the parties can be reconciled. Whatever it was that caused the disruption that led to war must be brought to the surface and fully addressed or the peace agreement will prove to be inadequate and peace will not last. Through His perfect life and sacrificial death, Jesus singlehandedly settled the accounts for all of humanity to have peace with God by fulfilling God's legal requirements for a peace offering. (see Leviticus 3, 7)

Isaiah 53:5: But He was pierced for our transgressions, He was crushed for our iniquities; **the punishment that brought us peace was on Him**, *and by His wounds we are healed.*

Colossians 1:19-20: For God was pleased to have all His fullness dwell in Him, and through Him to reconcile to Himself all things, whether things on earth or things in heaven, **by making peace through His blood, shed on the cross.**

Romans 5:1: Therefore, since we have been justified through faith, **we have peace with God through our Lord Jesus Christ.**

The way we accept the terms of peace that Jesus offers is to love Him and obey Him as our Lord. (see John 14:15, 21, 23; 1 John 5:3-4) In the end, on the Day of Judgment, anyone who does not accept Jesus' terms of peace will be destroyed. This said, when we accept the offer of peace with God that Jesus extends to us, we no longer need to be anxious about anything or be concerned that God is treating us like an enemy, no matter what may be happening in our circumstances.

Philippians 4:6-7: **Do not be anxious about anything**, *but in every situation, by prayer and petition, with thanksgiving, present your requests to God.* **And the peace of God**, *which transcends all understanding,* **will guard your hearts and your minds in Christ Jesus.**

Colossians 3:15: **Let the peace of Christ rule in your hearts**, *since as members of one body you were called to peace. And be thankful.*

Through the sacrifice of the Suffering Servant of Isaiah 53, God established us in righteousness. This means that we are settled in right standing with Him, have peace with Him, and are secure in His care. (See v. 53:14.) This also means that any enemy that attempts to attack us is not from God, including any natural or spiritual weapon forged against us and every tongue of accusation that contradicts the work of Christ on our behalf. (See v. 53:15-17.) Therefore, we have an assurance that no accusation against us is from God's mouth and that anything evil in our lives was not sent by Him. We no longer have to be concerned that anything has somehow disrupted the peace with God that Jesus secured for us and this means that we can have absolute confidence in our hearts and total security in our daily lives. Jesus paid the price for us to have perfect peace with God.

Help My Unbelief

There was a man who brought his demon-possessed son to Jesus to have the demon cast out of him. Jesus' disciples had been unable to expel the demon, so at first the man said to Jesus, "If you can do anything…please help us." Jesus rebuked him for this assertion that anything was impossible for God and the man corrected himself, crying out, "I do believe; help my unbelief!" (see Mark 9:24) At this, Jesus commanded the evil spirit to leave the boy and he was completely healed. When Jesus' disciples asked Him why they had not been able to drive the demon out of the boy, He told them it was because of their unbelief. (See Matthew 17:20.)

Unbelief prevents us from experiencing all of the blessings that are God's will for us. It occurs when we consider that our current circumstance is too difficult for God to handle or that our present problem has somehow not been addressed through the sacrifice and resurrection of Jesus. There are various types of unbelief and enemy attacks against our faith that seek to thwart our ability to receive the blessings God has for us. Understanding them can be helpful in assessing the condition of our hearts.

Disbelief is the inability or refusal to believe or trust in something. Disbelief says things like, "I do not believe that Jesus heals today." Just because we do not believe something does not mean it is not true. This said, if we do not believe something that Jesus died to give us, then we will be highly unlikely to receive it from God unless He dramatically intervenes in our lives—which He has been known to do.

Unbelief in its simplest form is *weakness of faith* or *faithlessness*. It stems from the same word used for an unbeliever because it indicates that we think something is too impossible or too *unbelievable* to be real. This does not always mean we have no faith but that we have been stretched in our faith past our ability to believe or accept something. For example, unbelief says, "I know that Jesus died for my sins, but I'm not sure He can provide for me financially." When we have varying levels of unbelief in our hearts, it is still possible to receive from God, but it will undoubtedly be inconsistent, unreliable, and feel more like a wrestling match than an easy flow of faith.

Misbelief is faith in something that is wrong. We have faith, but we have placed our faith in something that has no power to save us. Believing in anything other than the finished work of Jesus' sacrifice and resurrection as the solution to any circumstance, trial, or apparent problem is a misbelief. For example, misbelief says things like, "Time heals all wounds." Time does not heal, Jesus heals. Misbeliefs are also the result of ideas, strategies, or teachings that support the belief that Jesus is not God, did not come in the flesh, did not die, was not raised from the dead, or is not King of the Universe. This type of misbelief says things like, "I believe Jesus was a good teacher like many other religious leaders."

Self-righteousness is the most common and deadly misbelief. Simply put, self-righteousness is faith in our own record before God rather than in Jesus' perfect record. Self-righteousness says things like, "If I am a good person and do this or that, then God will…" or it may also say something like, "I deserve this problem because I did something bad." Self-righteousness can surface as pride or as self-pity by saying things like, "I deserve to be blessed," or, "I'm not good enough for God to bless me," or it can whine in exasperation, "I am a good person, why won't God bless me?"

Psychologizing our faith is another prevalent misbelief. Psychologizing points us to inspect our past for reasons why we feel disconnected from God or are not experiencing the fullness of His blessings. This kind of misbelief says things like, "I was unloved by my father, so it is hard for me to believe that God is a loving Heavenly Father." Unfortunately, this is the wrong basis for faith in God altogether. God's love for us is not based on our past but on the sacrifice of His Son in order to adopt us as His children. Everything about the person we used to be died on the cross with Christ so that we can live as a new creation and receive all of God's blessings. Digging into our past is the enemy's tactic of bringing to remembrance the very things Jesus blotted off the record through the shedding of His blood.

Unforgiveness is not the same as unbelief but it can be evidence of unbelief. This said, Jesus never refused to heal someone because they had unforgiveness in their lives. The blood of Jesus provides such complete forgiveness for our sins that He is not holding our unforgiveness against us. However, if we are believing God for something, we should not be surprised if opportunities to forgive others all of a sudden become prevalent in our life, including past wounds resurfacing and new offenses being inflicted by those around us. The state of our faith for receiving mercy from God is evidenced by how readily we extend mercy to those who hurt us.

Offense at God's ways is also not the same as unbelief but it can create resistance to what God wants to do in our lives. God's ways are much higher than our ways and sometimes, they seem nonsensical or even humiliating to us. For example, the people of Nazareth were offended by Jesus' humanity and, therefore, He could not do many miracles there because of their unbelief. (See Mark 6:5-6.) Religious people were offended by Jesus' approach and, therefore, He would not do any miracles for them to endorse their unbelief. When John the Baptist was uncertain if Jesus was truly the Messiah because His ways were so different than what he expected, Jesus said, "Blessed is the one who is not offended at me." (See Matthew 11:6.) If we find ourselves offended by Jesus or His ways of leading us, then we are in unbelief and will find it challenging to receive from Him.

Repent & Enter His Rest

In order to truly combat and conquer unbelief, misbelief, and disbelief, we must be willing to let go of everything we have ever thought to be true in order to be taught by the Holy Spirit. This will include challenging, refuting, and disproving common sense approaches of this world, beliefs that we were taught as a child, methods that may have worked for us in the past, and even some of the best known teachings in the Church. We have to allow the Holy Spirit to renew our mind, will, and emotions by demolishing our pride and our wrong ideas about God and His love for us.

In fact, Jesus taught that if our eye causes us to sin, we should pluck it out, and if our hand causes us to sin we should cut it off. (See Matthew 5:29-30.) Even though Jesus often spoke in parables, He was not using hyperbole or exaggeration in this passage as much as we would like to think. When Paul taught about not indulging our own desires, he went further than Jesus had and instructed believers to consider ourselves completely dead to all of our body parts so that we could live as slaves to the perfect will of God. (See Romans 6:11-18.) This is what repentance looks like and is part of what it means to take up our cross and follow Jesus by saying to God, "Not my will, but Yours be done."

It only takes a mustard seed of faith for mountains to be moved. Therefore, do not ever condemn yourself or anyone else for struggling with unbelief, and do not make faith into a self-righteous performance-driven way of meeting God's criteria for blessing. Jesus met all of God's requirements for you to be at peace with God. Your part is to enter into the rest He has provided for you. Start with the faith that you have and cry out to God to help your unbelief!

Basic Training Exercise

REST & REMEMBER

Deuteronomy 5:15 NIV – Remember that you were slaves in Egypt and that the LORD your God brought you out of there with a mighty hand and an outstretched arm. Therefore the LORD your God has commanded you to observe the Sabbath day.

DESCRIPTION

Rest is very important to God. Even God rested on the seventh day after He finished all of His work. Through faith in Christ, God invites us to enter His rest because Jesus finished all of the work of our salvation and redemption.

The Israelites had been slaves in Egypt, subjugated and driven by harsh task-masters. But by the blood of the Passover lamb, God delivered them out of slavery. Their historical reality gives us a beautiful prophetic picture of how we were slaves to sin, to this world, and to the evil one. But now by the blood of Jesus, we have been set free.

God called the Israelites to rest as a way of remembering that His leadership is not like the slave-masters they had experienced in Egypt. In fact, He had rescued them from that kind of abuse.

Therefore, practicing Rest & Remember is about stopping to rest from our tasks in order to remember the ways that God has redeemed us and set us free from the bondage this world, from our own nature, and from the evil one.

MEDITATION

Invite the Holy Spirit to speak to you and read the Deuteronomy passage above and the Additional Scriptures listed on the next page.

What stands out to you in these passages? How do these passages give you freedom for rest?

How have you viewed God as a harsh task-master? How is serving Him supposed to be different than this? What else do you sense the Lord speaking to you?

Basic TRAINING
SPIRITUAL EXERCISES

PURPOSE:

To enter into the rest that Jesus provides for our souls.

To recognize in our own lives how God has delivered us from the world, the flesh, and the devil.

To deepen our understanding of what Jesus has accomplished for us.

SPIRITUAL FRUIT:

Deeper rest in Christ.

Greater trust in God.

Increased peace in our hearts.

Genuine thankfulness and joy for what God has done for us.

More recognition of the work of Jesus.

PRAYER

Father, thank you sent Jesus to be my Passover Lamb who delivers me from the flesh, the world, and the devil. Help me to remember the ways that I was in bondage and the ways that you have rescued me and changed my heart since the day I first placed my faith in you. Fill me afresh with wonder at your mercy and grace. In Jesus' name, Amen.

PRACTICE

1. Stop and rest (literally) from the demands of life including business, community, household, family, and even ministry or church-related duties. If needed, schedule a time.

2. Consider your life before Jesus (i.e. your way of life, behavior, trusts, addictions, the path your life was on, etc.). Use the following questions as a guide for reflection:
   - What or who were you enslaved to before Jesus entered your life? How has God rescued you from this?
   - In what ways are you different now than your former life? How has life with God changed you?
   - How has God delivered you from subjugation to evil? Addictions? Oppression? Demons?
   - How has God delivered you from over-working or the burden of providing, performing, or producing to take care of yourself?
   - How has God saved you from the need to be busy or task-driven to feel accomplished or useful?
   - How has God freed you from finding your legitimacy in your work or in your ability to meet certain standards?

3. Take time to praise God for His mercy and kindness towards you. Praise God that He is a kind and loving leader, not a harsh task-master. Thank God for your new life with Him.
   - Begin afresh and enter into the rest (physical and spiritual) that God has provided for us in Jesus. Trust Him to continue His work in your life.
   - Considering your answers to these questions, in what areas is God calling you a deeper level of rest, trust, deliverance, and freedom in Him?

ADDITIONAL SCRIPTURES:

Genesis 2:2
Hebrews 4:1-11
Romans 4:1-8
Matthew 11:28-30
Philippians 1:6
Psalm 127:1-2
Isaiah 55:1-3
Revelation 21:6
Mark 6:31-32
Psalm 23
Psalm 81
Matthew 25:24-25

NOTES: _____

Basic Training Exercise

HELP MY UNBELIEF

Mark 9:21-24 NIV- Jesus asked the boy's father, "How long has he been like this?" "From childhood," he answered. "It has often thrown him into fire or water to kill him. But if you can do anything, take pity on us and help us." "If you can?" said Jesus. "Everything is possible for one who believes." Immediately the boy's father exclaimed, "I do believe; help me overcome my unbelief!"

DESCRIPTION

Unbelief prevents us from experiencing all of the blessings God has for us, including miracles. It occurs when we consider that our current circumstance is too difficult for God to handle or that our present problem has somehow not been addressed through the sacrifice and resurrection of Jesus. This does not mean we have no faith but that our faith has been stretched past our ability to believe.

This said, the free gift of salvation, deliverance, healing, and sustenance is ours to receive by faith. This means that when we have real faith in God, even if it is only the size of a mustard seed, everything is possible to us. We stop fearing anything or even thinking things like, "if you can..." to God because we start to truly entrust ourselves into His hands as our loving Heavenly Father no matter how grim our circumstances may appear to be.

Therefore, to practice Help My Unbelief is about recognizing that even though we have some faith, there are ways in which we are not fully trusting God. Recognizing these areas helps us turn them over the Lord, repent, and build our faith to receive from Him.

PRAYER

Father, I believe, help my unbelief! Show me the ways that I am not trusting you fully or am believing wrong things. Increase my faith in more areas of my life so that I can bring you greater glory. Show me how to exercise my faith by trusting you more in all things. In Jesus' name, Amen.

Category: Miracles

Basic TRAINING
SPIRITUAL EXERCISES

PURPOSE:

To resist and conquer various forms of unbelief.

To grow in faith and application of trusting God in our lives.

To experience more miracles because of greater faith.

SPIRITUAL FRUIT:

Strengthened faith and faithfulness.

Deeper experience of God's ways and work.

Repentance from self-reliance over trust in God.

Repentance from wrong beliefs.

Purified motives and approach to life.

CONSIDERATIONS

Consider these forms of unbelief, listed in no particular order:

- **Disbelief:** The inability or refusal to believe something. Says things like, "I do not believe that Jesus heals today."
- **Doubt/Unbelief:** Thinking something is too unbelievable to be real or having faith stretched past our ability to believe.
- **Misbelief:** Faith in something that is wrong. Says things like, "Time heals all wounds." Time does not heal, Jesus heals.
- **Self-Righteousness:** Faith in our own record before God rather than in Jesus' perfect record. Believes, "I deserve it."
- **Psychologizing:** Inspecting our past for reasons why we are unable to receive God's blessings. Says things like, "my father didn't love me so I doubt God does." "This is the wrong basis for faith altogether. Jesus did not come as a psychologist. He came as a Savior.

PRACTICE

1. Ask the Holy Spirit to highlight one of the unbeliefs above that is relevant to your life right now.

2. Ask the Lord to show you how this unbelief has infiltrated your thoughts. Talk to Him about:
   - When did this unbelief begin? Was there an event which triggered this? Was it from a disappointment?
   - Ask the Lord to reveal to you the real root of the issue. For example, pride, fear, intellectualism, theology, etc.

3. Repent. Ask the Lord to forgive your unbelief.
   - Ask the Lord to forgive your unbelief. Receive forgiveness.
   - Ask the Lord to help you change your approach.

4. Ask the Lord how He wants to help you overcome this unbelief through greater faith and trust in Him.
   - How will He transform your faith and renew your mind?
   - Is there something He is asking you to do to build your faith?

5. Do whatever He says.

NOTES:

Category: Miracles

ADDITIONAL SCRIPTURES:

Unbelief
Matthew 13:58
2 Kings 17:15-15
Psalm 78
Isaiah 65:2

Faith
Matthew 19:26
Philippians 4:13
Hebrews 11:1, 6
Romans 10:17
Mark 11:22-25
1 Corinthians 2:5
Romans 4:16

PERFECTION COURSE – UNIT 4.4 READING

Established Together

When the time came for all the tribes of Israel to inherit the Promised Land, there were a few tribes who received their inheritance on the east side of the Jordan. At first, when they requested their lands, Moses was appalled at the thought that they wanted to settle in their own inheritance while the rest of Israel went to war for their own lands. But then, these tribes agreed to go to war ahead of their brethren to aid in the battle against their enemies on their behalf until all of their brethren received their allotted inheritance. (See Numbers 32; Deuteronomy 3:12-22.)

As followers of Christ, we are in a war with this world, our flesh, and the evil one. The battle can be fierce and wearisome. When we are established in righteousness, we are settled with a peace in our hearts and no matter what circumstances may bring, we are at rest in our own souls. This is a blessing from God. But at the same time, our brothers and sisters in Christ who are not yet well established in the righteousness of Christ are still battling to enter into the fullness of their inheritance in Him. For us to be complacent while they are still at war is unloving and appalling.

After Peter first confessed that Jesus is the Messiah and Son of God, Jesus declared that upon this rock, HE would build His church. The work of the Lord in someone's life is something that only the Lord can do. This said, once we are established upon the Rock of Christ, we must co-labor with Jesus to help others be established in Him so that they also build upon the Rock rather than on sand. When the author of Hebrews wrote about exactly this, the community had grown battle weary from extended and severe persecution. Some were even on the verge of turning away from Christ to return to Judaism just to make their earthly lives easier. So the writer of Hebrews exhorted them to encourage one another daily and not to neglect meeting together so that they could stay focused on Christ and His eternal Kingdom without stumbling into sin, error, or unbelief. (See Hebrews 3, 10.)

The Purpose of the Church

God's purpose for His Church is to reveal His wisdom and love to the world. (See Ephesians 3:10; John 13:35.) This will be accomplished through believers who are so confident in Him that they will not bow down to the evil one and who will love one another so well that God's humble and selfless heart is put on display. When Jesus prayed His final High Priestly prayer in John 17, the depths of His heart was for oneness among believers. This unity will not happen by creed or doctrinal statement. It can only be done by the Lord through His Spirit working in the hearts of individual people to bring them together in like-mindedness.

Throughout history, the Church has taken various approaches to its purpose regarding the development of believers in Christ and the Christian faith. For example, the Roman Catholic approach has been more focused on the forgiveness of **sins**. People lived their lives, they were imperfect and they sinned so they needed forgiveness in order to be restored to right standing with God. They could go to the Catholic priest, confess their sins, say a few prayers and be cleansed and restored. The church became like a blood-bank for taking withdrawals from the wells of mercy while the priests maintained rituals to keep God happy. In contrast, the Protestant church focused more on the fact that Jesus came to save **sinners**. The whole person and all of their individual sins were forgiven and atoned for through the sacrifice of Jesus. Therefore, faith in God and independent study of His word for knowledge which aided this faith became the primary focus. The church became a center for the redeemed to study God and be encouraged in moral living.

However, the early Church gathered together to worship, pray, share, and teach one another and every believer had something to contribute. (See 1 Corinthians 14.) The people lived their lives by the power and guidance of the Holy Spirit in the midst of persecution and came together to share what God was doing, and strengthen one another to stand firm amidst the opposition of the world. Traveling apostles, prophets, and teachers were sent by God to various cities to bring the word of the Lord and teaching in the Scriptures to strengthen believers in their faith. Evangelists were sent out to gather lost souls into the Kingdom. Elders/pastors cared for the people in each local congregation. Everyone had their role within the Body of Christ and they worked together to spur one another on in the love and holiness of God.

The point is that in helping our brothers and sisters to be established in the righteousness of Christ, it is not one but ALL of these elements. Our duty is to encourage one another that our sins are forgiven through the sacrifice of Jesus. Our responsibility is to exhort one another to live as children of God and sinners who have been redeemed by the blood of the Lamb. The purpose of our gatherings must be to share with one another, to learn from one another, and to care for one another until we all attain maturity in Christ.

The Church has fallen far short of her calling and duty. I have heard it said that in every culture influenced by Christianity, the culture also influences the Christianity within it. In Jerusalem, Christianity became a religion. In Rome, Christianity became a government. In Greece, Christianity became a philosophy. In Europe, Christianity became a community center. In America, Christianity became an enterprise. Throughout history and in every culture, the Church has become distracted with the things of this world, with governments of nations, with philosophies and selfish ambitions of men. It should not be so.

Instead, let us press on to become so grounded in what Christ has done for us that we are unshaken by calamity and unmoved by any distraction. Let us press on ahead of our brothers and sisters in Christ to battle for them until they attain the full revelation of Christ and His righteousness for them. Let us not be complacent or stop encouraging one another as long as it is "Today" so that all of us will endure to the end and receive the rewards of our eternal inheritance.

KINGDOM WARRIOR EVALUATION

1 = Needs improvement	2 = In Refining Process	3 = Doing Well for Now

Kingdom/Boot Camp Training – *Are you training like an athlete to receive the prize of your King?*

Statement	1	2	3
Jesus is my King and the Commander of my life.	1	2	3
I demonstrate my allegiance to my King through obedience to His voice.	1	2	3
I understand the power and authority given to me by my King.	1	2	3
I honor my King who He died for me rather than use His authority for His own benefit.	1	2	3
I use the power and authority He has given me for His purposes and to be like Him.	1	2	3
I discipline my life in order to become increasingly useful to my King for His purposes.	1	2	3
I keep my life pure and holy.	1	2	3
I eliminate behaviors which are hazardous or unbeneficial to my Kingdom mission.	1	2	3
I reject my personal inclinations and preferences to serve the commands of my King.	1	2	3
I live my life according to the Word of God, the Holy Scriptures/Bible.	1	2	3
I reject and am victorious over sickness, oppression, demonic spirits, and anything cursed.	1	2	3
I do not tolerate unclean or demonic spirits in my life.	1	2	3
I separate myself from others whose behavior may corrupt my pursuit of God.	1	2	3
I rely on my King for everything I need.	1	2	3
I do not love money, strive for money, or make decisions based on money.	1	2	3
I am aware of and continually alert to my enemy's schemes and tactics.	1	2	3
I resist and am victorious over unbelief.	1	2	3
I am not bound by religion, legalism, or spiritual pride/superiority (like a Pharisee.)	1	2	3
I discern deception and "wisdom" which is not of God (i.e. earthly, sensual, demonic.)	1	2	3
I discern false teaching, teachers, and prophets and do not comply with their teaching.	1	2	3
I resist and am victorious over the urges of my flesh, including lusts for food and sex.	1	2	3
I have no fear of man. I do not wrongly submit myself or suppress truth in any way.	1	2	3
I do not use my God-given authority to tear people down but to build people up.	1	2	3
I use God's strength in my life to protect others, bring them to salvation, and equip them.	1	2	3
I handle conflicts with others directly, swiftly, and privately.	1	2	3
I aim for peace and regard conflicts with others to be a liability to my Kingdom mission.	1	2	3
I am willing to die in obedience to King Jesus so that others can live and know God.	1	2	3
I submit to the God-appointed authorities over me without grumbling or divisiveness.	1	2	3
My allegiance is exclusively to Jesus and no other person, organization, or nation.	1	2	3
I serve Jesus impartially/above any nationality, ethnicity, tribe, family, or relationship.	1	2	3

Do you not know that in a race all the runners run, but only one gets the prize?
Run in such a way as to get the prize. Everyone who competes in the games goes into strict training.
They do it to get a crown that will not last, but we do it to get a crown that will last forever.
1 Corinthians 9:24-25

Basic Training Exercise

HOLY SPIRIT: PROPHECY

Basic TRAINING
SPIRITUAL EXERCISES

1 Co 14:3, 24-25 NIV - The one who prophesies speaks to people for their strengthening, encouraging and comfort... But if an unbeliever or an inquirer comes in while everyone is prophesying, they are convicted of sin and are brought under judgment by all, as the secrets of their hearts are laid bare. So they will fall down and worship God, exclaiming, "God is really among you."

GIFTS OF THE HOLY SPIRIT

The Gifts of the Holy Spirit in 1 Corinthians 12 are gifts which are freely distributed by God when believers gather together. Jesus demonstrated that spiritual maturity includes operating in any and all of these gifts as God wills. Note: These gifts are different than those in Romans 12 and Ephesians 4.

DESCRIPTION

The Holy Spirit gift of Prophecy is distributed by the Holy Spirit when believers are gathered together. By definition, prophecy is "a discourse emanating from divine inspiration and declaring the purposes of God, whether by reproving and admonishing the wicked, or comforting the afflicted, revealing hidden things, or foretelling future events."* As such, the Holy Spirit gift of Prophecy is for edification, exhortation, comfort, and may also be used to expose or bring conviction of sin.

Any believer can function in this gift at any time as God grants them revelation. This said, the Scripture is clear that all hearers of prophecy must test/judge the word of prophecy for themselves before receiving it as from the Lord or taking action on the word. As a general guideline, words from the Lord will impart hope and restoration while words of condemnation or manipulation are not from God.

Practicing the Holy Spirit Gift of Prophecy is about listening to God when we are with people for anything He may desire to say to them and then speaking it forth on His behalf.

PURPOSE:

To speak forth God's words of encouragement, and alignment with His will.

To convey the heart of God towards others.

To discern accurately the situations in the lives of others so we can help them according to God's will.

SPIRITUAL FRUIT:

Speaking the truth in love to others.

Building up the Church.

Compassion coupled with words of exhortation to right action.

Considerate warnings and rebukes to those who need correction.

Comfort for the afflicted.

*Definition from Thayer's

PRAYER

Father, thank you that you desire to speak through me by your Spirit so that others may be brought into the fullness of your love and blessings. Help me to speak your words to others so that they can know you more. In Jesus' name, Amen.

PRACTICE

1. When you are with someone, take some time to ask the Lord if there is anything He desires to say to them.
   - While you are with the person, listen to them and listen to the Holy Spirit at the same time.

2. Pay careful attention to what the Holy Spirit reveals to you as you focus on the person you are with. Pay attention for things such as:
   - Scripture verses or passages that come to your mind.
   - Simple phrases which seem to come into your mind (which may hold significance to them even if not to you.)
   - Pictures or visions you see with the eyes of your heart (which you must then describe to them.)
   - Revelation of the call of God on their life or some aspect of how God has gifted them.
   - Discernment of the time or season of life with God that they are in and God's purpose in it.
   - Instructions from God for what they are to do next.
   - Insight into an area of their life which God desires to heal.
   - Invitations to deeper trust in God and His ways.
   - Warnings of danger ahead.
   - Calls to repentance for ungodliness or unbelief.
   - A scene or prophetic act the Lord wants you to do to demonstrate His message to them.

3. Share the insights you receive from the Lord with the person you are with or do what the Lord tells you to do.
   - Encourage them to test the word and take it to the Lord in prayer for application.
   - Give God all the glory for speaking through you!

NOTES:

ADDITIONAL SCRIPTURES:
1 Corinthians 14:1-5, 29-33, 39
Acts 11:28
Acts 13:1-2
Acts 21:8-14
Acts 21:9
1 Thessalonians 5:19-22
1 John 4:1

Category: Spiritual Gifts

ALL RIGHTS RESERVED © 2018 Wendy Bowen

Unit Four – Key Questions
Skilled in Righteousness

Use this worksheet to test your grasp of the material and exercises of Unit Four.

What does it mean to be skilled in the word of righteousness? (in your own words)	
How did Jesus' sacrifice establish us in righteousness?	**How can we be sure that Jesus paid it all?**
What is the role of faith in New Covenant righteousness?	**What must we do to enter into God's rest?**
What are some types of unbelief?	**What is the purpose of the Church?**
What is one thing you learned that you did not know before?	**What questions do you still have about this subject?**

UNIT FOUR: GROUP EXERCISES

Use the Established in Righteousness Chart to minister to one another. AND/OR Take communion.

Group Training Exercise

COMMUNION TOGETHER

DESCRIPTION

Jesus Christ is our eternal Passover Lamb. Like the Israelites painted the blood of the lamb on their doorposts to be protected from the destroyer, Jesus shed His blood so that our sins are forgiven. Through His blood painted on the doorposts of our hearts, we can be protected from destruction of sin, the world, the flesh, and the evil one. Jesus' body was broken so that we can freely enter into the presence of God to worship. When we take communion, we remember this great deliverance and what Jesus Christ did for us and receive in ourselves the life of God.

The first disciples of Christ took communion (or "broke bread") regularly. Consecrated bread and wine were made readily available for believers to serve themselves or take communion together. As a holy nation and a royal priesthood, every believer is a priest of God and able to administer the body and blood of Christ with due reverence. (1 Peter 2:9) This said, communion and the benefits of Christ's sacrifice are only available to those who believe that Jesus is Lord and that God raised Him from the dead. This means that if you do not yet believe in Jesus Christ as your Lord and Savior, you should abstain from communion or better yet, believe Jesus and partake.

Practicing the partaking of Communion is about commemorating Christ's sacrifice, renewing our faith in what He has done for us, and to looking forward to His return.

As you take communion together as a group, take a moment to look around the room at the people of God. These are your people. We are one nation, one people, one family, one body, one Kingdom chosen by God to be His. Hallelujah!

SCRIPTURE PORTION

Luke 22:19-20 NIV - And he took bread, gave thanks and broke it, and gave it to them, saying, "This is my body given for you; do this in remembrance of me." In the same way, after the supper he took the cup, saying, "This cup is the new covenant in my blood, which is poured out for you."

Category: Basics

GROUP PRACTICE

1. Prepare the bread and wine.
   - Consecrate the bread and wine to the Lord by praying over them. For example, "I consecrate this bread and wine to the Lord for holy use and purpose."
   - Do not use this bread or wine for casual snacking.

2. Perceive the body and blood of Jesus.
   - Jesus said of the bread and wine, "this **is** my body" and, "this **is** my blood" even when He still had a natural body.
   - Read the Communion Scriptures about what the body and blood of Jesus have done for us.
   - Believe that these Scriptures apply to the body and blood you are about to partake of.

3. Examine yourself and your faith.
   - Do you believe that Jesus Christ shed His blood for the forgiveness of your sins?
   - Do you believe that you are totally forgiven?
   - Do you believe that you can receive all of the benefits of Christ body and blood through faith in Jesus?

4. Optional: Have people share one aspect of Christ's sacrifice that they are focusing on as they take Communion today.

5. Remember the Lord's death and proclaim His return.
   - Praise God that because of Jesus's sacrifice, you are protected from the destroyer until Jesus returns.

6. Partake.
   - As you eat the body and drink the blood of Jesus, be consciously strengthened with the life and power of God in your inmost being. The indestructible life of Christ and the same power that raised Christ from the dead is in you.

7. Praise God and rejoice in His salvation!

Basic TRAINING — SPIRITUAL EXERCISES

PURPOSE:

To remember, honor, and revere Christ's sacrifice of atonement on our behalf.

To rejoice in God's salvation and the way that God has made for us to be saved.

To partake of the life of God.

GROUP SIZE:

Any size group.

SCRIPTURE PORTIONS:

John 1:29

1 Corinthians 5:7

Luke 22:15-20

Matthew 26:26-28

Mark 14:17-25

John 13:21-30

John 6:53-57

1 Corinthians 11:23-34

ALL RIGHTS RESERVED © 2019 Wendy Bowen

www.manifestinternational.com

UNIT FIVE: KINGDOM GOSPEL WITH SIGNS FOLLOWING

KEY SCRIPTURE VERSE FOR UNIT FIVE
He said to them, "Go into all the world and preach the gospel to all creation. Whoever believes and is baptized will be saved, but whoever does not believe will be condemned. And these signs will accompany those who believe: In my name they will drive out demons; they will speak in new tongues; they will pick up snakes with their hands; and when they drink deadly poison, it will not hurt them at all; they will place their hands on sick people, and they will get well." - Mark 16:15-18

CLASS 1: GOD'S PASSION FOR SOULS
1 Reading, 1 Scripture Worksheet, 2 Exercises
God spared no expense in giving His Son to buy humanity back for Himself. When we understand God's passion for souls, we will give everything to fulfill His purposes.

PRE-TEST: WHAT IS THE GOSPEL?

CLASS 2: GOSPEL OF THE KINGDOM
1 Reading, 1 Scripture Worksheet, 1 Exercise
God's eternal Gospel is being proclaimed to all of creation. Do you know what the Gospel is and how to share it with others?

CLASS 3: THESE SIGNS WILL FOLLOW
1 Reading, 2 Exercises
We have been given all power and authority to work miracles on the earth to bring glory to God through the name of Jesus Christ, His Son.

CLASS 4: IF YOU CONTINUE
1 Reading, 2 Scripture Worksheets, 1 Evaluation
Professing repentance and faith is not enough. Maturity calls for endurance all the way to Christ's return.

KEY QUESTIONS

GROUP EXERCISES

PERFECTION COURSE – UNIT 5.1 READING

God's Passion for Souls

God spared no expense for the redemption of the souls of mankind. The good news of Jesus Christ and all of the benefits of His salvation are available to anyone who will hear and believe that Jesus Christ is Lord and that God raised Him from the dead. Does this sound too good to be true? Then let us recall for a moment the state that we ourselves were in before we believed Jesus. We were dead in our inherited and ongoing sin, obeying the devil, without hope, outsiders, and excluded from God and His benefits. We were powerless, ungodly, sinners, and enemies of God. When we ourselves were in this horribly hopeless position, this is when Jesus Christ died for us. When we were in a spiritual state of death, Jesus restored us to right standing with God and gave us life.

> *Colossians 1:21-23: Once you **were alienated** from God and **were enemies** in your minds because of your evil behavior. **But now** he **has reconciled** you by Christ's physical body through death **to present you holy in his sight, without blemish and free from accusation**-- if you continue in your faith, established and firm, and do not move from the hope held out in the gospel. **This is the gospel** that you heard and that has been proclaimed to every creature under heaven, and of which I, Paul, have become a servant.*

> *Romans 5:6-10: You see, at just the right time, **when we were still powerless, Christ died for the ungodly**. Very rarely will anyone die for a righteous person, though for a good person someone might possibly dare to die. But God demonstrates his own love for us in this: **While we were still sinners, Christ died for us**. Since we have now been justified by his blood, how much more shall we be saved from God's wrath through him! For if, **while we were God's enemies, we were reconciled to him through the death of his Son, how much more, having been reconciled, shall we be saved through his life!***

> *1Timothy 4:10: That is why we labor and strive, because we have put our hope in the living God, who is **the Savior of all people, and especially of those who believe**.*

Jesus did not come to judge but to save everyone who will believe. The same salvation that was offered to us is available to every single person that we meet no matter what they have done. Jesus Christ destroyed death, bore our sickness, redeemed us from the curse, cancelled our sin-debt, and destroyed the works of the devil so that we could all be saved, healed, blessed, made holy, reign over the devil, and have eternal life in Him.

God So Loved that He Gave

God so loved the world that He gave His Son. The Gospel is a **free gift** of salvation and eternal life. The Gospel is **good news to the poor**. Jesus GAVE everything to save the souls of men. Jesus laid down His life so that others could live.

Unfortunately, many called into service for the Lord give way to the pollution of the things of this world, particularly the love of money. What a deadly threat to the message of eternal life! We cannot worship both God and money. Worship is service. Either we are serving for money or we are serving for the Lord. If we are truly serving the Lord, He guarantees that all of our needs will be taken care of. (See Matthew 6:25-33.) The laborer is deserving of food and shelter but the message of the Kingdom must never be perverted with matters of money.

Consider that the Apostle Paul labored as a tent-maker so as to never charge the Corinthians a dime for hearing the Gospel message or become a burden to any of them. He did this until Silas and Timothy arrived with an offering from the believers in Macedonia which freed him up financially to preach the Gospel full time. (See Acts 18:1-5; 2 Corinthians 11:9.) Paul was willing to receive offerings from other believers in order to support his work in the mission field but he humbled himself in order to preach the Gospel free of charge to those who did not yet know Jesus.

If we truly understand God's passion for souls we will not possibly see ministry as an opportunity for gain but a holy calling of pouring our lives out and sparing no expense so that just one more soul can come to know God and be saved. When we know what Jesus has done for us, we are not ashamed of our crucified King but are ready to be like Him. His love compels us to give of ourselves completely.

> *2 Corinthians 5:14-19:* **For Christ's love compels us**, *because we are convinced that* **one died for all, and therefore all died**. *And* **he died for all**, *that those who live should no longer live for themselves but for him who died for them and was raised again.* **So from now on we regard no one from a worldly point of view**. *Though we once regarded Christ in this way, we do so no longer. Therefore, if anyone is in Christ, the new creation has come: The old has gone, the new is here! All this is from* **God, who reconciled us to himself through Christ and gave us the ministry of reconciliation**: *For God was in Christ,* **reconciling the world to himself, no longer counting people's sins against them. And he gave us this wonderful message of reconciliation**.

> *Romans 1:16-17:* *For* **I am not ashamed of the gospel, because it is the power of God that brings salvation to everyone who believes**: *first to the Jew, then to the Gentile. For* **in the gospel the righteousness of God is revealed**--*a righteousness that is by faith from first to last, just as it is written: "The righteous will live by faith."*

When we truly understand what God has done for us and what Jesus has commissioned us to, we will be willing to GO so that the world can KNOW Jesus for themselves and be saved.

> *Romans 10:14-15:* *How, then, can they call on the one they have not believed in? And* **how can they believe in the one of whom they have not heard?** *And* **how can they hear without someone preaching to them?** *And how can anyone preach unless they are sent? As it is written: "How beautiful are the feet of those who bring good news!"*

My Witnesses

Ever since Adam's error, God has employed witnesses to testify about who He is, what He has done, and what He will do in times to come. Adam and Eve, eyewitnesses to Eden, testified about God, being in relationship with Him, and about the promise of a Son who would crush the head of the serpent. Noah was a preacher of righteousness who built an ark because of what he believed God had told him about the judgment that was to come. Later, when it seemed that all hope was lost and no one in the world worshipped or acknowledged God, God called upon Abraham to live a life of faith as a witness and testament of redemption by faith in the one true God. When God led the nation of Israel out of slavery, the story of His great miracle power spread throughout the earth that the God of Heaven had chosen a people for Himself. This said, God's original design for Israel was not outreach and evangelism. His intent was that through Israel's obedience to His righteousness, the nations would come to know the wisdom, power, and justice of the God who created heaven and earth. God designed His people to be a light to the nations so that all the earth would know that He is God and there is none other. They were to be His witnesses, testifying of His greatness and power, telling the stories of His redemption and holiness, and living according to His ways so as to demonstrate reverence for Him and represent Him on the earth.

But when Jesus came and established the New Covenant, He commissioned His disciples to go to the ends of the earth as His witnesses to tell of what God has done by sending His Son and to teach all peoples to obey Him until He returns. The only reason God has not yet sent Jesus to judge the earth with fire is to give more people time to repent, come to know Him, and be saved. (See 2 Peter 3:9.) We are His witnesses. We are called to testify of the great and wonderful salvation that God has made available to us through Jesus Christ. We are called to live lives of holy reverence for God, freedom from religious legalism and the curse of the law, miracle power and mostly, mercy and love. This is how the world will know that Jesus is King and that everything He said is true and will come to pass – including the day of judgment to come.

Each and every one of us as Christ's disciples have been commissioned by Jesus to declare a message of hope through repentance from sin and believing in Jesus so that everyone can hear the word of Christ and believe. We have a responsibility to deliver God's message and, significantly, Jesus will not return until we have accomplished our task as His witnesses to the ends of the earth.

> Matthew 24:14: And this **gospel of the kingdom will be preached** in the whole world **as a testimony to all nations, and then the end will come**.

The world needs to know about the love of God. The world needs to know that the day of His wrath is coming. The world needs to know that God has made a way to be saved from this wrath. We know the love of God because He gave His Son. The world will know the love of God when we spare no expense and give our all for them to know Him.

This is How We Know – 1 John
Scripture List & Worksheet

1 John 2:5-6: But if anyone obeys his word, love for God is truly made complete in them. **This is how we know we are in him**: Whoever claims to live in him must live as Jesus did.

1 John 2:18: Dear children, this is the last hour; and as you have heard that the antichrist is coming, even now many antichrists have come. **This is how we know it is the last hour.**

1 John 3:7-11: Dear children, do not let anyone lead you astray. The one who does what is right is righteous, just as he is righteous. The one who does what is sinful is of the devil, because the devil has been sinning from the beginning. The reason the Son of God appeared was to destroy the devil's work. No one who is born of God will continue to sin, because God's seed remains in them; they cannot go on sinning, because they have been born of God. **This is how we know who the children of God are and who the children of the devil are**: Anyone who does not do what is right is not God's child, nor is anyone who does not love their brother and sister. For this is the message you heard from the beginning: We should love one another.

1 John 3:16: **This is how we know what love is**: Jesus Christ laid down his life for us. And we ought to lay down our lives for our brothers and sisters.

1 John 3:19-24: **This is how we know that we belong to the truth** and how we set our hearts at rest in his presence: If our hearts condemn us, we know that God is greater than our hearts, and he knows everything. Dear friends, if our hearts do not condemn us, we have confidence before God and receive from him anything we ask, because we keep his commands and do what pleases him. And this is his command: to believe in the name of his Son, Jesus Christ, and to love one another as he commanded us. The one who keeps God's commands lives in him, and he in them. **And this is how we know that he lives in us**: We know it by the Spirit he gave us.

1 John 4:1-3: Dear friends, do not believe every spirit, but test the spirits to see whether they are from God, because many false prophets have gone out into the world. **This is how you can recognize the Spirit of God**: Every spirit that acknowledges that Jesus Christ has come in the flesh is from God, but every spirit that does not acknowledge Jesus is not from God. This is the spirit of the antichrist, which you have heard is coming and even now is already in the world.

1 John 4:6: We are from God, and whoever knows God listens to us; but whoever is not from God does not listen to us. **This is how we recognize the Spirit of truth and the spirit of falsehood.**

1 John 4:9: **This is how God showed his love among us**: He sent his one and only Son into the world that we might live through him.

1 John 4:13: **This is how we know that we live in him and he in us**: He has given us of his Spirit.

1 John 4:17: **This is how love is made complete among us** so that we will have confidence on the day of judgment: In this world we are like Jesus.

1 John 5:2: **This is how we know that we love the children of God**: by loving God and carrying out his commands.

Practical Application:

How do these Scriptures reveal the love of God for us?

List three misconceptions about what the love of God is or is not.
1.
2.
3.

How do these Scriptures help you to identify a true Gospel from a false Gospel?

How do these Scriptures help you to identify a true believer from one who only professes faith?

How is God asking you to personally respond to these Scriptures in your own life?

Basic Training Exercise

FREELY GIVE

Matthew 5:38-42 NIV - "You have heard that it was said, 'Eye for eye, and tooth for tooth.' But I tell you, do not resist an evil person. If anyone slaps you on the right cheek, turn to them the other cheek also. And if anyone wants to sue you and take your shirt, hand over your coat as well. If anyone forces you to go one mile, go with them two miles. Give to the one who asks you, and do not turn away from the one who wants to borrow from you.

DESCRIPTION

When Jesus sent His disciples out to proclaim the Kingdom of God, He reminded them that they had received from Him without cost. As such, they must give the gift of salvation and all of its benefits like healing, deliverance, and cleansing from sin for free.

God so loved the world that He GAVE His Son. Jesus so loved the world that He GAVE His life. Giving is not just about money. We can be generous with our time, service, counsel, forgiveness, and all of our possessions.

Giving can be a powerful way of connecting with people who do not yet know Jesus. However, when we charge for ministry or evangelism the integrity of the Gospel message is compromised.

Practicing Freely Give is about revealing the character of God through generosity so that others can come to know Jesus.

CONSIDERATIONS

How does giving gifts draw people to us and give us the opportunity to tell them about Jesus?

How does generosity reflect the character of God?

Why is it important not to dilute the Gospel message with requests for money? How could appealing for money contradict or distort the Gospel?

Do you have an internal resistance to giving to the poor? What is it? How does this NOT fit with the Gospel message?

Category: Evangelism

Basic TRAINING
SPIRITUAL EXERCISES

PURPOSE:

To share generously in practical ways in order to reveal Christ.

To be a demonstration of the love of God.

SPIRITUAL FRUIT:

Selfless, giving, love.

Increased willingness to share with others.

Greater confidence in sharing Jesus and the truth of His Kingdom with others.

Increase in being the light of the world to those who are in darkness.

PRAYER

Father, thank you that you gave your best and most valuable gift for me. Help me to give open-handedly to everyone who asks of me so that I can show your generosity and so that others may come to know you. In Jesus' name, Amen.

PRACTICE

1. Ask the Lord highlight to you someone who has recently asked you for something. As you do, consider:
   - What did they ask you for?
   - Did you give it to them? Why or why not?
   - Are you willing to give it to them now? Why or why not?
   - What is God asking you to do for them? How could this open up a conversation about Jesus with them?

2. Ask the Lord highlight to you a person you would like to share Christ with. As you do, keep the following in mind:
   - What are their goals in life? How can you contribute to them in a godly way?
   - Is there anything they have asked of you? Have you done it? Are you willing to do it for God?
   - What is God asking you to do for them? How could this open up a conversation about Jesus with them?

3. Ask the Lord to highlight to you a person in need or a homeless person who is asking for help.
   - What do you have that you can give to them?
   - What things other than money can you give? (i.e water bottle, sandwich, winter coat, blanket, etc.)
   - What is God asking you to do for them? How could this open up a conversation about Jesus with them?

4. Do whatever the Lord tells you to do. Take the time to share Jesus with the people you are freely giving to.

NOTES: _____

ADDITIONAL SCRIPTURES:

John 3:16

Matthew 10:8

Luke 6:30

1 Corinthians 9:11

1 Corinthians 9:18

Isaiah 55:1-2

Acts 8:20

Revelation 21:6

Revelation 22:17

2 Corinthians 8:9

Deuteronomy 15:7, 10

Category: Evangelism

Basic Training Exercise

GOD AND MONEY

Luke 16:13 NIV - No one can serve two masters. Either you will hate the one and love the other, or you will be devoted to the one and despise the other. You cannot serve both God and money.

DESCRIPTION

Everything we have is from God including our ability to make money. But somehow, money competes for our attention and affection. God delights to bless us as His children and to share His abundance with us. At the same time, He deserves to be the only one we worship and serve – not money.

Jesus was not afraid to talk about money and the potential hazards it can create for our walk of faith. If we turn our attention to money, it can choke out the work of God in our lives and create unneeded conflict. Money matters can stir up anxiety, fear, shame, and other wrong mindsets that Jesus desires to replace with certainty, joy, and freedom.

God desires to lead us into His abundance. We have to take steps to trust Him with our money. Therefore, the practice of God and Money is about trusting God with every aspect of our financial lives so that we worship and serve Him only.

TALK WITH GOD

In what ways have you based life decisions on money matters rather than obedience to God's guidance?

Do you find it difficult to include God in your finances? Your expenses? Your debts? Your hard-earned cash?

Do you believe God desires abundance for you?

PRAYER

Father, I worship you alone. Forgive me for the times I have made decisions based on finances rather than your guidance. Help me now to consecrate what I have to you and to trust you to guide me into your purposes and abundance. In Jesus' name, Amen.

Category: Basics

Basic TRAINING
SPIRITUAL EXERCISES

PURPOSE:
To grow in trusting God in our finances.

To discern and align our priorities with God and His purposes.

To turn our financial decisions over to God.

SPIRITUAL FRUIT:
Repentance from self-reliance and the love of money.

Proper stewardship of the resources God has given us.

Increased trust in God's provision for our needs.

PRACTICE

1. Consecrate your finances to God. Present to Him your bank accounts, assets, expenses, debts, needs, and desires, etc.
   - As an act of faith, dedicate all you have to the Lord. Say, "God, I dedicate all I have to you. What's mine is yours."
   - As an act of faith, put God in control of your finances.
   - From now on, **your money is God's money** and your finances are God's responsibility.

2. As you present your finances to God, take note of any fears, shame, guilt, or condemnation that arises in you.
   - Tell the Lord how you feel and why you feel this way.
   - Ask the Lord to reveal to you any wrong beliefs you have about money. Take note of what He says and talk with Him about it.
   - Ask the Lord to set you free from financial sin, bondage to money, pain or shame linked with your financial history, and any ungodly patterns or cycles of curse and blessing.
   - Ask the Lord to renew your mind about finances with His stability, abundance, joy, freedom, and blessing.

3. Every day, **before you spend** any money on anything, **ask** the Lord for His permission to spend **His money** on it. Obey what He tells you.
   - For one week (at least) journal daily about how God led you to spend. Is there anything that surprises you?
   - Take note of any resistance, rebellion, anger, or selfishness rises up in you as you do this. Ask the Lord to help you submit to His guidance and to deepen your trust in Him.

4. From now on, let God guide all of your financial decisions.
   - Continue to obey Him daily in all your spending.
   - Trust Him to guide you in managing your accounts, assets, debts, needs, and desires. (Remember that He manages the whole world, so He knows how to do this.)

NOTES:

ADDITIONAL SCRIPTURES:
Matthew 13:22
1 Timothy 6:9-10
Matthew 6:19-21
Luke 12:13-21
Deuteronomy 8:17-18
Matthew 7:9-11
Philippians 4:11-19
Hebrews 13:5
2 Corinthians 8:7
1 Kings 18:21
Proverbs 18:11
Proverbs 23:4
Proverbs 28:20
Proverbs 22:2
Proverbs 18:23

Category: Basics

WHAT IS THE GOSPEL?
Pre-Test

Answer the following questions. Examine what you know and believe about the Gospel.

What is the eternal Gospel of Jesus Christ? (In your own words.)

What are some key elements of the Gospel? Why are they important?		

What is an erroneous version of the Gospel you have heard? Why is it it a wrong Gospel?

PERFECTION COURSE – UNIT 5.2 READING

Gospel of the Kingdom

Repent for the Kingdom of God is at hand! The kingdoms of this world and the Kingdom of God are at war with each other. God's chosen King came to conquer the prince of this world – and triumphed. The ruler of this world knows that his time is short and works tirelessly to deceive all nations into worshipping him through worshipping themselves, indulging in pleasure, and denying God's existence and authority. The true and rightful King of all creation will return to judge all nations and people in the ultimate battle between the forces of good and evil and truth and lies.

The whole world stands condemned by God because of sin. Anyone who does not believe Jesus is still in their sins and will be subject to judgment, eternal condemnation, and the fires of hell. Jesus is coming back to avenge all evil. Until then, we have been given the keys to His Kingdom – making it accessible to anyone who will believe that Jesus is Lord and that God raised Him from the dead. Jesus is the only way to receive eternal life and salvation from the wrath of God. It is available to everyone who will repent and put their faith in Jesus.

The Eternal Gospel

The Gospel is the power of God for salvation, deliverance, healing, and sustenance to be received by FAITH. The Gospel is the wisdom of God which conquers every scheme of the evil one and the wisdom of this world. The Gospel is the good news of how Jesus, God's Son and anointed one, took the wrath of God upon Himself to crush the head of the serpent and conquer death to share eternal life with all who will believe and set themselves apart unto Him.

> *Revelation 14:6-12: Then I saw another angel flying in midair, and he had the **eternal gospel** to proclaim to those who live on the earth--to every nation, tribe, language and people. He said in a loud voice, "**Fear God and give him glory, because the hour of his judgment has come. Worship him who made the heavens, the earth, the sea and the springs of water.**" A second angel followed and said, "**Fallen! Fallen is Babylon the Great,**' which made all the nations drink the maddening wine of her adulteries." A third angel followed them and said in a loud voice: "**If anyone worships the beast and its image and receives its mark on their forehead or on their hand, they, too, will drink the wine of God's fury**, which has been poured full strength into the cup of his wrath. They will be tormented with burning sulfur in the presence of the holy angels and of the Lamb. And the smoke of their torment will rise for ever and ever. There will be no rest day or night for those who worship the beast and its image, or for anyone who receives the mark of its name." **This calls for patient endurance on the part of the people of God who keep his commands and remain faithful to Jesus**.*

The focus of the Gospel is on eternal life – life with God forever and the life of God made accessible. This is the life that Adam lost when he sold humanity into slavery to the evil one. God's promise to Eve was that one of her descendants would crush the head of the serpent forever. God's promise to Abraham was that his descendants would fill the earth, inherit the world, and be blessed. The purpose of the Laws God gave through Moses were to direct His people into righteousness so that they could attain eternal life and merit the world to come. When scribes and religious leaders approached Jesus, their questions were centered on the issue of how to attain eternal life. But Jesus came so that we might have eternal life – and life to the full measure. (See John 10:10.)

The Gospel is NOT about getting to heaven and going to the good place when you die. That is part of it but more so, the Gospel is the way God has made for us to have eternal life NOW dwelling inside of us. Jesus is LIFE. Jesus gives us the hope of eternal life and the indwelling life-power of God to strengthen us to resist the schemes of the evil one until Jesus returns to spend eternity with us in the world to come.

A Quick Synopsis of the Gospel

Throughout history, the Gospel has been perverted and distorted in various ways but the Gospel has not changed. Paul exhorted Timothy to remember the pure Gospel of Jesus Christ, the anointed King of Israel.

> *2 Timothy 2:8: Remember Jesus Christ, raised from the dead, descended from David.* **This is my gospel.**

Therefore, here is a quick synopsis of the Gospel.

Jesus Christ was born of a virgin by the power of the Holy Spirit into the lineage of King David of Israel. Israel was the only nation on earth that had a covenant relationship with the one and only true God, the Creator of Heaven and earth, and they were earnestly awaiting the Messiah or King that God promised them who would establish His Kingdom and set things right in the world. They were also the only people on earth with God's Law and standard of justice and righteousness which, if upheld, led to blessing, eternal life of fellowship with God, and inheriting all creation. Unfortunately, no man on earth has ever been able to live up to this standard of purity and godliness. As a consequence, all of mankind since the first man Adam has been separated from God because of falling short of perfect obedience to God's instructions. That is, until Jesus came along.

Because Jesus was conceived by the power of the Holy Spirit, He was born with the divine nature of God, His Father. He was simultaneously fully God and fully man, the exact image of His Father, and a full demonstration and incarnation of God in the flesh. Because Jesus followed the inclinations of His indwelling divine nature and not those of His flesh, He lived His life completely without sin according to the Law of God. His motives and actions always stemmed from God's perfect love, mercy, and justice so that He was completely righteous by God's standard. Additionally, God confirmed Jesus as His Son and the promised Messiah with power from heaven by enabling Jesus to supernaturally heal the sick, cast out demons, raise the dead, and work various other miracles, signs, and wonders.

However, instead of being accepted as a righteous man, the Son of God, the Messiah of Israel, and the Lord and King of all the earth, the religious leaders of Israel and the governmental authorities of this world unanimously mocked, rejected, and sentenced Jesus to death like a criminal, acting on behalf of all people. Jesus knew all of this in advance and willingly allowed Himself to be whipped and scourged, and to shed His blood, until He was ultimately nailed to a cross and crucified until He was dead. He was buried in a tomb and thought to be thoroughly defeated. In fact, for three days, it appeared that Jesus was the world's biggest failure and that He had horribly deceived all of His followers.

But God, with resurrection power by His Spirit, raised Jesus from the dead on the third day before His body had experienced decay. Jesus walked out of the grave in an imperishable resurrection body, having conquered death. For forty days, He revealed Himself to His disciples as proof that He is, indeed, alive from the dead and the Son of God who fulfills the prophecies concerning the Messiah of Israel.

After forty days of resurrection appearances, Jesus ascended in the clouds from Jerusalem to His Father in heaven, where He is now seated at the right hand of God, the position of all power and authority over all creation. At the appointed time, Jesus is coming back to judge the living and the dead, avenge all evil, abolish death, establish total dominion, restore all things, and hand the Kingdom back to His Father as He fulfills the remaining prophecies concerning Himself.

Until He returns, after Jesus ascended to heaven, He poured out the Holy Spirit into the hearts of all of us who believe in Him so that God's divine nature now dwells in us by faith. This means that we have Christ inside of us just like Jesus had God inside of Him when He was on the earth in the flesh. With Christ in us, we are empowered to live like Jesus lived, to love like He loved, and do the things that He did while we are still here on earth in these bodies. We are citizens of heaven and children of God, serving as His ambassadors with a message of His Kingdom, His goodness, and His love.

Therefore, we go to all nations to tell everyone everywhere that Jesus is Lord and that the way of salvation has been made for them.

Jesus' Kingdom Parables (Matthew 13)

Jesus' primary message everywhere He went was, "Repent for the Kingdom of God is at hand!" Like Jonah calling for Nineveh's repentance because judgment was imminent, Jesus proclaimed that the Kingdom of God was about to overthrow the kingdoms of the entire world. According to the Scriptures, all of Israel was awaiting the arrival of the Messiah who would shatter the kingdoms of this world and establish the eternal Kingdom of God for His holy ones. (See Daniel 2, 7.) However, when they saw Jesus working miracles for sinners and having dinner with outcasts rather than endorsing the religious leaders, they accused Him of working for the devil. Jesus rebuked their error and misunderstanding of God's Kingdom and, later that same day, sat down to share some of His primary parables about the Kingdom of God.

Jesus did not proclaim the Gospel the way Paul did. Jesus spoke in parables about His Kingdom. He did this deliberately so that only those with spiritual ears to hear would be able to understand His message and be drawn into His Kingdom. He only explained these parables to His disciples so that they would also be equipped to proclaim His Kingdom to the world.

In the parables of the soils, Jesus revealed that the Kingdom of God is not of this world, but it is a matter of the heart. The seed is the Word of God that is scattered about into all kinds of soils of the hearts of mankind. Some seeds become food for the birds as the enemy snatches the word out of a person's life. Some seeds do not take root and fall away when trial or difficulty comes. Some seeds take root but are choked by the thorns of the cares of this world and the love of money. But some receive the word of God with an open heart that understands. These ones will go on to produce a harvest for God and receive eternal life.

In the parable of the wheat and tares, Jesus made plain that good and evil will continue to dwell and grow together until the time of harvest comes. He did not come to judge the nations but to save them. Jesus did not come the first time to overthrow evil because that would disrupt the righteousness He desires to see growing in the fields of this world among the nations. But when He returns, the sickle will swing and the tares will be thrown into the eternal fire.

In the parable of the hidden treasure, the pearl of great price, and the net, Jesus explained that the Kingdom of God will be found by people who are not looking for it (Gentiles) in addition to those who have been searching for it for a long time (Jews) and that anyone who recognizes the value of the Kingdom of God will willingly give up everything they have to obtain it. The good news of God's Kingdom has been made available to everyone – a broad net has been cast into the sea. At the close of the age, the good from the bad will be divided and judged.

Therefore, let us fully understand the battle we are in and be strengthened with endurance until Jesus returns. Let us never compromise or water down the Gospel with worldliness or filth because upon such things the wrath of God is coming. Let us proclaim the real Jesus, descended from David, the King of Israel, and Savior of the whole world. And let us be wise in how we speak to outsiders, knowing that only those who have ears to hear will hear and know the truth and be saved.

BIBLICAL GOSPELS
Scripture List & Worksheet

Peter on the Day of Pentecost: Acts 2:14-47: Then Peter stood up with the Eleven, raised his voice and addressed the crowd: "Fellow Jews and all of you who live in Jerusalem, let me explain this to you; listen carefully to what I say. These people are not drunk, as you suppose. It's only nine in the morning! No, this is what was spoken by the prophet Joel: " 'In the last days, God says, I will pour out my Spirit on all people. Your sons and daughters will prophesy, your young men will see visions, your old men will dream dreams. Even on my servants, both men and women, I will pour out my Spirit in those days, and they will prophesy. I will show wonders in the heavens above and signs on the earth below, blood and fire and billows of smoke. The sun will be turned to darkness and the moon to blood before the coming of the great and glorious day of the Lord. And everyone who calls on the name of the Lord will be saved.' "Fellow Israelites, listen to this: Jesus of Nazareth was a man accredited by God to you by miracles, wonders and signs, which God did among you through him, as you yourselves know. This man was handed over to you by God's deliberate plan and foreknowledge; and you, with the help of wicked men, put him to death by nailing him to the cross. But God raised him from the dead, freeing him from the agony of death, because it was impossible for death to keep its hold on him. David said about him: " 'I saw the Lord always before me. Because he is at my right hand, I will not be shaken. Therefore my heart is glad and my tongue rejoices; my body also will rest in hope, because you will not abandon me to the realm of the dead, you will not let your holy one see decay. You have made known to me the paths of life; you will fill me with joy in your presence.' "Fellow Israelites, I can tell you confidently that the patriarch David died and was buried, and his tomb is here to this day. But he was a prophet and knew that God had promised him on oath that he would place one of his descendants on his throne. Seeing what was to come, he spoke of the resurrection of the Messiah, that he was not abandoned to the realm of the dead, nor did his body see decay. God has raised this Jesus to life, and we are all witnesses of it. Exalted to the right hand of God, he has received from the Father the promised Holy Spirit and has poured out what you now see and hear. For David did not ascend to heaven, and yet he said, " 'The Lord said to my Lord: "Sit at my right hand until I make your enemies a footstool for your feet." ' "Therefore let all Israel be assured of this: God has made this Jesus, whom you crucified, both Lord and Messiah." When the people heard this, they were cut to the heart and said to Peter and the other apostles, "Brothers, what shall we do?" Peter replied, "Repent and be baptized, every one of you, in the name of Jesus Christ for the forgiveness of your sins. And you will receive the gift of the Holy Spirit. The promise is for you and your children and for all who are far off--for all whom the Lord our God will call." With many other words he warned them; and he pleaded with them, "Save yourselves from this corrupt generation." Those who accepted his message were baptized, and about three thousand were added to their number that day. They devoted themselves to the apostles' teaching and to fellowship, to the breaking of bread and to prayer. Everyone was filled with awe at the many wonders and signs performed by the apostles. All the believers were together and had everything in common. They sold property and possessions to give to anyone who had need. Every day they continued to meet together in the temple courts. They broke bread in their homes and ate together with glad and sincere hearts, praising God and enjoying the favor of all the people. And the Lord added to their number daily those who were being saved.

Peter to Onlookers After Healing at the Temple: Acts 3:11-26: While the man held on to Peter and John, all the people were astonished and came running to them in the place called Solomon's Colonnade. When Peter saw this, he said to them: "Fellow Israelites, why does this surprise you? Why do you stare at us as if by our own power or godliness we had made this man walk? The God of Abraham, Isaac and Jacob, the God of our fathers, has glorified his servant Jesus. You handed him over to be killed, and you disowned him before Pilate, though he had decided to let him go. You disowned the Holy and Righteous One and asked that a murderer be released to you. You killed the author of life, but God raised him from the dead. We are witnesses of this. By faith in the name of Jesus, this man whom you see and know was made strong. It is Jesus' name and the faith that comes through him that has completely healed him, as you can all see. "Now, fellow Israelites, I know that you acted in ignorance, as did your leaders. But this is how God fulfilled what he had foretold through all the prophets, saying that his Messiah would suffer. Repent, then, and turn to God, so that your sins may be wiped out, that times of refreshing may come from the Lord, and that he may send the Messiah, who has been appointed for you--even Jesus. Heaven must receive him until the time comes for God to restore everything, as he promised long ago through his holy prophets. For Moses said, 'The Lord your God will raise up for you a prophet like me from among your own people; you must listen to everything he tells you. Anyone who does not listen to him will be completely cut off from their people.' "Indeed, beginning with Samuel, all the prophets who have spoken have foretold these days. And you are heirs of the prophets and of the covenant God made with your fathers. He said to Abraham, 'Through your offspring all peoples on earth will be blessed.' When God raised up his servant, he sent him first to you to bless you by turning each of you from your wicked ways."

Stephen's Proclamation: Acts 7:1-53: Then the high priest asked Stephen, "Are these charges true?" To this he replied: "Brothers and fathers, listen to me! The God of glory appeared to our father Abraham while he was still in Mesopotamia, before he lived in Harran. 'Leave your country and your people,' God said, 'and go to the land I will show you.' "So he left the land of the Chaldeans and settled in Harran. After the death of his father, God sent him to this land where you are now living. He gave him no inheritance here, not even enough ground to set his foot on. But God promised him that he and his descendants after him would possess the land, even though at that time Abraham had no child. God spoke to him in this way: 'For four hundred years your descendants will be strangers in a country not their own, and they will be enslaved and mistreated. But I will punish the nation they serve as slaves,' God said, 'and afterward they will come out of that country and worship me in this place.' Then he gave Abraham the covenant of circumcision. And Abraham became the father of Isaac and circumcised him eight days after his birth. Later Isaac became the father of Jacob, and Jacob became the father of the twelve patriarchs. "Because the patriarchs were jealous of Joseph, they sold him as a slave into Egypt. But God was with him and rescued him from all his troubles. He gave Joseph wisdom and enabled him to gain the goodwill of Pharaoh king of Egypt. So Pharaoh made him ruler over Egypt and all his palace. "Then a famine struck all Egypt and Canaan, bringing great suffering, and our ancestors could not find food. When Jacob heard that there was grain in Egypt, he sent our forefathers on their first visit. On their second visit, Joseph told his brothers who he was, and Pharaoh learned about Joseph's family. After this, Joseph sent for his father Jacob and his whole family, seventy-five in all. Then Jacob went down to Egypt, where he and our ancestors died. Their bodies were brought back to Shechem and placed in the tomb that Abraham had bought from the sons of Hamor at Shechem for a certain sum of money. "As the time drew near for God to fulfill his promise to Abraham, the number of our people in Egypt had greatly increased. Then 'a new king, to whom Joseph meant nothing, came to power in Egypt.' He dealt treacherously with our people and oppressed our ancestors by forcing them to throw out their newborn babies so that they would die. "At that time Moses was born, and he was no ordinary child. For three months he was cared for by his family. When he was placed outside, Pharaoh's daughter took him and brought him up as her own son. Moses was educated in all the wisdom of the Egyptians and was powerful in speech and action. "When Moses was forty years old, he decided to visit his own people, the Israelites. He saw one of them being mistreated by an Egyptian, so he went to his defense and avenged him by killing the Egyptian. Moses thought that his own people would realize that God was using him to rescue them, but they did not. The next day Moses came upon two Israelites who were fighting. He tried to reconcile them by saying, 'Men, you are brothers; why do you want to hurt each other?' "But the man who was mistreating the other pushed Moses aside and said, 'Who made you ruler and judge over us? Are you thinking of killing me as you killed the Egyptian yesterday?' When Moses heard this, he fled to Midian, where he settled as a foreigner and had two sons. "After forty years had passed, an angel appeared to Moses in the flames of a burning bush in the desert near Mount Sinai. When he saw this, he was amazed at the sight. As he went over to get a closer look, he heard the Lord say: 'I am the God of your fathers, the God of Abraham, Isaac and Jacob.' Moses trembled with fear and did not dare to look. "Then the Lord said to him, 'Take off your sandals, for the place where you are standing is holy ground. I have indeed seen the oppression of my people in Egypt. I have heard their groaning and have come down to set them free. Now come, I will send you back to Egypt.' "This is the same Moses they had rejected with the words, 'Who made you ruler and judge?' He was sent to be their ruler and deliverer by God himself, through the angel who appeared to him in the bush. He led them out of Egypt and performed wonders and signs in Egypt, at the Red Sea and for forty years in the wilderness. "This is the Moses who told the Israelites, 'God will raise up for you a prophet like me from your own people.' He was in the assembly in the wilderness, with the angel who spoke to him on Mount Sinai, and with our ancestors; and he received living words to pass on to us. "But our ancestors refused to obey him. Instead, they rejected him and in their hearts turned back to Egypt. They told Aaron, 'Make us gods who will go before us. As for this fellow Moses who led us out of Egypt--we don't know what has happened to him!' That was the time they made an idol in the form of a calf. They brought sacrifices to it and reveled in what their own hands had made. But God turned away from them and gave them over to the worship of the sun, moon and stars. This agrees with what is written in the book of the prophets: " 'Did you bring me sacrifices and offerings forty years in the wilderness, people of Israel? You have taken up the tabernacle of Molek and the star of your god Rephan, the idols you made to worship. Therefore I will send you into exile' beyond Babylon. "Our ancestors had the tabernacle of the covenant law with them in the wilderness. It had been made as God directed Moses, according to the pattern he had seen. After receiving the tabernacle, our ancestors under Joshua brought it with them when they took the land from the nations God drove out before them. It remained in the land until the time of David, who enjoyed God's favor and asked that he might provide a dwelling place for the God of Jacob. But it was Solomon who built a house for him. "However, the Most High does not live in houses made by human hands. As the prophet says: " 'Heaven is my throne, and the earth is my footstool. What kind of house will you build for me? says the Lord. Or where will my resting place be? Has not my hand made all these things?' "You stiff-necked people! Your hearts and ears are still uncircumcised. You are just like your ancestors: You always resist the Holy Spirit! Was there ever a prophet your ancestors did not persecute? They even killed those who predicted the coming of the Righteous One. And now you have betrayed and murdered him-- you who have received the law that was given through angels but have not obeyed it."

Philip Expounds the Scriptures: Acts 8:30-35: Then Philip ran up to the chariot and heard the man reading Isaiah the prophet. "Do you understand what you are reading?" Philip asked. "How can I," he said, "unless someone explains it to me?" So he invited Philip to come up and sit with him. This is the passage of Scripture the eunuch was reading: "He was led like a sheep to the slaughter, and as a lamb before its shearer is silent, so he did not open his mouth. In his humiliation he was deprived of justice. Who can speak of his descendants? For his life was taken from the earth." The eunuch asked Philip, "Tell me, please, who is the prophet talking about, himself or someone else?" Then Philip began with that very passage of Scripture and told him the good news about Jesus.

Peter to Gentiles: Acts 10:36-43: You know the message God sent to the people of Israel, announcing the good news of peace through Jesus Christ, who is Lord of all. You know what has happened throughout the province of Judea, beginning in Galilee after the baptism that John preached-- how God anointed Jesus of Nazareth with the Holy Spirit and power, and how he went around doing good and healing all who were under the power of the devil, because God was with him. "We are witnesses of everything he did in the country of the Jews and in Jerusalem. They killed him by hanging him on a cross, but God raised him from the dead on the third day and caused him to be seen. He was not seen by all the people, but by witnesses whom God had already chosen--by us who ate and drank with him after he rose from the dead. He commanded us to preach to the people and to testify that he is the one whom God appointed as judge of the living and the dead. All the prophets testify about him that everyone who believes in him receives forgiveness of sins through his name."

Paul in a Synagogue: Acts 13:16-41: Standing up, Paul motioned with his hand and said: "Fellow Israelites and you Gentiles who worship God, listen to me! The God of the people of Israel chose our ancestors; he made the people prosper during their stay in Egypt; with mighty power he led them out of that country; for about forty years he endured their conduct in the wilderness; and he overthrew seven nations in Canaan, giving their land to his people as their inheritance. All this took about 450 years. "After this, God gave them judges until the time of Samuel the prophet. Then the people asked for a king, and he gave them Saul son of Kish, of the tribe of Benjamin, who ruled forty years. After removing Saul, he made David their king. God testified concerning him: 'I have found David son of Jesse, a man after my own heart; he will do everything I want him to do.' "From this man's descendants God has brought to Israel the Savior Jesus, as he promised. Before the coming of Jesus, John preached repentance and baptism to all the people of Israel. As John was completing his work, he said: 'Who do you suppose I am? I am not the one you are looking for. But there is one coming after me whose sandals I am not worthy to untie.' "Fellow children of Abraham and you God-fearing Gentiles, it is to us that this message of salvation has been sent. The people of Jerusalem and their rulers did not recognize Jesus, yet in condemning him they fulfilled the words of the prophets that are read every Sabbath. Though they found no proper ground for a death sentence, they asked Pilate to have him executed. When they had carried out all that was written about him, they took him down from the cross and laid him in a tomb. But God raised him from the dead, and for many days he was seen by those who had traveled with him from Galilee to Jerusalem. They are now his witnesses to our people. "We tell you the good news: What God promised our ancestors he has fulfilled for us, their children, by raising up Jesus. As it is written in the second Psalm: " 'You are my son; today I have become your father.' God raised him from the dead so that he will never be subject to decay. As God has said, " 'I will give you the holy and sure blessings promised to David.' So it is also stated elsewhere: " 'You will not let your holy one see decay.' "Now when David had served God's purpose in his own generation, he fell asleep; he was buried with his ancestors and his body decayed. But the one whom God raised from the dead did not see decay. "Therefore, my friends, I want you to know that through Jesus the forgiveness of sins is proclaimed to you. Through him everyone who believes is set free from every sin, a justification you were not able to obtain under the law of Moses. Take care that what the prophets have said does not happen to you: " 'Look, you scoffers, wonder and perish, for I am going to do something in your days that you would never believe, even if someone told you.'"

Paul to Gentiles, after healing a man: Acts 14:15-17: "Friends, why are you doing this? We too are only human, like you. We are bringing you good news, telling you to turn from these worthless things to the living God, who made the heavens and the earth and the sea and everything in them. In the past, he let all nations go their own way. Yet he has not left himself without testimony: He has shown kindness by giving you rain from heaven and crops in their seasons; he provides you with plenty of food and fills your hearts with joy."

Paul to Gentiles: Acts 17:22-31: Paul then stood up in the meeting of the Areopagus and said: "People of Athens! I see that in every way you are very religious. For as I walked around and looked carefully at your objects of worship, I even found an altar with this inscription: to an unknown god. So you are ignorant of the very thing you worship--and this is what I am going to proclaim to you. "The God who made the world and everything in it is the Lord of heaven and earth and does not live in temples built by human hands. And he is not served by human hands, as if he needed anything. Rather, he himself gives everyone life and breath and everything else. From one man he made all the nations, that they should inhabit the whole earth; and he marked out their appointed times in history and the boundaries of their lands. God did this so that they would seek him and perhaps reach out for him and find him, though he is not far from any one of us. 'For in him we live and move and have our being.' As some of your own poets have said, 'We are his offspring.' "Therefore since we are God's offspring, we should not think that the divine being is like gold or silver or stone--an image made by human design and skill. In the past God overlooked such ignorance, but now he commands all people everywhere to repent. For he has set a day when he will judge the world with justice by the man he has appointed. He has given proof of this to everyone by raising him from the dead."

Practical Application:

List three things these Biblical Gospels have in common.
1.
2.
3.
How are these ways of telling the Gospel different than the way you have heard the Gospel told?
How will this change the way you share the Gospel with others?

Basic Training Exercise

SPEAKING IN PARABLES

Matthew 13:34-35 NIV - Jesus spoke all these things to the crowd in parables; he did not say anything to them without using a parable. So was fulfilled what was spoken through the prophet: "I will open my mouth in parables, I will utter things hidden since the creation of the world". (Quoting Psalm 78:1.)

DESCRIPTION

Jesus spoke in parables. Particularly when He spoke to "outsiders," He used parables to relate spiritual realities by comparing them to earthly subjects, objects, tasks, or stories. Jesus used parables when speaking to the masses, teaching in synagogues, or talking at dinner parties. Those with ears to hear realized that He was communicating spiritual truth.

As we share Jesus and His Kingdom with others, the Holy Spirit is able to guide us into sharing parables that the people we are speaking to can easily understand. As an evangelism tool, we can use parables to point to the eternal work of Jesus, to transition conversation from worldly things to the Kingdom of God, or to expose a problem without bringing condemnation. These metaphors are useful for bringing Kingdom perspective into almost any situation.

Practicing Speaking in Parables is about relating to others using examples from real life so that they can hear the Word of the Kingdom and turn to Jesus.

CONSIDERATIONS

How does a parable make things easier for people to understand? Particularly those not yet following Jesus? Why do you think Jesus taught in parables rather than explaining the Scriptures or giving rules to follow?

PRAYER

Father, thank you that you reveal yourself to people using examples we can understand. Help me to speak in parables the way Jesus speaks so that others may come to know you. In Jesus' name, Amen.

Category: Evangelism

Basic TRAINING
SPIRITUAL EXERCISES

PURPOSE:
To speak the way that Jesus spoke.

To share truths of Jesus and His Kingdom.

To communicate spiritual realities using practical examples from real life.

SPIRITUAL FRUIT:
Better communication with all kinds of people at any stage of life or faith.

Greater confidence in sharing Jesus and the truth of His Kingdom with others.

Increase in being the light of the world to those who are in darkness.

PRACTICE

1. Ask the Lord to help you create parables in one or more of the categories below. As you do, keep the following in mind:
   - What is the parable? What are you comparing?
   - What point, truth, or principle are you trying to convey?
   - What is the desired result, conviction, or action you desire the hearer to take from the parable?

2. Ask the Lord to help you share the parables in a way that:
   - States the comparison without unnecessary complexity.
   - Boldly but gently delivers the point, truth, or principle.
   - Brings conviction to the heart and motivates right action.
   - Glorifies God and points the hearers back to Jesus.

- Parables for Kingdom truth: Consider one aspect of life with Jesus, what He did/does for us, or what it means for mankind.
  - Ask the Lord to help you relate this aspect to something from normal life, something found in nature, or a made up story to express the point you want to convey. (Examples in Scripture include: light/darkness, Shepherd with sheep, Bride and Bridegroom, slavery/freedom, etc.)

- Parable as segue to salvation: As you participate in everyday conversation with people, take note of the topic of discussion.
  - In one word, what is the topic/theme of conversation?
  - Ask the Lord to help you see how this topic/theme could become an analogy for explaining a Kingdom truth. (Examples: Topic/Theme=War. Analogy=War for our soul; Topic= Marriage; Analogy=Marriage of the Lamb; etc.)

- Parable to expose a problem: When you listen to the troubles of others, try to pinpoint the problem from God's perspective.
  - Ask the Lord to identify the real issue or problem.
  - Ask the Lord to help you relate the real issue to something from normal life, something found in nature, or a made up story that exposes the problem. (Note: This is different than sharing a similar story from our own life.)

ADDITIONAL SCRIPTURES:

Matthew 13; 26

Luke 14; 15; 16

Psalm 78

Psalm 42:1-2

2 Samuel 12:1-4

Isaiah 5:1-7

2 Samuel 14:1-11

1 Corinthians 10:1-13

Galatians 4:21-31

NOTES: _____

Category: Evangelism

PERFECTION COURSE – UNIT 5.3 READING

These Signs will Follow

When Solomon prayed and dedicated the Temple of God in Jerusalem, his prayer reveals something about the heart of God for His people and for the people of the nations. Solomon prayed extensively for God's mercy and forgiveness when His own people when they fell into sin and error resulting in sickness, oppression, or enemy defeat. But when Solomon prayed for the foreigners who would come to the Temple to pray and seek the God of Israel, he asked God to grant whatever the foreigner asked. Through this, all the nations of the earth would know and exalt the name of the one true God. (See 1 Kings 8:41-43.)

God desires to make Himself known. He is willing to do just about anything to demonstrate the redemptive power of heaven in order to introduce Himself to those who do not know Him. The purpose of miracles is to demonstrate the power of God to the world so that they can see and believe and be saved. Jesus did not come to condemn, to judge, or to oppress but to forgive, show mercy, and set free.

*John 3:17: For God did not send His Son into the world to condemn the world, but **to save the world through Him**.*

*John 12:47: "If anyone hears my words but does not keep them, I do not judge that person. For I did not come to judge the world, but **to save the world**."*

With this same intent and purpose, Jesus bestowed upon His followers all power and authority to work miracles in His name to accompany the proclamation of His Kingdom. In fact, He said that miraculous signs would follow all who believe Him.

*John 14:12-13: Very truly I tell you, **whoever believes in Me will do the works I have been doing, and they will do even greater things than these**, because I am going to the Father. And **I will do whatever you ask in My name**, so that the Father may be glorified in the Son.*

The Miracles of Jesus

In order to do the works that Jesus did in the way that He did them, let us examine Jesus' ministry on earth to see what He did and how He did it. Jesus demonstrated the will of God to forgive, to heal, to deliver from oppression, and even to deliver from death – all revealing His purpose to save. Jesus' goodwill towards people was not hindered by their sins or anything that they had done. He did not inquire of anyone's worthiness or piety before healing or delivering them, and He did not go on religious sin-hunts to prove that the sufferer was suffering because of something that they had done to deserve it. Jesus knew that His sacrifice was totally sufficient to cover anything they may have done or not done and therefore, no matter what the problem was, when someone came to Him in faith, Jesus was moved with compassion and was willing and able to bring to earth for them. He did not drone on with long flowery prayers quoting a lot of Scripture to be impressive. Rather, He freely and succinctly forgave even blatant sin without condemnation, and He exercised His *power* and *authority* over sickness, demons, creation, and even over death.

*Luke 7:48: Then Jesus said to her, "**Your sins are forgiven**." (Jesus forgives immoral people.)*

*John 8:11: "No one, sir," she said. "**Then neither do I condemn you**," Jesus declared. "Go now and leave your life of sin." (Jesus forgives even egregious sin.)*

Luke 4:39: **So he bent over her and rebuked the fever, and it left her.** *She got up at once and began to wait on them. (Jesus commands sickness to leave.)*

John 9:3: "Neither this man nor his parents sinned," said Jesus, "but **this happened so that the works of God might be displayed in him.** *(Jesus heals without blaming the sufferer.)*

*Luke 5:12-13: While Jesus was in one of the towns, a man came along who was covered with leprosy. When he saw Jesus, he fell with his face to the ground and begged him, "***Lord, if you are willing,*** you can make me clean." Jesus reached out his hand and touched the man. "***I am willing***," he said. "***Be clean! [healed]***" And immediately the leprosy left him. (Jesus is willing.)*

Mark 9:22-23 NLT: The spirit often throws him into the fire or into water, trying to kill him. Have mercy on us and **help us, if you can**.*"* **"What do you mean, 'If I can'?"** *Jesus asked. "Anything is possible if a person believes."(Jesus is able.)*

Matthew 20:34: **Jesus had compassion on them** *and touched their eyes. Immediately* **they received their sight** *and followed him. (Jesus has compassion on the afflicted.)*

Matthew 8:31-32: The demons begged Jesus, "If you drive us out, send us into the herd of pigs." **He said to them, "Go!"** *So they came out and went into the pigs, and the whole herd rushed down the steep bank into the lake and died in the water. (Jesus commands demons with a single word.)*

Mark 4:39: He got up, **rebuked the wind and said to the waves, "Quiet! Be still!"** *Then the wind died down and it was completely calm. (Jesus commands creation.)*

*John 11:25: Jesus said to her, "***I am the resurrection and the life. The one who believes in me will live, even though they die***; (Jesus raises the dead.)*

Jesus did all of this to demonstrate His power and authority from God and reveal His identity as God's anointed one who has power over all the forces of evil – including death. But Jesus was not limited to these miracles. In fact, these examples are just the highlights that the writers of the Gospels chose to write about for our edification. However, these writers also made it definitively clear that Jesus healed ALL diseases for those who came to Him in faith.

Matthew 4:23-24: Jesus went throughout Galilee, teaching in their synagogues, proclaiming the good news of the kingdom, **and healing every disease and sickness among the people.** *News about Him spread all over Syria, and people brought to Him* **all who were ill with various diseases, those suffering severe pain, the demon-possessed, those having seizures, and the paralyzed; and He healed them.**

Matthew 9:35: Jesus went through all the towns and villages, teaching in their synagogues, proclaiming the good news of the kingdom and **healing every disease and sickness**.

Matthew 12:15: Aware of this, Jesus withdrew from that place. A large crowd followed Him, and **He healed all who were ill**.

Matthew 14:35-36: And when the men of that place recognized Jesus, they sent word to all the surrounding country. People brought **all their sick** *to Him and begged Him to let the sick just touch the edge of his cloak, and* **all who touched it were healed**.

Matthew 15:30-31: Great crowds came to Him, bringing **the lame, the blind, the crippled, the mute and many others, and laid them at His feet; and He healed them.** *The people were amazed when they saw the mute speaking, the crippled made well, the lame walking and the blind seeing. And they praised the God of Israel.*

Mark 1:32-34, 39: That evening after sunset the people brought to **Jesus all the sick and** *demon-possessed. The whole town gathered at the door, and **Jesus healed many who had various diseases. He also drove out many demons**, but He would not let the demons speak because they knew who He was. ... So He traveled throughout Galilee, preaching in their synagogues and **driving out demons.***

*Mark 6:54-56: As soon as they got out of the boat, people recognized Jesus. They ran throughout that whole region and carried the sick on mats to wherever they heard He was. And wherever He went--into villages, towns or countryside--they placed the sick in the marketplaces. They begged Him to let them touch even the edge of his cloak, and **all who touched it were healed.***

*Luke 4:40-41: At sunset, the people brought to Jesus **all who had various kinds of sickness, and laying His hands on each one, He healed them**. Moreover, **demons came out of many people**, shouting, "You are the Son of God!" But He rebuked them and would not allow them to speak, because they knew He was the Messiah.*

*Luke 6:17-19: He went down with them and stood on a level place. A large crowd of his disciples was there and a great number of people from all over Judea, from Jerusalem, and from the coastal region around Tyre and Sidon, who had come to hear Him and to be healed of their diseases. **Those troubled by impure spirits were cured, and the people all tried to touch Him, because power was coming from Him and healing them all**.*

*John 6:2: ...And a great crowd of people followed Him because they saw **the signs He had performed by healing the sick**.*

These healings and other miracles Jesus performed served as a sign to confirm Him as God's Son and the Messiah promised to Israel who is the Savior promised for all mankind. He did not work miracles for amusement or to pridefully put His power on display. He worked miracles to reveal His identity so that people might come to know Him, repent of their ways, and be saved.

Doing the Works that Jesus Did

Jesus shared His authority with His disciples while He was still with them to demonstrate to them beyond a doubt that it is His and God's will for the sick to be healed through faith in His name. Before His suffering, death, and resurrection, when the Lord had sent out His twelve disciples and later the seventy-two, He gave them authority over every disease, unclean spirits, and the power of the evil one.

*Matthew 10:1, 7-8: Jesus called His twelve disciples to Him and **gave them authority to drive out impure spirits and to heal every disease and sickness**... As you go, proclaim this message: 'The kingdom of heaven has come near.' **Heal the sick, raise the dead, cleanse those who have leprosy, drive out demons**. Freely you have received; freely give.*

*Luke 10:17, 19: The seventy-two returned with joy and said, "Lord, even the demons submit to us **in Your name** ... I have given you **authority to trample on snakes and scorpions and to overcome all the power of the enemy; nothing will harm you**.*

Now after His resurrection, Jesus sends His disciples out with ALL authority in heaven and on earth **in His name** to continue the work of bringing His Kingdom to earth as it is in heaven.

*Matthew 28:18-20: Then Jesus came to them and said, "**All authority in heaven and on earth has been given to Me**. Therefore go and make disciples of all nations, **baptizing them in the name of the Father and of the Son and of the Holy Spirit**, and teaching them to obey everything I have commanded you. And surely I am with you always, to the very end of the age."*

*Mark 16:17-18: And these signs will accompany those who believe: **In My name** they will **drive out demons**; they will speak in new tongues; they will pick up snakes with their hands; and when they drink deadly poison, it will not hurt them at all; they will **place their hands*** *on sick people, and they will get well.*

When the first disciples set out to obey Jesus' command after His ascension to , they continued to do the things Jesus had done during His ministry and what they had done when He previously shared His authority with them. They healed the sick, raised the dead, cleansed the lepers, and cast out demons with the same approach, authority, and power of God that Jesus would use if He was there in person. All the while, they pointed to Jesus as the one and only Messiah and Savior sent by God and the One who was truly responsible for all of the miracles and told people to repent so that they could be saved from the wrath of God to come.

> *Acts 3:6-8, 16: Then Peter said, "Silver or gold I do not have, but what I do have I give you.* ***In the name of Jesus Christ of Nazareth, walk.***" *Taking him by the right hand, he helped him up, and instantly the man's feet and ankles became strong. He jumped to his feet and began to walk. Then he went with them into the temple courts, walking and jumping, and praising God. ...* ***By faith in the name of Jesus****, this man whom you see and know was made strong.* ***It is Jesus' name*** *and the faith that comes through Him that has completely healed him, as you can all see."*

> *Acts 8:6-7, 12: When the crowds heard Philip and saw the signs he performed, they all paid close attention to what he said. For with shrieks,* ***impure spirits came out of many, and many who were paralyzed or lame were healed****. ... But when they believed Philip as he* ***proclaimed the good news of the kingdom of God and the name of Jesus Christ****, they were baptized, both men and women.*

> *Acts 9:34: "Aeneas," Peter said to him, "****Jesus Christ heals you****. Get up and roll up your mat." Immediately Aeneas got up.*

> *Acts 16:18: She kept this up for many days. Finally Paul became so annoyed that he turned around and said to the spirit, "****In the name of Jesus Christ I command you to come out of her!****" At that moment the [demonic] spirit left her.*

Practically speaking, in order to do the works that Jesus did in the way that He did them, we cannot simply imitate what He did. We must do what He did. It is impossible to replicate the works of Jesus by any formula because He never did anything the same way twice. For example, in different episodes of giving sight to the blind, Jesus touched their eyes, spit on their eyes, or made mud to put on their eyes. In spite of these different methods, each one received sight. In every miracle that Jesus did, He did what He saw God doing, acted on God's command, and said what God said.

In the same way, as Jesus sends us out to do the works that He did, He shows us or tells us through the Holy Spirit exactly what we are supposed to do with the person right in front of us. We will lay hands on the sick, we will command body parts to be healed, and we will command unclean spirits to flee in Jesus' name. As we wait for His spiritual direction, in our mind's eye we may see ourselves doing something such as laying hands on a person in a particular place, or we may experience a physical sensation somewhere in our bodies as an indication of where their pain is. In other instances, we may hear the Holy Spirit from our inmost being whispering to us, "foot pain" or, "anxiety," or we may experience a momentary onset of emotion to indicate how the person is feeling. As the Holy Spirit guides us, we may hear Jesus whispering things like, "Tell her I love her," or, "Tell her I am not ashamed of her." When we watch and listen for Jesus' instructions and step out to obey His promptings, we do only what we see Him doing and say what He says. We will do the things that He did in the way that He did them.

We who believe have been made citizens of heaven, even though we are still on the earth. We are sent by Christ as His ambassadors to do His will on earth, the way it is in heaven. In heaven, there is no lack, only abundance; there is no sickness, only health; there is no oppression, only freedom; there is no rejection, only acceptance; there is no depression, only joy; there is no stress, only peace. In heaven, there is no death, mourning, crying, or pain. In order to bring heaven to earth, we must keep our minds in heaven and do only what we see Jesus doing.

Resistance, Unbelief, & Demands

When Jesus walked on the earth and people did not believe in Him, He never defended Himself. He simply pointed to His miracles as proof that He had God's approval.

Jesus encountered people who did not believe Him and could not receive heaven on earth from Him. For example, in Nazareth, Jesus' boyhood hometown, people doubted His power. They scoffed, believing that He was just like everybody else, and they were deeply offended by Him. I imagine that they believed things such as this is the way things are in the world, and we get what we deserve, and Jesus is a good guy, but He is not able fix me, or my situation is too hard or impossible for Him. Jesus could not do many miracles in Nazareth because they could not receive from Him.

On the other hand, the religious leaders of the day had issues with Jesus' authority. They questioned if Jesus' authority came from God and accused Him of working for the devil. Other times, they demanded a miraculous sign from Jesus in order to prove that His authority was from God. When they did this, they were treating God like their servant and refused to believe Jesus unless they received what they wanted, the way they wanted it. Jesus did nothing for them.

Similarly, as we set out to do the works that Jesus did in the way that He did them, we will also encounter resistance from people who resist God's miracle working power or do not believe God still works miracles today the way He did in the Book of Acts. Many of these are well-meaning professing believers who have been incorrectly taught or who have had unfortunate experiences with those moving in spiritual power. Their teachings, like the religious leaders in Jesus' day, have a tendency to emphasize character through morality and good works as the demonstration of godliness and Christlikeness. However, Jesus Christ ministered in the power of God. To claim His likeness without His power is not quite like Him at all.

Moreover, the days are coming when the antichrist and the powers of darkness will fill the world with counterfeit signs and lying wonders to deceive all the nations into taking the mark of the beast. Scripture says he will work all manner of miracles including calling fire down from heaven. In the midst of the great apostasy, professing believers will even demand a signs to confirm that someone is working for the real Jesus. But we should take heed to what Jesus said about those who demand a sign.

> *Matthew 12:39-40: He answered, "A wicked and adulterous generation asks for a sign! But none will be given it **except the sign of the prophet Jonah**. For as **Jonah was three days and three nights in the belly of a huge fish, so the Son of Man will be three days and three nights in the heart of the earth**. (See also Matthew 16:4; Luke 11:29-30.)*

Therefore, let us press on to the fullness of all Jesus has died to give us – including His miracle power for bringing heaven to earth. But let us not be confused about who is God or who works for whom. We are the servants, Jesus is the King.

The works that Jesus did as the Son of God are the very same works that we are commissioned, authorized, and empowered to do as God's sons and daughters in Christ. The anointing of the Holy Spirit upon Jesus is the same anointing He has now shared with us. Jesus came to save. We go to save. Let's go!

> *Luke 4:18-19 **The Spirit of the Lord is on ME**, because he has **anointed ME** to **proclaim good news to the poor**. He has sent **ME** to proclaim **freedom for the prisoners** and **recovery of sight for the blind**, to **set the oppressed free**, to proclaim the **year of the Lord's favor**. (emphasis added for personal prayer)*

Basic Training Exercise

SPIRIT UPON ME

Luke 4:18-19 NIV - The Spirit of the Lord is on **me**, because he has anointed **me** to proclaim good news to the poor. He has sent **me** to proclaim freedom for the prisoners and recovery of sight for the blind, to set the oppressed free, to proclaim the year of the Lord's favor.

DESCRIPTION

In order to do the works that Jesus did, we need the Holy Spirit to come upon us. There are numerous examples from the Old Testament of the Spirit of the Lord coming upon normal people to give them supernatural power to fulfill God's work.

Now that the Holy Spirit has been poured out from heaven, the Spirit of the Lord comes to dwell inside of us when we believe Jesus. This is the internal anointing. When the Holy Spirit comes upon us at certain times in powerful ways to aid us in the works of God's Kingdom, it is the external anointing. Both the internal and external anointing are the Spirit of the Lord but they function in different ways for God's purposes.

It is by the Spirit coming upon us believers that they proclaimed the Gospel, prophesied, spoke in other tongues, healed the sick, cast out demons, and raised the dead. The Spirit of the Lord comes upon us today for the same purposes and more. This said, God's power is not to be used for the fulfillment of our own personal aims or for the manipulation of events. It is for the work of God and glorifying the name of Jesus.

Practicing Spirit upon Me is about engaging with the external anointing of God by inviting the Holy Spirit to come upon us as we fulfill God's purposes in the earth.

PRAYER

Father, I believe that you have anointed me to work the works of Jesus with your power from heaven. Allow me to experience your Spirit coming upon me so that I may move in your power and purposes. In Jesus' name, Amen.

Category: Miracles

PURPOSE:
To understand and experience the Spirit of the Lord coming upon us.

To work the works of Jesus by His guidance and power.

SPIRITUAL FRUIT:
Power of the Holy Spirit.

Increased faith and power for miracles.

Deeper experience of God's work for us and through us.

CONSIDERATIONS

In your life with the Holy Spirit, have you experienced more of God's internal power or His external power?

In what ways have you experienced the power of God coming upon you? What was this like for you?

In what ways do you think approaching the Holy Spirit **only for** internal power could be beneficial? Lacking?

In what ways do you think approaching the Holy Spirit **only for** external power could be beneficial? Lacking?

What do you think is the right approach to fulfilling God's purposes in cooperation with both the internal and external power? How will this affect your approach to the Holy Spirit?

PRACTICE

1. Read through the list of Additional Scriptures.
   - Take note that the power of God did not come upon anyone to fulfill their own selfish desires but to fulfill God's purposes.

2. Ask God to reveal to you a situation in your life in which He desires to pour His Spirit upon you to help you.
   - For example, living by faith in His salvation, deliverance, healing, miracles, or any other situation in your life.
   - Ask the Lord to give you one or two Scriptures for this area. (Note: Using only one or two will focus your faith.)

3. In your times of prayer, invite the Holy Spirit to come upon you. Say, "Holy Spirit, clothe me with power from heaven."
   - Briefly wait for anything the Lord may do or say before you begin to enter into prayer.
   - As you pray, alternate between speaking your Scriptures, singing your Scriptures, and speaking/singing in tongues until you sense the presence or power of God.

4. Once you sense the Spirit of the Lord upon you, listen to the Holy Spirit and do whatever you sense He tell you to do.
   - Praise God for what He does! To Him be all glory!

NOTES:

ADDITIONAL SCRIPTURES:
Acts 1:8

Acts 2:1-13

Acts 4:8, 31

Acts 9:17

Acts 10:38

Luke 11:13

Old Testament Examples:
Judges 3:10, 6:34, 11:29, 13:25, 14:6, 19, 15:14

1 Samuel 10:1, 6, 9, 11:6, 16:13

Numbers 11:16-30

Category: Miracles

Basic Training Exercise

HEAL THE SICK

Matthew 4:23-24 NIV - Jesus went throughout Galilee, teaching in their synagogues, proclaiming the good news of the kingdom, and healing every disease and sickness among the people. News about Him spread all over Syria, and people brought to Him all who were ill with various diseases, those suffering severe pain, the demon-possessed those having seizures, and the paralyzed; and He healed them.

DESCRIPTION

When Jesus died on the cross and said, "It is finished," His finished work included healing from all diseases and infirmities. By conquering sin by His blood and redeeming us from the curse of the Law through His death, we are made righteous by faith. The blessing of the righteous is health and healing from all sickness.

Jesus also gave His disciples authority over sickness and every infirmity. When He sent them out to proclaim the Kingdom of God, He also commanded them to demonstrate the benefits and blessings of the Kingdom by healing the sick in Jesus' name.

Therefore, to practicing Heal the Sick Demons is about aligning ourselves with God's will for us to be well and ministering healing to other people so that they can know the love of God for them in Christ Jesus.

TALK TO GOD

Do you believe that God still heals today? Have you ever been miraculously healed by God? Do you know someone who has?

What does Jesus' ministry reveal about God's will for healing?

In what ways have you turned to remedies other than believing God for your healing or wellness? Ask the Lord what He wants you to do about this.

How do you need to engage your faith to receive healing for yourself and minister healing to others?

Category: Miracles

Basic TRAINING
SPIRITUAL EXERCISES

PURPOSE:

To take authority over sickness in our own lives and in the lives of others.

To receive healing in Jesus' name.

To minister healing in Jesus' name.

SPIRITUAL FRUIT:

Deeper revelation of God's will to heal.

Greater functioning in God's authority for us as His children.

Deeper experience of God's ways and work on our behalf.

Deeper understanding and experience of God's healing power.

PRAYER

Father, thank you that you paid for my healing at the cross and have granted me authority in Jesus' name to heal the sick. Help me to believe and grant me power from heaven to be healed and heal for your glory. In Jesus' name, Amen.

PRACTICE – RECEIVING

1. Read through the Scriptures listed in the Additional Scriptures column.
   - Write down what you hear the Holy Spirit highlighting to you from these scriptures.
   - How do these prove that it is God's will to heal you?

2. Identify any kind of sickness, infirmity, weakness, or pain in your own body.
   - Believe in your heart that it is God's will for you to be well.
   - Open your heart to receive healing from God as a free gift.
   - Resist any unbelief with the Word of God, knowing you are the righteousness of God in Christ.

3. Praise God for your healing! Give Him all glory!

PRACTICE – MINISTERING

1. Identify sickness, infirmity, pain, and health issues in others.
   - Share with them that Jesus paid for their healing on the cross. Use the Scriptures and or testimonies of healing to build their faith.

2. If they are willing, pray healing for them the way Jesus did.
   - Don't ask God to heal it, command the sickness like this "In the name of Jesus, be healed," or "[Name of body part] be healed," or [Name of sickness] go, in Jesus' name.

3. Have them put their faith into practice by attempting to do something they previously could not do. For example, "take up your mat and walk…"

4. Praise God for their healing! Give Him all glory!

NOTES: _____

ADDITIONAL SCRIPTURES:

Matthew 8:1-4

Mark 3:1-6

Luke 7:1-17

John 5:1-9

Luke 14:1-6

Acts 9:32-35

Acts 3:1-10

Mark 10:46-52

Matthew 9:1-8

Matthew 10:1-8

Isaiah 53:1-12

1 Peter 2:24

Category: Miracles

PERFECTION COURSE – UNIT 5.4 READING

IF YOU CONTINUE

Professing to repent of your sins and believe Jesus is not a free pass to eternity. Actual repentance and belief is demonstrated by what we do. It is true that salvation is a free gift through faith in Christ. But it will also cost you everything you own if you truly know the value of the Kingdom that has been given to you. Our comprehension of the worth of Jesus is revealed when our faith is put to the test through trials and we stand the test through perseverance and faithfulness to Christ.

When Jesus told His disciples about the tribulation to come before His return, He made it explicitly clear that only those who endure to the very end will be saved. He also made clear that the tribulation before His return is going to be so terrible that nobody would be saved if the days were not shortened.

This is an absolute contradiction to the "salvation prayer" and "once saved, always saved" gospel that is being proclaimed today. The apostles did not believe or proclaim a pre-tribulation rapture. The argument has been made that Jesus said that no one can snatch any of us from His hand. This is true. (See John 10:28.) No one can snatch us out of God's hand but we at retain our free will to believe and to follow Jesus or to deny and renounce Him.

> 2 Timothy 2:11-13, 19: Here is a trustworthy saying: If we died with him, we will also live with him; if we endure, we will also reign with him. **If we disown him, he will also disown us**; if we are faithless, **he remains faithful, for he cannot disown himself**… Nevertheless, God's solid foundation stands firm, sealed with this inscription: "The Lord knows those who are his," and, **"Everyone who confesses the name of the Lord must turn away from wickedness."**

Our faith will be put to the test. God knows our hearts.

A Real Change of Heart

In the Book of John, there are two examples of Jesus putting to the proof those who had already professed faith in Him and were following Him.

After Jesus had fed the five thousand, a large crowd followed Him. But Jesus knew their hearts were not truly with Him. He openly rebuked them for following Him only because He had put food in their bellies. Their following of Jesus was actually service to a different god – their own stomach. Jesus challenged them by teaching that the real bread of life was His own body and real drink was His own blood. This was too disturbing for them. They did not truly grasp who Jesus was or what He was talking about. And so they abandoned Him, stopped following Him, and no longer believed Him to be the Messiah. Only the twelve remained with Him. (See John 6.)

A little later on, Jesus had pardoned the woman caught in adultery. Then, He proclaimed that He did not come to judge anyone and that they would die in their sins if they did not believe Him and so, many believed in Him. Simple enough. But Jesus turned to them and told them that they needed to abide or remain in Him and in His word to truly be His disciples – otherwise they were slaves. They immediately denied ever being enslaved to anyone. But Jesus pointed out that they were enslaved to sin and to lies. Instead of being the seed of the faithful Abraham, they were the offspring of the devil who is the father of lies. At this, their belief in Jesus abruptly ended, they accused Him of being a half-breed Samaritan and tried to stone Him to death. (See John 8.) They liked the message of freedom and forgiveness but were unable to see their own need for it.

Receiving a miracle and following Jesus because it meets our needs is immature belief. A profession of faith without a change of heart is not a real salvation. We must actually repent of our sins and live our lives for God in genuine repentance out of gratitude for Jesus' sacrifice.

The Example of Scripture

The example of Israel being delivered out of Egypt is an allegory for our deliverance from sin through the blood of Jesus. This said, within a few days of the Israelites walking through the Red Sea on dry ground, they grumbled out of hunger and thirst in unbelief that God was able to provide for them in the wilderness. They loathed this halfway state between the slavery of Egypt and the Promised Land and wanted to return to Egypt. It was these same people who had seen God's miracles in Egypt who did not believe that God was able to fulfill ALL of His promises to them. And so, they did not receive what was promised because of their own unbelief. Once we are saved, we have only just begun to walk with God and to have our faith shaped, developed, and tested through various trials and challenges that will come our way. The Israelites serve as our example so that we might be strengthened to stand the test of faith and receive all that Jesus died to give us.

> *Hebrews 3:14-19: We have come to share in Christ, if indeed we hold our original conviction firmly to the very end. As has just been said: "Today, if you hear his voice, do not harden your hearts as you did in the rebellion."* **Who were they who heard and rebelled? Were they not all those Moses led out of Egypt?** *And with whom was he angry for forty years?* **Was it not with those who sinned, whose bodies perished in the wilderness?** *And to whom did God swear that they would never enter his rest if not to those who disobeyed? So we see that they were not able to enter, because of their unbelief.*

> *1 Corinthians 10:1-13: For I do not want you to be ignorant of the fact, brothers and sisters, that our ancestors were* **all under the cloud** *and that they* **all passed through** *the sea. They were* **all baptized** *into Moses in the cloud and in the sea. They* **all ate the same spiritual food and drank the same spiritual drink**; *for they drank from the spiritual rock that accompanied them, and that rock was Christ.* **Nevertheless, God was not pleased with most of them; their bodies were scattered in the wilderness.**

> **Now these things occurred as examples to keep us from setting our hearts on evil things as they did.** *Do not be idolaters, as some of them were; as it is written: "The people sat down to eat and drink and got up to indulge in revelry." We should not commit sexual immorality, as some of them did--and in one day twenty-three thousand of them died. We should not test Christ, as some of them did--and were killed by snakes. And do not grumble, as some of them did--and were killed by the destroying angel.* **These things happened to them as examples and were written down as warnings for us, on whom the culmination of the ages has come.**

> *So,* **if you think you are standing firm, be careful that you don't fall!** *No temptation has overtaken you except what is common to mankind. And God is faithful; he will not let you be tempted beyond what you can bear. But when you are tempted, he will also provide a way out so that you can endure it.*

The letter of Hebrews was written to emphasize the supremacy of Christ and the life of true faithfulness. It was written to Jewish believers who had put their faith in Jesus as Messiah. For their faith in Jesus, they had been brutally rejected, disowned, and plundered by their families as heretics and blasphemers. (See Hebrews 10.) They had tasted the goodness of God, been indwelt with the Holy Spirit, and had already withstood much hardship for Christ. It's just that they had not anticipated just how long this persecution would continue before Christ's return. According to their own Scriptures, they expected His return at any moment to establish His Kingdom. But after ten years of hardship, they were worn out and considering returning to Judaism just to put an end to their earthly struggles. Therefore, the writer of Hebrews consistently encouraged these believers to stand firm until the very end. If they turned their backs on Christ they would not be able to return again. Their eternal souls were on the line.

> *Hebrews 6:4-8: It is impossible for those **who have once been enlightened**, who have tasted the heavenly gift, who have shared in the Holy Spirit, who have tasted the goodness of the word of God and the powers of the coming age **and who have fallen away, to be brought back to repentance**. To their loss they are crucifying the Son of God all over again and subjecting him to public disgrace. Land that drinks in the rain often falling on it and that produces a crop useful to those for whom it is farmed receives the blessing of God. But land that produces thorns and thistles is worthless and is in danger of being cursed. In the end it will be burned.*

Teachers who claim "once saved, always saved" refute this verse by saying that anyone who falls away must not have been saved in the first place. However, knowing the full context of the letter of Hebrews, this argument simply does not stand up.

Moreover, Peter also addressed believers who were vulnerable to falling away due to false teachers. He did not assert that the false teachers were never saved. Rather, he made clear that they had come to salvation but were perverting it to suit their own desires. Peter explains that it would have been better for them not to have been saved at all than to have been saved and then turn away. Clearly, this confirms that it is possible to be saved and fall away from the faith.

> *2 Peter 2:20-22: **If they have escaped the corruption of the world by knowing our Lord and Savior Jesus Christ and are again entangled in it and are overcome, they are worse off at the end than they were at the beginning. It would have been better for them not to have known the way of righteousness, than to have known it and then to turn their backs** on the sacred command that was passed on to them. Of them the proverbs are true: "A dog returns to its vomit," and, "A sow that is washed returns to her wallowing in the mud."*

Endure to the End

As tribulation and wickedness increases on the earth, it will become easier and more justifiable to carnal standards to look out for ourselves rather than pour ourselves out in service to God for the benefit of others. The persecution against Christians of the early church will be dwarfed by the persecution believers have yet to face on a global scale.

> *Matthew 24:12-13: Because of the increase of wickedness, the love of most will grow cold, but **the one who stands firm to the end will be saved**.*

> *Revelation 13:10: If anyone is to go into captivity, into captivity they will go. If anyone is to be killed with the sword, with the sword they will be killed." **This calls for patient endurance and faithfulness on the part of God's people**.*

Let us not live carelessly in hopes of being divinely airlifted off the earth before these trials come. Let us press on to know Christ and to continue in faithfulness to Him no matter what happens so that we can endure to the end and be saved.

www.manifestinternational.com

IF YOU CONTINUE...
Scripture List & Worksheet

Colossians 1:21-23: Once you were alienated from God and were enemies in your minds because of your evil behavior. But now he has reconciled you by Christ's physical body through death to present you holy in his sight, without blemish and free from accusation--**if you continue in your faith**, established and firm, and do not move from the hope held out in the gospel. This is the gospel that you heard and that has been proclaimed to every creature under heaven, and of which I, Paul, have become a servant.

1Corinthians 15:1-4: Now, brothers and sisters, I want to remind you of the gospel I preached to you, which you received and on which you have taken your stand. By this gospel you are saved, **if you hold firmly to the word** I preached to you. **Otherwise, you have believed in vain.** For what I received I passed on to you as of first importance: that Christ died for our sins according to the Scriptures, that he was buried, that he was raised on the third day according to the Scriptures,

1Timothy 4:16: Watch your life and doctrine closely. **Persevere in them**, because if you do, you will save both yourself and your hearers.

Romans 11:22: Consider therefore the kindness and sternness of God: sternness to those who fell, but kindness to you, **provided that you continue in his kindness. Otherwise, you also will be cut off.**

Galatians 3:2-3: I would like to learn just one thing from you: Did you receive the Spirit by the works of the law, or by believing what you heard? Are you so foolish? **After beginning by means of the Spirit, are you now trying to finish by means of the flesh?**

Hebrews 3:6, 14: But Christ is faithful as the Son over God's house. And we are his house, **if indeed we hold firmly to our confidence and the hope in which we glory**. ... We have come to share in Christ, **if indeed we hold our original conviction firmly to the very end**.

Hebrews 4:14: Therefore, since we have a great high priest who has ascended into heaven, Jesus the Son of God, **let us hold firmly to the faith we profess.**

Hebrews 6:11: We want each of you to **show this same diligence to the very end**, so that what you hope for may be fully realized.

Hebrews 10:23: Let us **hold unswervingly to the hope we profess**, for he who promised is faithful.

Practical Application:

What are three ways the Lord is asking you to respond to these Scriptures?
1.
2.
3.

Who Will & Will Not Enter
Scripture List & Worksheet

Matthew 5:3, 10, 18-20: "Blessed are the poor in spirit, for **theirs is the kingdom of heaven**. ... Blessed are those who are persecuted because of righteousness, for **theirs is the kingdom of heaven**. ... For truly I tell you, until heaven and earth disappear, not the smallest letter, not the least stroke of a pen, will by any means disappear from the Law until everything is accomplished. Therefore anyone who sets aside one of the least of these commands and teaches others accordingly will be called **least in the kingdom of heaven**, but whoever practices and teaches these commands will be called **great in the kingdom of heaven**. For I tell you that unless your righteousness surpasses that of the Pharisees and the teachers of the law, you will certainly **not enter the kingdom of heaven**.

Matthew 7:21-23: "**Not everyone who says to me, 'Lord, Lord,' will enter the kingdom of heaven**, but only the one who does the will of my Father who is in heaven. Many will say to me on that day, 'Lord, Lord, did we not prophesy in your name and in your name drive out demons and in your name perform many miracles?' Then I will tell them plainly, 'I never knew you. Away from me, you evildoers!'

John 3:3-8: Jesus replied, "Very truly I tell you, **no one can see the kingdom of God unless they are born again**." "How can someone be born when they are old?" Nicodemus asked. "Surely they cannot enter a second time into their mother's womb to be born!" Jesus answered, "Very truly I tell you, **no one can enter the kingdom of God** unless they are born of water and the Spirit. Flesh gives birth to flesh, but the Spirit gives birth to spirit. You should not be surprised at my saying, 'You must be born again.' The wind blows wherever it pleases. You hear its sound, but you cannot tell where it comes from or where it is going. So it is with everyone born of the Spirit."

Acts 14:22b: "We must go through **many hardships to enter the kingdom of God**," they said.

Mark 12:33-34a: To love him with all your heart, with all your understanding and with all your strength, and to love your neighbor as yourself is more important than all burnt offerings and sacrifices." When Jesus saw that he had answered wisely, he said to him, "**You are not far from the kingdom of God**."
Matthew 18:1-4: At that time the disciples came to Jesus and asked, "Who, then, is the **greatest in the kingdom of heaven**?" He called a little child to him, and placed the child among them. And he said: "Truly I tell you, **unless you change and become like little children, you will never enter the kingdom of heaven**. Therefore, whoever takes the lowly position of this child is the **greatest in the kingdom of heaven**.

Matthew 19:23-24: Then Jesus said to his disciples, "Truly I tell you, it is hard for someone who is rich **to enter the kingdom of heaven**. Again I tell you, it is easier for a camel to go through the eye of a needle than for someone who is rich **to enter the kingdom of God**."

Matthew 23:13: "Woe to you, teachers of the law and Pharisees, you hypocrites! **You shut the door of the kingdom of heaven** in people's faces. You yourselves do not enter, nor will you let those enter who are trying to.

Mark 9:43-48: If your hand causes you to stumble, cut it off. **It is better for you to enter life [in the Kingdom]** maimed than with two hands to go into hell, where the fire never goes out. And if your foot causes you to stumble, cut it off. It is better for you to enter life crippled than to have two feet and be thrown into hell. And if your eye causes you to stumble, pluck it out. **It is better for you to enter the kingdom of God** with one eye than to have two eyes and be thrown into hell, where " 'the worms that eat them do not die, and the fire is not quenched.'

Luke 9:57-62: As they were walking along the road, a man said to him, "I will follow you wherever you go." Jesus replied, "Foxes have dens and birds have nests, but the Son of Man has no place to lay his head." He said to another man, "Follow me." But he replied, "Lord, first let me go and bury my father." Jesus said to him, "Let the dead bury their own dead, but **you go and proclaim the kingdom of God**." Still another said, "I will follow you, Lord; but first let me go back and say goodbye to my family." Jesus replied, "No one who puts a hand to the plow and looks back is **fit for service in the kingdom of God**."

1 Corinthians 6:9-11: Or do you not know that wrongdoers **will not inherit the kingdom of God**? Do not be deceived: Neither the sexually immoral nor idolaters nor adulterers nor men who have sex with men nor thieves nor the greedy nor drunkards nor slanderers nor swindlers **will inherit the kingdom of God**. And that is what some of you were. But you were washed, you were sanctified, you were justified in the name of the Lord Jesus Christ and by the Spirit of our God.

1 Corinthians 15:48-50: As was the earthly man, so are those who are of the earth; and as is the heavenly man, so also are those who are of heaven. And just as we have borne the image of the earthly man, so shall we bear the image of the heavenly man. I declare to you, brothers and sisters, that **flesh and blood cannot inherit the kingdom of God**, nor does the perishable inherit the imperishable.
Galatians 5:19-21: The acts of the flesh are obvious: sexual immorality, impurity and debauchery; idolatry and witchcraft; hatred, discord, jealousy, fits of rage, selfish ambition, dissensions, factions and envy; drunkenness, orgies, and the like. I warn you, as I did before, that those who live like this **will not inherit the kingdom of God**.

Ephesians 5:5-6: For of this you can be sure: No immoral, impure or greedy person--such a person is an idolater--**has any inheritance in the kingdom of Christ and of God**. Let no one deceive you with empty words, for because of such things God's wrath comes on those who are disobedient.

Colossians 1:12-14: and giving joyful thanks to the Father, who has qualified you to share in the inheritance of his holy people in the kingdom of light. For he has rescued us from the dominion of darkness and brought us **into the kingdom of the Son he loves**, in whom we have redemption, the forgiveness of sins.

2 Thessalonians 1:4-5: Therefore, among God's churches we boast about your perseverance and faith in all the persecutions and trials you are enduring. All this is evidence that God's judgment is right, and as a result you will be **counted worthy of the kingdom of God**, for which you are suffering.
James 2:5: Listen, my dear brothers and sisters: Has not God chosen those who are poor in the eyes of the world to be rich in faith and **to inherit the kingdom** he promised those who love him?

2 Peter 1:10-11: Therefore, my brothers and sisters, make every effort to confirm your calling and election. For if you do these things, you will never stumble, and you will **receive a rich welcome into the eternal kingdom of our Lord and Savior Jesus Christ**.

Revelation 21:7-8: Those who are **victorious will inherit all this [the Kingdom]**, and I will be their God and they will be my children. But the cowardly, the unbelieving, the vile, the murderers, the sexually immoral, those who practice magic arts, the idolaters and all liars--they will be consigned to the fiery lake of burning sulfur. This is the second death."

Galatians 6:7-8: Do not be deceived: God cannot be mocked. A man reaps what he sows. Whoever sows to please their flesh, from the flesh will reap destruction; whoever sows to please the Spirit, from the Spirit will reap eternal life [in the Kingdom.]

Practical Application:

What do these Scriptures reveal to you about the Kingdom of God?

List three types of people or behaviors that qualify us for the Kingdom of God.
1.
2.
3.

List three types of people or behaviors that disqualify us for the Kingdom of God.
1.
2.
3.

In what ways does this challenge your concepts about the heart of God and His Kingdom?

How is God asking you to personally respond to these Scriptures in your own life?

Sermon on the Mount Inspection

1 = Needs improvement		2 = In Refining Process			3 = Doing Well for Now		

Sermon on the Mount – *based on Matthew 5-7, Luke 6*

I know my need for God.	1	2	3	I do not seek the praise of others.	1	2	3
I lament over sin and wickedness.	1	2	3	I give in secret.	1	2	3
I am meek, lowly.	1	2	3	I do not pray on display in public.	1	2	3
I am merciful.	1	2	3	I pray in the secret place of God.	1	2	3
My heart and motives are pure.	1	2	3	I do not heap up phrases in prayer.	1	2	3
I make peace at my own expense.	1	2	3	I forgive others their offenses.	1	2	3
I am persecuted for righteousness.	1	2	3	I do not fast to be seen/noticed.	1	2	3
I am reviled by others for Jesus.	1	2	3	I do not lay up treasures on earth.	1	2	3
I let my light shine before others.	1	2	3	I give generously to the poor.	1	2	3
I do not sin through anger.	1	2	3	I am not anxious about my life.	1	2	3
I quickly settle conflicts.	1	2	3	I do not focus on food & clothing.	1	2	3
I do not commit adultery.	1	2	3	I seek first the Kingdom of God.	1	2	3
I am not lustful in my heart.	1	2	3	I do not judge others.	1	2	3
I pluck out hindrances to eternity.	1	2	3	I take the log out of my own eye.	1	2	3
I do not swear falsely.	1	2	3	I do not throw pearls before pigs.	1	2	3
I do not take oaths.	1	2	3	I ask God in all things.	1	2	3
My yes is yes, my no is no.	1	2	3	I seek God in all things.	1	2	3
I do not resist evil people.	1	2	3	I knock for God for all things.	1	2	3
I turn the other cheek.	1	2	3	I do to others as I want to receive.	1	2	3
I go the extra mile.	1	2	3	I strive to enter by the narrow gate.	1	2	3
I give to everyone who asks of me.	1	2	3	I discern false teachers by fruit.	1	2	3
I do not demand back from takers.	1	2	3				
I love my enemies.	1	2	3	I hear the words of Jesus.	1	2	3
I bless those who curse me.	1	2	3	I DO the words of Jesus.	1	2	3

Now that you know these things, you will be blessed if you do them.
John 13:17

UNIT FIVE – KEY QUESTIONS
Kingdom Gospel with Signs

Use this worksheet to test your grasp of the material and exercises of Unit Five.

What is the eternal Gospel? (in your own words)	

How does God use witnesses to accomplish His purposes?	Why is it important to preach the Gospel free of charge?

What was Jesus' primary message?	What is God's purpose for miracles?

Does professing belief in Jesus qualify as salvation?	What happens to believers who turn away from Christ?

What is one thing you learned that you did not know before?	What questions do you still have about this subject?

UNIT FIVE: GROUP EXERCISES

Option One:
Using the Speaking in Parables exercise from Class Two, practice speaking to one another in parables about Jesus and His Kingdom. Offer constructive feedback about your parables.

AND/OR

Option Two:
Using the Heal the Sick exercise from Class Three, practice praying healing for one another and for anyone in the group who has any kind of sickness or infirmity.

UNIT SIX:
DISCERNMENT OF GOOD & EVIL

KEY SCRIPTURE VERSE FOR UNIT SIX
But solid food is for the mature, who by constant use have trained themselves to distinguish good from evil. - Hebrews 5:14

CLASS 1: DISCERNING THE SCHEMES OF THE ENEMY
1 Reading, 2 Exercises
Since the Garden of Eden, the enemy has been using every tactic he can to persuade believers off of the course of eternal life. The further we go on our spiritual journey, the more subtle the schemes of the enemy become.

CLASS 2: YEASTS OF JESUS' DAY & TODAY
1 Reading, 1 Scripture Worksheet, 1 Exercise
Jesus warned His disciples to beware of the yeasts of the false teachers in His day. In examining these yeasts, we will discover that the same false beliefs are still working to bring corruption today.

CLASS 3: DECEITFUL WORKERS & DOCTRINES OF DEMONS
1 Reading, 1 Scripture Worksheet, 1 Exercise
Approximately one third of the New Testament pertains to false teachers and how to avoid them. Let us examine the path of false teachers and their teachings so that we will not be led astray by doctrines of demons.

CLASS 4: ENDURING THROUGH THE GREAT APOSTASY
1 Reading, 1 Scripture Worksheet, 1 Prayer Guide
Before the return of Christ, many will fall away from the faith. Let us examine what Scripture actually says about the end times so that we can be prepared to endure in the truth.

KEY QUESTIONS

GROUP EXERCISES

PERFECTION COURSE – UNIT 6.1 READING

Discerning the Schemes of the Enemy

In the story of the prodigal son, the prodigal does not stop being a son. But the heart of the prodigal rejects his own sonship to exchange it for having his own way. It is a heart that says, "give it to me **now** so that I may do my will with it" rather than, "thank you father for all you have provided for me, how can I serve you?" I'm sure the freedom and fortune felt exhilarating for the prodigal at first. But it did not take long for him to lose all he had and find himself lost, alone, wasted, and useless. We have to consider for a moment, what was it in the heart of the prodigal that caused him to think and behave this way?

Before the world was created, Lucifer was designed by God to be the chief worshipping angel. Lucifer had experienced the bliss of unrestricted access to God and His throne. But after a while, worshipping God was not enough for him. He wanted to ascend to the throne of God for himself. He set out to do it. Iniquity, greed, and arrogance was found in him. He was thrown down.

In the Garden of Eden, Adam and Eve were believers – children of God. They had seen God, experienced God, fellowshipped with God, and clearly heard God's voice. They were made in God's image and appointed to rule the world with God. But then, Adam and Eve were faced with a choice. The serpent appealed to their desire to ascend to new heights of being like God. The devil did not say, "you will be like demons" or "you will be like me and my angels cast out of the presence of God." No. Instead, he said, "you will be like God." The serpent painted a picture of attaining their highest and truest objective in life which caused them to lust with ambition for greater things. At the same time, the evil one twisted and discounted God's Word which caused Adam and Eve to doubt, and ultimately negate, the consequences of disobedience. Desire was birthed in their hearts, the pros and cons were evaluated, and self-exaltation won the day over submission to God and His commands. Adam and Eve went prodigal in hopes of attaining their own desires but instead wound up separated from God and from the source of life.

The ancient serpent is still planting seeds of doubt and selfishness in the hearts of believers. The whole world is already under the power of the evil one and it takes little effort for him to keep them bound. It is believers who require specialized attention from the forces of evil and more subtle tactics which distort God's Word and ways to veer even the most sincere believers off their course for eternity. God allows us to retain our free will at all times. Though He longs for us to make right choices and not fall prey to deception, He allows us to set our own course and when we do, He waits for us to come to our senses and return to His wisdom and approach. We are most vulnerable when we feel most secure as those who consider ourselves to know God's love, salvation, fellowship, and peace. We must keep vigilant guard of our heart, mind, and will so as to continually discern the various tactics of the evil one.

Four Soils (See Matthew 13:1-23; Mark 4:1-24; Luke 8:4-18.)

Jesus said about his parable of the four soils that if we cannot understand this parable, we will be challenged to understand any of His other parables. This parable outlines the basis for the faithfulness required in a believer's heart to withstand the tactics and schemes of the enemy until we receive our ultimate eternal reward.

The seed is the Word of God. God sows seed liberally – throwing it everywhere on all kinds of soils, which represent the hearts of individuals and our ability to receive the Word of God.

The seed falls on top of the first soil. The birds of the air come to eat it before it penetrates. The heart is hard to the ways of God. On the one hand, this is a chastisement to keep our hearts soft and not quench the Holy Spirit or despise prophecies so that we do not miss out on what God desires to say to us. On the other hand, even when we do receive a word, we must be alert that the enemy's first line of attack is to try to snatch the seed out of our grasp. This usually comes through our own doubt, unbelief, or questioning, "Did God really say?" until we convince ourselves that God did not say what He said. Beware of this!

The seed which falls on the second soil is received with joy. We shout our hallelujah and amen with enthusiasm, ready to receive the blessing of God and set our course to obey Him. On our part, we may be excessively simple or naïve, not having counted the cost of following a crucified King. In the enemy's bag of tricks, he will try to kill the seed in our hearts through trials, troubles, persecution, humiliation, accusation, and any manner of tactics until ultimately, we ask ourselves, "Did God really say?" and we cannot conceive that God's path would be this challenging. Then, we abandon God's path by choosing ourselves and our own well-being.

The seed which falls on the third soil penetrates into our hearts and we start out well. The seed takes root. We are firm – or so we think. We know the voice of God and what He has said to us. But as we set out to see the Word of God fulfilled in our lives, temporal issues and priorities creep into our consciousness. Family obligations. Money. Time. Energy. Friends. Fellowship. Traditions. Reputation. Whatever it is, it causes us to settle into complacency rather than pushing further into all that God promised. The "good" and "godly" activities in our lives cause us to convince ourselves that this is sufficient service for God's Kingdom. "Did God really say?" becomes a dream we once had but not the reality of our existence. Even though we may appear to be serving God and flourishing in God's work, the enemy has succeeded in side-tracking us from God's true purpose for our lives.

But there is the fourth soil. The fourth soil perseveres through all of these challenges and tactics of the evil one. This is the heart that consistently chooses, "not my will but Yours be done," and is willing to give it all for God, even missing out on "opportunities" that seemed to be their ticket to "success" and recognition. This is the heart that receives and understands that God is worthy of all we have to give and that nothing of this world is worth departing from His ways. This heart knows that in the end, we will stand before Jesus and give account for what we have done with what He has given us.

Personally, what I have discovered about this parable is that it is not only true for our salvation in general but for every word of the Lord we receive as revelation and instruction from Him. All revelation will be tested in our hearts through our ability to live it out in our lives. All of God's instructions to us will be put to the test of whether or not we will choose to obey God or to indulge ourselves while convincing ourselves that we are doing it to serve Him. Knowing this can help us to discern the tactics of the enemy as we set ourselves to hear, receive, obey, and abide in the word of God until we see it come to pass in our lives.

Insights from the Book of Daniel

The enemy's tactics of deception have not changed much since creation. The Book of Daniel gives some insight into the methods the enemy uses to attempt to draw us off course.

> *Daniel 7:25 ESV - He shall **speak words against the Most High**, and shall **wear out the saints** of the Most High, and shall think to **change the times and the law**; and they shall be given into his hand for a time, times, and half a time.*

Speak against Most High: The serpent's first suggestion was, "Did God really say?" planting seeds of doubt. Then he launched an assault on God's character as if God was withholding something from Adam and Eve or had ordered them not to partake of something which would be beneficial for them. Even today, the enemy continuously aims to discredit God or cause us to doubt that God has given us everything we need to fulfill His purposes. The enemy accuses God of abandoning us, not speaking to us, not supplying our needs, not having paid the full price on the cross, and speaks against God's word as being unreliable, or that God will not fulfill His promises for us. The evil one persistently accuses God night and day to attempt to push us into taking matters into our own hands, rather than trusting God and waiting on Him in obedience to His commands.

<u>Wear out saints</u>: The word used here means persecute or constantly harass. It is easy to think that victory in "spiritual warfare" is attained with a simple command into the spirit realm. But we must realize that the enemy is persistent. Consider how Samson had great strength on numerous occasions to resist the temptations and enticements of doing what he should not. But over time and with constant pressure, even Samson caved into the plots of his enemies. Only with clear discernment and endurance will we stand in the strength of the Lord when the enemy has worn out all of our own strength and ability to stand.

<u>Change times</u>: The enemy knows his time is short and so, he likes to try to play with time. One of the ways the enemy attacks us is to convince us that we are behind schedule, that we are going to miss an appointed time of God, or that "our time" for exaltation has come. One of the most dangerous questions a Christian can ask is, "when is it MY time…" for blessing, honor, victory, exaltation or anything like this.

Moreover, the enemy himself is always attempting to set up his own times. The calendar of the world has been changed on numerous occasions by pagan emperors. The times of the Biblical feasts have been replaced with pagan holiday times. Even the Jewish calendar has been distorted by rabbis away from the pure Biblical prescription. It is God alone who changes the times and the seasons. It is God alone who will lead us in His perfect timing and whose timing never fails.

Additionally, the evil one will try to lure people into predicting the times of God and setting dates for the return of Christ. All of these predictions so far have failed to come to pass. Why? Because not even Jesus knows the time of His own return. Only the Father. The end will still come at the appointed time.

<u>Change laws</u>: The enemy also changes laws against and away from God's standard of righteousness. Legalizing things which God deems unlawful and outlawing things which God says are righteous. Just because something is legal does not mean that it is moral, let alone righteous in God's sight. Calling good evil and evil good is a sign of great depravity.

Religious commands and traditions can also be the enemy's way of changing laws. Adding to God's laws and establishing our own code of ethics is only done under the influence of the evil one who is yet again perverting God's word and its consequences as he did back in the Garden of Eden. Traditions of men nullify the power of the word of God.

> *Daniel 11:21, 23: "He will be succeeded by a contemptible person who has not been given the honor of royalty. He will invade the kingdom **when its people feel secure**, and **he will seize it through intrigue**. … After coming to an agreement with him, **he will act deceitfully**, and with only a few people he will rise to power.*

> *Daniel 11:32, 36: **With flattery he will corrupt** those who have violated the covenant, but the people who know their God will firmly resist him. … "The king will do as he pleases. **He will exalt and magnify himself above every god and will say unheard-of things against the God of gods**. He will be successful until the time of wrath is completed, for what has been determined must take place.*

<u>Feeling of Security</u>: The enemy knows when we feel we have attained a level of security in any aspect of our lives. This is when he loves to strike in the area where we think we have the least vulnerability. To promote this feeling of security, the enemy's mouthpieces and counterfeit spirits will constantly be saying, "peace, peace" when there is no peace and the true servants of God are issuing warnings. Those who succumb to the false peace will be unprepared for the seemingly sudden onslaught of attack that they were not expecting. If they had listened to God they would have remained vigilant and been prepared.

Intrigue, Flatteries: The word for intrigue and flatteries in this passage means smooth promises, slipperiness, and smoothness of speech. As previously stated, the enemy does not come and say, "you will be like demons" he says, "you will be like God." He knows how to appeal to our highest sense of what is right, particularly when we are feeling secure, and thus ensnares us by our own right desires into wrong actions.

Deception: The enemy is a counterfeiter and a fraud. He promises freedom but the result is bondage. He promises exaltation but the result is humiliation. He promises peace but the result is enmity. He promises abundance but the result is abasement. He is willing to take whatever form is necessary (i.e. strong for leadership, weak for entrapment, etc.) in order to allure and entice us into his schemes.

Self-exaltation: The primary motive of the evil one is to exalt himself. It is his nature. His motive in our lives is to cause us to exalt ourselves so that we fall from the grace God has given us in Christ or step beyond the bounds of what Christ has ordained for us. His words against the Most High are not often insulting because that would be too obvious. Instead, they are distortions of God's character, God's work, and the rightful place we have as God's children, causing us to want to ascend higher than we ought. Even though Jesus taught disciples to pray, "your will be done on earth as it is in heaven" it is wise for us to remember that the present heaven is the same one in which Lucifer exalted himself. This heaven will be rolled away like a scroll and a new heaven will be made which is completely pure of him.

> *Daniel 12:4 ESV - But you, Daniel, shut up the words and seal the book, until the time of the end. **Many shall run to and fro, and knowledge shall increase**.*"

Busyness: Busyness makes us feel important. The enemy loves to distract us with busyness – especially family, church, or service busyness. It is easy to persuade ourselves that we are doing something wonderful for God when we are praying, loving, caring, and serving. But we are only doing it for God if God has actually asked us to do it. Otherwise, we are doing work which will ultimately burn in the fire and will prove to have been a distraction from the work which would have passed through the test to eternity.

Knowledge: Knowledge makes us feel powerful and superior. The enemy loves to trick us into the pursuit of knowledge or mental ascent through enticing us to believe that special knowledge will elevate us and keep us from harm. The increase of knowledge in our days is prevalent everywhere. But instead of creating deeper knowledge and awareness of truth, it is numbing the minds of those infiltrated with excess information. The short term memory is chronically overused and the Holy Spirit's voice is snuffed out, if not forgotten. "Knowledge is power" is an enemy substitute for "the Gospel is the power." This is the end-times version of the tree of the knowledge of good and evil. It will only open our eyes to nakedness, fear, and shame while distancing us from the knowledge of the Holy One.

Double Mindedness

A double minded person is unstable in all their ways and should expect to receive nothing from God. As such, if we give way to double-mindedness, the enemy's scheme has succeeded in full. For example, when Adam and Eve experienced the first deception of believers on earth, the serpent was successful in persuading them from single-mindedness to double-mindedness. They had no other focus except God and His commands until an alternative was made available to them. The alternative appeared more promising for faster results and so, the choice was made. Adam and Eve concluded that the fruit was appealing, attractive, was beneficial for wisdom and success, and would advance them in their pursuits on earth. The results were sealed in their hearts before they even took a bite.

Worldliness (including the love of money) and pride are the greatest temptations to double-mindedness. But these very things are acts of treason against God. You cannot serve both God and mammon. We would be wise to remember that by the standards of this world, Jesus looked like a complete and total failure. But yet, through His obedience even unto death, Jesus is uncontested as the most famous person who ever lived and by God's standards, will be known in eternity as the most successful person who ever walked on earth. Not to mention that He is the wealthiest man in history because He owns the whole world. Riches will profit us nothing in the day of the Lord.

> *James 4:4-8: You adulterous people, don't you know that* **friendship with the world means enmity against God?** *Therefore, anyone who chooses to be a friend of the world becomes an enemy of God. Or do you think Scripture says without reason that he jealously longs for the spirit he has caused to dwell in us? But he gives us more grace. That is why Scripture says:* "**God opposes the proud but shows favor to the humble.**" **Submit yourselves, then, to God. Resist the devil,** *and he will flee from you. Come near to God and he will come near to you. Wash your hands, you sinners, and* **purify your hearts, you double-minded**.

> *1 John 2:15-17: Do not love the world or anything in the world.* **If anyone loves the world, love for the Father is not in them**. *For everything in the world--***the lust of the flesh, the lust of the eyes, and the pride of life--comes not from the Father but from the world**. *The world and its desires pass away, but whoever does the will of God lives forever.*

The enemy will always float the ways of the world before our faces to tempt us or allure us off of the path of obedience to God. His aim is to get us to strive to succeed by worldly standards and convince ourselves that worldly success is the mark of God's blessing. The result is that we feel blessed or cursed depending on our natural ability to measure up by the world's standards. What a lie from the pit of hell. The world, its ways, its luxuries, and its measurements of success are all passing away. Our Kingdom is not of this world.

Self-Deception

Self-deception occurs when the reality of our lives and conduct do not match what we think of ourselves. This is rooted in pride, ignorance, and lack of conviction from the Holy Spirit. Either the enemy has infiltrated our thoughts to the degree that we are not listening to the Holy Spirit anymore, or we have never fully repented from our former ways of doing things so as to extract ourselves from the influence of the world, the flesh, and the devil. Whatever ground we have yielded to deception must be regained in our lives through truth and repentance. Lies must be replaced and the truth must be applied to our lives. Self-awareness and honesty with ourselves and before God as we take the planks out of our own eyes is absolutely necessary to our spiritual advancement and endurance.

> *James 1:22, 26: Do not merely listen to the word, and so* **deceive yourselves**. *Do what it says. ... Those who consider themselves religious and yet do not keep a tight rein on their tongues* **deceive themselves**, *and their religion is worthless.*

Those who hear the Word but do not do it are self-deceived. They may have much learning about God and much knowledge of Him but they do not actually know God or His ways. They may be able to quote many Scriptures and are usually quite good at judging other people's faults and wrongdoings but when a trial hits their own life, their faith is powerless and useless.

> *1 John 1:8: If we* **claim to be without sin, we deceive ourselves** *and the truth is not in us.*

Those who claim to be without sin are self-deceived. Anyone claiming to be without sin is lacking in conviction from the Holy Spirit. This means they are either not saved at all or are not listening to God. This can also evidence itself by people who make excuses for their sin, treat it lightly, or blame-shift by pointing the finger at someone else to escape responsibility for their own sin. The only one without sin is Jesus. Even the most perfect saint on this side of heaven is imperfect in their thoughts, actions, motives, or perceptions from time to time. If we think otherwise, we make God to be a liar but we ourselves are the ones who lie. God is not fooled.

> *Galatians 3:1-3: You foolish Galatians!* **Who has bewitched you?** *Before your very eyes Jesus Christ was clearly portrayed as crucified. I would like to learn just one thing from you: Did you*

*receive the Spirit **by the works of the law, or by believing** what you heard? Are you so foolish? **After beginning by means of the Spirit, are you now trying to finish by means of the flesh?***

Those who think they can perfect through actions of the flesh what only God can do by His Spirit are self-deceived. We can add nothing to the finished work of Christ or it was not finished when He finished it. ANY attempt to add anything to the finished work of the cross through our own efforts and striving is a lie from the pit of hell.

*Galatians 6:3-4: If anyone **thinks they are something when they are not, they deceive themselves**. Each one should test their own actions. Then they can take pride in themselves alone, without comparing themselves to someone else,*

Those who think they are something when they are not are self-deceived. None of us bring anything to the table except a body of flesh willing to serve the Lord. If we think we are standing strong enough to not be tempted by the sins and snares that other believers fall into, we will prove sorely mistaken. If we think we have attained some standing or title or position within the Body of Christ other than that of a servant, we are self-important and self-deceived.

*1 Corinthians 3:18: Do not **deceive yourselves. If any of you think you are wise** by the standards of this age, you should become "fools" so that you may become wise.*

Those who consider themselves wise by the standards of this world are self-deceived. The wisest wisdom the world has to offer killed the King of Creation on a cross. If we think that we will have anything to contribute to the work of God, or ways which are superior to God's, we are self-deceived.

*1 Corinthians 6:9: Or do you not know that wrongdoers will not inherit the kingdom of God? **Do not be deceived**: Neither the sexually immoral nor idolaters nor adulterers nor men who have sex with men.*

*1 Corinthians 15:33: **Do not be misled**: "Bad company corrupts good character."*

Those who think they can carouse with or participate with lawlessness without losing their inheritance in the Kingdom of God are self-deceived.

*2 Corinthians 11:3: But I am afraid that just as **Eve was deceived by the serpent's cunning**, your minds may somehow be led astray from your sincere and pure devotion to Christ.*

Most sadly, self-deception still occurs among those who seem to be spiritually advanced. The Corinthians were gifted will all manner of spiritual gifts and had extensive knowledge of God and His ways. But they were prone to the teachings and promises of the false apostles who relentlessly persecuted the Apostle Paul and tried to dissuade them from Paul's teachings. When we try to be self-important spiritually, we will find ourselves self-deceived. Our King is the only One who ever was something, but He became nothing to show us the way of humility.

Counterfeits

The enemy is an excellent counterfeiter. The first word to describe the serpent is "subtle." He is exceptionally subtle and knows how to deceive even the most seasoned saint, if it is possible to deceive them. Only those who know the truth will be able to discern the difference between the counterfeit and the real thing. What makes this most challenging is that a fake is always pretty close to the real thing. The evil one does not come along and present a bottle of poison to one who can read the label. No. He finds something good and mixes poison into it so that a consumer who consumes enough will be imbibed and eventually overthrown. One percent pollution of ninety-nine percent purity is enough to begin to infiltrate the minds of the well intentioned. His objective is to gain a bit of ground in our hearts so that we become confused, unstable, or double-minded until we take hold of the polluted Word of God for our own purposes until we have aligned with a wrong spirit altogether.

Consider, for example, that when the northern and southern kingdom divided, the king of the northern kingdom was concerned that his people would go to Jerusalem in the southern kingdom to worship God in the only place where God had chosen for sacrifices to be made. So, he set up centers of worship for the people within the territory of the northern kingdom, ordained priests who did not meet God's requirements of the sons of Aaron or Levites, and appointed feasts which were in times close to the times of God's appointed feasts. To unbelievers from outside nations, the differences between the northern kingdom and southern kingdom appeared minimal. They were all "people of the God of Israel" claiming to worship Him. Their worship even looked alike in many ways. But those who knew the commands of the Lord knew the differences between the fake and the real thing. Therefore, many priests and Levites moved to the southern kingdom to keep themselves aligned with the truth. There may have been others who inwardly knew that the northern kingdom's worship was unsanctioned by God, but as a matter of personal convenience, submitted themselves to it and engaged in counterfeit worship. Soon, the whole kingdom had given way to worshipping Baal (which means lord) thinking themselves to still be the faithful people of the Most High God.

In the most convincing ways possible, the enemy counterfeits the best aspects of God to lure us into obedience to the lie rather than the truth. In Paul's day, so called "super apostles" used big boasts and swelling words to make great promises to those who were eager to hear of God's greatness, power, and willingness to bless. But these "apostles" were not proclaiming the real Jesus. They proclaimed a fabrication of their own minds backed by spiritual power supplied by a spirit other than the Holy Spirit.

> *2 Corinthians 11:4 ESV - For if someone comes and proclaims **another Jesus** than the one we proclaimed, or if you receive **a different spirit** from the one you received, or if you accept **a different gospel** from the one you accepted, you put up with it readily enough.*

Counterfeit Jesus: The counterfeit Jesus can take many and various forms but in one way or another will not resemble the Jesus of the Gospels. Undoubtedly, a counterfeit Jesus will reflect some form of the wisdom of man as we make Jesus in our image rather than knowing Him as He really is. For example, psychology Jesus, political Jesus, etc. Another Jesus we create in our own imagination is one who paid the price for us to such a degree that He no longer rebukes, chastises, or tells us to take up our cross. A very popular counterfeit Jesus comes in the form of a "lover" or "bridegroom" who is so madly in love with all people that He has lost His senses and is dripping with unrestrained passion. None of these are the Jesus of the Gospels who is the same yesterday, today, and forever.

Counterfeit Spirit: There is only one Holy Spirit. The Holy Spirit exists to bring glory to Jesus and conviction of sin, righteousness, and judgment. This said, there are multitudes of other spirits in the spirit realm all wanting to have a voice for the evil one. These spirits love to introduce all manner of unrighteous thoughts into our minds, particularly and all sorts of imaginations about God, Jesus, and ourselves. False spirits aim to endorse our flesh, mental ascent, worldly wisdom; to drive us to godless activities or activities God did not assign us to; to push us into religious observances or performance mentality of measuring up for God; or to give us a false peace (which we think is the peace of God) but it is designed by the spirit to keep us complacent, lukewarm, and ineffective.

Counterfeit Gospel: A gospel without a day of judgment is not the real Gospel. A gospel without sin is not the real Gospel. A gospel which claims Jesus is not God incarnate or without Jesus' death and resurrection is not the real Gospel. A gospel lacking the cross of Christ and necessitating the cross of the believer is not the real Gospel. A gospel focusing its ultimate aim on wealth in this world or a takeover of the nations before Christ's return is not the real Gospel. There are many more false gospels out there.

Counterfeit God: A god who does not require faith in His Son is not the real God. A god who accepts all people of all religions without requiring repentance and conversion to Christ is not the real God. A magnanimous loving "Father" who will desperately do anything for His children's comfort or happiness as a result of emotional passion or easy persuasion away from truth and righteousness is not the real God. A god who is angry and whose wrath has not been appeased by Christ's atoning blood is not the real God.

<u>Counterfeit Presence</u>: A counterfeit spiritual presence in the atmosphere is often mistaken for being the presence of God. It can be felt by the senses of the body like in physical sensations like waves of power or feelings of wind. It is typically weighty, sweet or soothing to the emotions, and attached with feelings of peace, love, and acceptance tailored to the ideals and desires of the person experiencing it. Those who crave love and attention will be most vulnerable to the counterfeit presence because it appeases their flesh. At the same time, they are convinced in deeper measure that God loves them the way they are, without requiring repentance from sin and error. A counterfeit presence can also cause obsessions in the mind for the "feeling" of God's presence rather than a pursuit of the truth. The victims of this are unknowingly training themselves to confirm the Word of God by a physical manifestation or sensation rather than by the indwelling Spirit of the Lord issuing His "amen" to the truth spoken in love.

<u>Counterfeit Miracles</u>: God works miracles and still works miracles today. However, the evil one is also capable of working miracles. The antichrist will have power to work all manner of signs and wonders for the purpose of deceiving the whole world through his miraculous powers. The enemy can counterfeit visions, dreams, spiritual encounters with the Father and the Son, healings, deliverances, and baptism of the Holy Spirit. There are demonic tongues and prophesies which emanate from wrong spirits. None of these eliminate the fact that the genuine version of all of these things exist. In fact, if they were not real and from God, the enemy would not be trying to imitate them. This calls for discernment of the truth. There are also other miracles which lack any redemptive value but serve to distract and allure people away from Christ such as stigmata, apparitions, speaking to those gone to glory, gem stones, gold dust, and omniscient "prophecies" of phone numbers and non-redemptive information. These can all be very impressive to spectators, particularly those who have opened themselves up to the spiritual realm of God and its possibilities. Unfortunately, these types of things appeal to the greedy, carnal, and soulish parts of our humanity. Jesus never once worked any of these types of miracles and never once appealed to anyone's carnal greed. But the Holy Spirit only issues His "amen" to the truth of the Word of God and miracles worked by the power of God for God's purposes.

What can be confusing about counterfeit miracles is that they are often executed in the name of Jesus or in the "presence" of the "anointing" of "God." Many people may even profess their faith in Jesus because they have seen a miracle – even a counterfeit one. What we have to remember is that the evil one's house is already divided against itself and will ultimately fall. In the meantime, he cares nothing for anyone other than himself and his own exaltation as he attempts for all eternity to usurp the throne of God and maintain his dominion in the hearts of mankind. The evil one does not care who gets healed or delivered, who feels loved and appeased, or who is oppressed and tormented. His only ambition is to sidetrack all of us away from God and from the truth.

Temptations

The temptations of Jesus in the wilderness are another classic example of the schemes the enemy uses to attempt to allure us into his agenda. First, the enemy tempted Jesus to use miracle power and authority to serve the cravings of His stomach. Second, the enemy tempted Jesus to take unnecessary risk in the name of trusting in God's Word. Third, the enemy promised exaltation over the whole world in exchange for compromised worship.

Generally, the temptations were to force Jesus to prove Himself and His identity. If Jesus had caved to any of these temptations, the nature of the self-exalting evil one would have been found in Him. Instead, by the power of the Holy Spirit and the truth of the Word of God, the evil one found no place in Him.

Following Jesus' example, we must learn to discern the schemes of the evil one so that we give no place to him in our hearts and do not allow his lies to penetrate deeper into our lives.

Basic Training Exercise

ENEMY TACTICS

2 Corinthians 2:11 NIV – in order that Satan might not outwit us. For we are not unaware of his schemes.

DESCRIPTION

In the Garden of Eden, the serpent was described as more subtle than any other of God's creatures. Even today, this subtlety makes the evil one an expert deceiver, distracter, and destroyer if we are not aware enough to discern his schemes. Sometimes, it is an event in our lives that triggers an enemy infiltration of our thoughts. Other times, it is a persistent and gradual wearing down and decline of our faith or endurance.

Regardless of how the enemy is attacking us or attempting to divert or deceive us, Jesus conquered it at the cross. Everything we need for victory, godliness, and the fulfillment of God's plans for us was provided through the work of Jesus. We receive it as a free gift, by grace through faith in what Jesus accomplish for us. In fact, when we do identify the real root of what the enemy is attacking in our lives, we realize that what the enemy is working against us is exactly what God is working in our favor. For example, if the enemy attack is discouragement, God is working courage in us.

To put Enemy Tactics into practice is about allowing the Lord to reveal the subtle ways that the evil one is laying temptations before us or has worked his way into our thoughts so that we can renew our faith, hope, trust, and freedom in Jesus and the work He finished for us through His death and resurrection.

PRAYER

Father, thank you that you sent your Son, Jesus, to destroy the works of the enemy including everything that attempts to separate me from you or discourage and distract me from your plans and purposes. Help me now to discern the tactics of the enemy in my life so that he has no place in me. In Jesus' name. Amen.

Category: Discernment

PURPOSE:

To discern the tactics of the enemy.

To remain faithful to Christ and God's purpose for us.

To live established in the truth and hope of the Gospel.

SPIRITUAL FRUIT:

Increased discernment of the attacks of the enemy.

Renewed identity in Christ and the finished work of the cross.

Restored faith and hope.

Repentance from focus on self.

Purging of evil, pride, and discouragement.

CONSIDERATIONS

Consider these enemy tactics, listed in no particular order:

- **Doubt/Unbelief:** particularly in God's goodness or grace
- **Discouragement:** looking to the size of the problem rather than the ability of God
- **Diversion:** turning from God's instructions or greater purpose
- **Failure:** looking at apparent failure, not trusting God for redemption and victory
- **Frustration:** losing patience, not trusting God's timing
- **Flesh:** temptation to do things in our own strength
- **Performance:** thinking God's plan can be thwarted by us
- **Condemnation:** guilty feelings over sins from past or present
- **Success:** accepting exaltation of man out of God's order
- **Shortcuts:** trying to skip stages of God's plan development
- **Weakness:** losing strength due to extended battles/service

PRACTICE

1. Ask the Holy Spirit to highlight one of the enemy tactics above that is relevant to your life right now.

2. Ask the Lord to show you how the enemy has subtly infiltrated your thoughts using this tactic. Talk to Him about:
   - When did the enemy start attacking you in this way? Was there an event which triggered this or was it gradual?
   - Ask the Lord to reveal to you the real root of the issue in your present situation. (i.e. pride, fear, a past wound, etc.)

3. Ask the Lord to show you how He conquered this enemy tactic through His death and resurrection.
   - What else do Scripture and the Holy Spirit say about this?

4. Ask the Lord how He wants you to humble yourself before Him and resist the devil so that he flees from you.
   - How is He guiding you into faith and rest in Him?
   - Is there something He is asking you to do in your situation?

5. Do whatever He says.

NOTES:

_____

_____

Category: Discernment

ADDITIONAL SCRIPTURES:

Enemy Schemes
Genesis 3:1
Daniel 7:25
Genesis 16
2Chronicles 26:16
1 Samuel 15

Focus/Faith
Luke 4:1-13
Colossians 2:13-14
Hebrews 12:1-2
1 John 1:7
Romans 8:1
Colossians 1:9-14
John 6:15
Galatians 6:9
2 Corinthians 4:16
James 4:7

Basic Training Exercise

FLATTERY & INGRATIATING

Daniel 11:21, 32 KJV - And in his estate shall stand up a vile person, to whom they shall not give the honour of the kingdom: but he shall come in peaceably, and obtain the kingdom by flatteries. ... And such as do wickedly against the covenant shall he corrupt by flatteries: but the people that do know their God shall be strong, and do exploits.

DESCRIPTION

Flattery is a deadly toxin that can lead us into all types of wrong decisions. It will be the primary tactic of the antichrist in the last days to deceive even the most sincere servants of God if it is possible for them to be deceived. Until then, we can grow in our discernment of flattery as others function in this manner towards us.

Flattery is not as simplistic as it seems. There are various techniques of ingratiating favor which can be used in tandem with each other to get our attention, puff us up, distract us from the word and work of God, or get us to do things that God never told us to do. An expert flatterer will use multiple methods in their attempts to obtain what they want from us.

A flatterer always has a selfish motive, whether they are aware of it or not. This is part of discerning flattery correctly. For example, one person compliments us because they appreciate us while another person gives the same compliment because they want something. One is sincere, the latter is ingratiating.

To put Flattery & Ingratiating into practice is about asking the Lord to reveal the actions and intents of those who may be trying to flatter or deceive us for their own purposes or in ways which distract us from the truth and peace of God in Christ Jesus.

PRAYER

Father, thank you that you know the hearts of all men and are never fooled by flattery. Help us to discern the techniques and motives of flattery so that we may stand firm in your truth. In Jesus' name, Amen.

Basic TRAINING
SPIRITUAL EXERCISES

PURPOSE:
To discern flattery in order to not be ensnared by evil and stand firm in the truth.

To turn from flatterers and walk according to the wisdom of God.

SPIRITUAL FRUIT:
Increased discernment of the attacks of the enemy.

Faithfulness to God and His voice and purposes.

Distinguishing flattering motives from sincerity.

Wise as a serpent, harmless as a dove.

CONSIDERATIONS
Consider these aspects and purposes of flattery & ingratiating:

Ways Flatterers Ingratiate:
- **Compliments:** Praising for who we are or what we do.
- **Conformity of thought or actions:** Behaving like us.
- **Self-praise:** Highlighting their best aspects or success.
- **Rendering favors or gifts:** Generosity or special treatment.
- **Self-deprecation:** Putting themselves down, false humility.
- **Humor:** Finding what makes you laugh and using it.
- **Neediness/Dependence:** Triggering compassion and care.
- **Name-dropping:** Feigning success through affiliation.

For the Purpose of:
- **Obtaining reward or position:** getting something from you
- **Preventing punishment:** preventing negative consequences
- **Cultivating approval or love:** being or feeling loved

PRACTICE

1. Ask the Lord to highlight to you a person who wants something from you. Consider the ways this person is seeking your favor. Write down your observations.

2. Ask the Lord to give you wisdom and discernment as you consider their actions.
   - Do their actions line up with the tactics of flattery?
   - Are they doing what they are doing freely or for the purpose of gaining something from you?

3. Now, ask the Lord to highlight someone YOU want something from. Consider the ways you are approaching this person to gain their favor. Write down your observations.

4. Ask the Lord to give you wisdom and discernment as you consider your own actions.
   - Are you being sincere or flattering?
   - If you are engaging in flattery, repent.

5. Ask the Lord to give you wisdom for how to proceed with these situations. Listen to what He says. Do what He says.

NOTES: _____

ADDITIONAL SCRIPTURES:

Psalm 5:9

Psalm 12:2

Psalm 36:2

Proverbs 29:5

Jude 1:16

Romans 16:18

1 Thessalonians 2:5

PERFECTION COURSE – UNIT 6.2 READING

Yeasts of Jesus' Day and Today

In the days leading up to Jesus' day, there were various groups who were each equally awaiting the Messiah's arrival. In different ways, these groups readied themselves for the Messiah to come and establish righteous order by overthrowing Gentile oppressors and handing the Kingdom over to Israel. Each group started off with sincere motives and focus on the pursuit of God. But as their movements blossomed and Jesus arrived, none of them recognized God when He was standing right in front of them.

Literally speaking, yeast is a self-reproducing fungus which spreads aggressively throughout whatever it is added to and changes its character through fermentation and decay. Jesus said to beware of the yeast of the Pharisees, Sadducees, and Herod. The teachings of these groups and others permeated the hearts of men until the whole purpose was off course.

> *Matthew 16:11-12: How is it you don't understand that I was not talking to you about bread?* ***But be on your guard against the yeast of the*** *Pharisees* ***and*** *Sadducees*.*" Then they understood that he was not telling them to guard against the yeast used in bread,* ***but against the teaching [doctrine] of the Pharisees and Sadducees****. (See also Luke 12:1.)*

> *Mark 8:15: "Be careful," Jesus warned them.* ***"Watch out for the yeast of the Pharisees and that of*** *Herod*.*"*

In the Scriptures, yeast (which is also called leaven) is symbolic of sin, wickedness, or gain attained unjustly through wrongdoing or violence. In the New Testament, yeast also symbolizes false teachings of religion, unbelief, and worldliness which have the potential to spread through believers and draw us away from the truth of Christ.

Pharisees

The Pharisees started their movement shortly after the return of the exiles from Babylonian captivity. The word which the name Pharisees comes from means "separated." Ezra had instituted religious reforms and demanded separation from pagan customs, wives, and children. Out of fear of another exile and desiring to be ready in righteousness for Messiah's arrival, the Pharisees instituted rules and regulations requiring common people to adhere to priestly standards of purity and holiness. Various rabbis interpreted the Scriptures and created "houses" or "schools" of thought, typically named after themselves. Common people would follow them by adhering to their teachings of holiness and good works. Their teachings became known as the "oral Torah" or spoken law, which they considered to be equal with the Law of God in Scripture. At times, there teachings were excessively binding including over thirty-nine different classes of work which were forbidden on the Sabbath. Other times, their interpretations were loose including easy divorce for any reason whatsoever. Their approach to Scripture was often metaphoric or combining passages that were not actually inter-related to create their own "special" knowledge or revelation of the text. Moreover, they considered that anyone who did not adhere to their teachings would be condemned and that the resurrection would be their greatest triumph as they assumed that they would be proven right about everything. In their self-righteousness, they anticipated their reward and to see their opponents cursed and trampled.

When Jesus stood before the Pharisees, they rejected Him because He did not adhere to their man-made regulations and called them out as hypocrites. (See Matthew 23.) They sought to put Him to death for denouncing their teachings and stewardship of the Kingdom of God.

The Pharisees ultimately became the foundation for what known today as rabbinic Judaism and their "oral Torah" is known as the Talmud. To this day, they do not believe that Jesus is the Messiah and have written many teachings for the purpose of deliberately disqualifying Jesus from being the Jewish King.

The yeast of the Pharisees also lives today in the hearts of believers who follow teachers or teachings rather than the pure and simple pursuit of Jesus. It can also be found in those who have given way to self-righteousness and reliance on their own holiness and good works for obtaining the grace of God. The righteous will live by faith. Victory is not to those who will or run, but those to whom God shows mercy. (See Romans 9:16.)

Sadducees

The Sadducees mostly consisted of affluent members of the priestly class. The name Sadducees is rooted in the name Zadok, who was the faithful priestly line from the days of King David. They controlled the High Priesthood and the majority of the Sanhedrin which was the ruling counsel of the Jewish people. The Sadducees did not believe in the spiritual realm or the resurrection from the dead and only accepted the first five books of the Scriptures. Without eternal hope or focus, their sights became set on the things of this world. After the exiles returned, Jerusalem remained set apart to God and refused to participate in world commerce in order to remain holy. But the Sadducees pushed to "Hellenize" Jerusalem, open it up as a crossroads, and participate in the global marketplace. They even allowed a nudist gymnasium to be built in Jerusalem and were the ones who put the marketplace in the Temple of God. Their theology blended with popular philosophies of the day and rejected the "oral Torah" of the Pharisees. As they ruled the people of Judah while under Rome's governing authority, they found it beneficial to compromise and submit to Rome's way of doing things in order to keep the peace and maintain their position of religious authority over the people.

Jesus was enflamed that God's House had been turned into a marketplace and so, the Sadducees challenged His authority. Jesus rebuked them for their lack of understanding of the Scriptures and their failure to comprehend the power and eternality of God. (See Matthew 22.) They were quite mistaken in their views and their ways.

The Sadducees lost their power and disbanded when the Temple was destroyed by the Romans in 70 AD. But the yeast of unbelief, compromise, and blending with the world's marketplace is still active today in the hearts of many believers who have lost sight of eternal things for the pursuit of worldly impact. God's House was never intended to be a marketplace or to take over the marketplace of this world.

Herod

Herod was the appointed "King of the Jews" in the days of Jesus but was completely worldly in all his ways, no matter how pious and religious he pretended to be. He may have built a glorious and marvelous Temple for God but inwardly he was paranoid and a murderer of those who posed any threat to him. He is also credited with being and extremely sharp businessman, a master tradesman of global commerce in his day, and a magnificent builder of palaces and cities. He was fascinated with Jewish culture and messengers of God like John the Baptist and stories of Jesus and His miracles but rejected all rebukes for holiness or submission to God's righteous standard.

As Herod established his own palaces of luxury and lawlessness, he killed God's messengers. He wanted God's miracle power for his own purposes but when Jesus would not indulge him, Herod mocked and ridiculed Jesus' kingship, dressed Him in a royal robe, and sent Him off to be executed.

Herod's life ended when he received praise as a god and did not give God glory. Arrogance is at the root of this type of yeast and its fruit is personal indulgence, luxury, and self-glorification. Needless to say, this yeast is still alive and active today. Life is not measured in the abundance of possessions. The things which are esteemed by men are worth nothing in God's Kingdom.

Zealots

The Zealots were a group of rebels who desired to use force to regain Jewish independence. They named themselves after the Scripture pertaining to the zeal of Phineas who was commended by God for killing sinners to put a stop to a plague. (See Numbers 25.) They wanted to overthrow their Roman oppressors and hated paying taxes. Their hope was for victory in this world. They eagerly awaited the Messiah's arrival to bring conflict, war, and demolition to everyone not aligned with God. They lived by the sword and felt completely justified in doing so.

The Zealot's impression of Jesus was probably centered around whether or not He was going to establish the Kingdom of God NOW on earth and reject Rome's authority. When Jesus ordered people to pay taxes to Caesar and allowed Himself to be crucified rather than killing those who opposed Him, I'm pretty sure this did not line up with the Zealot's theology.

The Zealots started the revolt against Rome in 66 AD but this was only the beginning of the unrest which ultimately led to the destruction of the Temple in 70 AD. The Zealots came to their end on Masada in a mass suicide to avoid Roman capture, torture, or execution. With no eternal hope, they fell on their swords like King Saul. This exhibited their lack of faith in God's sovereignty and lack of hope in His deliverance.

This yeast is still active today in those who use God's word to revolt against the governing authorities in this world or claim that because self-defense is legal that it is acceptable in the sight of God. Those who live by the sword will die by the sword. We follow a crucified King.

Essenes

The Essenes were a group who were so disillusioned with the Pharisees, Sadducees, Temple system and everything else about how God's people had declined in sincere holiness and pursuit of God that they went to live in caves in the desert to prepare themselves through purity for the great war and tribulation that was to come with the Messiah's arrival. Because the Temple had become corrupt in their sight, they set up their own sacrifices and considered themselves to be the righteous remnant of God's holy people. They held themselves to strict rituals of multiple daily washings, prayer, worship, meditation on Scripture, and abstinence from all worldly pleasures, including marriage, in order to prepare themselves as the holy ones worthy of receiving the Kingdom of God from the Messiah. It is rumored that John the Baptist may have spent time with the Essenes in the years before his public ministry began.

While there is much good to be said of sincere personal devotion, it is possible to be so set apart that you miss God. It is not known whether the Essenes learned of or became followers of Jesus because even though they are noted by Josephus as being a major sect of Judaism in that day, there is no mention of them in Scripture. Perhaps they may have become so consumed with cave life and ritual that when Messiah arrived, they carried on devotedly waiting for Him.

This yeast is still active today in those who mean well but set themselves apart to the extent that they may have actually missed God's greater purpose. God so LOVED the world that He sent His Son into it to serve and to save it and to give His life for all who would believe.

False Teaching

False teaching is no different today than it has been since the beginning. Adam and his wife were made in God's image to be like God. Then, the evil one came along with a lie that if they disobeyed God's command, they would be like God. Similarly, Jesus is the King of all the kingdoms of the world. Then, the devil came along with a lie that if Jesus disobeyed God and worshipped him instead, Jesus would receive all the kingdoms of the world. In both instances, the devil's deception promised what they already had through a false path which would subject them to the enemy and, ultimately, lead them to death. For us today, as in any day, we have to beware of the yeasts of false teachings which seek to lead us away from the simplicity of devotion to Jesus.

www.manifestinternational.com

New Testament Woes
Scripture List & Worksheet

Luke 6:24-26: "But **woe** to you who are rich, for you have already received your comfort. **Woe** to you who are well fed now, for you will go hungry. **Woe** to you who laugh now, for you will mourn and weep. **Woe** to you when everyone speaks well of you, for that is how their ancestors treated the false prophets.

Matthew 23:13, 15-16, 23, 25-26, 27-29: "**Woe** to you, teachers of the law and Pharisees, you hypocrites! You shut the door of the kingdom of heaven in people's faces. You yourselves do not enter, nor will you let those enter who are trying to. ... "**Woe** to you, teachers of the law and Pharisees, you hypocrites! You travel over land and sea to win a single convert, and when you have succeeded, you make them twice as much a child of hell as you are. "**Woe** to you, blind guides! You say, 'If anyone swears by the temple, it means nothing; but anyone who swears by the gold of the temple is bound by that oath.' ... "**Woe** to you, teachers of the law and Pharisees, you hypocrites! You give a tenth of your spices--mint, dill and cumin. But you have neglected the more important matters of the law--justice, mercy and faithfulness. You should have practiced the latter, without neglecting the former. ... "**Woe** to you, teachers of the law and Pharisees, you hypocrites! You clean the outside of the cup and dish, but inside they are full of greed and self-indulgence. Blind Pharisee! First clean the inside of the cup and dish, and then the outside also will be clean.... "**Woe** to you, teachers of the law and Pharisees, you hypocrites! You are like whitewashed tombs, which look beautiful on the outside but on the inside are full of the bones of the dead and everything unclean. In the same way, on the outside you appear to people as righteous but on the inside you are full of hypocrisy and wickedness. "**Woe** to you, teachers of the law and Pharisees, you hypocrites! You build tombs for the prophets and decorate the graves of the righteous. (Also Luke 11:42-52.)

Matthew 26:24: The Son of Man will go just as it is written about him. But **woe** to that man who betrays the Son of Man! It would be better for him if he had not been born." (Also Mark 14:21; Luke 22:22.)

Matthew 11:21: "**Woe** to you, Chorazin! **Woe** to you, Bethsaida! For if the miracles that were performed in you had been performed in Tyre and Sidon, they would have repented long ago in sackcloth and ashes. (Also Luke 10:13.)

Matthew 18:7: **Woe** to the world because of the things that cause people to stumble! Such things must come, but **woe** to the person through whom they come! (Also Luke 17:1.)

Jude 1:11: **Woe** to them! [False Teachers.] They have taken the way of Cain; they have rushed for profit into Balaam's error; they have been destroyed in Korah's rebellion.

Revelation 12:12: Therefore rejoice, you heavens and you who dwell in them! But **woe** to the earth and the sea, because the devil has gone down to you! He is filled with fury, because he knows that his time is short."

Revelation 18:9-20 NIV - "When the kings of the earth who committed adultery with her and shared her luxury see the smoke of her burning, they will weep and mourn over her. Terrified at her torment, they will stand far off and cry: " '**Woe! Woe** to you, great city, you mighty city of Babylon! In one hour your doom has come!' "The merchants of the earth will weep and mourn over her because no one buys their cargoes anymore-- cargoes of gold, silver, precious stones and pearls; fine linen, purple, silk and scarlet cloth; every sort of citron wood, and articles of every kind made of ivory, costly wood, bronze, iron and marble; cargoes of cinnamon and spice, of incense, myrrh and frankincense, of wine and olive oil, of fine flour and wheat; cattle and sheep; horses and carriages; and human beings sold as slaves. "They will say, 'The fruit you longed for is gone from you. All your luxury and splendor have vanished, never to be recovered.' The merchants who sold these things and gained their wealth from her will stand far off, terrified at her torment. They will weep and mourn and cry out: " **'Woe!** Woe to you, great city, dressed in fine linen, purple and scarlet, and glittering with gold, precious stones and pearls! In one hour such great wealth has been brought to ruin!' "Every sea captain, and all who travel by ship, the sailors, and all who earn their living from the sea, will stand far off. When they see the smoke of her burning, they will exclaim, 'Was there ever a city like this great city?' They will throw dust on their heads, and with weeping and mourning cry out: " **'Woe! Woe** to you, great city, where all who had ships on the sea became rich through her wealth! In one hour she has been brought to ruin!' "Rejoice over her, you heavens! Rejoice, you people of God! Rejoice, apostles and prophets! For God has judged her with the judgment she imposed on you."

Practical Application:

How do these Scriptures reveal God's justice?

List three things God is displeased with, as revealed by these Scriptures.
1.
2.
3.

To pronounce a woe is to pronounce a curse on something. In what ways does this challenge your concepts about the heart of God to love and bless?

How is God asking you to personally respond to these Scriptures in your own life?

Basic Training Exercise

BEWARE OF YEASTS

Matthew 16:5 NIV - When they went across the lake, the disciples forgot to take bread. "Be careful," Jesus said to them. "Be on your guard against the yeast of the Pharisees and Sadducees."

DESCRIPTION

In the times of Jesus, there were various groups who were all equally awaiting the Messiah's arrival. In the meantime, they had created their own concepts of what God's anointed one would be like and how He would approach teaching and ministry.

Jesus warned His disciples that these influences could negatively impact our faith in Him if we are do not keep watch and stand guard against them. He compared this to yeast spreading through a batch of dough until the whole dough was ruined.

To put Beware of Yeasts into practice is about allowing the Lord to expose these yeasts so that we can repent and return to unleavened faith in Christ alone.

YEASTS OF JESUS' DAY & TODAY

Pharisees – Religion: Believing that God's blessings or curses are earned or deserved through my behavior or obedience rather than Christ's. Placing hope in tradition of man-made regulations.

Sadducees - Unbelief: Not believing the whole counsel of God or having eternal hope. Aiming to attain the things of this world or placing hope in money as security.

Herod - Worldliness: Measuring success and influence by the world's standards. Aiming to attain the things of this world or placing hope in money as security.

Zealots – Politics: Emphasizing or focusing on the governments of this world rather than on Christ. Imposing Kingdom values on unbelieving people.

Essenes – Seclusion: Hypervigilant separation from everything in the world. Placing faith in preparation and purity.

Category: Discernment

PURPOSE:

To discern the harmful yeasts which can be damaging to pure faith.

To maintain pure faith and live established in the truth and hope of the Gospel.

SPIRITUAL FRUIT:

Increased discernment of error.

Restored faith and hope in Christ alone.

Repentance from focus on self and this world.

PRAYER

Father, thank you that you sent your Son, Jesus, to demonstrate pure faith for me. Help me now to discern the yeasts in my own life of faith so that I can repent and be set free by your truth, in Jesus' name, Amen.

PRACTICE

1. Ask the Lord to highlight one of the yeasts that is relevant to your life right now.

2. Ask the Lord to show you why this focus is off balance or against what the cross of Christ. Talk to Him about:
   - How does this nullify the need for the cross?
   - How does this take my eyes off of eternity?
   - How does this cause me to function in my flesh?
   - How does this distract me from God's Kingdom purpose?
   - How might this cause me to miss what God is doing?

3. Ask the Lord to reveal to you how this yeast has infiltrated your life, beliefs, and activities.

4. Ask the Lord to show you how Jesus addressed this matter in the course of His ministry.
   - What does Scripture and the Holy Spirit say about this?
   - Does Scripture endorse any aspects of this approach?
   - How does Scripture prove that this approach is missing the mark?

5. Ask the Lord how He wants you to eradicate this yeast from your life and beliefs.
   - How is He guiding you into faith and trust in Him?
   - What beliefs, focus areas, or activities do you need to repent from in order to eliminate this yeast from your life?

6. Do whatever He says.

NOTES:
_____

ADDITIONAL SCRIPTURES:

Yeasts:
Matthew 16:6
Mark 8:15
Luke 12:1

Other Verses
1 Corinthians 5:6
Matthew 3:7
Matthew 23:13-39
Mark 12:18-27
Acts 12:22-23
Matthew 22:15-22
Matthew 26:55
John 18:36
Luke 13:1-5

Category: Discernment

PERFECTION COURSE – UNIT 6.3 READING

DECEITFUL WORKERS & DOCTRINES OF DEMONS

False prophets and teachers have been a challenger of God's people throughout history. The first false prophet was Satan in the Garden of Eden who told Adam's wife a lie about what she would gain for herself if she disregarded God's command. They failed the test. Later, the same serpent in a different garden, the devil relentlessly attempted to entice Jesus through false promises to worship him instead of God but Jesus did not succumb to his false promises. He passed the test. Jesus is worthy of a bride who knows the truth, discerns lies of the evil one and does not give way to false prophecies and teachings because of her love for the truth. He deserves a bride who passes the test of deceitful workers and doctrines of demons.

> *1 Timothy 4:1: The Spirit clearly says that **in later times some will abandon the faith and follow deceiving spirits and things taught by demons**.*

Unfortunately, the false spiritual practices and powers of this world can be alluring and seem to produce easier and faster results than waiting for God, repenting of sin, and enduring on the path of holiness. Blending the practices of false spirituality with the name of God is an abomination but it is not always easy to discern. For this reason, God commanded His people NOT to learn the practices of the nations and their forms of worship and spirituality and not to worship Him in the way that they worship their gods. (Read Deuteronomy 12:1-32.) He warned the people against the false spiritual practices of the nations including necromancy (talking to the dead,) divination and mediums (false prophecy, fortune-telling, psychic power,) soothsaying and smooth talk (speaking peace and blessing rather than exhortation to righteousness and warning of judgment,) witchcraft and sorcery (manipulation of the will of others, curses, spells, and spiritual power used to enact a will other than God's.) He warned in advance that even as they waited for the prophet like Moses who would speak the word of truth, other so-called prophets would come in God's name, presumptuously using His name for their own purposes. (See Deuteronomy 18:9-22.)

When Jesus was asked about signs preceding His return, He warned His disciples that many false prophets, teachers, and messiahs will come attempting to deceive God's people – even in His name.

> *Matthew 24:4-5, 10-13, 23-24: Jesus answered: "Watch out that no one deceives you. For many will come **in my name**, claiming, 'I am the Messiah,' and **will deceive many**. ... At that time **many will turn away from the faith** and will betray and hate each other, and **many false prophets will appear and deceive many people**. Because of the increase of wickedness, the love of most will grow cold, but the one who stands firm to the end will be saved. ... At that time if anyone says to you, 'Look, here is the Messiah!' or, 'There he is!' do not believe it. **For false messiahs and false prophets will appear and perform great signs and wonders to deceive, if possible, even the elect**.*

It may be easy to think that we will discern someone claiming to be a messiah as if they are walking around claiming to be Jesus. While there are people who do this, not many people are convinced by them. We would be wise to notice, however, that messiah means *anointed one*. There are many falsely anointed ones already on the earth functioning in false "anointings" which are not the Holy Spirit. There are those who "honor the anointing" on a person's life because they function in omniscient prophetic gifting or miracle power even though their lives are full of sin. Jesus warned us not to do this and that true prophets would be known by their fruit. This said, a person of good morals can also be the enemy's ideal target for infiltration with a false anointing because it is a convincing package. Even outwardly upright people can have their doctrine infiltrated with heresy. The bottom line is that anyone who uses the power of the name of Jesus to work their own will or their own concept of God's will are actually working iniquity and lawlessness against God.

> *Matthew 7:15-16, 21-23:* **Watch out for false prophets. They come to you in sheep's clothing,** *but inwardly they are ferocious wolves.* **By their fruit you will recognize** *them. Do people pick grapes from thornbushes, or figs from thistles? ... Not everyone who says to me, 'Lord, Lord,' will enter the kingdom of heaven, but* **only the one who does the will of my Father** *who is in heaven. Many will say to me on that day, 'Lord, Lord,* **did we not prophesy in your name and in your name drive out demons and in your name perform many miracles?'** *Then I will tell them plainly, 'I never knew you. Away from me, you evildoers!'*

The purpose of discerning truth from error and true workers from deceitful ones is NOT for the purpose of accusation or denouncement. Those who give way to this temptation find themselves on the side of the accuser of the brethren. However, discernment of the truth is absolutely key in the end times so that it is not possible to deceive us, even if great signs and wonders are attached to the doctrines of demons.

On that note, when we discern a false prophet or teacher, it should only enhance our love for the truth and God's word and ways and renew our humility and awe at God's gift of discernment and keeping us from falling into error ourselves. If we are responding correctly, we will be again enflamed with devotion and entrusting ourselves to the one who is keeping us from stumbling.

False Prophets are a Test

False prophets are raised up by God. This sounds bizarre and ungodly but it is absolutely true. All things were created by God for His purposes and none can escape His sovereignty. God clearly warned Israel about false prophets and what His purpose is in sending them, and even allowing their signs, wonders, and prophetic words to come to pass. Sending false prophets is God's way of proving whether our hearts are fully aligned with Him or if selfish desire remains in us.

> *Deuteronomy 13:1-5: If a* **prophet, or one who foretells by dreams**, *appears among you and announces to you a sign or wonder,* **and if the sign or wonder spoken of takes place, and the prophet says, "Let us follow other gods"** *(gods you have not known) "and let us worship them," you must not listen to the words of that prophet or dreamer.* **The LORD your God is testing you to find out whether you love him with all your heart and with all your soul. It is the LORD your God you must follow, and him you must revere. Keep his commands and obey him; serve him and hold fast to him.** *That prophet or dreamer must be put to death for inciting rebellion against the LORD your God, who brought you out of Egypt and redeemed you from the land of slavery.* **That prophet or dreamer tried to turn you from the way the LORD your God commanded you to follow.** *You must purge the evil from among you.*

Again, it seems obvious enough that if a prophet comes along and does a miracle and then tells us to follow the god of some other religion, we will see through it. However, the enemy is a counterfeiter and blasphemer of God's name. The evil one will use God's name to promote teachings that abuse God's character, reject or divert people from His ways, or deny His stated conditions. We must know God not only by name but also by His truth and His ways. If we love God, we will keep His commandments and not be enticed to follow after false promises. Ezekiel furthered this revelation of God's intent to purge evil from His people to the level of their hearts. If they had set up idols in their hearts and then inquired of a prophet of God, God would answer them according to the idol in their heart. God, Himself would put the stumbling block before His own people so that they could fall into the error in their hearts and ultimately, repent and turn to Him with all their heart and soul. (Read Ezekiel 14:3-11.)

In the final days before the return of Christ, believers will be put to the ultimate test of faithfulness and love of God. God will raise up the ultimate false prophet – the man of lawlessness who sets Himself up as god but is actually the antichrist. This man will rule the whole world and be accompanied by all manner of signs and wonders as he promotes teachings which defy the ways of God and the real Christ.

> 2 Thessalonians 2:9-12 ESV: *The coming of the lawless one is by the activity of Satan* **with all power and false signs and wonders, and with all wicked deception** *for those who are perishing,* **because they refused to love the truth** *and so be saved. Therefore* **God sends them a strong delusion, so that they may believe what is false, in order that all may be condemned who did not believe the truth but had pleasure in unrighteousness.**

In the end, the test will be whether we love the truth or have pleasure in disobeying the truth. It is the Garden of Eden all over again but in magnified form as the age comes to its culmination. It is a strong delusion – not a weak one – because Jesus is worthy of a strong and faithful bride. Therefore, we must discern misuse and abuse of the name of God and the name of Jesus as blasphemy. We must discern erroneous teachings which do not align with the words of Christ and the life and ministry of Jesus and His first followers as heresy. We must keep our own hearts pure from the love of self, money, and the world so that our own idols do not become a snare to us as we enter into the time of testing.

The Fall into Falsehood

The true workers for Jesus follow the path of the crucified King who died for our sins, calls us to repentance, and tells us to put our faith in God while taking up our cross to follow Him. False workers attempt to use God for their own gain and prey on weaker believers who desire blessing rather than sacrifice.

> 1 Timothy 6:3-5: **If anyone teaches otherwise and does not agree to the sound instruction of our Lord Jesus Christ and to godly teaching, they are conceited and understand nothing.** *They have an* **unhealthy interest in controversies and quarrels about words** *that result in envy, strife, malicious talk, evil suspicions and constant friction between people of corrupt mind, who have been robbed of the truth and who* **think that godliness is a means to financial gain.**

The beginning of the end of the genuine devotion in any believer or teacher is when they begin to refuse sound doctrine and its application in their lives. This is the point at which the narrow way of following Christ and enduring in simple faithfulness seems to become boring or pointless or they become obsessed with a certain aspect of God, whether blessing, gifts, or requirements. As a result, they seek out fresh revelation or special knowledge which appeases their desires and flesh. This all continues to appear outwardly like the pursuit of God. And as they give way to self-deception, they believe that they are pursuing God. But in reality, they are pursuing a god of their own design, a Jesus who suits their preferences, and a spirit which empowers them to do things that God did not author.

> 2 Timothy 4:3-4: *For the time will come when* **people will not put up with sound doctrine.** *Instead, to* **suit their own desires***, they will gather around them a great number of teachers to say* **what their itching ears want to hear. They will turn their ears away from the truth** *and* **turn aside to myths.**

These professing believers are still rebellious at heart. They refuse to submit themselves any further to the crucifixion process of following Jesus even though outwardly they appear to be very pious and devoted to Him and claim to know Him well. They say they want disciples of Jesus but actually, their aim is followers for themselves or their doctrines. They say they love the truth but actually, they delight in "special" knowledge and human precepts which reject the truth of Christ. They claim to live in sacrificial obedience but have at some point strayed from obedience through choosing themselves rather than death to self.

> *Titus 1:10-11, 16: For there are many **rebellious people, full of meaningless talk and deception**, especially those of the circumcision group. They must be silenced, because they are disrupting whole households by **teaching things they ought not to teach**--and that **for the sake of dishonest gain**. ... **They claim to know God, but by their actions they deny him**. They are detestable, **disobedient** and unfit for doing anything good.*

<u>Rebellious</u>: Not truly submitted. Disobedient. Veering off the way of truth for self-protection or exaltation. They may put on a good show of seeming obedience and submission to God but at the root their hearts are self-seeking and their obedience is based on their own thoughts, will, and desires.

<u>Meaningless talk</u>: Empty words with no eternal weight or rooting in Scripture. False peace. Rambling on with stories or even "testimonies" or worldly talk which has no eternal value even though it is presented in a spiritual manner as a metaphor, parable, or spiritual lesson from a natural experience.

<u>Deception</u>: Seduction through promises of blessing or benefit. Painting a picture of success to lure others into lust and steps of rebellion. Deception invites the unsuspecting into a quest of discovery for more of whatever they think they need in order to succeed or advance to the next level – usually knowledge, power, "anointing," money, etc. The enemy's first deceptions were, "surely, you will not die," and "you will be like God," which could be rephrased as, "it is safe to stray from the narrow way," and "it will give you what you need to be exalted."

These professing believers embark on the path of deception, not realizing that they have given way to self-deception through their own concepts of God over the actual truth of God. As they become more fully persuaded that they have discovered something of God that has been missed by others, they become the false teachers of their day. Savage wolves are not just outsiders who come in as obvious snake-oil salesmen. False teachers arise from the ranks of believers.

> *Acts 20:29-31a: I know that after I leave, **savage wolves will come in among you** and will not spare the flock. Even **from your own number men will arise and distort the truth in order to draw away disciples after them**. So be on your guard!*

<u>Distort the truth</u>: Twisting Scripture out of context. Denying or diminishing essential elements of the faith. Building principles or theologies based on stacking Scriptures like a house of cards for self-serving purposes.

<u>Draw disciples after themselves</u>: Desiring to build ministries for recognition, money, fame, following, etc.

These people have departed from taking up their cross in order to avoid further suffering to their pride, ego, flesh, or circumstances. They adopt a new theology which releases them from the obligation of true faithfulness to our crucified King so that they can enjoy peace with worldly people rather than rejection.

> *Galatians 6:12: Those who want to **impress people by means of the flesh** are trying to compel you to be circumcised. The only reason they do this is **to avoid being persecuted** for the cross of Christ.*

<u>Piety to impress people</u>: Putting on a show of morality, goodness, and religious observance.

<u>Compromise to avoid persecution</u>: Watering down the Gospel, its power, or its requirements by synchronizing with worldliness, lawlessness, or legalism.

We must stand guard, both for ourselves and watch for changes and shifts in those we love to prevent them from slipping into self-deception. The saddest thing is to watch someone we love who has taken up their cross for some time but grows weary in doing so and reasons to themselves that, "if I stay on this cross any longer, it is going to damage my spiritual life and heart." Imagine if Jesus had said that. None of us would be saved. We must be willing to embrace the cross God has given us to carry for as long as He has ordained for us to carry it so that the new life we walk in is actually resurrection life and not a false spirituality which has come to the aid of our uncrucified flesh.

False Workers

False Christian teachers have existed since the early church. The apostles warned disciples about the schemes and characteristics of false workers so that they could be alert and not fall into their deceptions.

> *Galatians 3:1: You foolish Galatians!* **Who has bewitched you?**

Bewitch: Feigning praise to charm or lead others into error by wicked arts.

> *1 Timothy 1:3-7: As I urged you when I went into Macedonia, stay there in Ephesus so that you may* **command certain people not to teach false doctrines any longer or to devote themselves to myths and endless genealogies.** *Such things* **promote controversial speculations rather than advancing God's work--which is by faith.** *The goal of this command is love, which comes from a pure heart and a good conscience and a sincere faith.* **Some have departed from these and have turned to meaningless talk.** *They want to be* **teachers of the law,** *but they do not know what they are talking about or what they so confidently affirm.*

Myths and genealogies: Sayings, clichés, fables. This is something said, quoted, and repeated so often that it is believed to be true or even believed to be Scripture when in reality, it is a contradiction of Scripture or a proverb of man. For example, "God helps those who help themselves." This can also include apocryphal writings, stories, or testimonies that never actually happened but which make the unsuspecting believe that they have some kind of special knowledge or insight. It can even include stories or testimonies of things that did occur but have become the basis for teaching, practice, or belief for those attempting to replicate the same results or outcome.

Promote speculation rather than faith: Special knowledge, unlocking "mysteries," etc. If our confidence is in special knowledge or we feel that special knowledge will be the key to our deliverance, our eyes have been diverted off of Christ who said that we must become like a child.

Meaningless talk: Vain discussions, debates, arguments, conjecture, opinions. Rambling "stories" that do not tie back to the truth of God or Christ. Promotion of man-made approach and dogma rather than Christ. Empty, worldly conversation.

Claim to teach Scripture/Law: Abusing Scripture without regard for the whole counsel of God. Piecing Scriptures together to mean something God did not intend. Wrenching Scripture out of context. Over-emphasizing numbers, formulas, or seeming patterns of God in Scripture as a measurement or prediction of spiritual things or current events.

> *Colossians 2:16: Therefore do not let anyone judge you by* **what you eat or drink***, or with regard to a* **religious festival, a New Moon celebration or a Sabbath day.**

> *Colossians 2:16, 20-23: Therefore do not let anyone judge you by* **what you eat or drink***, or with regard to a* **religious festival, a New Moon celebration or a Sabbath day.** *... Since you died with Christ to the elemental spiritual forces of this world, why, as though you still belonged to the world, do you submit to its rules:* **"Do not handle! Do not taste! Do not touch!"?** *These rules, which have to do with things that are all destined to perish with use, are* **based on merely human commands and teachings.** *Such regulations indeed have an* **appearance of wisdom,** *with their* **self-imposed worship,** *their* **false humility and their harsh treatment of the body,** *but they lack any value in restraining sensual indulgence.*

Impose religious observances and regulations: Commanding observance to Old Covenant requirements.

Human commands and teachings: Commanding observance of human doctrines and traditions.

Appearance of wisdom: Presented as logical, good things for believers to do for godliness and blessing.

Self-imposed worship: Misdirected zeal. Self-made worship. Much of what we call "worship" today is actually more like a pep-rally for Jesus full of hype which satiates our flesh rather than honoring our King. Many "worship" songs are actually self-indulgent, soulish, lovesick emotional displays of sensuality rather than anything that will ever be sung in heavenly places. Some "worship" songs are mediumistic, chanting, or looping in endless mantras which create a sensation of a spiritual atmosphere but the spirit present is NOT the Holy Spirit.

False humility: Imitating Christ's lowliness through self-deprecation or self-abasement. Jesus never self-deprecated or feigned lowliness. He willingly took the lowest place, was born in a manger, lived an invisible life for thirty years, and then faithfully fulfilled the ministry and purpose God had given Him.

Asceticism: Harsh treatment of the body done to attain favor with God. This can be obviously seen in those who would whip themselves with spiked cords to "suffer" for Christ or "beat their flesh like Paul," as these are more obviously wrong interpretations and applications of God's intended meaning. However, this can also occur with excessive fasting or any kind of self-imposed abstinence which God has not ordained and which we do in order to win His favor, approval, anointing, or blessing. God sees the heart.

> *Colossians 2:18-19: Do not let anyone who **delights in false humility** and the **worship of angels** disqualify you. Such a person also **goes into great detail about what they have seen**; they are **puffed up** with idle **notions by their unspiritual mind**. They have lost connection with the head, from whom the whole body, supported and held together by its ligaments and sinews, grows as God causes it to grow.*

Worship of Angels: Excessive focus on angelic beings and their assistance. Using Christ-given authority to command angels. Glorifying angels or angelic activity. Engaging in the spiritual realm or work of angels.

Goes into great detail about visions: Expresses details of visions of heaven, hell, angels, the spiritual realm, and other spiritual things. By contrast, Paul had visions and revelations which surpassed anyone in the world but refused to speak of them because he said they were too sacred for human words. Though Paul could have built his ministry by fascinating people with stories of his spiritual experiences, he instead made it his aim to know nothing except Jesus Christ and Him crucified and to boast in nothing but the cross. (See 1 Corinthians 2:2; Galatians 6:14.)

Puffed up: Think themselves to be special or superior because of their advanced spirituality and spiritual experiences. Look down on others who have not had the same experiences.

Notions of their flesh: Serving and comforting their beastly nature rather than Christ. Observing natural things as spiritual parables which God did not ordain.

> *1 Timothy 4:2-5: Such teachings come through **hypocritical liars**, whose consciences have been seared as with a hot iron. They **forbid people to marry and order them to abstain from certain foods**, which God created to be received with thanksgiving by those who believe and who know the truth. For everything God created is good, and nothing is to be rejected if it is received with thanksgiving, because it is consecrated by the word of God and prayer.*

Hypocrisy: Acting, putting on a show, lying through words and actions.

Forbidding marriage and foods: Dishonoring God's pattern for marriage and making the Kingdom of God into a matter of food and drink.

> *2 Timothy 2:14-18: Keep reminding God's people of these things. Warn them before God against **quarreling about words**; it is of no value, and only ruins those who listen. Do your best to present yourself to God as one approved, a worker who does not need to be ashamed and who correctly handles the word of truth. Avoid **godless chatter**, because those who indulge in it will become more and more ungodly. Their **teaching will spread like gangrene.***

> *Among them are Hymenaeus and Philetus, who have departed from the truth. They **say that the resurrection has already taken place**, and they **destroy the faith of some**.*

Quarreling about words: Over-focus on words and their meaning as essential to "real" understanding. Straining out a gnat and swallowing the camel. Can also be in the form of "connect dots" based on the root origins of certain words in worldly matters which seems like special insight but is actually worthless.

Godless chatter: Worldly conversation and babbling. Common talk like common people, politics, etc. Honoring men, ministers, or famous people to appear important or influential. Using many words.

Miscalculate God's times and purposes: Steering away from eternal focus to temporal living.

> *2Peter 2:1-3: But there were also **false prophets among** the people, just as there **will be false teachers among you**. They will **secretly introduce destructive heresies**, even **denying the sovereign Lord** who bought them--bringing swift destruction on themselves. **Many will follow their depraved conduct and will bring the way of truth into disrepute**. In their **greed** these teachers will **exploit you with fabricated stories**. Their condemnation has long been hanging over them, and their destruction has not been sleeping.*

Destructive heresies, denying the Lord: Perverting the Gospel and requirement of repentance and faith in Christ alone for salvation. Emphasizing aspects of piety, faith, or techniques of prayer as the "key" to obtaining blessing from God, or using Christ-given authority for self-ordained purposes.

Depraved conduct: Sensually indulgent, lustful, licentious, permissive, lawless, godless, fleshly, and carnal.

Malign the way of truth: Speak against or persecute those who stand firm in the truth of Christ and the life of holiness. Accuse the faithful of ignorance, judgmentalism, religiosity, Phariseeism, and "limiting" God.

Greed and exploitation: Self-serving, love of money, using others for advancement or advantage. Using techniques for fundraising such as encouraging people to "sow" finances into their ministries in order to "reap" blessing and rewards from God. This is in sharp contrast to Jesus' instruction to imitate the birds who neither sow nor reap but trust God to supply all their needs and that through genuine seeking of the Kingdom of God, we can be assured that all our true needs for fulfilling God's plans will be supplied.

Fabricated Stories: Molded words (formed like pottery,) feigned speech, attempting to present as divine nature, wisdom, or love. Typically couched in smooth talk of the "love of God" or "love" for the hearers as the promise of blessing.

> *2 Peter 2:10-14, 18-19:. This is especially true of those who **follow the corrupt desire of the flesh** and **despise authority**. Bold and arrogant, they are not afraid to **heap abuse on celestial beings**; yet even angels, although they are stronger and more powerful, do not heap abuse on such beings when bringing judgment on them from the Lord. But these people **blaspheme in matters they do not understand**. They are like **unreasoning animals, creatures of instinct,** born only to be caught and destroyed, and like animals they too will perish. They will be paid back with harm for the harm they have done. **Their idea of pleasure is to carouse in broad daylight**. They are blots and blemishes, reveling in their pleasures while they feast with you. With **eyes full of adultery, they never stop sinning; they seduce the unstable; they are experts in greed**--an accursed brood!... These people are springs without water and mists driven by a storm. Blackest darkness is reserved for them. For **they mouth empty, boastful words and, by appealing to the lustful desires of the flesh, they entice people who are just escaping from those who live in error**. They **promise them freedom, while they themselves are slaves of depravity**--for "people are slaves to whatever has mastered them."*

Despise authority: Disdain and refuse to submit to authorities of the world or the Church. Promote rebellion.

Heap abuse on celestial beings: Use Christ-given authority to rebuke spiritual forces in heavenly realms rather than the proclamation of the Gospel for salvation. (i.e. principalities, strongholds, forces, etc.)

Blaspheme things they do not understand: Abuse the name of Jesus in ways that Jesus did not command or demonstrate.

Instinctual: Beastial rather than spiritual. Sniffing for spiritual opportunity rather than waiting on God.

Carousing in daylight: Putting revelry on display as God's "favor," "freedom," or blessing.

Adulterous eyes: Unfaithful to Jesus and His way. Full of lust and covetousness for self-serving techniques to serve their own lusts, purposes, and agenda.

Experts in greed: Abuse God's offerings to advance their own ministries. Entice others to financial giving through manipulative promises of blessing or breakthrough. Loving money and teaching others to love it.

Boastful words: Self-exaltation, superiority, use of hype, and self-praise to present themselves as having superior connection to God or spiritual revelation or power. May also boast in the miracles, testimonies, or work of others rather than their own work or experiences, even though they may at times present the miracles as if they were their own experience. Done to titillate, fascinate, and distract from truth.

Appealing to lustful desires of flesh: Presenting a picture of the fulfillment of human and worldly desires, particularly for money, influence, opportunity, promotion, authority, spiritual gifts, spiritual power, and all other forms of self-indulgence. Also, negating the need for taking up cross to follow Jesus, crucifying flesh for sanctification, and personal sacrifice.

Seduce the unstable, new believers: Prey on those who are not firmly grounded in the truth of Christ and His ways. Allure them with promises of the abundant life rather than taking up their cross.

Promise freedom: Appealing to base side of humanity and need by promising breakthrough or restoration rather than leading people through death to self into true life in Christ.

Jude's letter to believers was also an emphatic warning to stay on the straight and narrow way of truly following Christ rather than giving way to false teachers.

> *Jude 1:4, 8, 16: For certain individuals whose condemnation was written about long ago have secretly slipped in among you. They are **ungodly** people, who **pervert the grace of our God into a license for immorality** and **deny Jesus Christ our only Sovereign and Lord**. ... In the very same way, **on the strength of their dreams** these ungodly people **pollute their own bodies, reject authority and heap abuse on celestial beings**. ... These people are **grumblers and faultfinders**; they **follow their own evil desires**; they **boast about themselves and flatter others for their own advantage**.*

Pervert God's grace for lawlessness: Abuse "knowledge" and "freedom" in Christ for self-indulgence.

Live by dreams: Led by dreams, visions, or spiritual encounters which are not from the Lord.

Grumblers, faultfinders: Despise and persecute those who are standing in the truth of Christ.

Boast about themselves: Praise themselves and their experiences with their own speech.

Flatter others for advantage: Use techniques of flattery to seduce others to follow them.

Balaam, Cain, Korah, Jezebel

Peter, Jude, and John each referenced characters from the Old Testament as examples of the spirit that false prophets and teachers function in. These same spirits are at work in false ministries today.

> *2 Peter 2:15-16: They have **left the straight way and wandered off to follow the way of Balaam son of Bezer, who loved the wages of wickedness**. But he was rebuked for his wrongdoing*

by a donkey--an animal without speech--who spoke with a human voice and restrained the prophet's madness.

Jude 1:11-12: Woe to them! **They have taken the way of Cain; they have rushed for profit into Balaam's error; they have been destroyed in Korah's rebellion.** *These people are blemishes at your love feasts,* **eating with you without the slightest qualm--shepherds who feed only themselves.**

Balaam: Balaam was a false prophet who used the techniques of divination to speak with God. A pagan king hired Balaam, the prophet for profit, in the fortieth year of Israel's time in the wilderness when Israel was conquering territories on the west side of the Jordan River and readying themselves to take the Promised Land. Though Balaam used false techniques, he did actually converse with God and was given words from God to speak. In fact, Balaam was one of the first people in Scripture to prophesy about the Messiah to come through revelation and a prophetic word that God had given him. However, because Balaam was not God's prophet and had been hired by a pagan king, God only allowed Balaam to bless His people. Balaam also taught Israelite women how to entice the men into sexual immorality and false worship. In contrast, the prophets God sent throughout Israel's history were used by God to rebuke His people when they were going astray, exhort them to return to and remain on the righteous path, and promise them blessing for enduring in faithfulness to God.

Some things we can garner from this: Those who charge money for ministry are not God's servants. Those who insist that prophecy is only for blessing people without warnings, rebukes, or exhortations to righteousness are not God's prophets. Just because someone has heard a true word of blessing from the Lord may not be God's servant. Sometimes, false prophets attack the most in the time imminently preceding blessing and breakthrough. As such, we must also be alert in these end times that the ministry of the spirit of Balaam will be alive and well, as the evil one tries to divert us from our eternal inheritance. The antichrist will undoubtedly hire many Balaam-type prophets who will speak true things from God even though they are not God's prophets and will entice people into lawlessness and false worship. We need not fear the words of these prophets because they will be accurate from God but we should beware not to learn their techniques or follow their teachings into heresy, error, and destruction.

Cain: Cain was the first murderer in the Bible. He offered an offering which was not by faith and then became infuriated when his brother's offering was accepted while his was not. He was unable to rule over the sin in his heart and it converted into brutality against his brother.

Things we can garner from this: Those who have departed from the path of faith in Christ, even if they outwardly appear to continue in God's service, will hate and persecute those who remain faithful.

Korah: Korah was a Levite who wanted the High Priesthood for himself. He led the leaders of Israel in rebellion against God's appointed leaders, Moses and Aaron. Korah had already been given a special position of service in the Tabernacle of God but it was not enough for him. He wanted more. Korah asserted his right to rule based on the fact that Moses and Aaron did not have an exclusive on being the only ones who could hear God even though God had appointed them as His mouthpieces. Korah grumbled that Moses and Aaron had not fulfilled the promise of taking Israel into the Promised Land even though God had said they would be in the wilderness for forty years. Korah wanted to lead the people back to life in Egypt even though God said not to return there. Korah appealed to the base nature of humanity in the elders of Israel to assert themselves and their own desires to get out of the wilderness while at the same time establishing a following for himself, away from God's appointed leaders.

Things we can garner from this: Those who are ambitious in ministry may seek to usurp authority or conduct a hostile takeover of other's ministries which have been established by God. Another Biblical example of this type of thing is the story of David's son Absalom who promised the people blessings while diverting their loyalty away from David to himself.

Revelation 2:20: Nevertheless, I have this against you: **You tolerate that woman Jezebel, who calls herself a prophet.** *By her teaching she* **misleads my servants into sexual immorality and the eating of food sacrificed to idols.**

Jezebel: Jezebel was a Phoenician princess who became queen of Israel as the wife of Ahab, King of Israel. She worshipped Baal, the pagan god of prosperity, fertility, and harvest, whose name means "lord." Jezebel led worship of Baal, promoted and supported prophets of Baal, and attempted to kill all true prophets of God. She used sensuality and manipulation to advance her husband's kingdom, authority, and dominion. In the Book of Revelation, the spirit of Jezebel enticed believers into sexual immorality and eating foods offered to idols in the name of Christian liberty. Jezebel's worship of Baal lingered on through these unsanctified pagan practices.

Things we can garner from this: Those within the body of Christ functioning in the spirit of Jezebel will endorse and promote false teachers, prosperity gospels, the love of money, messages of "peace peace," and everything else contrary to sound doctrine. They may openly reject or refute the need for sound doctrine with the appeal to spirituality, the spiritual realm, revival, and freedom from religion. At the same time, they will detest, mock, persecute, diminish, reject, and try to destroy the ministries of those carrying the word of truth and emphasizing the need for sound doctrine.

Do Not Be Alarmed

When Jesus' disciples inquired about how to handle the Pharisees, Jesus said to leave them alone because they are blind guides who will fall into a pit. (See Matthew 15:14.) When they inquired about how to handle people who were ministering in Jesus' name but were not one of their group, Jesus said not to stop them. (See Mark 9:39.) When Jesus' disciples wanted to call down fire from heaven as judgment upon those who did not receive them, He rebuked them for functioning in a wrong spirit. (See Luke 9:55.) When Jesus spoke of the end-times false prophets and tribulations, He said that they MUST happen before He returns. (See Luke 21:9.) When the people asked Moses what to do when a prophet's word did not come to pass, he told them the prophet must have spoken presumptuously and not to be alarmed. (See Deuteronomy 18:22.) When people were concerned about false workers preaching the Gospel for gain, Paul said he rejoiced as Christ was proclaimed. (See Philippians 1:18.)

The world will continue to increase in lawlessness and wickedness until Christ returns. The time of our exodus from this world will be similar to the days of Israel's exodus from Egypt. In those days, the wise men and sorcerers of Egypt were able to counterfeit the miracles of God just as the antichrist and his hoards will be able to work all manner of signs and wonders.

2 Timothy 3:1-9: But mark this: **There will be terrible times in the last days.** *People will be lovers of themselves, lovers of money, boastful, proud, abusive, disobedient to their parents, ungrateful, unholy, without love, unforgiving, slanderous, without self-control, brutal, not lovers of the good, treacherous, rash, conceited, lovers of pleasure rather than lovers of God-- having a form of godliness but denying its power.* **Have nothing to do with such people.** *They are the kind who worm their way into homes and gain control over gullible women, who are loaded down with sins and are swayed by all kinds of evil desires,* **always learning but never able to come to a knowledge of the truth.** *Just as Jannes and Jambres opposed Moses, so also* **these teachers oppose the truth.** *(See Exodus 7:11-12, 22, 8:7, 18-19.)*

In these end-times before Christ's return, we must be alert that false spiritual practices do not penetrate our own spiritual lives and the lives of those believers we love and have influence over. We must guard our lives and our doctrine carefully so that we are able to stand by the power of the Holy Spirit to the very end. We must keep our eyes open and on the Lord. This is a call for endurance of the saints!

Comparison Table

True Apostle, Prophet, Teacher	False Apostle, Prophet, Teacher
Sacrificial living, self-denial	Greedy, working for profit, love of $$
Exalting Jesus to make disciples of Christ	Exalting themselves for fame and following
Commanding repentance from sin and separation from the world	Endorsing pleasure as God's blessing and promoting collaboration with the world
Releasing sinners into freedom from the law of sin and death into grace	Commanding adherence to man-made regulations, doctrines, or traditions
Not being a burden to anyone	Using others for support and service
Laying life down for other's benefit	Using others for their own benefit
Teaching the whole counsel of God and sound doctrine, rightly using the Scriptures	Teaching revelation from their own mind, twisting God's Word
Demonstrating the power of God to glorify the name of Jesus	Displaying miracles without redemptive value to gain a following for themselves
Suffering persecution, hardship, rejection by the world and organized religion	Rejecting suffering and hardship as "not the will of God," acceptance of the world
Following the pattern of Jesus	Following the pattern of this world

www.manifestinternational.com

False Prophets
Scripture List & Worksheet

Jeremiah 6:13-15: "From the least to the greatest, all are greedy for gain; prophets and priests alike, all practice deceit. They dress the wound of my people as though it were not serious. 'Peace, peace,' they say, when there is no peace. Are they ashamed of their detestable conduct? No, they have no shame at all; they do not even know how to blush. So they will fall among the fallen; they will be brought down when I punish them," says the LORD.

Jeremiah 14:14-16: Then the LORD said to me, "The prophets are prophesying lies in my name. I have not sent them or appointed them or spoken to them. They are prophesying to you false visions, divinations, idolatries and the delusions of their own minds. Therefore this is what the LORD says about the prophets who are prophesying in my name: I did not send them, yet they are saying, 'No sword or famine will touch this land.' Those same prophets will perish by sword and famine. And the people they are prophesying to will be thrown out into the streets of Jerusalem because of the famine and sword. There will be no one to bury them, their wives, their sons and their daughters. I will pour out on them the calamity they deserve.

Jeremiah 23:9-40: Concerning the prophets: My heart is broken within me; all my bones tremble. I am like a drunken man, like a strong man overcome by wine, because of the LORD and his holy words. The land is full of adulterers; because of the curse the land lies parched and the pastures in the wilderness are withered. The prophets follow an evil course and use their power unjustly. "Both prophet and priest are godless; even in my temple I find their wickedness," declares the LORD. "Therefore their path will become slippery; they will be banished to darkness and there they will fall. I will bring disaster on them in the year they are punished," declares the LORD. "Among the prophets of Samaria I saw this repulsive thing: They prophesied by Baal and led my people Israel astray. And among the prophets of Jerusalem I have seen something horrible: They commit adultery and live a lie. They strengthen the hands of evildoers, so that not one of them turns from their wickedness. They are all like Sodom to me; the people of Jerusalem are like Gomorrah." Therefore this is what the LORD Almighty says concerning the prophets: "I will make them eat bitter food and drink poisoned water, because from the prophets of Jerusalem ungodliness has spread throughout the land." This is what the LORD Almighty says: "Do not listen to what the prophets are prophesying to you; they fill you with false hopes. They speak visions from their own minds, not from the mouth of the LORD. They keep saying to those who despise me, 'The LORD says: You will have peace.' And to all who follow the stubbornness of their hearts they say, 'No harm will come to you.' But which of them has stood in the council of the LORD to see or to hear his word? Who has listened and heard his word? See, the storm of the LORD will burst out in wrath, a whirlwind swirling down on the heads of the wicked. The anger of the LORD will not turn back until he fully accomplishes the purposes of his heart. In days to come you will understand it clearly. I did not send these prophets, yet they have run with their message; I did not speak to them, yet they have prophesied. But if they had stood in my council, they would have proclaimed my words to my people and would have turned them from their evil ways and from their evil deeds. "Am I only a God nearby," declares the LORD, "and not a God far away? Who can hide in secret places so that I cannot see them?" declares the LORD. "Do not I fill heaven and earth?" declares the LORD. "I have heard what the prophets say who prophesy lies in my name. They say, 'I had a dream! I had a dream!' How long will this continue in the hearts of these lying prophets, who prophesy the delusions of their own minds? They think the dreams they tell one another will make my people forget my name, just as their ancestors forgot my name through Baal worship. Let the prophet who has a dream recount the dream, but let the one who has my word speak it faithfully. For what has straw to do with grain?" declares the LORD. "Is not my word like fire," declares the LORD, "and like a hammer that breaks a rock in pieces? "Therefore," declares the LORD, "I am against the prophets who steal from one another words supposedly from me. Yes," declares the LORD, "I am against the prophets who wag their own tongues and yet declare, 'The LORD declares.' Indeed, I am against those who prophesy false dreams," declares the LORD. "They tell them and lead my people astray with their reckless lies, yet I did not send or appoint them. They do not benefit these people in the least," declares the LORD. "When these people, or a prophet or a priest, ask you, 'What is the message from the LORD?' say to them, 'What message? I will forsake you, declares the LORD.' If a prophet or a priest or anyone else claims, 'This is a message from the LORD,' I will punish them and their household. This is what each of you keeps saying to your friends and other Israelites: 'What is the LORD's answer?' or 'What has the LORD spoken?' But you must not mention 'a message from the LORD' again, because each one's word becomes their own message. So you distort the words of the living God, the LORD Almighty, our God. This is what you keep saying to a prophet: 'What is the LORD's answer to you?' or 'What has the LORD spoken?' Although you claim, 'This is a message from the LORD,' this is what the LORD says: You used the words, 'This is a message from the LORD,' even though I told you that you must not claim, 'This is a message from the LORD.' Therefore, I will surely forget you and cast you out of my presence along with the city I gave to you and your ancestors. I will bring on you everlasting disgrace--everlasting shame that will not be forgotten."

Ezekiel 13:1-23: The word of the LORD came to me: "Son of man, prophesy against the prophets of Israel who are now prophesying. Say to those who prophesy out of their own imagination: 'Hear the word of the LORD! This is what the Sovereign LORD says: Woe to the foolish prophets who follow their own spirit and have seen nothing! Your prophets, Israel, are like jackals among ruins. You have not gone up to the breaches in the wall to repair it for the people of Israel so that it will stand firm in the battle on the day of the LORD. Their visions are false and their divinations a lie. Even though the LORD has not sent them, they say, "The LORD declares," and expect him to fulfill their words. Have you not seen false visions and uttered lying divinations when you say, "The LORD declares," though I have not spoken? " 'Therefore this is what the Sovereign LORD says: Because of your false words and lying visions, I am against you, declares the Sovereign LORD. My hand will be against the prophets who see false visions and utter lying divinations. They will not belong to the council of my people or be listed in the records of Israel, nor will they enter the land of Israel. Then you will know that I am the Sovereign LORD. " 'Because they lead my people astray, saying, "Peace," when there is no peace, and because, when a flimsy wall is built, they cover it with whitewash, therefore tell those who cover it with whitewash that it is going to fall. Rain will come in torrents, and I will send hailstones hurtling down, and violent winds will burst forth. When the wall collapses, will people not ask you, "Where is the whitewash you covered it with?" " 'Therefore this is what the Sovereign LORD says: In my wrath I will unleash a violent wind, and in my anger hailstones and torrents of rain will fall with destructive fury. I will tear down the wall you have covered with whitewash and will level it to the ground so that its foundation will be laid bare. When it falls, you will be destroyed in it; and you will know that I am the LORD. So I will pour out my wrath against the wall and against those who covered it with whitewash. I will say to you, "The wall is gone and so are those who whitewashed it, those prophets of Israel who prophesied to Jerusalem and saw visions of peace for her when there was no peace, declares the Sovereign LORD." ' "Now, son of man, set your face against the daughters of your people who prophesy out of their own imagination. Prophesy against them and say, 'This is what the Sovereign LORD says: Woe to the women who sew magic charms on all their wrists and make veils of various lengths for their heads in order to ensnare people. Will you ensnare the lives of my people but preserve your own? You have profaned me among my people for a few handfuls of barley and scraps of bread. By lying to my people, who listen to lies, you have killed those who should not have died and have spared those who should not live. " 'Therefore this is what the Sovereign LORD says: I am against your magic charms with which you ensnare people like birds and I will tear them from your arms; I will set free the people that you ensnare like birds. I will tear off your veils and save my people from your hands, and they will no longer fall prey to your power. Then you will know that I am the LORD. Because you disheartened the righteous with your lies, when I had brought them no grief, and because you encouraged the wicked not to turn from their evil ways and so save their lives, therefore you will no longer see false visions or practice divination. I will save my people from your hands. And then you will know that I am the LORD.' "

Micah 2:6-13: "Do not prophesy," their prophets say. "Do not prophesy about these things; disgrace will not overtake us." You descendants of Jacob, should it be said, "Does the LORD become impatient? Does he do such things?" "Do not my words do good to the one whose ways are upright? Lately my people have risen up like an enemy. You strip off the rich robe from those who pass by without a care, like men returning from battle. You drive the women of my people from their pleasant homes. You take away my blessing from their children forever. Get up, go away! For this is not your resting place, because it is defiled, it is ruined, beyond all remedy. If a liar and deceiver comes and says, 'I will prophesy for you plenty of wine and beer,' that would be just the prophet for this people! "I will surely gather all of you, Jacob; I will surely bring together the remnant of Israel. I will bring them together like sheep in a pen, like a flock in its pasture; the place will throng with people. The One who breaks open the way will go up before them; they will break through the gate and go out. Their King will pass through before them, the LORD at their head."

Micah 3:1-12: Then I said, "Listen, you leaders of Jacob, you rulers of Israel. Should you not embrace justice, you who hate good and love evil; who tear the skin from my people and the flesh from their bones; who eat my people's flesh, strip off their skin and break their bones in pieces; who chop them up like meat for the pan, like flesh for the pot?" Then they will cry out to the LORD, but he will not answer them. At that time he will hide his face from them because of the evil they have done. This is what the LORD says: "As for the prophets who lead my people astray, they proclaim 'peace' if they have something to eat, but prepare to wage war against anyone who refuses to feed them. Therefore night will come over you, without visions, and darkness, without divination. The sun will set for the prophets, and the day will go dark for them. The seers will be ashamed and the diviners disgraced. They will all cover their faces because there is no answer from God." But as for me, I am filled with power, with the Spirit of the LORD, and with justice and might, to declare to Jacob his transgression, to Israel his sin. Hear this, you leaders of Jacob, you rulers of Israel, who despise justice and distort all that is right; who build Zion with bloodshed, and Jerusalem with wickedness. Her leaders judge for a bribe, her priests teach for a price, and her prophets tell fortunes for money. Yet they look for the LORD's support and say, "Is not the LORD among us? No disaster will come upon us." Therefore because of you, Zion will be plowed like a field, Jerusalem will become a heap of rubble, the temple hill a mound overgrown with thickets.

2 Corinthians 11:1-15: I hope you will put up with me in a little foolishness. Yes, please put up with me! I am jealous for you with a godly jealousy. I promised you to one husband, to Christ, so that I might present you as a pure virgin to him. But I am afraid that just as Eve was deceived by the serpent's cunning, your minds may somehow be led astray from your sincere and pure devotion to Christ. For if someone comes to you and preaches a Jesus other than the Jesus we preached, or if you receive a different spirit from the Spirit you received, or a different gospel from the one you accepted, you put up with it easily enough. I do not think I am in the least inferior to those "super-apostles." I may indeed be untrained as a speaker, but I do have knowledge. We have made this perfectly clear to you in every way. Was it a sin for me to lower myself in order to elevate you by preaching the gospel of God to you free of charge? I robbed other churches by receiving support from them so as to serve you. And when I was with you and needed something, I was not a burden to anyone, for the brothers who came from Macedonia supplied what I needed. I have kept myself from being a burden to you in any way, and will continue to do so. As surely

as the truth of Christ is in me, nobody in the regions of Achaia will stop this boasting of mine. Why? Because I do not love you? God knows I do! And I will keep on doing what I am doing in order to cut the ground from under those who want an opportunity to be considered equal with us in the things they boast about. For such people are false apostles, deceitful workers, masquerading as apostles of Christ. And no wonder, for Satan himself masquerades as an angel of light. It is not surprising, then, if his servants also masquerade as servants of righteousness. Their end will be what their actions deserve.

Practical Application:

List three things these Scriptures reveal about false prophets.
1.
2.
3.
How have you experienced or witnessed these types of things in "prophets" today?
How is God asking you to personally respond to these Scriptures in your own life?

Basic Training Exercise

FALLING FROM GRACE

Galatians 5:4 NIV - You who are trying to be justified by the law have been alienated from Christ; you have fallen away from grace.

DESCRIPTION

Salvation is by grace through faith in Jesus Christ. We cannot earn it or maintain it by what we do. But we can choose to stand by faith in Jesus' perfect record or by works with our own record of righteousness. If we choose our own record, we have fallen from grace.

Falling from grace is a serious thing. We fall from grace when we depart from the undeserved favor of God's New Covenant through faith in Jesus by subjecting ourselves to the requirements of the Old Covenant or any other form of mandatory religious piety, legalism, rule-keeping, or believing that God's blessing is based on our personal performance.

Unfortunately, our flesh and Adamic nature has a strong tendency towards rules and regulations. The knowledge of good and evil has been the greatest temptation and downfall of mankind since the Garden of Eden. It is tempting to create or subscribe to systems for self-advancement and blessing rather than becoming like a child to be blessed by simple faith.

However, Jesus lived the perfect life that **no one** born of Adam has ever been able to live. Then, Jesus offered Himself as a sacrifice for our sin. God raised Him on the third day. Jesus is now seated at the right hand of God. Anyone who believes this in their hearts and confesses that Jesus is Lord is declared righteous before God by faith. Nothing more. Nothing less.

To put Falling from Grace into practice is about listening closely to our own thoughts in order to discern if we are placing our faith in Christ's righteousness or our own works or rule-following. Similarly, we can listen to the words and teachings of others to discern if their words are encouraging us in the Lord or tempting us to fall from grace.

Category: Discernment

Basic TRAINING SPIRITUAL EXERCISES

PURPOSE:

To be established and in grace without being led astray by false teaching.

To guard our hearts and minds in the purity of Christ's righteousness as a free gift.

To be strengthened in our faith and endurance in Christ.

SPIRITUAL FRUIT:

Increased discernment of good and evil.

Greater revelation of righteousness.

Deeper knowledge of God and what Jesus accomplished for us.

Increased purity of faith.

Expanded love for Jesus.

PRAYER

Father, I believe that you sent Jesus so that I can be saved by grace through faith in Him and what He did for me. Grant me the ability to discern when I am tempted towards legalism or rules. In Jesus' name, Amen.

CONSIDERATIONS

Consider what you believe about the following statements. True or False?

- T/F – There is nothing I can do to make God love me more/less.
- T/F – Good things happen to good people. Bad things to bad.
- T/F – God blesses people when they pray, read Scripture, etc.
- T/F – I can earn God's blessings through my obedience.
- T/F – People get what they deserve.

PRACTICE

1. This week, take note of your thoughts/motives for why you do the things you do. Ask God to reveal areas where you are trusting in your own performance, rule-keeping, etc.
   - Are you doing something or not doing something in order to be approved of by God?
   - Are you doing what you do in order to earn favor or blessing from God? To get God to give you something?
   - Take note of how these things are contrary to receiving God's blessings as free gift through faith in Jesus.

2. As the Lord reveals areas for repentance, confess the ways you have fallen from grace by trying to justify yourself by what you do or do not do.
   - Receive His forgiveness by faith. Be restored afresh.

3. As you listen to others speak, listen to what they emphasize as the way of blessing or right-standing with God.
   - Are they promoting steps or rules to earn God's favor?
   - If so, how does this contradict righteousness as a free gift?
   - How could this be dangerous for your faith?

NOTES: _____

Category: Discernment

ADDITIONAL SCRIPTURES:

Hebrews 12:15
2 Peter 3:17
Ephesians 2:8-10
1 Corinthians 10:12
Romans 6:14
Romans 3:23-24
Romans 7:8-25
Hebrews 4:1

 PERFECTION COURSE – UNIT 6.4 READING

Enduring through the Great Apostasy

Abraham looked for a city whose builder and maker was God. In fact, all of the heroes of faith did, including Jesus. This city is the Bride, the New Jerusalem, who will come down out of heaven from God. These are the regenerated ones who have clothed themselves in white linen through their righteous deeds done by the power of the Spirit of the Lord. These are the remnant of faithful ones who have endured through testing and trials until their faith was proven genuine and worthy of inheriting the Kingdom of God. These are the holy ones of God who will dwell with Him for eternity.

In the Bible, the first person to build a city was Cain after he had been banished to wander the earth with a mark on him preventing anyone from killing him. Another renowned city builder and mighty one was Nimrod, one of the earliest pre-figures of the antichrist. Nimrod built the tower of Babel and called it the gate of God. Nimrod ruled the world as one people, with one language, and one mission – to build a fortress reaching to the heavens in order to make a name for themselves and avoid the judgment of God.

We follow a crucified King who came longing to be received by an earthly city but instead was rejected, mocked, and killed. The example our King set for us is absolute uncompromising righteousness in the face of immense opposition, religious pressure, and brutal, torturous death. But His eyes were on the eternal prize and so, He paid the price willingly. All of His twelve apostles were also martyred for their faith. It is said that some of the believers in the early church sought out martyrdom as an opportunity to testify about Christ and show their willingness to pay the ultimate price for Him.

Are we ready to follow Jesus for eternal purposes even unto death? Or will we choose ourselves for the sake of our lives on earth? Will we keep our eyes on the eternal city built by God? Or will we join with the whole world in worship of a counterfeit Christ who sets himself up on earth as God and against God? These are the question of the end times.

Jesus said to expect persecution and the possibility of martyrdom if we truly wanted to follow Him. The world hates Jesus and will hate us if we are truly like Him. In the time before His return, all nations will hate true followers of Jesus. This will cause many believers to fall away from the faith by giving way to false prophets who do not require such faithfulness to eternity.

> *Matthew 24:9-14:* Then **you will be handed over to be persecuted and put to death,** and **you will be hated by all nations because of me.** At that time **many will turn away from the faith** and will betray and hate each other, and many false prophets will appear and deceive many people. Because of the increase of wickedness, **the love of most will grow cold, but the one who stands firm to the end will be saved.** And this gospel of the kingdom will be preached in the whole world as a testimony to all nations, and then the end will come.

> *John 15:18-20:* **If the world hates you, keep in mind that it hated me first. If you belonged to the world, it would love you as its own.** As it is, you do not belong to the world, but I have chosen you out of the world. That is why the world hates you. Remember what I told you: 'A servant is not greater than his master.' **If they persecuted me, they will persecute you also.** If they obeyed my teaching, they will obey yours also.

In the times of the end, the world will unite under one world-ruler who will exalt himself above every leader and call himself god. The world will be united with one religion under one "god" and will worship the antichrist and take the mark of the beast. Many people spend time trying to figure out what the mark of the beast will be and how to avoid taking it. We would be wiser to seek and pursue the will of God so that we may be sealed with His seal and kept for eternity by His mercy and grace.

Insights of the End

Jesus' first followers would also have been well aware of the apocalyptic writings of Daniel which foretold the end of days through dramatic visions given to Daniel while he was in Babylonian exile. The people of God longed to see God's Kingdom be established on the earth and therefore, awaited Jesus' imminent return to conquer the Gentile kingdoms for their vindication. Here are some of the passages they would have been familiar with:

> *Daniel 7:21-25: As I watched, this horn was **waging war against the holy people and defeating them**, until the Ancient of Days came and pronounced judgment in favor of the holy people of the Most High, and the time came when they possessed the kingdom. "He gave me this explanation: 'The fourth beast is a fourth kingdom that will appear on earth. It will be different from all the other kingdoms and will devour the whole earth, trampling it down and crushing it. The ten horns are ten kings who will come from this kingdom. After them another king will arise, different from the earlier ones; he will subdue three kings. He will **speak against the Most High and oppress his holy people and try to change the set times and the laws. The holy people will be delivered into his hands for a time, times and half a time**.*

<u>World ruler waging war against the holy people and defeating them; oppressing the holy people who are delivered into his hands</u>: We must let this Scripture penetrate our understanding. Our victory is eternal even at the expense of our earthly lives. If we become fixated on a "victory" theology pertaining to earthly things rather than the conquering of sin and freedom from religion, fear, and condemnation through the truth of Christ, we will be sorely disappointed when the reality of the end times hits our lives. If we do not grasp this, our faith will be vulnerable to shattering because we did not know or love the truth.

<u>Speaking against the Most High</u>: Blasphemy against God includes distortions of His character, Word, ways, truth, or conditions for salvation. For example, the name of God was blasphemed among the nations because of the behavior and exile of the people of Israel. The nations did not understand the worldly behavior or people with a righteous God or how such a powerful God could allow exile to happen to His people. Therefore, God's character was maligned, His righteousness was misassessed, and stories of His power became regarded like fables and fairy tales. Blasphemy is not always obvious insults or abuse.

> *Daniel 8:23-26: In the latter part of their reign, when rebels have become completely wicked, a fierce-looking king, a master of intrigue, will arise. **He will become very strong, but not by his own power**. He will cause astounding devastation and will succeed in whatever he does. **He will destroy those who are mighty, the holy people. He will cause deceit to prosper**, and he will consider himself superior. When they feel secure, he will destroy many and **take his stand against the Prince of princes**. Yet he will be destroyed, but not by human power. "The vision of the evenings and mornings that has been given you is true, but **seal up the vision, for it concerns the distant future**.*

<u>Supernatural strength and power; causing deceit to prosper</u>: The delusion of the end times will be beyond natural comprehension. There will be a driving spiritual force behind the lies of the antichrist which causes most people to believe him and his deceptions and turn themselves over to following him out of fear of his great power. Like Nimrod the mighty hunter who dominated people with his adept warrior skills, the fierce king will command respect and demand worship by force.

<u>Destroying the holy people</u>: The word for destroy can mean destruction as we normally think of it but can also mean to corrupt, pervert, ruin, spoil, or decay. The holy people is us - the people of God.

Taking his stand against Jesus: This counterfeit Christ will present himself as the alternative to Jesus while most likely using Jesus' name to his own advantage to advance his own agenda.

Vision sealed for the end: Daniel was told that this vision was for the end times. Though many of the events in this prophetic vision took place in the times before Jesus' first time on earth, the Scripture expressly links it to the times of the end.

> *Daniel 11:14: In those times many will rise against the king of the South.* **Those who are violent among your own people will rebel** *in fulfillment of the vision, but without success.*

Violent believers rise up in rebellion: Jesus said those who live by the sword will die by the sword. Those who believe that the battle can be won in political battles or through violent rebellions will be sorely mistaken. Our King is a slaughtered Lamb who kept silent rather than defend Himself. He will come as the Lion with a vengeance in the end but until then, all vengeance belongs to Him. Those who know Him follow the Lamb wherever He goes. We must learn to participate with the divine nature of the Lamb.

> *Daniel 11:32-35:* **With flattery he will corrupt those who have violated the covenant, but the people who know their God will firmly resist him.** *Those who are wise will instruct many, though for a time* **they will fall by the sword or be burned or captured or plundered.** *When they fall, they will receive a little help, and many who are not sincere will join them.* **Some of the wise will stumble, so that they may be refined, purified and made spotless until the time of the end,** *for it will still come at the appointed time.*

Flattery to corrupt believers into violating the covenant: Smooth talk and false promises will corrupt those who have previously been committed to Jesus. The end times tribulation will force people into desperate situations where their faith is vulnerable to giving way to error. Like Esau who was so hungry that he sold his birthright for a bowl of lentils, or like Judas who sold out Jesus for thirty pieces of silver, we too will be pushed to the limit of what we can endure and tempted to sell out.

People who know their God will resist: Only through knowing God and His faithfulness and trusting Him even unto death, will we be able to resist the flatteries and persuasions of the evil ruler of the world. In fact, the times will be so severe that people who resist will appear to be moronic idiots for turning down the benefits offered through submission to the antichrist. But if we know God we will resist.

Wise will fall by the sword or be burned, captured, plundered: The wise among believers will be martyred. They will be targeted, hunted down, plundered, and put to death to silence them.

Wise will stumble to be refined, purified, made spotless: Other wise ones will stumble into error but this will serve to purify their faith and make them worthy to receive our King and be counted as His Bride.

> *Daniel 12:1-4: At that time Michael, the great prince who protects your people, will arise.* **There will be a time of distress such as has not happened from the beginning of nations** *until then.* **But at that time your people--everyone whose name is found written in the book--will be delivered.** *Multitudes who sleep in the dust of the earth will awake: some to everlasting life, others to shame and everlasting contempt. Those who are wise will shine like the brightness of the heavens, and those who lead many to righteousness, like the stars for ever and ever. But you, Daniel,* **roll up and seal the words of the scroll until the time of the end.** *Many will go here and there to increase knowledge."*

Time of distress: Jesus also clearly stated that we will not be gathered up to Him until AFTER the events of the tribulation. (See Matthew 24:29-31.) We will not be here for the time of God's wrath after the seventh trumpet sounds off and the bowls of wrath begin to be poured out. But we will remain on earth during the plagues detailed in the Book of Revelation through the opening of the seals of the scroll and the sounding of the trumpets. This is a call for the endurance of the saints.

Ultimate deliverance in resurrection: In God's timing, we will be delivered. The dead in Christ will rise first and those who remain alive will be supernaturally transformed into an imperishable body to dwell with the Lord forever.

Roll up and seal the scroll: Daniel's visions were for the end-times. In heaven, no one was found worthy to open the eternal scrolls which would usher in the judgments of God and tribulation upon the earth. Only Jesus was found worthy in perfect righteousness and obedience even unto death. The Lamb that was slain and the eternal King is the only one worthy to open the scroll.

Paul and John echo Daniel's visions, saying almost the same things of the end times ruler and his wicked acts against the holy ones of God.

> *2 Thessalonians 2:3-4, 9-12 ESV: Let no one deceive you in any way. For that day will not come, **unless the rebellion comes first**, and the **man of lawlessness is revealed, the son of destruction, who opposes and exalts himself against every so-called god or object of worship, so that he takes his seat in the temple of God, proclaiming himself to be God**. ... The coming of the lawless one is **by the activity of Satan with all power and false signs and wonders**, and **with all wicked deception** for those who are perishing, because they **refused to love the truth and so be saved**. Therefore **God sends them a strong delusion, so that they may believe what is false, in order that all may be condemned who did not believe the truth but had pleasure in unrighteousness**.*

Rebellion: The Greek word apostasia meaning apostasy falling away, defection, or forsaking of the truth.

Strong delusion: It will be a strong delusion – not a weak one – a strong one. It is one thing if a counterfeit is produced by a counterfeiter; but imagine if a counterfeit was created by the producer of the genuine article. How convincing would that be! According to this Scripture, the strong delusion will be raised up by God Himself. Corruptions and distortions of the truth will be presented in marvelously convincing ways to persuade even the most well-intentioned believers into error. As in the Garden of Eden, it will not come in the form of pure evil but will be presented in the form of attaining godliness, peace, and unity.

Man of lawlessness, son of destruction: The word perdition is the same word Jesus used to describe Judas. Judas had walked closely with Jesus for three years, doing all the things that the other disciples did, working miracles in Jesus' name, and even controlling the treasury of Jesus' ministry. But Judas saw and seized an opportunity to advance the Kingdom of God on earth for his own benefit. He turned Jesus over to the religious authorities hoping that this would force Jesus into combat and the fulfillment of the Daniel prophecies pertaining to the establishment of the Kingdom. If Jesus had acted on this, rather than going to His death on the cross, Judas may very well have become the treasurer of the whole world because he had already been serving as the treasurer of Jesus' ministry. He had more than thirty pieces of silver on his mind. All of this is to say that the man of lawlessness will rebel against Jesus with the motive of ruling the global economies of the world. (This is similarly referenced in Ezekiel 28:5, 16.)

False signs and wonders and deception: The antichrist will counterfeit every miracle of God and also put on displays of spiritual power to deceive the whole world. The antichrist will even set up an image of himself in the Temple of God and cause it to speak. All who refuse to worship the image will be killed. (See Revelation 13:14-15.)

Love of the truth or pleasure in unrighteousness: This is a matter of the heart. Jesus is the truth and there is nothing deceitful or crooked in Him. Our love for the truth is a direct reflection of our love for God. Either our hearts love the truth of Jesus Christ and all it entails more than our own lives or our hearts have iniquity in them which sets itself up against God. Those who have iniquity in their hearts will be led astray into believing the lie. Jesus deserves a pure Bride.

Revelation 13:4-10: People worshiped the dragon because he had given authority to the beast, and they also worshiped the beast and asked, "Who is like the beast? Who can wage war against it?" **The beast was given a mouth to utter proud words and blasphemies and to exercise its authority for forty-two months. It opened its mouth to blaspheme God, and to slander his name and his dwelling place and those who live in heaven. It was given power to wage war against God's holy people and to conquer them.** *And it was given authority over every tribe, people, language and nation. All inhabitants of the earth will worship the beast--all whose names have not been written in the Lamb's book of life, the Lamb who was slain from the creation of the world. Whoever has ears, let them hear.* **"If anyone is to go into captivity, into captivity they will go. If anyone is to be killed with the sword, with the sword they will be killed." This calls for patient endurance and faithfulness on the part of God's people.**

<u>Waging war against God's holy people and conquering them</u>: In case anyone wanted to dismiss Daniel's prophecies as having already been fulfilled, this nullifies that assertion. This is still yet to come.

<u>Captivity & killed with sword</u>: This echoes the words of Jeremiah in preparing the people of Judah for the Babylonian invasion that was about to come upon them. (See Jeremiah 15:2.) As followers of the Lamb, we submit ourselves to whatever God has for us, praying for and blessing those who persecute us and treat us shamefully, and hoping that even in our death, they might come to recognize Jesus as Lord.

<u>Patient endurance</u>: As believers fall into apostasy and martyrdom left and right, we will need great endurance to persevere in our faith in Christ. Only the Holy Spirit can supply this. This is why most apostolic prayers are centered around believers truly knowing God through Jesus Christ to be strengthened with power to endure in holiness, righteousness, and faithfulness until the end.

Prayer in the End Times

Abraham's intercession on behalf of Sodom and Gomorrah is often used as a model for prayer, appealing to God on behalf of a city or nation. But we have to remember that God did ultimately judge and destroy Sodom and Gomorrah. Jewish tradition states that Abraham stopped negotiating with God when he reached ten righteous ones because he based his calculation on the fact that Lot, his wife, daughters, and potentially sons-in-law lived in Sodom. His prayer was looking out for the protection of his own and the city would simply benefit from it. God did honor Abraham's prayer – but probably not in the way Abraham expected. God made a way of escape for Abraham's family members, who were the righteous ones in Sodom but then, God judged the cities because their time of judgement had come.

Much later in history, God told Jeremiah NOT to pray for the people of Judah because their lack of repentance after repeated warnings had brought them to the point that intercession would make no difference. (See Jeremiah 7:16, 11:14, 14:11.) Ezekiel was also told by God that the people's actions had determined the consequences which God was forced in righteousness to pour out upon them and that even the prayers of Noah, Daniel, and Job could not save them. (See Ezekiel 14:12-23.)

No doubt, it is God's will for all people to be saved. But not all will be saved. Salvation comes only through knowledge of the truth resulting in faith in Jesus Christ which is demonstrated by repentance from sin. Abraham, Jeremiah, Ezekiel, and other prophets did not pray for God not to send the disasters. They knew that they had heard God decree the disasters. God only relents disasters when people repent of their sins. (See Jeremiah 18:7-10.) Interceding against disasters that God has ordained is effectively robbing people of their opportunity to cry out to God in desperation. (See Isaiah 26:9-10.)

God does nothing on the earth without revealing it to His servants, the prophets. He is not obligated in any way to do this but He does it to continually glorify His name as the only one who knows the end from the beginning. God revealed His intentions for Sodom and Gomorrah to Abraham because Abraham was His friend and He wanted Abraham to understand the full ramifications of the set-apart life God had called him to. Jesus calls us His friends if we do what He commands us. As His friends, He tells us everything the Father told Him so that we might not fall away in the time of testing.

All of this is to say that while I am all for prayer and intercession, I am also for prayer which is directed by God and by revelation of what God is actually doing in a situation. Praying according to what we THINK is God's will can lead us into exasperation, fatigue, and disillusionment because we have not accurately understood God's plan. These prayers appeal to our flesh and carnal notions of the love of God and what that looks like but they are not rooted in both the kindness and severity of God. The severity of God's wrath makes the salvation we have in Christ all the sweeter and all the more urgently needed to be shared with the lost world. If we spend ourselves in countless hours of intercession for nations, against plagues, or for our own rendition of God's righteousness, we will swiftly find ourselves praying against God and against the events clearly detailed as God's will in the Book of Revelation and prophetic Scriptures. Moreover, these types of prayers will make us extremely susceptible to the flatteries and persuasions of the antichrist who will present the love of God in a perverted manner to serve his own agenda of world domination. If we do not know the truth, his words will sound right to us.

This is why the apostolic prayers of the New Testament have very little to do with details of everyday life and common needs but stress the importance of truly KNOWING God through Jesus Christ and having genuine revelation of who Christ is and what He has done for us so that we will have power to stand in faithfulness against all schemes of the enemy even until the very end.

The Real Apostates

When Jesus came and people followed Him and His teachings, they were accused of apostasy against Moses. (See Acts 21:21.) In the end times, followers of the real Jesus will be accused of apostasy for standing firm in the truth without bowing down to the false religion of the antichrist.

> John 16:1-2: All this **I have told you so that you will not fall away.** They will **put you out of the synagogue**; in fact, the time is coming when **anyone who kills you will think they are offering a service to God**.

Put you out of the synagogue: This literally means, they will excommunicate you from the assembly of the congregation. Though in the days of Jesus and even now it did and can literally mean Jewish synagogues. However, this phrase is not limited to Jewish synagogues. Church history makes this abundantly clear.

Think they are offering a service to God: Jesus was presented for the death penalty by religious leaders who accused Him as a blasphemer and excommunicated Him from the people of God. Many of the martyrs of the past seventeen hundred years died at the hands of worldly church leaders who thought they were serving God by purging evil heretics from the church. History has made plain the reality of their stories. These are the times we will endure before Christ returns to claim us as His Bride.

Apostates will be the majority in the end times. MANY will fall away from the faith. These are not unbelievers. You cannot fall away from something you were never in. The love of MOST will grow cold. Selflessness and charity will perish from the lives of those who are not empowered by the agape love of God. Those who fall away will do so to follow what suits their own temporal needs and desires. It will be totally understandable from a worldly perspective but totally abominable from eternity's viewpoint.

The antichrist will build and unite a world for himself, attempting to ascend to the heights of heaven's authority. His prophets will be saying, "peace peace," "bless bless," and "victory victory" as they try to take over the world "for God."

Jesus died for the truth to bring not peace but a sword and to receive the world from God as His reward with all authority for all eternity. His prophets will be warning people of the day of judgment to come and salvation in Him alone.

The question remains: In the end, which side will you be on?

www.manifestinternational.com

REVELATION CHURCHES
Worksheet

Churches of Revelation	Commendation	Rebuke	Action Steps
Ephesus 2:1-7	Good works & endurance. Vigilance against false teachers. Not grown weary.	Abandoned first love.	Remember from where you have fallen. Repent and do the works as at first.
Smyrna 2:8-11	Enduring persecution, slander. Rich in faith.		Do not fear trials. Stand firm even unto death.
Pergamum 2:12-17	Holding to Christ's name and faith even to martyrdom.	Tolerating false prophets causing people to stumble.	Repent.
Thyatira 2:18-29	Increasing in love, faith, service, and endurance.	Tolerating false prophets and not repenting.	Repent. Hold fast to the truth to the end.
Sardis 3:1-6	A few loyal people who have not soiled their garments.	Works incomplete.	Repent and remember what you received. Wake up.
Philadelphia 3:7-13	Patiently enduring. Keeping God's word. Not denying God's name.		Hold fast.
Laodicea 3:14-22		Spiritually poor, blind, bankrupt, naked, lukewarm.	Be zealous and repent.

Practical Application:

Which of the Commendations do you sense the Holy Spirit is applying to your walk and life with Christ?

Which of the Rebukes do you sense the Holy Spirit is applying to your walk and life with Christ?

What action steps is God giving you to apply in your own life? (Whether listed or not.)

APOSTOLIC PRAYERS
Growing in Knowing God

KNOWLEDGE OF GOD'S WILL (COLOSSIANS 1:9-14)

And so, from the day we heard, we have not ceased to pray for you, asking that you may be filled with the knowledge of his will in all spiritual wisdom and understanding, so as to walk in a manner worthy of the Lord, fully pleasing to him: bearing fruit in every good work and increasing in the knowledge of God; being strengthened with all power, according to his glorious might, for all endurance and patience with joy; giving thanks to the Father, who has qualified you to share in the inheritance of the saints in light. He has delivered us from the domain of darkness and transferred us to the kingdom of his beloved Son, in whom we have redemption, the forgiveness of sins.

SPIRIT OF WISDOM & REVELATION (EPHESIANS 1:16-23)

I do not cease to give thanks for you, remembering you in my prayers, that the God of our Lord Jesus Christ, the Father of glory, may give you the Spirit of wisdom and of revelation in the knowledge of him, having the eyes of your hearts enlightened, that you may know what is the hope to which he has called you, what are the riches of his glorious inheritance in the saints, and what is the immeasurable greatness of his power toward us who believe, according to the working of his great might that he worked in Christ when he raised him from the dead and seated him at his right hand in the heavenly places, far above all rule and authority and power and dominion, and above every name that is named, not only in this age but also in the one to come. And he put all things under his feet and gave him as head over all things to the church, which is his body, the fullness of him who fills all in all.

FULLNESS OF GOD & HIS LOVE (EPHESIANS 3:14-21)

For this reason I bow my knees before the Father, from whom every family in heaven and on earth is named, that according to the riches of his glory he may grant you to be strengthened with power through his Spirit in your inner being, so that Christ may dwell in your hearts through faith--that you, being rooted and grounded in love, may have strength to comprehend with all the saints what is the breadth and length and height and depth, and to know the love of Christ that surpasses knowledge, that you may be filled with all the fullness of God. Now to him who is able to do far more abundantly than all that we ask or think, according to the power at work within us, to him be glory in the church and in Christ Jesus throughout all generations, forever and ever. Amen.

ABOUNDING LOVE WITH DISCERNMENT (PHILIPPIANS 1:9-11)

And it is my prayer that your love may abound more and more, with knowledge and all discernment, so that you may approve what is excellent, and so be pure and blameless for the day of Christ, filled with the fruit of righteousness that comes through Jesus Christ, to the glory and praise of God.

WALKING WORTHY OF GOD (2 THESSALONIANS 1:11-12)

To this end we always pray for you, that our God may make you worthy of his calling and may fulfill every resolve for good and every work of faith by his power, so that the name of our Lord Jesus may be glorified in you, and you in him, according to the grace of our God and the Lord Jesus Christ.

EFFECTUAL KINGDOM WORK (PHILEMON 1:6)

I pray that the sharing of your faith may become effective for the full knowledge of every good thing that is in us for the sake of Christ.

GOD'S WILL & KINGDOM (MATTHEW 6:9-13)

Pray then like this: "Our Father in heaven, hallowed be your name. Your kingdom come, your will be done, on earth as it is in heaven. Give us this day our daily bread, and forgive us our debts, as we also have forgiven our debtors. And lead us not into temptation, but deliver us from evil.

UNIT SIX – KEY QUESTIONS
Discernment of Good & Evil

Use this worksheet to test your grasp of the material and exercises of Unit Six.

What is the difference between the knowledge of good and evil and discernment of good and evil? (in your own words)	
What is the enemy's primary objective of deception?	**How do good intentions become polluted with error?**
How does false teaching appeal to soulish desires?	**What is the common characteristic of false teachers?**
What is God's purposes in allowing false teachers?	**How will believers endure through the great apostasy?**
What is one thing you learned that you did not know before?	**What questions do you still have about this subject?**

UNIT SIX: GROUP EXERCISES

Option One:
1. Based on the various exercises in this Unit have each person in the group share something they have learned about discerning the schemes of the enemy and how to discern good from evil.
2. Discuss what impact this will have on your perspective of teachers, prophets, and ministries today.

AND/OR

Option Two
1. Use the Apostolic Prayer Guide and select one prayer to pray for your group.
2. Have each member of the group select one of the prayers on the Apostolic Prayer Guide as a prayer for themselves. Pair up and commit to praying that prayer for your partner for one week. Check back with one another to discuss what God does!

UNIT SEVEN:
FULFILLING MINISTRY
TO PREPARE THE BRIDE

KEY SCRIPTURE VERSE FOR UNIT SEVEN
So Christ himself gave the apostles, the prophets, the evangelists, the pastors and teachers, to equip his people for works of service, so that the body of Christ may be built up until we all reach unity in the faith and in the knowledge of the Son of God and become mature, attaining to the whole measure of the fullness of Christ. - Ephesians 4:11-13

CLASS 1: MAKING DISCIPLES
1 Reading, 2 Prayer Guides, 1 Exercise
The Great Commission is to make disciples...not just converts. God calls and uses all kinds of people to build His Kingdom and His aim is for us to work together to grow to spiritual maturity.

CLASS 2: THE WORK OF MINISTRY
1 Reading, 1 Evaluation, 2 Prayer Guides
Each believer has been called by God into ministry service. Our callings will be different (apostles, prophets, evangelists, shepherds, and teachers) but our job description is the same: to equip the saints for the work of ministry.

CLASS 3: BRIDAL LOVE MADE READY
1 Reading, 2 Evaluations, 1 Exercise
In the end, all of humanity will be judged as the whore or the Bride. Follow the Bride into selfless love that surrenders all in expectation of her Bridegroom King.

KEY QUESTIONS

GROUP EXERCISES

PERFECTION COURSE – UNIT 7.1 READING

Make Disciples

God's plan for changing the world was to fully train twelve men and replicate Himself in them. He made disciples by spending time with them and allowing them to spend time with Him. They were with Jesus when He taught in the synagogues and the Temple, when He shared parables about the Kingdom of God, and when He proclaimed the need for repentance. They were with Jesus when He healed the sick, cast out demons, and worked marvelous miracles. They were with Jesus when He rebuked the Pharisees and religious leaders. They were with Jesus when He was tired, hungry, and did basic menial things that no one else noticed. They were with Jesus in the storm and when He rested, in His trials and His triumphs, and through His betrayal, conviction, and death. And they were the ones who were with Him after He was resurrected.

Jesus lived thirty years on earth before beginning His public ministry. Even though He was already able to refute the religious scholars at the Temple by the age of twelve, He submitted Himself to His parents for another eighteen years before it was time for His ministry to begin. Through this time, He lived in perfect righteous obedience to God's Law. He never told a lie or did anything self-serving, His motives were always right, and He patiently sat through thirty years of bad synagogue sermons listening to their erroneous theologies and interpretations of God's Word.

John the Baptist also waited upon God's perfect timing to begin ministry. Once John started proclaiming repentance and baptizing people, it was not long before Jesus came to John to be baptized. John recognized Him as the Son of God and Messiah and a voice from heaven confirmed Jesus' identity as the Holy Spirit descended upon Jesus from above. Immediately after this confirmation, Jesus was driven into the wilderness to be tested and tempted by Satan. He came out of the wilderness with His identity proven by His impenetrable divine nature and in the power of the Most High God.

After all of this, Jesus began to call His first disciples. Their call to follow Jesus was a call to drop everything in order to learn His ways and teachings and put them into practice. The call is the same today as it was then. If He really is the Messiah and Son of God then nothing in this world could possibly compare to knowing Him, spending time with Him, and learning from Him to do His will.

Disciples of All Kinds

As Jesus walked by the Sea of Galilee, He called out to Peter and Andrew saying, "Follow Me." They immediately dropped everything to follow Him. Then Jesus called out to John and James saying, "Follow Me." They immediately dropped everything to follow Him. (See Matthew 4:18-22.) These were simple fishermen who may or may not have been literate or proper in any way and were certainly not trained as religious scholars. Simple, hardworking people are loved by God and can be useful to His service.

Around this same time, Jesus found Philip and said, "Follow Me." Philip also found Nathanael to join them. As Nathanael approached in unbelief, Jesus prophetically spoke to him pertaining to his character and activities. Both were persuaded that Jesus was the Son of God and King of Israel. (See John 1:43-51.) And so they followed Him. Those who have lived with integrity and honesty will be invited by Jesus into a whole new life of discovering the righteous ways of God.

Jesus went from there to perform His first miracle at the wedding feast in Cana. His disciples believed Him all the more because of this miracle. God loves to make Himself known to us to confirm our choice in trusting Him. Even today, God will do marvelous things for us when we first come to faith in Him. I like to refer to it as a person's Red Sea season when God is demonstrating Himself to them in ways that they cannot deny, which will be a remembrance to them when following Jesus becomes more challenging, and which they will ultimately give account for in the event of wavering away from the faith.

Jesus ministered to great crowds, proclaiming the Kingdom of God and commanding repentance. Many people followed Him because of this. Then, after arriving at Capernaum, Jesus walked by Matthew in his tax booth and said, "Follow Me." Matthew dropped everything to follow Jesus. Matthew was a business and money-minded man, intelligent, skilled with numbers, and ready to be hated for doing his job. Tax collectors were loathed by Israelites because they worked for the Romans whose taxes oppressed their people. But tax collectors and business people were not hated by God and are welcomed in His service.

Jesus was also criticized for keeping company with prostitutes, sinners, lepers, and all other rebels and outcasts of society. In Him, they found acceptance. He spent time with the rich, the poor, the religious, and the rejected. Everyone was invited to repent of their ways and come into His Kingdom. Those who received the invitation followed Him, but many made worldly excuses for why they could not.

When Jesus made His way to Jerusalem for the Passover feast, He turned over the tables in the Temple out of zeal for the House of God. At night, under cover of darkness, a Pharisee named Nicodemus came to Jesus to inquire of Him because he was almost certain that Jesus must be the Messiah. Jesus' answer challenged Nicodemus' religious understanding. Nicodemus did not follow Jesus at first and remained in his religious order. But later, Nicodemus did speak up for Jesus to the religious leaders and ultimately, he openly believed Jesus and assisted with His burial. Sometimes, religious people, whether Christian or from other faiths, recognize something holy about Jesus, but it takes some time for them to come into alignment and faith in Him. When they are ready, Jesus is ready for them.

Disciples of John the Baptist were confused to see Jesus and His disciples baptizing people. But John did not hesitate to point them to Jesus as the anointed Messiah of God and the only one to follow. Sometimes, those who have been following an incomplete version of Christianity need to leave what they have known to follow to the fullest the One appointed by God.

Large crowds and masses of people followed Jesus to hear His teaching and experience His miracles. Jesus had many disciples, both men and women, who faithfully followed Him. But when it came time to choose the twelve who would be near to Him, Jesus stayed up all night in prayer to be certain to know from God those who were chosen for the task, even the one who would betray Him. God knows in advance who will endure and who will fall away, who will remain faithful and who will betray Him. He calls us anyway so that God's perfect will may be fulfilled.

The twelve chosen by Jesus were the ones who would have the special privilege of serving Him by doing the works that He did the way that He did them. Later, He added seventy others whom He sent out to do the works of the Kingdom of God. It was Jesus' greatest joy and satisfaction to see His followers come into revelation and understanding of the ways and power of God. This was the beginning of making disciples by replicating Himself in them.

Another thing to notice is that Jesus did not chase people down to force them to follow Him. Either they were willing to follow or they were not. Many who followed Him and openly professed their belief and devotion, He challenged, rebuked, or made the barrier of entry so high or controversial that they went away not knowing what to make of Him. He made Himself available to everyone but He revealed Himself to those who were willing to follow Him closely.

After His resurrection, Jesus commissioned His disciples to make disciples the same way that He had made disciples out of them. Now that Jesus had died for the sins of the whole world, people from every nation, tribe, and tongue were welcomed into the Kingdom of God through faith in Jesus Christ as demonstrated by repentance from sin. The disciples were commissioned to baptize new believers and to teach them everything that Jesus had taught them. But first, they had to wait for the Holy Spirit to be poured out from heaven upon them to equip them with God's power for their work. Sometimes, even after we have experienced wonderful things with God, and in service to Him, we must wait for Him to usher us into our next season of service.

After the Holy Spirit was poured out, the disciples proclaimed the Gospel with a passion and thousands of people believed in Jesus because of their message. But there was one in particular who did not believe them and who set his face to eradicate them and their message from the face of the earth. His name was Saul.

Saul was a brilliant man with the best theological training in the world. He was zealously on fire for God and the purity of God's Word – or so he thought. But after a dramatic encounter with Jesus on the way to Damascus to imprison some more Christians, his life was changed forever. This of course, is the apostle Paul who went on to be the greatest voice for Christianity the world has ever known. God is not offended by people who don't believe Him at first. God does not only choose simple people or those whose sins are obvious by their ungodly behavior. God can take even a genius and religious zealot and transform their knowledge, skills, and fiery passion into something that will impact the world for eternity.

Where were you and what were you doing when Jesus called you? There are many others out there today who are just like you were, doing the same things you were doing before Jesus called you to follow Him. There are many more who are nothing like you were and they are in need of Jesus, too. Will you drop everything to follow Jesus and go and make disciples?

Making Disciples

Every disciple of Jesus is commissioned to make more disciples of Jesus.

> *Matthew 28:18-20: Then Jesus came to them and said, "All authority in heaven and on earth has been given to me. Therefore* **go and make disciples of all nations**, *baptizing them in the name of the Father and of the Son and of the Holy Spirit, and* **teaching them to obey everything I have commanded you**. *And surely I am with you always, to the very end of the age."*

The first part of Jesus' command is, "Go." It means go. We cannot make disciples while sitting on our butts in the comforts of our homes – even in the age of technology. Not everyone is called to go out on the mission field or to travel around the world. But everyone is called to "Go" somewhere to do something for God, even it is only down the street.

Disciples are made by doing life together, the way Jesus walked with His disciples. Disciples are made as we bear with each other's failures, rejoice in one another's victories, encourage one another in righteousness, and speak the truth in love to one another as we grow together in Christ. Jesus did not say, "Go and make converts," or "Go and get people to say they believe," or "Go and get people to pray a prayer so they believe they are saved from hell." He said, "Go and make disciples," and "Teach them to obey everything I have commanded you."

As disciples of Jesus, first we have to learn His teachings and apply them to our lives. Before we can make disciples for Christ, we have to be a disciple of Christ. Jesus lived out and demonstrated for us perfect theology in action. How He handled situations and people is our model for how He wants us to handle the same scenarios in modern life and how He wants us to make disciples.

In line with this, Paul did not say "follow Christ as I follow my own ideas." He said, "Follow me as I follow Christ." (See 1 Corinthians 11:1.) All of us are on a journey on the way to the perfection of Christ and none of us will attain perfection on this side of heaven. Nevertheless, we must commit ourselves to following Christ to the best of our ability at whatever stage of life or faith we may be at so as to set the example for others to recognize Christ in us and follow Him alongside us. We have to allow the people God has given to us to disciple to see our compassion, love, and miracle power in addition to vulnerabilities, imperfections, and humanity so that we can reveal to them the mercy, love, and kindness of God poured out to us as we rightly respond with humility, honesty, and sincere repentance through God's dealings with us. Christ forever and always deserves all glory. Our imperfections, if handled correctly, can be a greater testimony to those truly pursuing the truth and grace of God than eloquent speech or power miracle displays could ever be.

The aim of Paul's ministry was to produce genuine selfless love in the sincere hearts of faith of actual followers of Jesus who knew that they had been redeemed from darkness through the forgiveness of their sins. (See 1 Timothy 1:5.) His objective was not to create superstars who made millions of dollars or spoke to millions of people as evidence of their spiritual power of persuasion. His objective was not to spiritually empower people to work miracles which were out of alignment with God's character or purposes. Paul's objective was to connect people with Jesus in such a way that Jesus' teachings would come alive in their hearts and lives producing a sincere willingness to surrender all and suffer anything at any cost for the sake of following the crucified King or for the sake of one soul being snatched from the fires of hell.

As such, if you are teaching or modeling anything other than the teachings of Jesus, you are not making disciples of Jesus. If you are teaching or modeling anything in Jesus' name about how to have a better life or material gain on earth, you are making disciples of this world and the tree of the knowledge of good and evil. If you have gained a following for yourself through teaching and displaying man-made principles and religious traditions, keys to spiritual advancement, or unsanctioned spiritual practices, no matter how much "anointing" you may have, you are making disciples of the devil.

Consider for a moment that the New Testament had to be written because the first Christians were falling into all these same errors and away from the pure teachings of Jesus. Thank God they were weak! If they had not struggled the way they did, Peter, Paul, James, John, and Jude would not have felt the need to write such wonderful letters of correction! The writers of the New Testament were completely focused on the finished work of Christ, the proper and holy application of this revelation in the lives of Christ followers, and the endurance required through the testings and tribulations of the times before Christ's return.

Moreover, they did not leave the disciples with a free pass to salvation because they had professed a belief in Christ to avoid the fires of hell. Instead, with genuine love they did everything they could to chastise, rebuke, exhort, and encourage the believers into right conduct and warn them of the eternal consequences if they did not change their ways. They did not write fluff letters to encourage them in their otherwise worldly lives or to blend in or take over the world as some form of "light" or preparation of the world for Jesus' return. Rather, in love, they continuously called them into deeper personal devotion and separation from the world and all of its ways and that the true preparation for Christ's return was holiness, purity, and readiness to die at the hands of the world for the sake of His name.

Therefore, as a check of your own discipleship, teachings, and what you are modeling for others about Christ, refresh yourself by the Commands of Jesus chart in Unit One: Class Four and the Sermon on the Mount chart in Unit Five: Class Four of this course. These are the commands of our King. These are the things He commissioned us to teach others. These are the basis for all genuine discipleship.

Surely I am With You

The first disciples had the advantage of walking with Jesus in a literal, physical body, everywhere He went. Once the Holy Spirit was poured out, Jesus dwells within believers' hearts to guide us by His Spirit. Though at times, Jesus feels distant, He is as close as our next breath and ever willing to guide us as if He were with us in person. He will never leave us or forsake us. It is His delight to guide us, shepherd us, teach us His ways, and impart to us His power for His purposes. We are never alone when He is with us.

Therefore, go and be a disciple of Christ. Go and make disciples of Christ. Go and make disciples who make disciples…

Becoming a Mature Disciple
Prayer Guide & Attributes

LED BY THE SPIRIT OF THE LORD, WISE & DISCERNING
- Mind set on and led by the Holy Spirit. Wisdom proven by actions. (Romans 8:5-6,14; James 3:13; Matthew 11:19)
- Full of the Holy Spirit. Prophesying, seeing visions, dreaming dreams. (Acts 2:17-18, 6:3; Ephesians 5:18)
- Skilled in the word of righteousness. Trained senses to discern good from evil. (Hebrews 5:13-14)
- Wise as a serpent, harmless as a dove. Wise for good; innocent regarding evil. (Matthew 10:16; Romans 16:19)

SKILLED IN THE WORD OF GOD
- Mind opened by the Holy Spirit to understand the Scriptures. (Luke 24:27, 45)
- Rightly handling the word of truth to teach, rebuke, correct, and train from the Scriptures. (2Timothy 2:15, 3:16)
- Skilled in the word of righteousness. Boldly declaring the whole counsel of God. (Hebrews 5:13; Acts 20:27)

WALKING & LIVING BY FAITH
- Not ashamed of the Gospel of Jesus Christ. Righteous living by faith. (Romans 1:16-17; Habakkuk 2:4)
- Christ within as hope of glory. Walking by faith and not by sight. (2Corinthians 5:7; Hebrews 11:1,6)
- Receiving miracles. Followed by signs and wonders. (John 11:40,14:12; Mark 16:17-18; Acts 14:3)

OBEDIENT, TAKING UP CROSS
- Crucified flesh. Living for God. Denying self. Taking up cross daily. Following Jesus. (Galatians 2:20; Luke 9:23)
- Taking no vengeance. Not reviling in return. Not threatening. Entrusting self to God. (1Peter 2:23)
- Rejoicing in trials. Enduring successfully. Learning obedience through suffering. (James 1:2-4; Hebrews 5:8)

GENUINE LOVE, FRUITFULNESS, GODLINESS
- Genuine love from a pure heart, good conscience, sincere faith. (1Timothy 1:5; 1Corinthians 13; Romans 12:9-21)
- Abounding in the fruit of the Spirit. Control of the tongue. (Galatians 5:16, 22-23; 2Peter 1:3-7; James 3:2)
- Loving enemies and praying for those who persecute. Perfect/mature as our heavenly Father. (Matthew 5:44,48)

DOING THE WILL OF GOD
- Not conformed to this world. Renewed mind. Able to discern the perfect and pleasing will of God. (Romans 12:2)
- Rejoicing always. Praying without ceasing. Giving thanks in all circumstances. (1Thessalonians 5:16-18)
- Abstaining from sexual immorality, controlling own body in holiness and honor. (1Thessalonians 4:3-5)
- Doing good which silences the ignorance of foolish people. (1Peter 2:14b-15)
- Enduring in the will of God to receive what is promised. (Hebrews 10:36)

EQUIPPED FOR CALLING & GOOD WORKS
- Knowing and functioning in ministry gift to bring the Church to unity and maturity. (Ephesians 4:11-13)
- Cleansed self of what is dishonorable. Useful and ready for every good work. (2Timothy 2:21)
- Purified from lawlessness. Zealous for good works. (Titus 2:14)

VICTORIOUS IN CHRIST
- Overcoming the world by faith. More than a conqueror. Led in victory. (1John 5:4; Romans 8:37; 1Corinthians 15:57)
- Spreading the fragrance of the knowledge of Christ everywhere. (2Corinthians 2:14)

SPIRITUALLY MATURE
- Fully trained to be like the Teacher, Jesus. Presentable as mature in Christ. (Luke 6:40; Romans 8:29; Colossians 1:28)
- Christ within, the hope of glory. Filled with the fullness of God. (Colossians 1:27; Galatians 4:19; Ephesians 3:19)

www.manifestinternational.com
ALL RIGHTS RESERVED © 2020 Wendy Bowen

LOVE ONE ANOTHER

OUR COMMANDMENT	OUR EXAMPLE
A new command I give you: Love one another. As I have loved you, so you must love one another. By this all will know that you are my disciples. (John 13:35)	All the believers were one in heart and mind. No one claimed that any of their possessions was their own, but they shared everything they had. (Acts 4:32)

CONSIDER OTHERS BETTER THAN YOURSELF & SUBMIT TO ONE ANOTHER
- Accept one another as Christ accepted you. (Romans 15:5-7)
- Do nothing out of selfish ambition. Value others above yourself. Have the mindset of Christ. (Philippians 2:3,5)
- Honor others above yourself. Do not be conceited. Have the attitude of Christ. (Romans 12:10,16; Galatians 5:26)
- Submit to one another out of reverence for Christ. (Ephesians 5:21)

DO NOT JUDGE ONE ANOTHER
- First, take the plank out of your own eye, then you will be able to help your brother. (Matthew 7:5; Luke 6:41-42)
- Stop passing judgment. Do not put stumbling blocks before others. (Romans 14:13; 1Corinthians 8:1-13)
- Do not judge or you will be judged with the measure you use. (Matthew 7:1-2; Luke 6:37-38)
- Who are you to judge someone else's servant? There is only One Judge. (Romans 14:4; James 4:12)

FORGIVE ONE ANOTHER
- Be kind and compassionate, forgiving as Christ forgave you. (Ephesians 4:32; Colossians 3:13)
- Do not slander one another. Do not grumble against one another. (James 4:11,5:9; 1Peter 4:9)
- Confess your sins to one another so that you may be healed. (James 5:16)
- If you do not forgive other's sins, neither will your Father forgive you. (Matthew 6:15; 18:21-35)

BEAR ONE ANOTHER'S BURDENS & SERVE ONE ANOTHER
- Carry one another's burdens. Be completely humble and gentle with one another. (Galatians 6:2; Ephesians 4:2)
- Serve one another humbly in love. Consider nothing to be your own. (Galatians 5:13; Acts 4:32)
- Wash one another's feet. (John 13:14)

ENCOURAGE ONE ANOTHER & BE COMPASSIONATE
- Be mutually encouraged in faith. Provoke one another to good works. (Romans 1:12; Hebrews 3:13,10:24-25)
- Speak the truth in love to one another. Do not lie to one another. (Ephesians 4:15,25; Colossians 3:9)
- Build each other up. Do not pay back wrong for wrong. Do what is good for each other. (1Thessalonians 5:11,15)
- Clothe yourselves with compassion, kindness, humility, gentleness, and patience. (Colossians 3:12; 1Peter 5:5)

LIVE IN UNITY & BE AT PEACE WITH ONE ANOTHER AS ONE BODY
- Be of one heart and mind, without divisions. (Acts 4:32; 1Corinthians 1:10, 3:1-9; 12:25)
- Strive for full restoration....live in peace. Be in harmony. (2Corinthians 13:11; Romans 12:16; Mark 9:50)
- Be as one body with many parts with different functions. (Romans 12:3-8; 1Corinthians 12:4-25; Ephesians 4:11-13)
- If one member suffers, all suffer together. If one member is honored, all rejoice together. (1Corinthians 12:26)

LOVE ONE ANOTHER
- Love one another because God so loved us. (John 15:12,17; 1John 3:11,23, 4:7,11,12)
- Let your love increase and overflow to one another as brothers and sisters. (1Thessalonians 3:12; Hebrews 13:1)
- Love one another sincerely and deeply from the heart. Let love be genuine. (1Peter 1:22, 3:8; Romans 12:9-21)

Love is patient & kind; does not envy or boast; is not proud or arrogant or rude;
Love does not insist on its own way; is not easily angered & keeps no record of wrongs...
Love always protects, trusts, hopes, perseveres. Love never fails. (1 Corinthians 13:4-8)

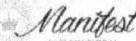

www.manifestinternational.com
ALL RIGHTS RESERVED © 2020 Wendy Bowen

Basic Training Exercise

3, 12, 70, MASSES

Luke 6:12-13 NIV - One of those days Jesus went out to a mountainside to pray, and spent the night praying to God. When morning came, he called his disciples to him and chose twelve of them, whom he also designated apostles:

DESCRIPTION

Jesus stayed up all night on only one occasion. It was the night before He chose the 12 who would be closest to Him during His time of ministry and going to the cross. Up to that point, Jesus already had many people following Him. But now, He chose 12 to walk closely with Him. These twelve would share life with Him and be with Him everywhere He went. Nothing was hidden form them and He explained everything to them. Peter, James, and John had experiences with Jesus that the others did not. Jesus also shared access and privileges with others including women who followed Him. 70 of these were also appointed for special service and experiences with Jesus.

God is a loving Father and as such, He wants us to have friends and enjoy them, as long as they do not influence us away from Him. Friendship with Jesus is the most important friendship of our life. When we first come to faith in Christ, our friendships may change in order for God to take His rightful place in our life. As we grow spiritually, we need to check in with God about the people who He wants to remain in our life and how close He wants us to be to them.

As such, putting 3, 12, 70, Masses into practice is about seeking the Lord for His wisdom and discernment about the people in our lives, especially those closest to us so that we can keep our eyes and hearts on Him.

PRAYER

Father, thank you that you sent Jesus to demonstrate true friendship. Teach me how to be a friend and who you want me to be a friend to so that I can keep my eyes on you. In Jesus' name, Amen.

Category: Christlike Care

PURPOSE:

To love others well.

To discern from the Lord who He wants us to be closely connected with.

To be free to invest fully in the lives of the people God has given us.

SPIRITUAL FRUIT:

Love for others.

Brotherly fellowship for mutual encouragement.

Discernment of safe and unsafe people.

Freedom of time and energy to obey God.

CONSIDERATIONS

What has been your experience with peer pressure? Has there ever been a time when a "friend" influenced you in a negative way to do something which you would not have otherwise done?

Has there ever been a time when you may have done something you shouldn't but a friend prevented you?

PRACTICE

1. Make a list of the people in your life. Include: family members, friends, acquaintances, work associates, etc.

2. Talk with the Lord about the time you spend with people and their influence on your life and walk with Him.
   - Who is a positive, godly influence in your life?
   - Who is a negative, ungodly influence on your life?

3. Create a chart for 2, 12, 70, and the masses. Ask the Lord to help you put the people in your life into these categories.
   - **The Three:** Trustworthy people of integrity in the Lord who you can trust with your secrets and who will speak the truth in love to you.
   - **The Twelve:** People who you can share your life with who love God, pray for you, and want what is best for you according to God's plan for your life.
   - **The Seventy:** Are people who have a similar mission, purpose, or season to yours with whom you can be mutually encouraged and edified.
   - **The Masses:** Is everyone else.

4. Ask the Lord to help you adjust your life to more accurately reflect the friendships He desires to be closest to you.
   - Is there anyone you need to spend more time with?
   - Is there anyone you need to spend less time with?
   - How can you put these changes into practice?

5. Thank God for being such a loving Father to help you choose your friends. Enjoy your friends and love them well.

NOTES: _____

ADDITIONAL SCRIPTURES:

Mark 4:10-12
Proverbs 12:26
1 Corinthians 15:33
John 15:13-15
1 John 1:7
1 John 2:19

Category: Christlike Care

The Work of Ministry

Ministry begins when we echo the words of Isaiah, "Here I am, send me!" We have already heard the call to discipleship and have pursued the Lord in our hearts. Then, we hear and recognize the need God has for willing laborers to do His work on the earth. Our heart responds with the Spirit's willingness, "Here I am, send me!" Then, God proceeds to tell us the type of work we are called to for Him.

> *Isaiah 6:9-10:* He said, "Go and tell this people: " 'Be ever hearing, but **never understanding**; be ever seeing, but **never perceiving**.' **Make the heart of this people calloused**; make their ears dull and close their eyes. Otherwise they might see with their eyes, hear with their ears, understand with their hearts, and turn and be healed."

We are sent out to people who think they understand but do not, who think they see but are blind. We are sent to speak the truth until their ears and hearts are calloused and hardened to hearing it anymore and their eyes go blind to the truth of God's word and work. Then, God tells us the duration of our ministry and the type of response we can expect for doing His work.

> *Isaiah 6:11-13:* Then I said, "For how long, Lord?" And he answered: "**Until the cities lie ruined and without inhabitant, until the houses are left deserted and the fields ruined and ravaged, until the LORD has sent everyone far away and the land is utterly forsaken. And though a tenth remains in the land, it will again be laid waste**. But as the terebinth and oak leave stumps when they are cut down, so **the holy seed will be the stump in the land**."

Until Christ returns to judge the world, through every calamity, plague, disaster, war, and tribulation, we must keep proclaiming the truth of God to people who refuse to listen. Only one-tenth will remain and even that will be re-purified. What is left is the remnant of God.

Are you still ready to raise your hand for ministry? Recall our Savior, Jesus, who came to His own and His own did not recognize Him as God. He spoke the truth and demonstrated perfect righteousness but they accused Him of blasphemy, heresy, and working for the devil. Are you ready for this kind of service? Or do you think that ministry is a call to fame, fortune, and having masses of followers?

One of the Greek words for minister in the New Testament means, "To serve at one's own expense." Have you counted the cost of ministry? We must recognize that executing true ministry in the likeness of Jesus will cost everything we have and things we do not yet have, plus things that God will give us for the purpose of handing them over to someone else. Of course, this is in addition to the physical, mental, and emotional anguish of serving, supporting, and nurturing those who prefer themselves to God, lies to truth, false spiritual power to the way of the cross, and who are constantly stumbling into all sorts of pits and snares in need of rescue and realignment.

Once you have accepted this reality of ministry and are willing to do it in the attitude of expressing all the truth, love, and mercy, you have received from the Lord for yourself, you might be ready to begin.

Servants of God

One of the things the apostles made abundantly clear in their letters is that they knew themselves to be servants of God and NOT of men. Jesus did not serve the whims and demands of people. Jesus served God, no matter what people thought or wanted because He knew He had one master to whom He would ultimately give account. While we are all called to submit to God's appointed authorities, we must also remember that we will stand before the throne of Jesus alone to review what we alone have done.

Moreover, the apostles did not use their apostleship as a title to lord over people or abuse their authority for self-serving purposes. They often called themselves slaves of God, emphasizing God's total ownership of them in heart, mind, soul, and body to whatever He pleased with their lives.

As we enter into ministry, we may be tempted to think that our lives are given to serve the people. This will not go well for us. God loves people. God also knows that people are fickle, needy, co-dependent, possessive, and often looking for a human to rescue them from their problems or to support them in their problems in perpetuity because they are not yet ready to repent of the issue that is causing the problem. Jesus did not cave into the needs and demands of the ones He came to serve. This is love. There are times when, in God's wisdom and love, the best way to minister to someone is to cut them off or leave them in their problem until they realize that they are the problem so that they can turn to God. (See 1 Corinthians 5:5; 1 Timothy 1:20.) The point is that if we serve people rather than serving God to serve people, we will be stuck in a whirlwind of human need with nothing but our own strength to sustain us.

Only by God's wisdom and direction in each situation will we rightly serve Him – and the people – for His purposes. We will give our all in service to God and lay our lives down for other people's benefit and God will give us the strength we need to do it. Jesus obeyed God even unto death at the hands of the ones He came to serve. Are you ready for this kind of service?

Ministry of Reconciliation

The ministry calling of every believer is the ministry of reconciliation. Our function is not to become the answer to someone's issues but to connect them with God so that He can be their Savior, Redeemer, Deliverer, Defender, Provider, and all the other roles He does so well for all of us.

> *2 Corinthians 5:18-19: All this is from God, who reconciled us to himself through Christ and gave us the* **ministry of reconciliation: that God was reconciling the world to himself in Christ, not counting people's sins against them**. *And he has committed to us* **the message of reconciliation**.

Everyone is invited into salvation and all of its benefits. The Gospel must be proclaimed to the whole world before the end will come. Everyone must hear of the eternal salvation afforded to us through God's Son so that they will give an account before God of having heard and believed or refused the word of truth. Until Jesus returns, no matter what someone has done or even how many times they have refused to believe Jesus, our ministry is to make sure they know that their sins have been forgiven through the cross of Christ and that this invitation can be accepted and received by FAITH that Jesus Christ is the Son of God and that God raised Him from the dead. Even after they have been saved, our ministry is to continually remind one another of the finished work of Christ. Our sins have been forgiven.

There is no other message. Though Paul had superior revelation, more knowledge, and better relationship with God than any other person on earth, he made it his aim to know nothing when he was ministering except Jesus Christ and Him crucified. (See 1 Corinthians 2:2.)

> *Romans 1:5: Through him we received grace and apostleship* **to call all the Gentiles to the obedience that comes from faith for his name's sake**.

> *Titus 1:1: Paul, a servant of God and an apostle of Jesus Christ* **to further the faith of God's elect and their knowledge of the truth that leads to godliness**

> *2 Timothy 1:1 NLT: This letter is from Paul, chosen by the will of God to be an apostle of Christ Jesus.* **I have been sent out to tell others about the life he has promised through faith in Christ Jesus**.

As we enter into ministry, we must align ourselves with God's heart and eternal plan of redemption. We become co-laborers with God to do His work, His way, and the way Jesus demonstrated for us when He walked on earth. The term co-laboring is rooted in synergy, meaning doing something together in sync with someone else. We do not work for God by serving Him through our own ideas and initiative. We must be willing to be led by Jesus into His plans, in His timing, and in His way of doing things in order to be in sync with His heart so as to carry out His work. The first disciples spent so much time with Jesus that they became like Him and were in sync with His way of doing things. This is also our call to co-laboring: to spend so much time with Jesus that we become like Him and know how to do things the way He does them.

Until Jesus returns, we are called to co-labor with Him as soldiers in a war that is not of this world. The kingdom of darkness contends aggressively against us as the light of the world and we will face battles of good versus evil, truth versus deception, hope versus despair, and faith in eternal life versus the fear of death. Moreover, as servants whose Kingdom is not of this world, Paul specifically exhorted that we not become entangled in worldly pursuits of any kind which drain the time, energy, and resources that we could be using for God's Kingdom. (See 2 Timothy 2:4.) For example, Jesus never prayed about or involved Himself in activist causes or in world politics even though His fellow countrymen wanted a Messiah who would do so and take over the world on their behalf. He never addressed issues like the death penalty, although He may have avoided the cross for doing so. He never discussed matters like homosexuality or abortion, even though those things were happening when He was on earth. When He discussed family matters, He did not make it the priority of Christian life, but made it clear that members of our own households might become our enemies. Jesus was singularly focused on proclaiming the Kingdom of God and warning people to repent and believe the good news of God's salvation.

Our Job Description

In Jesus' parable about the workers in the vineyard, each worker is called to work by the vineyard's owner and everyone is working to harvest the produce of the vineyard. As such, every single follower of Jesus has been commissioned by the Lord for ministry and all of us have the same job description.

> *Ephesians 4:11-13 ESV: And he gave the apostles, the prophets, the evangelists, the shepherds and teachers, to* **equip the saints for the work of ministry, for building up the body of Christ**, *until we all attain to the unity of the faith and of the knowledge of the Son of God, to mature manhood, to the measure of the stature of the fullness of Christ*

To **equip** means to furnish and make perfect. This entails becoming a source of supply for those who are not perfect yet. If those around us are not yet mature in Christ, our job is to give them what they need to help them grow to maturity and the likeness of Jesus. This could be teaching and training, counsel by the Holy Spirit to align them with truth or bring healing from wounds, or it could mean material supply of their needs to fulfill what God is giving them to do. For example, Paul wished to visit the Thessalonians again so that he could supply what was lacking in their faith. (See 1 Thessalonians 3:10.)

The **work** means the business or employment of doing or producing something, whether by hand, industry, or mind. While there is much to be said for resting and soaking in the presence of the Lord, if we are spending time with the real Jesus, He will put us to work and give us something to do. I don't imagine any laborers in a vineyard were paid wages for soaking in the sun while others put their hands to the plow. Being a minister of the Lord is a call to work for God and not look back. (See Luke 9:62.)

The work of **ministry** is service. The word for ministry in this passage is the same word used for deacons, which describes the role of a waiter. The primary meaning of ministry is to execute the commands of another. The ministry of the Law of Moses was to execute the commands of God through Moses. The ministry of Jesus was to execute the commands of God and fulfill His purpose. Our ministry is to execute the commands of Christ as our King by being like Him and doing the things He did the way He did them in service to others. Jesus came not to be served by people but to serve them and to give His life for them. Jesus took the lowest place and washed His disciple's feet.

The motive and intent of **building up** the Body is the promotion and edification of someone else's growth in the Lord. We are each called to exhort, encourage, impart wisdom, share, and assist one another. For example, if we were building a physical building, we would not just bless a shoddy old shack and put it into service. We would check its foundation, plumb the walls, re-plaster the ceilings, re-wire the electrical fixtures, scrub down the floors, fix the plumbing, etc. This is what we are called to do for one another spiritually as God's spiritual building – His Temple.

Putting all of this together, we can see that each of us is called to furnish others with what they need to fulfill their work in obeying the commands of Jesus so that they can in turn build up others. If this is different than the definition of ministry than you had pictured, then your concept of ministry needs to be reset.

Our Ministry Roles

All of God's laborers are called to His vineyard but not all workers have the same exact job. Some will be up on a ladder picking grapes, some will be down on the ground doing the same. Some laborers will be carrying barrels of grapes to the designated center for storage. Some servants may be sorting through the grapes to pick off the leaves, branches, and bugs. Others might be carrying water or preparing a meal for the laborers to be fed and strong for their work. Some may be caring for or mending those who have blisters, injuries, fatigue, or heatstroke so that they can recuperate and be sent back out into the vineyard again. Others might be training new vineyard workers on how to pluck grapes properly so they are not damaged. Some servants might be in charge of counting and taking inventory so that not a single grape is lost or wasted. There might also be foremen or overseers who ensure that everything is running smoothly, according to the owner's wishes. As such, even though our aim as God's laborers is the same, the way we serve God in our various ministries will be different.

> *Ephesians 4:11-13 ESV: And he gave the **apostles, the prophets, the evangelists, the shepherds and teachers**, to equip the saints for the work of ministry, for building up the body of Christ, until we all attain to the unity of the faith and of the knowledge of the Son of God, to mature manhood, to the measure of the stature of the fullness of Christ*

According to Ephesians 4:7, each one of us has been gifted with one of these gifts, according to the measure that Christ has given us. I do not agree with teachings that say that only special people are called to the "fivefold ministry" because it contradicts what Scripture says. This said, the measure of the gift any one of us has received from Christ will be different and therefore, will evidence itself in our lives in various ways as we serve Him. Jesus expressed this same concept through the parable of the talents. For example, one person may be called as a prophet with only two talents while another is called as a prophet but has ten talents. We are each responsible to the Lord and will give an account based on what we have done with what we have been given. To whom much is given much is required.

Additionally, let the record reflect that there is very little Scriptural information upon which to build any of our own theologies about the five ministry gifts, even though they are real and very important elements to proper service in the Body of Christ. Therefore, as with all things, we will look to Jesus as our example.

Jesus is the **apostle** and High Priest of our faith. (See Hebrews 3:1.) An apostle is defined as "one sent forth with orders." Jesus knew from God what His mission was. He did a new thing on the earth, instituted the New Covenant, and fulfilled the first stage of God's eternal redemptive plan of salvation. He will return to finish the work. Jesus longed for the day of judgment but knew that He must first undergo the baptism of death for others to join Him in eternity. He gathered followers through the proclamation of the Gospel and demonstration of the Kingdom of God. But as soon as followers received real revelation of His identity, from then on, He told them in advance about the need for His suffering, death, and resurrection. His hope was eternal and not of this world. He gave everything, including His life to implement God's new order and make God's old order obsolete. He lacked any of the qualifications of the priesthood of the old order but fulfilled a priesthood in the everlasting order of Melchizedek.

Those called to this ministry will have clear calling and direction from God Himself. Generally, God will call apostles to a people group or nation who have not yet heard the Gospel and/or to bring reform within the church by rejecting its present evil practices and demonstrating true worship. Apostles will be trained by God and sent by God, even though they may receive confirmation of their revelation from men and others in authority, or be sent and supplied by churches for their work. They will find it very difficult to tolerate erroneous church practices and the status quo because God will have revealed a new pattern to them for implementation. They will endure much hardship, rejection, and accusation for being out of order to the extent that they will be considered by most to be the least likely servants of Christ or on display as the scum of the earth. The call to apostleship is not only a call to great authority and position but a call to great responsibility and the lowest possible position of service. The former is only genuinely attained through the latter. God will not have it any other way.

Jesus is the **prophet** promised by Moses whom all people must listen to and obey. (See Deuteronomy 18:18.) Jesus spoke ONLY the words that God put in His mouth and He said ALL that God commanded Him to say. In exact alignment with every other Biblical prophet of God, Jesus called upon people to repent. If they did not repent, they remained under condemnation and would suffer the wrath of God. Jesus told His disciples what was to come in world events so that they would be strengthened in their faith and not fall away. He prophesied the times of the end including the calamities, wars, plagues, and apostasy that would happen before His return. He assured His hearers of God's ultimate plan and the rewards which the faithful would receive in eternity. Those who had ears heard and obeyed the words of God's prophet, Jesus.

Those truly called to this ministry will have deep conviction of their call to speak the word of the Lord and a deep love for the truth. They will typically have felt like outcast black sheep their whole lives but this is God's design of preparing them for the intensity of standing alone as the one proclaiming truth in the midst of a world and church full of lies and deception. They need to walk the full course of crucifying their flesh and everything soulish and worldly in them to prevent their ministry from being polluted with error. This also entails much emotional healing from many wounds inflicted upon them throughout their lives for being messengers of truth. They oscillate between being very bold and extremely submissive and can tend to be socially a bit awkward or lacking in social graces. While God works Himself into their hearts, minds, will, and emotions, their lives may appear for a time to be complacent, inconsistent, loner-ish, and will sometimes show up to a meeting wearing or carrying bizarre accouterment for prophetic purposes. Have patience with them. God and their assigned apostle will train them to become mature prophets who will not pander to anyone's flesh and will not display their gift like a psychic power of predicting world events. Their purpose will be fixed on proclaiming the truth and exhorting all people into obedience to the truth so that those with ears may be free in Christ and receive their eternal inheritance.

Jesus is the **evangelist** who brings the good news and demonstrates heaven's power. Jesus proclaimed the message of God's salvation through repentance and faith. This message was confirmed by miracles, healings, casting out demons, prophecies, and the distribution of spiritual gifts. When Jesus had finished evangelizing in a city or village, He swiftly moved on to the next place, even if people begged Him to stay. God kept Him moving from place to place so that the message could be proclaimed everywhere and to everyone within His assigned territory, even though He was willing to minister to those not within His assigned people group when they specifically sought Him out.

Those called to this ministry will have a deep, ravenous hunger for lost souls to be found. They will be very black and white about sin. They will find it difficult to sit in church meetings for too long because there are people out in the world going to hell and they want to be out there reaching them. They will usually be drawn to a specific type of person but are not limited by it because a lost soul is a lost soul and it needs to get saved. God will keep the evangelist moving in service activities and will grant them an anointing to confirm their message of salvation with miracles and help others come to faith in Him. This anointing is to help with the work of salvation, not a confirmation of the evangelist's maturity. In fact, it is important for the evangelist to be nurtured with good doctrine in order to keep their message pure and to foster their repentance from sin so that they do not grow into hypocrisy in spite of spiritual power.

Jesus is the **shepherd** who oversees the flock of God with righteousness. (See 2 Peter 2:25.) He laid down His life for the sheep. He fed the sheep with natural food and nourishment. He fed the sheep with spiritual food of good doctrine, wisdom, and understanding. He saw people as sheep without a shepherd and longed with love to gather them to His flock and sheepfold for their own security, health, and well-being. His greatest joy was to see His sheep genuinely functioning in His teachings and truth. He loved the sheep up to the very end, no matter if they betrayed or abandoned Him, used or abused Him, or didn't understand a word He was saying to them. He loved them, knew them by name, and called them His own. He gave His sheep His peace.

Those called as true shepherds or elders are nurturers touched with a deep compassion for people. They are willing to bear with people through any stage of life, growth, pain, loss, sickness, health, riches, poverty, and anything else that may happen to them. They will typically emphasize encouragement but are not afraid to use the shepherd's staff to bring correction when someone steps outside the bounds of truth and godliness. They love people. They love spending time with people. They take time to get to know people and genuinely care about their welfare and progress in the Lord. Their joy is to see the sheep grow in righteousness, truth, and love. They will serve to the point of exhaustion to be sure that their sheep are comforted in times of need and distress. They will lead their sheep to the way of peace in Jesus.

Jesus is the **teacher** who taught endlessly in the synagogues and at the Temple. Every word Jesus ever spoke was the truth and was in complete alignment with God's Word. He recognized when God's Word was being misused or misinterpreted by other teachers and brought correction through proper use of the holy Scriptures. He rejected anything man-made that was not rooted in correct understanding of the Word of God. He had compassion on the people who had been poorly and incorrectly taught and so, this compassion led Him to teach them many things. He taught His disciples everything in detail and shared with them everything the Father had taught Him.

Those called as teachers will love the Word of God. If something isn't working, they will seek the answer in God's Word. If they or someone else has a problem, they will find a Scripture about it. They use what they discover in Scripture to create teachings on topics about God and His Word which take into account the whole counsel of God. They have very little tolerance for irreverent spiritual babble or frivolity and will instead separate themselves from the crowd to study the Word. They will go through challenges in life and there will be times when their theological framework seems to be shattered. But these times only serve to drive them ever deeper into God's Word. They will sometimes struggle to sort through apparent contradictions in the Word, or when to apply which teaching at what time, but if they learn to submit to the guidance of the Holy Spirit, they will know how to speak a word in season to refresh the weary.

While this gives us a general outline of the ministry gifts given by Christ to the church, it is important to note that there are many ministries established today on the basis of the gift of the primary minister. They typically teach only what they know to anyone who will follow them and this creates the possibility of someone being trained by an evangelist for evangelistic ministry who is actually called by God as a prophet...and things like this. Spiritual maturity includes knowing our own ministry calling and functioning in God-given discernment to assist others in discovering and fulfilling their ministry callings even if it is different than our own and even if we need to send them to someone else for training that we are unable to give them. This type of selflessness and discerning service are some of the marks of maturity in ministry.

Functioning properly together also entails honoring those with ministry gifts different than ours as long as they are sanctified and grounded in the truth. For example, God may send a prophet to a teaching ministry to knock them out of their theological construct or may send a teacher to a prophetic ministry to align them with the truth and prevent them from mixing with wrong spirits. If the ministry rejects the servant of God because they were not functioning in their particular "style" or dogma, they have rejected Jesus. Beware of this.

Unity & Maturity

The work of ministry will continue until the Church attains unity and maturity in Christ. The last time I checked the church was neither united nor mature, so there must still be work to be done.

> *Ephesians 4:11-13 ESV: And he gave the apostles, the prophets, the evangelists, the shepherds and teachers, to equip the saints for the work of ministry, for building up the body of Christ,* **until we all attain to the unity of the faith and of the knowledge of the Son of God, to mature manhood, to the measure of the stature of the fullness of Christ.**

True unity cannot and will not come through doctrinal creeds, statements of faith, or the attempts of man to unite for Christ. Unity by the Spirit is an unexplainable phenomena which occurs only when brothers and sisters in the Lord have received the same revelation understanding of who God is and how He wants things done which are in exact accord with one another even if they have never previously met. This will occur regardless of nationality, ethnicity, background, or ministry training. It comes from God.

In the times of the end, this genuine unity will span the globe as God moves by His Spirit to unite His remnant Bride in holy love and abounding truth. While the world is drawing together in a counterfeit unity of worship for the antichrist in the name of God, the truly mature in the Lord will set themselves apart from the world and its false peacemaking. There is ONE Body, Spirit, hope, Lord, faith, baptism, God, and Father. (See Ephesians 4:4-6.)

Until then, we aim for unity through building one another up by speaking the truth in love to one another. An infant believer does not yet know what they believe and they have to be taught. An adolescent believer needs freedom to discover truth from error and to test the boundaries of their revelation without being abandoned to error. A mature believer needs to be reminded of the simplicity of devotion to Jesus and that without love, they are nothing.

> *Ephesians 4:14-15: Then we will no longer be infants, tossed back and forth by the waves, and blown here and there by every wind of teaching and by the cunning and craftiness of people in their deceitful scheming. Instead,* **speaking the truth in love, we will grow to become in every respect the mature body of him who is the head, that is, Christ.**

> *Colossians 1:28-2: He [Christ] is the one we* **proclaim, admonishing and teaching everyone with all wisdom, so that we may present everyone fully mature in Christ.** *To this end I strenuously contend with all the energy Christ so powerfully works in me.*

If we continue to encourage one another through the stages of spiritual life, we will grow to maturity. The mature in Christ can discern truth from error and are governed by the Spirit of the Lord into right action and divine wisdom. The mature in Christ will make every effort to maintain unity in the Spirit but will never compromise truth for the sake of peace. (See James 3:17.) The mature in Christ will be unified together by their own revelation and experiential knowledge of the truth of God and His ways. The mature Bride will be ready for her King.

Laborers Rewards

In Jesus' parable of the laborers in the vineyard, each laborer receives the same pay: a day's wage. God shows no favoritism. However, in the Luke version of the parable of the talents, Jesus made it explicitly clear that His laborers who aptly use the talents He has given them to produce a return for His Kingdom will be rewarded with eternal rewards and honor. Those who have been good stewards of their resources for God's Kingdom purposes on earth, will be trusted with true riches in heaven. (See Luke 16:11.) Those who have wisely used what they have for God's Kingdom purposes in this world will be given cities to rule over in the world to come. (See Luke 19:17.) Those who have buried their talents or who have wasted their resources for the things of this world will receive no heavenly reward.

First of all, we must be found **faithful**. (See 1 Corinthians 4:2.) God is looking for those whom He can trust. Those who do their dealings with integrity, even to the minutest detail, and from a sincere heart. God is looking for those He can rely upon to do what He wants done on the earth in righteousness and purity. He needs people who obey Him from a submitted heart. He needs people to do what He says, the way that He says it, in a timely manner, with the right attitude, to the best of our ability.

Faithful people will learn to **know how to keep rank**. (See 1 Chronicles 12:33, 38.) God is a God of order. His vineyard is not a democracy, it's a monarchy – there is a King. Everyone has to know how to do their own job and do it to the best of their ability. If a grape-picker decides one day that he'd rather be a water-bearer, the productivity of the whole vineyard is thrown off and the laborers get agitated. Rightfully so. God is looking for those who will stay within the bounds of what He has assigned them to in each season of their lives. Our submission and keeping rank with God is often reflected in how well we do so with others.

Faithful people who keep rank become **useful** to God. (See 2 Timothy 2:21.) Once our lives become cleansed of our own arrogance and approach to things and we stop doing other people's jobs or things that God did not ask us to do, God can use us for His purposes. When we recognize that our lives are not our own and that we exist to serve God and His purposes, God is able to put us to good use. Even though we might still be imperfect in many ways, God knows our hearts are set on Him, to do what is pleasing to Him, and to serve for His glory. A cleansed vessel He can use for honorable purposes.

Useful people become **fully equipped for any good work** (See 2 Timothy 3:17.) As we walk faithfully with God and remain pliable and submissive to Him, He will continue to work with us in additional areas of devotion and service, give us deeper revelation and understanding of His Word and His ways, walk us through tests and trials, and release us into new levels of ministry. There is no aspect of Jesus' life and ministry that God will not invite us into as we pursue Him to the fullest.

Fully equipped people become **fully trained servants who are like the Master**. (See Luke 6:40.)

The most faithful, useful, and fully equipped person who ever lived was Jesus. For His service to God, He was rejected, mocked, ridiculed, and ultimately killed. But God raised Him to eternal life and He ascended to heaven to receive the eternal reward His Father ordained for Him. He has the name above all names and will rule the world for all eternity.

Paul was a close second to Jesus. When his ministry was being falsely accused by false apostles, Paul did not justify himself or his service to God through spiritual revelation, prophetic powers or visions, angelic activity, or even the remarkable miracles God had worked through him. No. He proved the genuineness of his ministry by the integrity of godly character and listing out his sufferings for Christ. (See 2 Corinthians 6:3-10, 11:23-27.) He was willing to suffer anything for the sake of the elect and even wished to give up his own salvation so that his own people could be saved. (See Colossians 1:24; Romans 9:3.) Paul was beheaded for his service to God and is in heaven now under the altar shouting out, "how long until you avenge my blood?"

We may not all be called to martyrdom but all of us are called to give our lives. We may not all be called to seemingly great levels of ministry service but all of us are called to be faithful, useful, and equipped for the Master's purposes. No matter what level of service or role of ministry we have been called to, when we arrive in eternal dwellings and stand before Jesus to be welcomed to His banqueting table and receive our rewards, we not feel as if we have done too much for God. We will with the deepest humility and gratitude look upon the fulfilled promises of God and say, "I have only done my duty."

WILLING SERVANT INSPECTION						
1 = Needs improvement		*2 = In Refining Process*		*3 = Doing Well for Now*		
Am I willing to NOT be esteemed?				1	2	3
Am I willing to NOT be secure?				1	2	3
Am I willing to NOT be in control?				1	2	3
Let this mind be in you which was also in Christ Jesus, who, being in the form of God, did not consider it robbery to be equal with God, but made Himself of no reputation, taking the form of a bondservant, and coming in the likeness of men. — Philippians 2:5-7						

*Based on questions of Trappist Monks when entering service to the Lord.

Prayer Guide for Laborers
Workers in God's Vineyard & Harvest Field

Sent into the Harvest Field to Make Disciples of Christ
- Knowing that the harvest is plentiful and the laborers are few. (Matthew 9:37-38)
- Not putting hand to the plow and looking back. Counting the world's things as dung. (Luke 9:62; Philippians 3:7-8)
- Proclaiming the good news of God's salvation and the ministry of reconciliation. (Luke 4:18; 2Corinthians 5:18-19)
- Making disciples by baptizing them and teaching them the teachings of Jesus. (Matthew 28:19-20)
- Calling people to the obedience of faith and eternal life in Christ. (Romans 1:1-5; 2Timothy 1:1)

Open Doors for the Message to Spread
- Open doors for effectual work and rapid spread. (Colossians 4:3-4; 1Corinthians 16:9; 2Thessalonians 3:1)
- Fearlessness and boldness to speak the word of Christ. (Colossians 4:3-4; Acts 4:29-30; Ephesians 6:19-20)
- New territories opened where Christ has not yet been preached. (2Corinthians 10:15-16)
- The message spreading rapidly by those who have been changed. (1Thessalonians 1:8-10; Romans 1:8)

Holy Conduct & Pure Ministry
- Exhibiting conduct worthy of the household of God. (1Timothy 3:1-13; 2Timothy 2:19-21; Titus 1:5-16; 2Peter 1:5-7)
- Putting no stumbling block in anyone's way. Fighting with spiritual weapons. (2Corinthians 6:3; Romans 14:13)
- Declaring the whole counsel of God and rightly dividing the word of truth. (Acts 20:27; 2Timothy 2:15)

Encouraging & Praying for Believers
- Furthering the faith of the elect and their knowledge of the truth that leads to godliness. (Titus 1:1-3)
- Being mutually encouraged and refreshed in fellowship with other believers. (Romans 1:9-12, 15:32)
- Praying for the Lord's people everywhere to become spiritually mature in Christ. (Ephesians 6:18; Colossians 4:12)
- Supplying believers with everything needed for life in Christ. (1Thessalonians 3:10; 2Peter 1:3-4)
- Acknowledging leaders and laborers and supplying their needs. (1Thessalonians 5:12-13; 3John 1:8)

God-Guided Travel
- Going by faith based on God's command and by His guidance. (Matthew 10:7-14; Acts 16:6-10)
- God making the way in His timing. (1Thessalonians 3:10-11; Romans 1:9-10; Acts 9:6, 10:20, 14:6, 18:9-10)
- Blocked by the Holy Spirit but not blocked by the evil one. (Acts 16:6, 1Thessalonians 2:18; Romans 15:22)
- Prophetic insight and protected lives even in shipwreck. (Acts 27:27-44)

Discerning False Laborers
- Watching out for those who rise up with false teachings. (Acts 20:28-30; Galatians 1:8-9; Jude 1:10-12; 2Peter 2:1-3)
- Gently instructing opponents in the hope that God will grant them repentance. (2Timothy 2:25-26; Jude 1:22)
- Avoiding those whose teaching is ungodly or causes strife. (1Timothy 6:3-5; 2Timothy 2:16-18)
- Not showing them hospitality. Warning others about them. (2John 1:10-11; 1Timothy 1:20; 2Timothy 4:14-15)

Deliverance from Persecutors
- Kept safe from wicked people and protected from the evil one. (2Thessalonians 3:2-3; Romans 15:30-32)
- Deliverance from evil attacks of those opposing the Gospel message. (2Timothy 4:16-18; 2Corinthians 1:8-11)
- Forgiving those functioning in ignorance. (2Timothy 4:16-18; Luke 23:34; Acts 7:60)

Rejoicing in Suffering for Christ
- Willing to suffer or die for Jesus and His Kingdom. (2Timothy 2:3; Colossians 1:24; 2Corinthians 11:23-27; Acts 20:24)
- Enduring through trials. Relying on God who raises the dead. (2Timothy 4:7-8; 2Corinthians 1:8-11)

www.manifestinternational.com
ALL RIGHTS RESERVED © 2020 Wendy Bowen

THE WORK OF MINISTRY
Scriptures for Servants of the Lord

USEFUL TO THE MASTER FOR EVERY GOOD WORK
- 2 Timothy 3:16-17: All Scripture is breathed out by God and profitable for teaching, for reproof, for correction, and for training in righteousness, that the man of God may be complete, equipped for every good work.
- 2 Timothy 2:20-21: Now in a great house there are not only vessels of gold and silver but also of wood and clay, some for honorable use, some for dishonorable. Therefore, if anyone cleanses himself from what is dishonorable, he will be a vessel for honorable use, set apart as holy, useful to the master of the house, ready for every good work.

FULLY TRAINED, LIKE THE MASTER
- Luke 6:40: A disciple is not above his teacher, but everyone when he is fully trained will be like his teacher.
- Mark 10:43-45: But whoever would be great among you must be your servant… For even the Son of Man came not to be served but to serve, and to give his life as a ransom for many.
- John 15:20: Remember the word that I said to you: 'A servant is not greater than his master.' If they persecuted me, they will also persecute you. If they kept my word, they will also keep yours.

SETTING THE EXAMPLE OF GODLINESS & DOCTRINE
- 1 Timothy 4:12: Set the believers an example in speech, in conduct, in love, in faith, in purity.
- 2 Timothy 2:22-25: Flee youthful passions and pursue righteousness, faith, love, and peace, along with those who call on the Lord from a pure heart…And the Lord's servant must not be quarrelsome but kind to everyone, able to teach, patiently enduring evil, correcting his opponents with gentleness.
- 2 Timothy 2:15: Do your best to present yourself to God as one approved, a worker who has no need to be ashamed, rightly handling the word of truth.
- Corinthians 4:1-2: This is how one should regard us, as servants of Christ and stewards of the mysteries of God. Moreover, it is required of stewards that they be found faithful.

SHEPHERDING THE FLOCK OF GOD
- John 10:11-13: I am the good shepherd. The good shepherd lays down his life for the sheep. He who is a hired hand and not a shepherd, who does not own the sheep, sees the wolf coming and leaves the sheep and flees, and the wolf snatches them and scatters them. He flees because he is a hired hand and cares nothing for the sheep.
- Acts 20:28: Pay careful attention to yourselves and to all the flock, in which the Holy Spirit has made you overseers, to care for the church of God, which he obtained with his own blood.

MINISTER OF THE GOSPEL
- Romans 15:16: To be a minister of Christ Jesus to the Gentiles in the priestly service of the gospel of God, so that the offering of the Gentiles may be acceptable, sanctified by the Holy Spirit.
- 2 Corinthians 3:6: Who has made us sufficient to be ministers of a new covenant, not of the letter but of the Spirit. For the letter kills, but the Spirit gives life.
- Acts 26:18: I am sending you to open their eyes, so that they may turn from darkness to light and from the power of Satan to God, that they may receive forgiveness of sins and a place among those who are sanctified by faith in Me.

FULFILLING THE DUTIES OF MINISTRY
- Ephesians 4:11-13: And he gave the apostles, the prophets, the evangelists, the shepherds and teachers, to equip the saints for the work of ministry, for building up the body of Christ, until we all attain to the unity of the faith and of the knowledge of the Son of God, to mature manhood, to the measure of the stature of the fullness of Christ.
- 2 Timothy 4:5: Always be sober-minded, endure suffering, do the work of an evangelist, fulfill your ministry.
- Colossians 4:17: See that you fulfill the ministry that you have received in the Lord.
- 2 Timothy 4:7: I have fought the good fight, I have finished the race, I have kept the faith.

www.manifestinternational.com
ALL RIGHTS RESERVED © 2020 Wendy Bowen

PERFECTION COURSE – UNIT 7.3 READING

Bridal Love Made Ready

Jesus is worthy of a pure Bride who has prepared herself for Him. He is worthy of a Bride who has not given way to the whoredoms of the world, of religion, or of false spirits. He is worthy of a Bride who has proven her faithfulness and devotion to Him through her perseverance in her love for Him through trials and tests and temptations to give up on Him and turn to other things. He is worthy of a Bride who crowns Him all the glory He deserves.

When we first come to faith in Jesus, we experience of rush of love and a sense of heartfelt eternal devotion and gratitude. Like falling in love, we can hardly contain ourselves and our newfound joy. But as this phase passes and the trials of the narrow way begin, our faithfulness is put to the test. These tribulations prove the sincerity of our devotion and the genuineness of our faith. If we respond correctly to God's dealings with us, these tribulations produce in us the maturity that God is seeking in a Bride for His Son. When we rejoice in our sufferings for righteousness' sake and continually submit ourselves to the chastisement of God, we will be made perfect, mature, complete, and ready for our Bridegroom King.

In Jesus' parable of the wedding banquet, a king issues invitations to a feast. The first people invited give worldly and self-centered excuses for why they cannot come. So, the king invites others, who also give excuses. The king finally compels all sorts of people to come – both good and bad people – so that his feast is full with anyone who will accept the invitation. But when the feast begins, there is one there who is wearing the wrong garments and is thrown out. The parable ends with the words, "Many are called but few are chosen."

It is a Bride's responsibility to make herself ready. Some people never leave the whoredoms of this world to become the Bride of Christ. People who do not know that they are whores do not see the need to repent. In fact, whoredom keeps them very busy because they believe that excelling in whatever whoredom they are in will be their path to freedom. There are those who recognize that they have been whores in the world system, repent from the heart, and put on the righteous deeds of holiness to make themselves ready. But there are those who receive the invitation without recognizing the depths of their own depravity and so, they do not see the need to change their garments in order to attend the wedding feast. They will show up for the feast ready to celebrate but will wind up being sorely disappointed.

Biblical Whoredom

Whoredom is in the heart. Any one of us is vulnerable to giving way to whoredom because it always presents itself like a good idea or the only option. When challenges mount up against us, compromising through sin, hidden acts, wrong spirits, worldliness, or disobedience can seem like a viable solution.

No little girl ever dreams of being a whore when she grows up. But if life becomes too difficult, turning herself over may seem like the only option. The first time, which she promises herself will be the last time, brings such shame and sorrow to her. But when the payday comes, she starts to consider that it was worth it. For others in difficulty, taking shelter in the protection of a pimp seems like a wise decision for survival. These convince themselves that forgoing their chastity, dignity, and self-respect is a justifiable price worth paying in order to remain alive. They compromise as a matter of choice and then try to work the system to their own advantage, promising themselves that someday, they will make their escape. Others see that whores profit more than they do by working an honest job. They give themselves over to whoredom as a way of personal advancement while convincing themselves that they are in control of the situation and that they will stop once they have amassed enough of a fortune to retire.

The first whore in the Bible was Eve. Eve sold herself out. I'm sure it seemed like a good idea at the time. It was going to benefit her and make her wise. It was going to make her powerful and like God. It was going to help her and Adam achieve their purpose in ruling the earth. It was a compromise that cost the human race our fellowship with God.

When Hosea was told to purchase a wife out of whoredom, he did so. Hosea took her as his own, cleaned her up, fed her, provided for her, clothed her, and restored her dignity by giving her the status of a wife. But in spite of this, she could not help herself. Whoredom was so deeply rooted in her that she went back to it and even sold herself to a pimp after she was married to Hosea. While she was at it, she boasted and displayed all she had as if she had attained it through her own whoredoms. She gave credit to her lovers as her providers even though it was Hosea who had given her everything. The depths of her whoring heart were exposed when she was met with trial. Instead of calling and reaching out for Hosea, she called upon her lovers to save her. She chased after them but no one came to help her. (Read Hosea 2-3.)

While we may have received salvation and been redeemed by Jesus from the whoredoms of this world, our whoring nature does not automatically depart from us. We will be tempted to return to the only ways we have known because being cared for in the love of God is so foreign to us. We will be tempted to steal glory from God by showing off what He has blessed us with as if we attained it through our own wisdom or labor. When trials come, whatever we reach out to for help is the god we are worshipping. This could include money, comfort food, sex, alcohol, other people, hard work, religion, politics, or anything else we place our hope in, justify ourselves with, or do in attempts to be our own god.

Ezekiel also talks of the faithless bride who whores herself out. Ezekiel describes the path of an unwanted infant girl who was taken in, washed, and cared for. As she grew to the age of love, she was treated with dignity and respect as she became a bride of a loving and honorable husband. He gave her marvelous gifts, clothed her with fine clothes and jewels, and she became well known for her extraordinary beauty. But she began to trust in her beauty and used it to advance her own desires rather than her husband's. She lavished gifts on other men, gave them the jewels her husband had given her, and spread her legs for any passerby to ravish her. She sold herself out, forgetting her humble beginnings and the hopeless life she had been redeemed from. Her delight in whoring became so overpowering that she used her husband's riches as bribes to entice people into bed with her. (Read Ezekiel 16.) She became utterly defiled and worthless.

Many of us start with God with pure and simple devotion to Jesus. He cleanses us and we begin to grow in our life with Him. Then, our hearts are moved into ministry and we recognize the seriousness of being one of His representatives. God clothes us with dignity for service. We start out very well and sincerely committed to Jesus and the real Gospel. As God advances and blesses us, He increases His blessings in our lives and enlarges the sphere of our influence. We become more and more appealing because of the grace God has put on our lives and people are drawn in to us and to Him. But we have to be watchful that we do not begin to trust in our own persona or give way to compromise because we feel established in the blessing of God. We can be a blessing to many people as long as we remain submitted to the direction and purposes of God. We can become all things to all people but not to the extent that the words of Christ or purity of devotion to Him are diluted or perverted. If the attention or focus of our ministry becomes notoriety, money, influence, fame, or giving the people what they want rather than giving God what He wants, we have become a whore. If we display and distribute God's blessings, miracles, or spiritual powers to entice people to follow us rather than reveal the love of God to them, we have become a whore. If we entangle ourselves with matters of this world so that we look influential but it is not advancing God's Kingdom, we have become a whore.

In the end, the whole world will have sold itself out in whoredoms because it will be the only way to remain alive. Babylon, the Beast, and the systems of this world will have deceived those who can be deceived and corrupted all those who can be corrupted.

> *Revelation 17:1, 5 KJV: And there came one of the seven angels which had the seven vials, and talked with me, saying unto me, Come hither; I will shew unto thee* **the judgment of the great whore** *that sitteth upon many waters: ... And* **upon her forehead was: a name written, MYSTERY, BABYLON THE GREAT, THE MOTHER OF HARLOTS** AND ABOMINATIONS OF THE EARTH.

Only those who endure in faithfulness to Jesus and do not give way to the justifications or false promises of whoredom will be counted worthy as His Bride.

Agape Love of the Bride

The sum of the Law of God is to love the Lord your God with all your heart, soul, mind, and strength and to love your neighbor as yourself. The Holy Spirit's role in our lives is to write this Law upon our hearts and work this love into our hearts so that we can love Jesus with the love He deserves and reflect His likeness.

When Jesus sat with Peter by the sea of Galilee after Peter had denied Him three times, He asked, "Do you love me?" In the Greek language, there are multiple words for love. I wish we had these distinctions in English because it truly separates the intent of the heart.

Eros love is lust. The motive of eros love is, "I love you because I want something from you." Many people start to follow Jesus because He has done a wonderful miracle for them or they want Him to do a miracle for them. They want something from Him. Their love is selfish and paper-thin.

Phileo love is preference. The motive of phileo love is, "I love you because you are my type." Each of us has personal preferences, cultural influences, and characteristics we enjoy in other people. If we love Jesus because He fits into our lifestyle and way of thinking or because we simply prefer His company to that of others, we probably do not yet fully know Him, and we certainly do not love Him as He actually is.

Agape love is selfless charity. The motive of agape love is, "I love you because I love you." Agape love puts itself aside and pours itself out for the benefit of the one being loved. True love for Christ means loving Him with all our heart and soul with selfless, reckless abandon of ourselves and all we have to Him and His purposes, without insisting on our own way or expecting anything in return.

By the sea of Galilee, the first two times Jesus asked Peter, "Do you **agape** me?" meaning, do you love me with all your heart and soul, and are you willing to die for me? By this point, the same Peter who had proudly sworn of his love and devotion and that he would never deny Jesus had now come to recognize the nature of the whore in himself. He could not honestly answer that he agape loved Jesus – only **phileo** loved Him. The third time, Jesus asked, "Do you phileo me?" meaning do you prefer me to others and do I fit into your life? Peter was hurt that Jesus had lowered the bar for Peter's ineptitude but nonetheless, affirmed his love for Jesus. Jesus' command to Peter in this exchange was, "Feed my sheep." If we love Jesus, even if we only prefer Jesus in brotherly love, He calls upon us to feed His sheep and tend His lambs.

There is no greater agape than to lay down our life for the sheep of God. (See John 15:13.) The heart that says, "Take my life instead of theirs," or "Let me die so that they can live" is the type of selfless, self-giving, unending love, charity, and benevolence Jesus is looking for in our hearts.

When Israel was in the wilderness, God was ready to annihilate them from the face of the earth for their stubborn rebellion against Him. He told Moses that He was going to obliterate Israel and start over with Moses, making Moses' descendants into a people for Himself. Though this sounds like a great honor for Moses and he could have taken it as divine honor, Moses was more concerned about the glory of God and how the welfare of the people reflected God's nature. Moses begged God not to destroy the people and offered himself in their place. Similarly, when the fullness of time came, the whole world stood condemned before Him and He would have been justified in ending it all in a fiery day of judgment. But Jesus, in agape love for us, offered Himself in our place.

God is looking for a Bride for His Son who reflects this nature of agape love. It is the standard set by Jesus when He came in the flesh and it is the standard He is worthy of in His wife. We may not all be called to martyrdom but each of us is called to take up our cross and die to ourselves by crucifying our flesh including the flimsy eros and phileo love within us. God is looking for a Bride who will offer her own life, preferences, desires, needs, and all she has for the sake of others knowing God. God is looking for a Bride who will put our lives on the altar like a whole burnt offering and pour our lives out in service like a drink offering for people who do not deserve our love and can never pay us back. God is looking for a Bride who will not resort to prayer techniques for manipulating situations, no matter how godly we consider our motives to be. God is looking for a Bride who for the sake of His name will speak the truth in love and be willing to be put to death while forgiving the very ones who are killing them. God is looking for a Bride who agape loves Him so much that she is willing to give all of heart, soul, mind, and strength to Him for His glory. This is the Bride Jesus deserves.

My Sister, My Bride

This bridal love relationship is most vividly portrayed in the Song of Solomon. At first, the Shulamite girl is unwilling to follow her beloved when He calls her into the hills of myrrh and suffering. (v. 2:17.) She prefers the comforts of His embrace and the specialness she feels when she is with Him. But in time, it is revealed to her who He truly is – the King – and she agrees to go with Him even if it is costly to her or entails suffering. She agrees to stick with Him whatever may come. (v. 3:7; 4:6.) This is the likeness He was looking for in her and this level of heartfelt devotion deeply moves the heart of the Beloved. He expresses His adoration.

> *Song of Songs 4:9-15:* **You have stolen my heart, my sister, my bride**; *you have stolen my heart with one glance of your eyes, with one jewel of your necklace.* **How delightful is your love, my sister, my bride!** *How much more pleasing is your love than wine, and the fragrance of your perfume more than any spice! Your lips drop sweetness as the honeycomb, my bride; milk and honey are under your tongue. The fragrance of your garments is like the fragrance of Lebanon.* **You are a garden locked up, my sister, my bride**; *you are a spring enclosed, a sealed fountain. Your plants are an orchard of pomegranates with choice fruits, with henna and nard, nard and saffron, calamus and cinnamon, with every kind of incense tree, with myrrh and aloes and all the finest spices. You are a garden fountain, a well of flowing water streaming down from Lebanon.*

Up to this point, He has referred to her as His "darling" or "companion." But now, He repeatedly refers to her as His sister. He sees the likeness of His Father in her and they have become equal in status as if born of the same parents with the same rights and privileges. It is not incestuous. It is a term of endearment and likeness of heart and mind. This is also the first time that He refers to her as His "bride."

Also up to this point, the Shulamite has been expressing and professing her love openly and unashamedly even though her actions were not previously in alignment with her words. But now, she has committed to Him with her eyes opened and willing to pay the cost of being His. For the first time, He expresses His love for her using the word for love/beloved which is only used between husband and wife. They are committed to one another. He continues on to praise her chastity and delights in the way she has reserved her virginity and intimacy exclusively for Him.

When we first put our faith in Jesus, we have the right to become children of God but it is those who are led by the Spirit of the Lord who are the sons of God. (See John 1:12; Romans 8:14.) As we mature and allow God to work His divine nature in us, our resistance breaks away and we become more willing to offer ourselves to God no matter the cost. This renewal of our minds, emotion, and willingness to be selfless rather than self-serving is the beginning of being set apart as the Bride rather than the whore.

Bridal Praise

The Shulamite settles into new life with her Bridegroom King. But as she becomes comfortable, she finds herself confused and unresponsive to His advances. (v. 5:2.) When she recognizes that she has missed His call, her heart drops within her in the agony of the thought of missing or disappointing Him. (v. 5:6.) She sets out into the night to find Him and be with Him. But she does not find Him. Instead, she encounters the watchmen of the city who treat her like whoring wife or prostitute because a dignified woman would not be out at night. They beat her, took away her royal robe, and beat her some more until daylight. (v. 5:7.) In the morning when the women of the city see her distressed condition, they wonder what makes her Beloved so different than any other man and why He would be worth enduring such a beating. (v. 5:9.) She describes Him to them as a god worthy of worship and beyond compare to anything of this world.

> *Song of Songs 5:10-16: She:* **My beloved is radiant and ruddy, outstanding among ten thousand.** *His head is* **purest gold**; *his hair is wavy and black as a raven. His eyes are like doves by the water streams, washed in milk,* **mounted like jewels.** *His cheeks are like beds of* **spice yielding perfume.** *His lips are like* **lilies** *dripping with myrrh. His arms are* **rods of gold set with topaz.** *His body is like* **polished ivory** *decorated with lapis lazuli. His legs are pillars of* **marble set on bases of pure gold.** *His appearance is like Lebanon, choice as its cedars. His mouth is sweetness itself;* **he is altogether lovely. This is my beloved, this is my friend,** *daughters of Jerusalem.*

The words she uses to describe her beloved echo the description of an idol of a god made of polished ivory, pure gold, and fine jewels. In her sight, He stands out from every other man beyond any comparison. Her girlish professions of love have matured into marital faithfulness and even worship. The fantasies of love have passed but now, He has become her lover and her friend. He is worth everything to her.

As we advance in our spiritual walk through phases of trials and sufferings on display for all to see, many will wonder what we are doing or how we could possibly follow a God who would allow this to happen to His Beloved ones. But we know better. This is the way of the cross. This is the pursuit of devoting ourselves completely to Him no matter who misunderstands us, falsely accuses us, maligns our character, rejects us, or beats us. We have put away childish fantasies of what following Jesus is truly about and what royal bridal authority is to be used for. He has become not only our King and access to blessing and comfort, but our lover and our friend. Nothing in this world compares to the joy of knowing Him. There is no one else like Him in heaven or on earth.

A Sealed Heart

After the Shulamite finds her Beloved, His praise and adoration for her is heightened beyond compare. She has demonstrated sincere and pure devotion through her willingness to endure such hardship to find Him and be with Him. He can hardly contain His love and praise for her. (v. 6:4-7:9.) Then, He makes a request of her to establish their love forever.

> *Song of Songs 8:5b-7: Place me* **like a seal over your heart, like a seal on your arm;** *for* **love is as strong as death, its jealousy unyielding as the grave.** *It burns like blazing fire, like a mighty flame. Many waters cannot quench love; rivers cannot sweep it away.* **If one were to give all the wealth of one's house for love, it would be utterly scorned.**

He asks her to set Him as a seal on her heart. A seal is like a signet ring which would be pressed into melted wax to indicate the owner's mark and authority. He wants His mark alone to be on her heart as His possession for all eternity. He is not looking for outward displays or professions of devotion but an inner heart which is totally committed to Him for His purposes. He also asks her to set Him as a seal on her arm which is the mark and indication of slavery. He desires for her to submit herself to Him in holy reverence and respect, forsaking her own will and making Him and their love the most important master in her life. His love for her will prove to be stronger than death and unyielding to the grave. All of the riches in the world cannot compare to the value of this love.

As we continue in our relentless pursuit of Jesus, He calls us to an absolute abandonment of ourselves to Him and His Kingdom. We recognize that we are not our own and have been bought with a price but now, we are ready to yield fully to Him of our own free will. We have put aside our slavery to sin and our flesh in order to make ourselves willing and obedient slaves to His direction and guidance. We are willing to give up everything we have and even our own lives because we know that the love of Jesus is the only thing which will pass through death to resurrection and eternal life. Our eternal hope consumes us in the adoration of God and everything of this world looks like dung by comparison.

Through the Song of Solomon, the love of the Bride progresses from childish professions of love to the commitment of marital faithfulness, to friendship, worship, and willing slavery. The love of the Bridegroom progresses from companionship to sisterly love and respect, to marital love, total adoration, and zealous, jealous possession. This is our journey of growing love, faithfulness, and intimacy with our loving Lord Jesus.

Worthy Worship

When our hearts have been given totally over to Jesus in adoration, our praise joins with the chorus of heaven and is completely consumed with His worthiness.

> *Revelation 4:8-11: Each of the four living creatures had six wings and was covered with eyes all around, even under its wings. Day and night they never stop saying: "* **'Holy, holy, holy is the Lord God Almighty,' who was, and is, and is to come.** *" Whenever the living creatures give glory, honor and thanks to him who sits on the throne and who lives for ever and ever, the twenty-four elders fall down before him who sits on the throne and worship him who lives for ever and ever. They lay their crowns before the throne and say: "* **You are worthy, our Lord and God, to receive glory and honor and power, for you created all things, and by your will they were created and have their being.** *"*

> *Revelation 5:12-13: In a loud voice they were saying: "* **Worthy is the Lamb, who was slain, to receive power and wealth and wisdom and strength and honor and glory and praise!** *" Then I heard every creature in heaven and on earth and under the earth and on the sea, and all that is in them, saying: "* **To him who sits on the throne and to the Lamb be praise and honor and glory and power, for ever and ever!** *"*

Until Jesus returns we will pour our lives out in service to Him for the sake of telling all people about our wonderful King and raising them up to maturity in Him. But the day will come when we will join with all of heaven to rejoice at the downfall of the great prostitute.

> *Revelation 19:1-8: After this I heard what sounded like the roar of a great multitude in heaven shouting: "Hallelujah! Salvation and glory and power belong to our God, for true and just are his judgments.* **He has condemned the great prostitute who corrupted the earth by her adulteries. He has avenged on her the blood of his servants.** *" And again they shouted: "Hallelujah! The smoke from her goes up for ever and ever." The twenty-four elders and the four living creatures fell down and worshiped God, who was seated on the throne. And they cried: "Amen, Hallelujah!" Then a voice came from the throne, saying: "* **Praise our God, all you his servants, you who fear him, both great and small!** *" Then I heard what sounded like a great multitude, like the roar of rushing waters and like loud peals of thunder, shouting: "* **Hallelujah! For our Lord God Almighty reigns. Let us rejoice and be glad**

and give him glory! For the wedding of the Lamb has come, and his bride has made herself ready. Fine linen, bright and clean, was given her to wear." *(Fine linen stands for the righteous acts of God's holy people.)*

The Bride will have made herself ready through steadfast perseverance and pursuit of her Beloved. The Bride will have stood the test of the temptations to whoredom without giving way to the lusts of her flesh, this world, or the deceptions of the evil one. The Bride will have the seal of God impressed upon her heart like a seal of ownership for all eternity. The Bride will be spotless, without wrinkle or blemish, dressed in white and ready to receive her King.

Let us press on to maturity in His likeness so that we may join with Him at the wedding feast of the Lamb. Our Bridegroom King is forever the only one worthy of our devotion. He is worth everything.

PROCESS WORKSHEET
SUFFICIENCY

www.manifestinternational.com

INSTRUCTIONS

God is all sufficient and almighty. As His children, His desire is for us to depend on Him for all we need. In fact, Jesus said that unless we become like little children, we cannot inherit the Kingdom of God. This said, relying on an invisible God can often be more challenging for us than relying on ourselves or our own methods.

Use this worksheet as a guide for allowing God to shed light on your level of self-sufficiency vs. finding sufficiency in Him. Pray through and write down a summary of each of the following points.

1. **How much do you rely on your own abilities in the following areas? Rate each area from 1 to 5.**
   1 = I do not rely on this – 5 = I rely on this heavily

   - Ability to Work: Work-ethic, willingness to work hard, do whatever it takes… ___
   - Ability to Provide: Capacity for making money, having enough, making things stretch/last… ___
   - Social Skills: Use of your personality, looks, humor, or charisma to appeal to others… ___
   - Personal Expertise: Areas of skill, capability, knowledge, know-how, experience/wisdom… ___
   - Personal Strength: Bodily strength, emotional strength, spiritual strength, ability to "handle it"… ___
   - Use of Technology: Use of technological tools to resolve issues independently… ___
   - Use of Treatments: Use of methods, routines, practices, medicines, remedies that work for you… ___

2. **In what ways is your sense of security reliant upon your ability to do things for yourself?**

   Do you have anxiety or fears about not being able to take care of yourself?

   Describe a time when you were not able, capable, or strong enough to take care of yourself or a situation in your life. What was that like for you? Did you enjoy it or find it challenging? How so?

   What do you think are some potential dangers of self-reliance and/or self-sufficiency?

3. **In what ways does your sense of security depend on other people? On experts or authorities?**

   How much do you rely upon your spouse, parents, family, friends, or social groups for your needs?
   - Share a time when you felt secure because of other people.
   - Share a time when your reliance on other people proved to be problematic or disastrous.

   How much do you rely on of the guidance/approval of professionals, experts, authority figures, ministers, or people who know God better than you?
   - Share a time when you felt secure or safe because of the counsel of a professional or "expert."
   - Share a time when an "expert," authority figure, or person you revered led you in the wrong direction.

   What do you think are some potential dangers of trusting in other people, even experts?

4. **In what ways are you at ease because of your beliefs, principles, and/or following the rules?**

   How does knowing you are "being a good person" or "doing the right thing," help you to feel secure?

Do you believe God blesses you more for being good? Punishes you for not doing the right thing?
- Share a time when you felt that God blessed you because you had been obedient.
- Share a time when you became angry/upset because God blessed someone you considered bad/wrong.

What do you think are some potential dangers of self-righteousness?

5. **How did Jesus demonstrate for us the life of reliance upon God in all things?**

   Jesus said, "By myself I can do nothing," or "I say only what the Father tells me," or "I do nothing on my own initiative." (See John 5:19,30, 8:28, 12:49.) What did He mean?

   List at least three examples of how Jesus had to live by faith. In what ways did He rely on God?
   1. _____
   2. _____
   3. _____

   How do these examples of Jesus' dependence on the Father reveal how God wants us to rely on Him as His sons and daughters?

6. **What would it be like to trust God with every aspect of your life?**

   What concerns, fears, or anxieties rise up in you at the thought of trusting God in all things?

   How do you think your life would be different if you gave up control in order to do only what God said?

   Is there a particular area of your life that Jesus is asking you to trust Him with right now? How so?

   In what ways have you been striving to perform or earn something apart from the Lord?

7. **How is Jesus asking you to trust and rely on His sufficiency in your life right now?**

   How is God calling you to rest? Trust in His provision? How is He calling you to co-labor with Him rather than just laboring?

   (See Isaiah 55; Matthew 7:11; Matthew 11:28-30; Luke 12:22-32; Romans 4:3-5; Mark 8:36.)

   How is God asking you to do and speak only what He reveals by His Spirit rather than your own personality or approach to people?

   (Consider 1 John 2:27; Luke 12:12; John 6:29 & 63; Romans 8:7-8 & 32.)

   How is God asking you to trust His expertise and strength rather than "handling" things yourself, or trusting in experts, or trusting in principles/rules?

   (See 1 Corinthians 1:12; 1 Corinthians 3:18-23; Luke 18:9-14; Galatians 3:2-3; Revelation 3:17.)

   How does God want you to turn to Him as the One to resolve your issues, answer your questions, give you direction, and heal your body, soul, and mind?

   (Consider 1 Peter 2:25; 2 Corinthians 1:9; John 14:26; Hebrews 11:6.)

8. What are your next steps for trusting in God's sufficiency for your life?

AGAPE LOVE INSPECTION

1 = Needs improvement				2 = In Refining Process				3 = Doing Well for Now		

I am patient.	1	2	3	I keep no record of wrongs.	1	2	3
I am kind.	1	2	3	I do not delight in evil.	1	2	3
I am not envious.	1	2	3	I rejoice with the truth.	1	2	3
I am not boastful.	1	2	3	I always protect others.	1	2	3
I am not proud.	1	2	3	I always trust.	1	2	3
I do not dishonor others.	1	2	3	I always hope.	1	2	3
I am not self-seeking.	1	2	3	I always persevere.	1	2	3
I am not easily angered.	1	2	3	My love never fails.	1	2	3

Greater love has no one than this: to lay down one's life for one's friends. – John 15:13

Eros Love: motivated by selfish desires = "I love you because I want you for something…"

Phileo Love: brotherly love, preferential treatment = "I love you because I you're my type"

Agape Love: pure charity & good will with no expectation of anything in return = selfless benevolence

*Based on 1 Corinthians 13.

Basic Training Exercise

WORTHY OF IT ALL

Revelation 5:12-13 NIV - In a loud voice they were saying: "Worthy is the Lamb, who was slain, to receive power and wealth and wisdom and strength and honor and glory and praise!" Then I heard every creature in heaven and on earth and under the earth and on the sea, and all that is in them, saying: "To him who sits on the throne and to the Lamb be praise and honor and glory and power, for ever and ever!"

DESCRIPTION

The commandment of God is summarized as "love the Lord your God with all your heart, soul, mind, and might, and love your neighbor as yourself." The Holy Spirit dwelling within us works to make this a reality in our lives and our worship.

Sometimes, we praise God or thank Him because He has done something for us or because we want Him to do something for us. There is a time and place for this. But the multitudes in heaven never stops singing of the worthiness of Jesus just for who He is and what He has done to redeem mankind from wrath and death.

Jesus is truly worthy of all we could ever possibly give Him and all we could ever say to praise Him.

To put Worthy of It All into practice is about partnering with the Holy Spirit to join with the praises in heaven about the worthiness of Jesus to praise Him exclusively for who He is and what He has done to redeem us.

Praise the Lord!

PRAYER

Father, you alone are worthy of all of my praise. Thank you for who you are and all you have done for me. Help me now to praise you in the way heaven sings your praises. Let my worship be pleasing to you. In Jesus' name, Amen.

PURPOSE:

To give God the type of praise He deserves.

To connect our hearts with the worthiness of Jesus.

SPIRITUAL FRUIT:

Genuine and unselfish worship of God.

Real appreciation for Jesus' sacrifice.

Worshipping the way we will in heaven for eternity.

A deeper personal connection with God.

CONSIDERATIONS

Why is Jesus worthy of all praise?

How is Jesus worthy of all power? What would it look like to praise Jesus with your power?

How is Jesus worthy of all wealth? What would it look like to praise Jesus with your wealth?

How is Jesus worthy of all wisdom? What would it look like to praise Jesus with your wisdom?

How is Jesus worthy of all strength? What would it look like to praise Jesus with your strength?

How is Jesus worthy of all honor? What would it look like to praise Jesus with your honor?

How is Jesus worthy of all glory? What would it look like to praise Jesus with your glory?

How does knowing that heaven praises a slain Lamb change your perspective of what God values?

PRACTICE

1. Use the Considerations above to contemplate the love and goodness of God.

2. Ask the Lord to highlight a particular aspect of Jesus' worthiness to you.
   - Use this aspect as a basis for praising God.
   - Praise God out loud with your words or with song.

3. Move on to another aspect of the worthiness of Jesus and repeat #2.

4. Listen to anything God may say to you when your time of praise is complete. Do whatever He says. Praise the Lord!

NOTES:

_____
_____
_____
_____
_____

ADDITIONAL SCRIPTURES:

Revelation 5

Revelation 4:8-11

Revelation 7:10-12

Revelation 11:16-18

Revelation 19:3-8

Unit Seven – Key Questions
Preparing the Bride

Use this worksheet to test your grasp of the material and exercises of Unit Seven.

What is the evidence of someone being a disciple of Christ? (in your own words)	
What types of people does Jesus call to follow Him?	**What does it mean to make disciples?**
What is the work of ministry?	**What are the five ministry gifts to the Church?**
What is the beginning of whoredom?	**How does the Bride prove her worthiness?**
What is one thing you learned that you did not know before?	**What questions do you still have about this subject?**

UNIT SEVEN: GROUP EXERCISES

Have a group discussion about the five ministry gifts and the known callings within your group. Use the Work of Ministry and Prayer Guide for Laborers to pray for one another's ministries.

AND/OR

Have a time of worship together. Find music which truly emphasizes Christ's worthiness the way heaven praises Him.

ABOUT THE AUTHOR

Wendy Bowen has lived entirely by faith for many years in the *literal* application of what is today known as the Manifest International Approach, (see manifestinternational.com/approach) God has never failed her. She proclaims Jesus, the whole counsel of God, and spreads the message of God's faithfulness all over the world. She equips followers of Jesus to live by faith in these end-times so as to endure to the end and be saved.

www.manifestinternational.com

www.ingramcontent.com/pod-product-compliance
Lightning Source LLC
Chambersburg PA
CBHW080433110426
42743CB00016B/3156